Jetpack Compose Essentials

Jetpack Compose Essentials

Contents

Table of Contents

1. Start Here... 1

   1.1 For Kotlin programmers 1

   1.2 For new Kotlin programmers 1

   1.3 Downloading the code samples... 1

   1.4 Download the eBook 2

   1.5 Feedback... 2

   1.6 Errata.. 2

2. Setting up an Android Studio Development Environment.. 3

   2.1 System requirements... 3

   2.2 Downloading the Android Studio package 3

   2.3 Installing Android Studio.. 4

      2.3.1 Installation on Windows 4

      2.3.2 Installation on macOS 4

      2.3.3 Installation on Linux... 5

   2.4 The Android Studio setup wizard 5

   2.5 Installing additional Android SDK packages 6

   2.6 Making the Android SDK tools command-line accessible....................... 9

      2.6.1 Windows 8.1 9

      2.6.2 Windows 10 10

      2.6.3 Windows 11 10

      2.6.4 Linux 10

      2.6.5 macOS.. 10

   2.7 Android Studio memory management 11

   2.8 Updating Android Studio and the SDK 11

   2.9 Summary 11

3. A Compose Project Overview 13

   3.1 About the project... 13

   3.2 Creating the project 14

   3.3 Creating an activity 14

   3.4 Defining the project and SDK settings 15

   3.5 Previewing the example project 16

   3.6 Reviewing the main activity.. 18

   3.7 Preview updates.. 22

   3.8 Summary 22

4. An Example Compose Project 23

   4.1 Getting started 23

   4.2 Removing the template Code 23

   4.3 The Composable hierarchy 24

   4.4 Adding the DemoText composable 24

   4.5 Previewing the DemoText composable 26

   4.6 Adding the DemoSlider composable... 26

4.7 Adding the DemoScreen composable 27
4.8 Previewing the DemoScreen composable... 29
4.9 Testing in interactive mode.. 30
4.10 Completing the project.. 31
4.11 Summary 31

5. Creating an Android Virtual Device (AVD) in Android Studio 33

5.1 About Android Virtual Devices 33
5.2 Starting the emulator 34
5.3 Running the application in the AVD 35
5.4 Running on multiple devices 37
5.5 Stopping a running application 38
5.6 Supporting dark theme... 38
5.7 Running the emulator in a separate window.. 39
5.8 Enabling the device frame.. 40
5.9 AVD command-line creation 41
5.10 Android Virtual Device configuration files 43
5.11 Moving and renaming an Android Virtual Device... 43
5.12 Summary 43

6. Using and Configuring the Android Studio AVD Emulator 45

6.1 The emulator environment 45
6.2 The emulator toolbar options 45
6.3 Working in zoom mode.. 47
6.4 Resizing the emulator window 47
6.5 Extended control options 47
6.5.1 Location.. 48
6.5.2 Displays.. 48
6.5.3 Cellular 48
6.5.4 Battery.. 48
6.5.5 Camera... 48
6.5.6 Phone 48
6.5.7 Directional pad 48
6.5.8 Microphone.. 48
6.5.9 Fingerprint 48
6.5.10 Virtual sensors 49
6.5.11 Snapshots... 49
6.5.12 Record and playback.. 49
6.5.13 Google Play 49
6.5.14 Settings 49
6.5.15 Help.. 49
6.6 Working with snapshots 49
6.7 Configuring fingerprint emulation 50
6.8 The emulator in tool window mode.. 51
6.9 Summary 52

7. A Tour of the Android Studio User Interface 53

7.1 The Welcome screen 53
7.2 The main window.. 54
7.3 The tool windows 55
7.4 Android Studio keyboard shortcuts.. 58

7.5 Switcher and recent files navigation...59

7.6 Changing the Android Studio theme 60

7.7 Summary 60

8. Testing Android Studio Apps on a Physical Android Device.. 61

8.1 An overview of the Android Debug Bridge (ADB) 61

8.2 Enabling USB debugging ADB on Android devices 61

8.2.1 macOS ADB configuration 62

8.2.2 Windows ADB configuration 63

8.2.3 Linux adb configuration 64

8.3 Resolving USB connection issues...64

8.4 Enabling wireless debugging on Android devices 65

8.5 Testing the adb connection 67

8.6 Summary 67

9. The Basics of the Android Studio Code Editor... 69

9.1 The Android Studio editor 69

9.2 Code mode 71

9.3 Splitting the editor window..72

9.4 Code completion 72

9.5 Statement completion 74

9.6 Parameter information 74

9.7 Parameter name hints 74

9.8 Code generation 74

9.9 Code folding..75

9.10 Quick documentation lookup 77

9.11 Code reformatting...77

9.12 Finding sample code 78

9.13 Live templates 78

9.14 Summary 79

10. An Overview of the Android Architecture 81

10.1 The Android software stack 81

10.2 The Linux kernel...82

10.3 Android runtime – ART 82

10.4 Android libraries 82

10.4.1 C/C++ libraries..82

10.5 Application framework...83

10.6 Applications 83

10.7 Summary 83

11. An Introduction to Kotlin... 85

11.1 What is Kotlin? 85

11.2 Kotlin and Java..85

11.3 Converting from Java to Kotlin 85

11.4 Kotlin and Android Studio 86

11.5 Experimenting with Kotlin 86

11.6 Semi-colons in Kotlin 87

11.7 Summary 87

12. Kotlin Data Types, Variables and Nullability 89

Table of Contents

12.1 Kotlin data types...89
    12.1.1 Integer data types...90
    12.1.2 Floating point data types..90
    12.1.3 Boolean data type...90
    12.1.4 Character data type...90
    12.1.5 String data type...90
    12.1.6 Escape sequences..91
12.2 Mutable variables..92
12.3 Immutable variables..92
12.4 Declaring mutable and immutable variables...92
12.5 Data types are objects...92
12.6 Type annotations and type inference...93
12.7 Nullable type...94
12.8 The safe call operator..94
12.9 Not-null assertion...95
12.10 Nullable types and the let function...95
12.11 Late initialization (lateinit)..96
12.12 The Elvis operator...97
12.13 Type casting and type checking...97
12.14 Summary..98

13. Kotlin Operators and Expressions **99**

13.1 Expression syntax in Kotlin...99
13.2 The Basic assignment operator...99
13.3 Kotlin arithmetic operators...99
13.4 Augmented assignment operators...100
13.5 Increment and decrement operators..100
13.6 Equality operators...101
13.7 Boolean logical operators..101
13.8 Range operator..102
13.9 Bitwise operators..102
    13.9.1 Bitwise Inversion...102
    13.9.2 Bitwise AND..103
    13.9.3 Bitwise OR...103
    13.9.4 Bitwise XOR..103
    13.9.5 Bitwise left shift...104
    13.9.6 Bitwise right shift...104
13.10 Summary..105

14. Kotlin Control flow **107**

14.1 Looping control flow...107
    14.1.1 The Kotlin *for-in* Statement..107
    14.1.2 The *while* loop..108
    14.1.3 The *do ... while* loop..109
    14.1.4 Breaking from Loops..109
    14.1.5 The *continue* statement..110
    14.1.6 Break and continue labels...110
14.2 Conditional control flow..111
    14.2.1 Using the *if* expressions..111
    14.2.2 Using *if ... else ...* expressions..112

14.2.3 Using *if ... else if ...* Expressions 112
14.2.4 Using the *when* statement 112
14.3 Summary 113

15. An Overview of Kotlin Functions and Lambdas 115

15.1 What is a function? 115
15.2 How to declare a Kotlin function 115
15.3 Calling a Kotlin function 116
15.4 Single expression functions 116
15.5 Local functions 116
15.6 Handling return values 117
15.7 Declaring default function parameters 117
15.8 Variable number of function parameters 117
15.9 Lambda expressions 118
15.10 Higher-order functions 119
15.11 Summary 120

16. The Basics of Object-Oriented Programming in Kotlin 121

16.1 What is an object? 121
16.2 What is a class? 121
16.3 Declaring a Kotlin class 121
16.4 Adding properties to a class 122
16.5 Defining methods 122
16.6 Declaring and initializing a class instance 122
16.7 Primary and secondary constructors 122
16.8 Initializer blocks 125
16.9 Calling methods and accessing properties 125
16.10 Custom accessors 125
16.11 Nested and inner classes 126
16.12 Companion objects 127
16.13 Summary 129

17. An Introduction to Kotlin Inheritance and Subclassing 131

17.1 Inheritance, classes, and subclasses 131
17.2 Subclassing syntax 131
17.3 A Kotlin inheritance example 132
17.4 Extending the functionality of a subclass 133
17.5 Overriding inherited methods 134
17.6 Adding a custom secondary constructor 135
17.7 Using the SavingsAccount class 135
17.8 Summary 135

18. An Overview of Compose 137

18.1 Development before Compose 137
18.2 Compose declarative syntax 137
18.3 Compose is data-driven 138
18.4 Summary 138

19. Composable Functions Overview 141

19.1 What is a composable function? 141
19.2 Stateful vs. stateless composables 141

19.3 Composable function syntax 142
19.4 Foundation and Material composables 144
19.5 Summary 145

20. An Overview of Compose State and Recomposition **147**

20.1 The basics of state 147
20.2 Introducing recomposition 147
20.3 Creating the StateExample project 148
20.4 Declaring state in a composable 148
20.5 Unidirectional data flow 151
20.6 State hoisting 153
20.7 Saving state through configuration changes 155
20.8 Summary 156

21. An Introduction to Composition Local **157**

21.1 Understanding CompositionLocal 157
21.2 Using CompositionLocal 158
21.3 Creating the CompLocalDemo project 159
21.4 Designing the layout 159
21.5 Adding the CompositionLocal state 160
21.6 Accessing the CompositionLocal state 161
21.7 Testing the design 161
21.8 Summary 164

22. An Overview of Compose Slot APIs **165**

22.1 Understanding slot APIs 165
22.2 Declaring a slot API 166
22.3 Calling slot API composables 166
22.4 Summary 168

23. A Compose Slot API Tutorial **169**

23.1 About the project 169
23.2 Creating the SlotApiDemo project 169
23.3 Preparing the MainActivity class file 169
23.4 Creating the MainScreen composable 170
23.5 Adding the ScreenContent composable 171
23.6 Creating the Checkbox composable 172
23.7 Implementing the ScreenContent slot API 173
23.8 Adding an Image drawable resource 174
23.9 Writing the TitleImage composable 175
23.10 Completing the MainScreen composable 176
23.11 Previewing the project 178
23.12 Summary 179

24. Using Modifiers in Compose **181**

24.1 An overview of modifiers 181
24.2 Creating the ModifierDemo project 181
24.3 Creating a modifier 182
24.4 Modifier ordering 184
24.5 Adding modifier support to a composable 184
24.6 Common built-in modifiers 188

24.7 Combining modifiers...188
24.8 Summary...189

25. Composing Layouts with Row and Column 191

25.1 Creating the RowColDemo project 191
25.2 Row composable...192
25.3 Column composable..192
25.4 Combining Row and Column composables..193
25.5 Layout alignment 194
25.6 Layout arrangement positioning..196
25.7 Layout arrangement spacing..198
25.8 Row and Column scope modifiers..199
25.9 Scope modifier weights 203
25.10 Summary...204

26. Box Layouts in Compose.. 205

26.1 An introduction to the Box composable...205
26.2 Creating the BoxLayout project 205
26.3 Adding the TextCell composable 205
26.4 Adding a Box layout..206
26.5 Box alignment...207
26.6 BoxScope modifiers 209
26.7 Using the clip() modifier 209
26.8 Summary...211

27. Custom Layout Modifiers... 213

27.1 Compose layout basics 213
27.2 Custom layouts 213
27.3 Creating the LayoutModifier project...213
27.4 Adding the ColorBox composable...214
27.5 Creating a custom layout modifier 215
27.6 Understanding default position..215
27.7 Completing the layout modifier...215
27.8 Using a custom modifier 216
27.9 Working with alignment lines 217
27.10 Working with baselines 219
27.11 Summary...220

28. Building Custom Layouts... 221

28.1 An overview of custom layouts 221
28.2 Custom layout syntax 221
28.3 Using a custom layout...222
28.4 Creating the CustomLayout project 223
28.5 Creating the CascadeLayout composable 223
28.6 Using the CascadeLayout composable 225
28.7 Summary...226

29. A Guide to ConstraintLayout in Compose 227

29.1 An introduction to ConstraintLayout 227
29.2 How ConstraintLayout works..227
29.2.1 Constraints..227

29.2.2 Margins..228
29.2.3 Opposing constraints...228
29.2.4 Constraint bias..229
29.2.5 Chains...230
29.2.6 Chain styles 230
29.3 Configuring dimensions..231
29.4 Guideline helper..231
29.5 Barrier helper..232
29.6 Summary..233

30. Working with ConstraintLayout in Compose **235**

30.1 Calling ConstraintLayout..235
30.2 Generating references...235
30.3 Assigning a reference to a composable..235
30.4 Adding constraints..236
30.5 Creating the ConstraintLayout project 236
30.6 Adding the ConstraintLayout library..237
30.7 Adding a custom button composable...237
30.8 Basic constraints...238
30.9 Opposing constraints...239
30.10 Constraint bias..240
30.11 Constraint margins..241
30.12 The importance of opposing constraints and bias...............................242
30.13 Creating chains..245
30.14 Working with guidelines..246
30.15 Working with barriers..247
30.16 Decoupling constraints with constraint sets..250
30.17 Summary..252

31. Working with IntrinsicSize in Compose... **253**

31.1 Intrinsic measurements...253
31.2 Max. vs Min. Intrinsic Size measurements 253
31.3 About the example project...254
31.4 Creating the IntrinsicSizeDemo project..255
31.5 Creating the custom text field...255
31.6 Adding the Text and Box components..256
31.7 Adding the top-level Column...256
31.8 Testing the project...257
31.9 Applying IntrinsicSize.Max measurements 257
31.10 Applying IntrinsicSize.Min measurements 258
31.11 Summary..258

32. An Overview of Lists and Grids in Compose **259**

32.1 Standard vs. lazy lists 259
32.2 Working with Column and Row lists 259
32.3 Creating lazy lists 260
32.4 Enabling scrolling with ScrollState 261
32.5 Programmatic scrolling..261
32.6 Sticky headers 263
32.7 Responding to scroll position...264
32.8 Creating a lazy grid..265

32.9 Summary 267

33. A Compose Row and Column List Tutorial 269

33.1 Creating the ListDemo project 269
33.2 Creating a Column-based list 269
33.3 Enabling list scrolling 271
33.4 Manual scrolling 271
33.5 A Row list example 274
33.6 Summary 274

34. A Compose Lazy List Tutorial 275

34.1 Creating the LazyListDemo project 275
34.2 Adding list data to the project 275
34.3 Reading the XML data 277
34.4 Handling image loading 278
34.5 Designing the list item composable 280
34.6 Building the lazy list 281
34.7 Testing the project 281
34.8 Making list items clickable 282
34.9 Summary 284

35. Lazy List Sticky Headers and Scroll Detection 285

35.1 Grouping the list item data 285
35.2 Displaying the headers and items 285
35.3 Adding sticky headers 286
35.4 Reacting to scroll position 287
35.5 Adding the scroll button 289
35.6 Testing the finished app 291
35.7 Summary 291

36. Compose Visibility Animation 293

36.1 Creating the AnimateVisibility project 293
36.2 Animating visibility 293
36.3 Defining enter and exit animations 296
36.4 Animation specs and animation easing 297
36.5 Repeating an animation 299
36.6 Different animations for different children 299
36.7 Auto-starting an animation 300
36.8 Implementing crossfading 301
36.9 Summary 302

37. Compose State-Driven Animation 303

37.1 Understanding state-driven animation 303
37.2 Introducing animate as state functions 303
37.3 Creating the AnimateState project 304
37.4 Animating rotation with animateFloatAsState 304
37.5 Animating color changes with animateColorAsState 307
37.6 Animating motion with animateDpAsState 309
37.7 Adding spring effects 312
37.8 Working with keyframes 313
37.9 Combining multiple animations 314

37.10 Using the Animation Inspector 316

37.11 Summary 318

38. Canvas Graphics Drawing in Compose **319**

38.1 Introducing the Canvas component 319

38.2 Creating the CanvasDemo project.. 319

38.3 Drawing a line and getting the canvas size 319

38.4 Drawing dashed lines.. 321

38.5 Drawing a rectangle 321

38.6 Applying rotation 325

38.7 Drawing circles and ovals... 326

38.8 Drawing gradients... 327

38.9 Drawing arcs 330

38.10 Drawing paths 331

38.11 Drawing points... 332

38.12 Drawing an image 333

38.13 Summary 335

39. Working with ViewModels in Compose **337**

39.1 What is Android Jetpack? 337

39.2 The "old" architecture 337

39.3 Modern Android architecture 337

39.4 The ViewModel component.. 337

39.5 ViewModel implementation using state.. 338

39.6 Connecting a ViewModel state to an activity... 339

39.7 ViewModel implementation using LiveData... 340

39.8 Observing ViewModel LiveData within an activity 341

39.9 Summary 341

40. A Compose ViewModel Tutorial.. **343**

40.1 About the project.. 343

40.2 Creating the ViewModelDemo project 344

40.3 Adding the ViewModel 344

40.4 Accessing DemoViewModel from MainActivity... 345

40.5 Designing the temperature input composable 346

40.6 Designing the temperature input composable 347

40.7 Completing the user interface design... 350

40.8 Testing the app.. 351

40.9 Summary 352

41. An Overview of Android SQLite Databases **353**

41.1 Understanding database tables.. 353

41.2 Introducing database schema 353

41.3 Columns and data types 353

41.4 Database rows 354

41.5 Introducing primary keys 354

41.6 What is SQLite?... 354

41.7 Structured Query Language (SQL)... 354

41.8 Trying SQLite on an Android Virtual Device (AVD) 355

41.9 The Android Room persistence library... 357

41.10 Summary.. 357

42. Room Databases and Compose **359**

42.1 Revisiting modern app architecture 359
42.2 Key elements of Room database persistence 359
    42.2.1 Repository 359
    42.2.2 Room database 360
    42.2.3 Data Access Object (DAO) 360
    42.2.4 Entities 360
    42.2.5 SQLite database 360
42.3 Understanding entities 361
42.4 Data Access Objects 363
42.5 The Room database 364
42.6 The Repository.. 365
42.7 In-Memory databases 366
42.8 Database Inspector.. 367
42.9 Summary 367

43. A Compose Room Database and Repository Tutorial **369**

43.1 About the RoomDemo project.. 369
43.2 Creating the RoomDemo project.. 370
43.3 Modifying the build configuration 370
43.4 Building the entity.. 370
43.5 Creating the Data Access Object.. 372
43.6 Adding the Room database... 373
43.7 Adding the repository... 374
43.8 Adding the ViewModel 376
43.9 Designing the user interface 378
43.10 Completing the MainScreen function.. 380
43.11 Testing the RoomDemo app 383
43.12 Using the Database Inspector 383
43.13 Summary 384

44. An Overview of Navigation in Compose **385**

44.1 Understanding navigation... 385
44.2 Declaring a navigation controller.. 387
44.3 Declaring a navigation host 387
44.4 Adding destinations to the navigation graph 387
44.5 Navigating to destinations.. 388
44.6 Passing arguments to a destination... 390
44.7 Working with bottom navigation bars 391
44.8 Summary 393

45. A Compose Navigation Tutorial **395**

45.1 Creating the NavigationDemo project 395
45.2 About the NavigationDemo project 395
45.3 Declaring the navigation routes 395
45.4 Adding the home screen 396
45.5 Adding the welcome screen... 397
45.6 Adding the profile screen 398
45.7 Creating the navigation controller and host.. 399
45.8 Implementing the screen navigation 399

45.9 Passing the user name argument...400
45.10 Testing the project...401
45.11 Summary...403

46. A Compose Bottom Navigation Bar Tutorial **405**

46.1 Creating the BottomBarDemo project...405
46.2 Declaring the navigation routes 405
46.3 Designing bar items 406
46.4 Creating the bar item list..406
46.5 Adding the destination screens 407
46.6 Creating the navigation controller and host 409
46.7 Designing the navigation bar...410
46.8 Working with the Scaffold component...411
46.9 Testing the project...412
46.10 Summary...412

47. Detecting Gestures in Compose...**413**

47.1 Compose gesture detection...413
47.2 Creating the GestureDemo project..413
47.3 Detecting click gestures..413
47.4 Detecting taps using PointerInputScope...415
47.5 Detecting drag gestures 416
47.6 Detecting drag gestures using PointerInputScope..418
47.7 Scrolling using the scrollable modifier..419
47.8 Scrolling using the scroll modifiers 420
47.9 Detecting pinch gestures...422
47.10 Detecting rotation gestures...423
47.11 Detecting translation gestures 424
47.12 Summary...425

48. Detecting Swipe Gestures in Compose **427**

48.1 Swipe gestures and anchors 427
48.2 Detecting swipe gestures 427
48.3 Declaring the anchors map 428
48.4 Declaring thresholds...428
48.5 Moving a component in response to a swipe 428
48.6 About the SwipeDemo project 429
48.7 Creating the SwipeDemo project 429
48.8 Setting up the swipeable state and anchors...429
48.9 Designing the parent Box..430
48.10 Testing the project..433
48.11 Summary...433

49. Working with Compose Theming...**435**

49.1 Material Design 2 vs Material Design 3 435
49.2 Material Design 2 Theming 435
49.3 Material Design 3 Theming 438
49.4 Building a Custom Theme..439
49.5 Summary 440

50. A Material Design 3 Theming Tutorial **441**

50.1 Creating the ThemeDemo project 441
50.2 Adding the Material Design 3 library 441
50.3 Designing the user interface 441
50.4 Building a new theme 443
50.5 Adding the theme to the project 444
50.6 Enabling dynamic colors 445
50.7 Summary 447

51. Creating, Testing, and Uploading an Android App Bundle.................................. **449**

51.1 The release preparation process 449
51.2 Android app bundles 449
51.3 Register for a Google Play Developer Console account.. 450
51.4 Configuring the app in the console... 451
51.5 Enabling Google Play app signing 452
51.6 Creating a keystore file 452
51.7 Creating the Android app bundle 454
51.8 Generating test APK files 455
51.9 Uploading the app bundle to the Google Play Developer Console 456
51.10 Exploring the app bundle... 457
51.11 Managing testers 458
51.12 Rolling the app out for testing... 458
51.13 Uploading new app bundle revisions 459
51.14 Analyzing the app bundle file 460
51.15 Summary... 460

52. An Overview of Gradle in Android Studio... **463**

52.1 An Overview of Gradle 463
52.2 Gradle and Android Studio 463
52.2.1 Sensible Defaults 463
52.2.2 Dependencies... 463
52.2.3 Build Variants 464
52.2.4 Manifest Entries 464
52.2.5 APK Signing... 464
52.2.6 ProGuard Support.. 464
52.3 The Property and Settings Gradle Build Files 464
52.4 The Top-level Gradle Build File... 465
52.5 Module Level Gradle Build Files 466
52.6 Configuring Signing Settings in the Build File... 468
52.7 Running Gradle Tasks from the Command-line 469
52.8 Summary 470

Index **471**

Chapter 1

1. Start Here

The goal of this book is to teach you how to build Android applications using Jetpack Compose, Android Studio, and the Kotlin programming language.

Beginning with the basics, this book explains how to set up an Android Studio development environment.

The book also includes in-depth chapters introducing the Kotlin programming language including data types, operators, control flow, functions, lambdas, and object-oriented programming.

An introduction to the key concepts of Jetpack Compose and Android project architecture is followed by a guided tour of Android Studio in Compose development mode. The book also covers the creation of custom Composables and explains how these functions are combined to create user interface layouts including the use of row, column, box, and list components.

Other topics covered include data handling using state properties, key user interface design concepts such as modifiers, navigation bars, and user interface navigation. Additional chapters explore building your own re-usable custom layout components.

The book also includes chapters covering graphics drawing, user interface animation, transitions, and gesture handling.

Chapters are also included covering view models, SQLite databases, Room database access, the Database Inspector, live data, and custom theme creation.

Finally, the book explains how to package up a completed app and upload it to the Google Play Store for publication.

Along the way, the topics covered in the book are put into practice through detailed tutorials, the source code for which is also available for download.

Assuming you already have some rudimentary programming experience, are ready to download Android Studio and the Android SDK, and have access to a Windows, Mac, or Linux system, you are ready to get started.

1.1 For Kotlin programmers

This book has been designed to address the needs of both existing Kotlin programmers and those who are new to both Kotlin and Jetpack Compose app development. If you are familiar with the Kotlin programming language, you can probably skip the Kotlin specific chapters.

1.2 For new Kotlin programmers

If you are new to programming in Kotlin then the entire book is appropriate for you. Just start at the beginning and keep going.

1.3 Downloading the code samples

The source code and Android Studio project files for the examples contained in this book are available for download at:

https://www.ebookfrenzy.com/retail/compose/index.php

Start Here

The steps to load a project from the code samples into Android Studio are as follows:

1. From the Welcome to Android Studio dialog, click on the Open button option.

2. In the project selection dialog, navigate to and select the folder containing the project to be imported and click on OK.

1.4 Download the eBook

Thank you for purchasing the print edition of this book. Your purchase includes a color copy of the book in PDF format.

If you would like to download the PDF version of this book, please email proof of purchase (for example a receipt, delivery notice or photo of the physical book) to *feedback@ebookfrenzy.com* and we will provide you with a download link.

1.5 Feedback

We want you to be satisfied with your purchase of this book. If you find any errors in the book or have any comments, questions or concerns please contact us at *feedback@ebookfrenzy.com*.

1.6 Errata

While we make every effort to ensure the accuracy of the content of this book, inevitably, a book covering a subject area of this size and complexity may include some errors and oversights. Any known issues with the book will be outlined, together with solutions at the following URL:

https://www.ebookfrenzy.com/errata/compose.html

If you find an error not listed in the errata, please let us know by emailing our technical support team at *feedback@ ebookfrenzy.com*.

2. Setting up an Android Studio Development Environment

Before any work can begin on the development of an Android application, the first step is to configure a computer system to act as the development platform. This involves several steps consisting of installing the Android Studio Integrated Development Environment (IDE) which also includes the Android Software Development Kit (SDK), the Kotlin plug-in and OpenJDK Java development environment.

This chapter will cover the steps necessary to install the requisite components for Android application development on Windows, macOS, and Linux-based systems.

2.1 System requirements

Android application development may be performed on any of the following system types:

- Windows 8/10/11 64-bit

- macOS 10.14 or later running on Intel or Apple silicon

- Chrome OS device with Intel i5 or higher

- Linux systems with version 2.31 or later of the GNU C Library (glibc)

- Minimum of 8GB of RAM (see below)

- Approximately 8GB of available disk space

- 1280 x 800 minimum screen resolution

Although Android Studio will run on computers with 8GB of RAM, performance will be greatly improved on systems containing more memory. This is particularly an issue if you plan to test your apps using the Android Virtual Device emulator (AVD).

2.2 Downloading the Android Studio package

Most of the work involved in developing applications for Android will be performed using the Android Studio environment. The content and examples in this book were created based on Android Studio Bumble Bee 2021.1.1 using the Android API 32 SDK which, at the time of writing, are the current versions.

Android Studio is, however, subject to frequent updates so a newer version may have been released since this book was published.

The latest release of Android Studio may be downloaded from the primary download page which can be found at the following URL:

https://developer.android.com/studio/index.html

If this page provides instructions for downloading a newer version of Android Studio it is important to note that there may be some minor differences between this book and the software. A web search for "Android Studio Bumble Bee" should provide the option to download the older version if these differences become a problem.

Alternatively, visit the following web page to find Android Studio Bumble Bee 2021.1.1 in the archives:

https://developer.android.com/studio/archive

2.3 Installing Android Studio

Once downloaded, the exact steps to install Android Studio differ depending on the operating system on which the installation is being performed.

2.3.1 Installation on Windows

Locate the downloaded Android Studio installation executable file (named *android-studio-<version>-windows.exe*) in a Windows Explorer window and double-click on it to start the installation process, clicking the *Yes* button in the User Account Control dialog if it appears.

Once the Android Studio setup wizard appears, work through the various screens to configure the installation to meet your requirements in terms of the file system location into which Android Studio should be installed and whether or not it should be made available to other users of the system. When prompted to select the components to install, make sure that the *Android Studio* and *Android Virtual Device* options are all selected.

Although there are no strict rules on where Android Studio should be installed on the system, the remainder of this book will assume that the installation was performed into *C:\Program Files\Android\Android Studio* and that the Android SDK packages have been installed into the user's *AppData\Local\Android\sdk* sub-folder. Once the options have been configured, click on the *Install* button to begin the installation process.

On versions of Windows with a Start menu, the newly installed Android Studio can be launched from the entry added to that menu during the installation. The executable may be pinned to the taskbar for easy access by navigating to the *Android Studio\bin* directory, right-clicking on the *studio64* executable, and selecting the *Pin to Taskbar* menu option (on Windows 11 this option can be found by selecting *Show more options* from the menu).

2.3.2 Installation on macOS

Android Studio for macOS is downloaded in the form of a disk image (.dmg) file. Once the *android-studio-<version>-mac.dmg* file has been downloaded, locate it in a Finder window and double-click on it to open it as shown in Figure 2-1:

Figure 2-1

To install the package, simply drag the Android Studio icon and drop it onto the Applications folder. The Android Studio package will then be installed into the Applications folder of the system, a process that will typically take a few seconds to complete.

To launch Android Studio, locate the executable in the Applications folder using a Finder window and double-click on it.

For future, easier access to the tool, drag the Android Studio icon from the Finder window and drop it onto the dock.

2.3.3 Installation on Linux

Having downloaded the Linux Android Studio package, open a terminal window, change directory to the location where Android Studio is to be installed and execute the following command:

```
unzip /<path to package>/android-studio-ide-<version>-linux.zip
```

Note that the Android Studio bundle will be installed into a subdirectory named *android-studio*. Assuming, therefore, that the above command was executed in */home/demo*, the software packages will be unpacked into */home/demo/android-studio*.

To launch Android Studio, open a terminal window, change directory to the *android-studio/bin* sub-directory and execute the following command:

```
./studio.sh
```

When running on a 64-bit Linux system, it may be necessary to install some 32-bit support libraries before Android Studio will run. On Ubuntu these libraries can be installed using the following command:

```
sudo apt-get install libc6:i386 libncurses5:i386 libstdc++6:i386 lib32z1 libbz2-
1.0:i386
```

On Red Hat and Fedora-based 64-bit systems, use the following command:

```
sudo yum install zlib.i686 ncurses-libs.i686 bzip2-libs.i686
```

2.4 The Android Studio setup wizard

If you are installing Android Studio for the first time the initial dialog that appears once the setup process starts may resemble that shown in Figure 2-2 below:

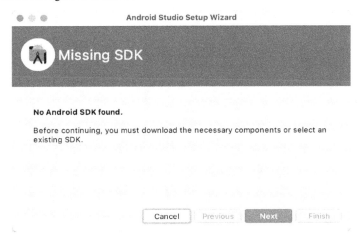

Figure 2-2

If this dialog appears, click the Next button to display the SDK Components Setup dialog (Figure 2-3). Within this dialog, make sure that the Android SDK option is selected along with the latest API package before clicking on the Next button:

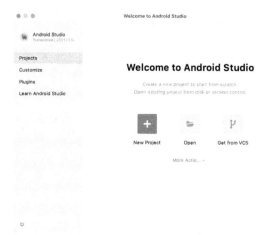

Figure 2-3

After clicking Next, Android Studio will download and install the Android SDK and tools.

If you have previously installed an earlier version of Android Studio, the first time that this new version is launched, a dialog may appear providing the option to import settings from a previous Android Studio version. If you have settings from a previous version and would like to import them into the latest installation, select the appropriate option and location. Alternatively, indicate that you do not need to import any previous settings and click on the OK button to proceed.

After these initial setup steps have been taken, click the Finish button to display the Welcome to Android Studio screen:

Figure 2-4

2.5 Installing additional Android SDK packages

The steps performed so far have installed the Android Studio IDE and the current set of default Android SDK packages. Before proceeding, it is worth taking some time to verify which packages are installed and to install any missing or updated packages.

This task can be performed by clicking on the *More Actions* link within the welcome dialog and selecting the *SDK Manager* option from the drop-down menu. Once invoked, the *Android SDK* screen of the Preferences dialog will appear as shown in Figure 2-5:

Figure 2-5

Immediately after installing Android Studio for the first, time it is likely that only the latest released version of the Android SDK has been installed. To install older versions of the Android SDK simply select the checkboxes corresponding to the versions and click on the *Apply* button.

Most of the examples in this book will support older versions of Android as far back as Android 8.0 (Oreo). This is to ensure that the apps run on a wide range of Android devices. Within the list of SDK versions, enable the checkbox next to Android 8.0 (Oreo) and click on the Apply button. In the resulting confirmation dialog click on the OK button to install the SDK. Subsequent dialogs will seek the acceptance of licenses and terms before performing the installation. Click Finish once the installation is complete.

It is also possible that updates will be listed as being available for the latest SDK. To access detailed information about the packages that are ready to be updated, enable the *Show Package Details* option located in the lower right-hand corner of the screen. This will display information similar to that shown in Figure 2-6:

Name	API Level	Revision	Status
Android TV Intel x86 Atom System Image	25	6	Not installed
Android Wear for China ARM EABI v7a System Image	25	3	Not installed
Android Wear for China Intel x86 Atom System Image	25	3	Not installed
Android Wear ARM EABI v7a System Image	25	3	Not installed
Android Wear Intel x86 Atom System Image	25	3	Not installed
Google APIs ARM 64 v8a System Image	25	8	Not installed
Google APIs ARM EABI v7a System Image	25	8	Not installed
Google APIs Intel x86 Atom System Image	25	8	Not installed
Google APIs Intel x86 Atom_64 System Image	25	6	Update Available: 8
Android 7.0 (Nougat)			
Google APIs	24	1	Not installed

Figure 2-6

The above figure highlights the availability of an update. To install the updates, enable the checkbox to the left of the item name and click on the *Apply* button.

In addition to the Android SDK packages, several tools are also installed for building Android applications. To view the currently installed packages and check for updates, remain within the SDK settings screen and select the SDK Tools tab as shown in Figure 2-7:

Setting up an Android Studio Development Environment

Figure 2-7

Within the Android SDK Tools screen, make sure that the following packages are listed as *Installed* in the Status column:

- Android SDK Build-tools

- Android Emulator

- Android SDK Platform-tools

- Google Play Services

- Intel x86 Emulator Accelerator (HAXM installer)

- Google USB Driver (Windows only)

- Layout Inspector image server for API S

Note the Intel x86 Emulator Accelerator (HAXM installer) cannot be installed on Apple silicon-based Macs.

If any of the above packages are listed as *Not Installed* or requiring an update, simply select the checkboxes next to those packages and click on the *Apply* button to initiate the installation process. If the HAXM emulator settings dialog appears, select the recommended memory allocation:

Figure 2-8

Once the installation is complete, review the package list and make sure that the selected packages are now listed as *Installed* in the *Status* column. If any are listed as *Not installed,* make sure they are selected and click on the *Apply* button again.

2.6 Making the Android SDK tools command-line accessible

Most of the time, the underlying tools of the Android SDK will be accessed from within the Android Studio environment. That being said, however, there will also be instances where it will be useful to be able to invoke those tools from a command prompt or terminal window. For the operating system on which you are developing to be able to find these tools, it will be necessary to add them to the system's *PATH* environment variable.

Regardless of operating system, the PATH variable needs to be configured to include the following paths (where *<path_to_android_sdk_installation>* represents the file system location into which the Android SDK was installed):

```
<path_to_android_sdk_installation>/sdk/tools
<path_to_android_sdk_installation>/sdk/tools/bin
<path_to_android_sdk_installation>/sdk/platform-tools
```

The location of the SDK on your system can be identified by launching the SDK Manager and referring to the *Android SDK Location:* field located at the top of the settings panel as highlighted in Figure 2-9:

Figure 2-9

Once the location of the SDK has been identified, the steps to add this to the PATH variable are operating system dependent:

2.6.1 Windows 8.1

1. On the start screen, move the mouse to the bottom right-hand corner of the screen and select Search from the resulting menu. In the search box, enter Control Panel. When the Control Panel icon appears in the results area, click on it to launch the tool on the desktop.

2. Within the Control Panel, use the Category menu to change the display to Large Icons. From the list of icons select the one labeled System.

3. In the Environment Variables dialog, locate the Path variable in the System variables list, select it and click on the *Edit...* button. Using the *New* button in the edit dialog, add three new entries to the path. For example, assuming the Android SDK was installed into C:\Users\demo\AppData\Local\Android\Sdk, the following entries would need to be added:

```
C:\Users\demo\AppData\Local\Android\Sdk\platform-tools
C:\Users\demo\AppData\Local\Android\Sdk\tools
C:\Users\demo\AppData\Local\Android\Sdk\tools\bin
```

4. Click on OK in each dialog box and close the system properties control panel.

Open a command prompt window by pressing Windows + R on the keyboard and entering *cmd* into the Run dialog. Within the Command Prompt window, enter:

```
echo %Path%
```

The returned path variable value should include the paths to the Android SDK platform tools folders. Verify that the *platform-tools* value is correct by attempting to run the *adb* tool as follows:

```
adb
```

The tool should output a list of command-line options when executed.

Similarly, check the *tools* path setting by attempting to run the AVD Manager command-line tool (don't worry if the avdmanager tool reports a problem with Java - this will be addressed later):

```
avdmanager
```

If a message similar to the following message appears for one or both of the commands, it is most likely that an incorrect path was appended to the Path environment variable:

```
'adb' is not recognized as an internal or external command,
operable program or batch file.
```

2.6.2 Windows 10

Right-click on the Start menu, select Settings from the resulting menu and enter "Edit the system environment variables" into the *Find a setting* text field. In the System Properties dialog, click the *Environment Variables...* button. Follow the steps outlined for Windows 8.1 starting from step 3.

2.6.3 Windows 11

Right-click on the Start icon located in the taskbar and select Settings from the resulting menu. When the Settings dialog appears, scroll down the list of categories and select the "About" option. In the About screen, select *Advanced system settings* from the Related links section. When the System Properties window appears, click on the *Environment Variables...* button. Follow the steps outlined for Windows 8.1 starting from step 3.

2.6.4 Linux

On Linux, this configuration can typically be achieved by adding a command to the *.bashrc* file in your home directory (specifics may differ depending on the particular Linux distribution in use). Assuming that the Android SDK bundle package was installed into */home/demo/Android/sdk*, the export line in the *.bashrc* file would read as follows:

```
export PATH=/home/demo/Android/sdk/platform-tools:/home/demo/Android/sdk/tools:/
home/demo/Android/sdk/tools/bin:/home/demo/android-studio/bin:$PATH
```

Note also that the above command adds the *android-studio/bin* directory to the PATH variable. This will enable the *studio.sh* script to be executed regardless of the current directory within a terminal window.

2.6.5 macOS

Several techniques may be employed to modify the $PATH environment variable on macOS. Arguably the cleanest method is to add a new file in the */etc/paths.d* directory containing the paths to be added to $PATH. Assuming an Android SDK installation location of */Users/demo/Library/Android/sdk*, the path may be configured by creating a new file named *android-sdk* in the */etc/paths.d* directory containing the following lines:

```
/Users/demo/Library/Android/sdk/tools
/Users/demo/Library/Android/sdk/tools/bin
/Users/demo/Library/Android/sdk/platform-tools
```

Note that since this is a system directory it will be necessary to use the *sudo* command when creating the file. For example:

```
sudo vi /etc/paths.d/android-sdk
```

2.7 Android Studio memory management

Android Studio is a large and complex software application that consists of many background processes. Although Android Studio has been criticized in the past for providing less than optimal performance, Google has made significant performance improvements in recent releases and continues to do so with each new version. These improvements include allowing the user to configure the amount of memory used by both the Android Studio IDE and the background processes used to build and run apps. This allows the software to take advantage of systems with larger amounts of RAM.

If you are running Android Studio on a system with sufficient unused RAM to increase these values (this feature is only available on 64-bit systems with 5GB or more of RAM) and find that Android Studio performance appears to be degraded it may be worth experimenting with these memory settings. Android Studio may also notify you that performance can be increased via a dialog similar to the one shown below:

Figure 2-10

To view and modify the current memory configuration, select the *File -> Settings...* (*Android Studio -> Preferences...* on macOS) menu option and, in the resulting dialog, select the *Memory Settings* option listed under *System Settings* in the left-hand navigation panel as illustrated in Figure 2-11 below.

When changing the memory allocation, be sure not to allocate more memory than necessary or than your system can spare without slowing down other processes.

Figure 2-11

2.8 Updating Android Studio and the SDK

From time to time new versions of Android Studio and the Android SDK are released. New versions of the SDK are installed using the Android SDK Manager. Android Studio will typically notify you when an update is ready to be installed.

To manually check for Android Studio updates, use the *Help -> Check for Updates...* menu option from the Android Studio main window (*Android Studio -> Check for Updates...* on macOS).

2.9 Summary

Before beginning the development of Android-based applications, the first step is to set up a suitable development environment. This consists of the Android SDKs and Android Studio IDE (which also includes the OpenJDK development environment). In this chapter, we have covered the steps necessary to install these packages on Windows, macOS, and Linux.

Chapter 3

3. A Compose Project Overview

Now that we have installed Android Studio, the next step is to create an Android app using Jetpack Compose. Although this project will make use of several Compose features, it is an intentionally simple example intended to provide an early demonstration of Compose in action and an initial success on which to build as you work through the remainder of the book. The project will also serve to verify that your Android Studio environment is correctly installed and configured.

This chapter will create a new project using the Android Studio Compose project template and explore both the basic structure of a Compose-based Android Studio project and some of the key areas of Android Studio. In the next chapter, we will use this project to create a simple Android app.

Both chapters will briefly explain key features of Compose as they are introduced within the project. If anything is unclear when you have completed the project, rest assured that all of the areas covered in the tutorial will be explored in greater detail in later chapters of the book.

3.1 About the project

The completed project will consist of two text components and a slider. When the slider is moved, the current value will be displayed on one of the text components, while the font size of the second text instance will adjust to match the current slider position. Once completed, the user interface for the app will appear as shown in Figure 3-1:

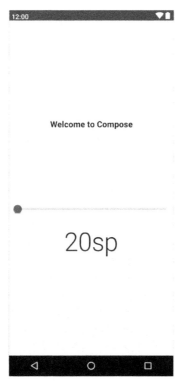

Figure 3-1

3.2 Creating the project

The first step in building an app is to create a new project within Android Studio. Begin, therefore, by launching Android Studio so that the "Welcome to Android Studio" screen appears as illustrated in Figure 3-2:

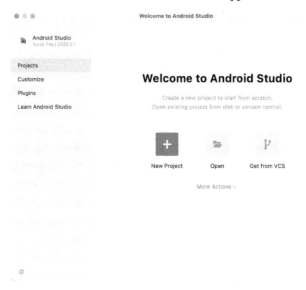

Figure 3-2

Once this window appears, Android Studio is ready for a new project to be created. To create the new project, click on the *New Project* button to display the first screen of the *New Project* wizard.

3.3 Creating an activity

The next step is to define the type of initial activity that is to be created for the application. The left-hand panel provides a list of platform categories from which the *Phone and Tablet* option must be selected. Although a range of different activity types is available when developing Android applications, only the *Empty Compose Activity* template provides a pre-configured project ready to work with Compose. Select this option before clicking on the *Next* button:

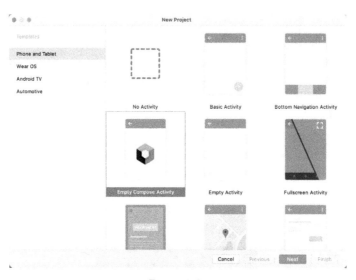

Figure 3-3

3.4 Defining the project and SDK settings

In the project configuration window (Figure 3-4), set the *Name* field to *ComposeDemo*. The application name is the name by which the application will be referenced and identified within Android Studio and is also the name that would be used if the completed application were to go on sale in the Google Play store:

Figure 3-4

The *Package name* is used to uniquely identify the application within the Google Play app store application ecosystem. Although this can be set to any string that uniquely identifies your app, it is traditionally based on the reversed URL of your domain name followed by the name of the application. For example, if your domain is *www.mycompany.com*, and the application has been named *ComposeDemo*, then the package name might be specified as follows:

```
com.mycompany.composedemo
```

If you do not have a domain name you can enter any other string into the Company Domain field, or you may use *example.com* for testing, though this will need to be changed before an application can be published:

```
com.example.composedemo
```

The *Save location* setting will default to a location in the folder named *AndroidStudioProjects* located in your home directory and may be changed by clicking on the folder icon to the right of the text field containing the current path setting.

Set the minimum SDK setting to API 26: Android 8.0 (Oreo). This is the minimum SDK that will be used in most of the projects created in this book unless a necessary feature is only available in a more recent version. The objective here is to build an app using the latest Android SDK, while also retaining compatibility with devices running older versions of Android (in this case as far back as Android 8.0). The text beneath the Minimum SDK setting will outline the percentage of Android devices currently in use on which the app will run. Click on the *Help me choose* link to see a full breakdown of the various Android versions still in use:

Figure 3-5

Since Compose only works with Kotlin, the *Language* menu is preset to *Kotlin* and cannot be changed. Click on the *Finish* button to create the project.

3.5 Previewing the example project

At this point, Android Studio should have created a minimal example application project and opened the main window.

Figure 3-6

The newly created project and references to associated files are listed in the *Project* tool window located on the left-hand side of the main project window. The Project tool window has several modes in which information can be displayed. By default, this panel should be in *Android* mode. This setting is controlled by the menu at the top of the panel as highlighted in Figure 3-7. If the panel is not currently in Android mode, use the menu to switch mode:

Figure 3-7

The code for the main activity of the project (an activity corresponds to a single user interface screen or module within an Android app) is contained within the *MainActivity.kt* file located under *app -> java -> com.example. composedemo* within the Project tool window as indicated in Figure 3-8:

Figure 3-8

Double-click on this file to load it into the main code editor panel. The editor can be used in different modes when writing code, the most useful of which when working with Compose is Split mode. The current mode can be changed using the buttons marked A in Figure 3-9. Split mode displays the code editor (B) alongside the Preview panel (C) in which the current user interface design will appear:

```
MainActivity.kt

                                                                              Code  Split  Design
      package com.ebookfrenzy.composedemo              Analyzing...                A

      import ...

      class MainActivity : ComponentActivity() {
          override fun onCreate(savedInstanceState: Bundle?) {
              super.onCreate(savedInstanceState)
              setContent {
                  ComposeDemoTheme {
                      // A surface container using the 'background' color f
                      Surface(color = MaterialTheme.colors.background) {
                          Greeting( name: "Android")
                      }
                  }                                         A successful build is needed before the preview can be
              }
          }                                                     Build & Refresh... (⌥⇧⌘R)
      }
                                        B
                                                                   C
      @Composable
      fun Greeting(name: String) {
          Text(text = "Hello $name!")
      }

      @Preview(showBackground = true)
      @Composable
      fun DefaultPreview() {
          ComposeDemoTheme {
              Greeting( name: "Android")
          }
      }
```

Figure 3-9

To get us started, Android Studio has already added some code to the *MainActivity.kt* file to display a Text component configured to display a message which reads "Hello Android".

If the project has not yet been built, the Preview panel will display the message shown in Figure 3-10:

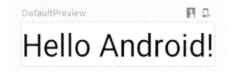

Figure 3-10

If you see this notification, click on the *Build & Refresh* link to rebuild the project. After the build is complete, the Preview panel should update to display the user interface defined by the code in the *MainActivity.kt* file:

DefaultPreview

Hello Android!

Figure 3-11

3.6 Reviewing the main activity

Android applications are created by bringing together one or more elements known as *Activities*. An activity is a single, standalone module of application functionality that either correlates directly to a single user interface screen and its corresponding functionality, or acts as a container for a collection of related screens. An appointments application might, for example, contain an activity screen that displays appointments set up for the current day. The application might also utilize a second activity consisting of multiple screens where new appointments may be entered by the user and existing appointments edited.

When we created the ComposeDemo project, Android Studio created a single initial activity for our app, named it MainActivity, and generated some code for it in the *MainActivity.kt* file. This activity contains the first screen that will be displayed when the app is run on a device. Before we modify the code for our requirements in the next chapter, it is worth taking some time to review the code currently contained within the *MainActivity.kt* file.

The file begins with the following line (keep in mind that this may be different if you used your own domain name instead of *com.example*):

```
package com.example.composedemo
```

This tells the build system that the classes and functions declared in this file belong to the *com.example. composedemo* package which we configured when we created the project.

Next are a series of *import* directives. The Android SDK is comprised of a vast collection of libraries that provide the foundation for building Android apps. If all of these libraries were included within an app the resulting app bundle would be too large to run efficiently on a mobile device. To avoid this problem an app only imports the libraries that it needs to be able to run:

```
import android.os.Bundle
import androidx.activity.ComponentActivity
import androidx.activity.compose.setContent
import androidx.compose.material.MaterialTheme
import androidx.compose.material.Surface
import androidx.compose.material.Text
.
.
```

Initially, the list of import directives will most likely be "folded" to save space. To unfold the list, click on the small "+" button indicated by the arrow in Figure 3-12 below:

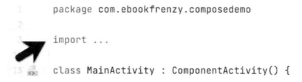

Figure 3-12

The MainActivity class is then declared as a subclass of the Android ComponentActivity class:

```
class MainActivity : ComponentActivity() {
.
.
}
```

The MainActivity class implements a single method in the form of *onCreate()*. This is the first method that is called when an activity is launched by the Android runtime system and is an artifact of the way apps used to be developed before the introduction of Compose. The *onCreate()* method is used here to provide a bridge between the containing activity and the Compose-based user interfaces that are to appear within it:

```
override fun onCreate(savedInstanceState: Bundle?) {
    super.onCreate(savedInstanceState)
    setContent {
        ComposeDemoTheme {
```

A Compose Project Overview

.

.

```
        }
    }
}
```

The method declares that the content of the activity's user interface will be provided by a composable function named *ComposeDemoTheme*. This composable function is declared in the *Theme.kt* file located under the *app -> <package name> -> ui.theme* folder in the Project tool window. This, along with the other files in the *ui.theme* folder defines the colors, fonts, and shapes to be used by the activity and provides a central location from which to customize the overall theme of the app's user interface.

The call to the ComposeDemoTheme composable function is configured to contain a Surface composable. Surface is a built-in Compose component designed to provide a background for other composables:

```
ComposeDemoTheme {
    // A surface container using the 'background' color from the theme
    Surface(
        modifier = Modifier.fillMaxSize(),
        color = MaterialTheme.colors.background

    .

    .

}
```

In this case, the Surface component is configured to fill the entire screen and with the background set to the standard background color defined by the Android Material Design theme. Material Design is a set of design guidelines developed by Google to provide a consistent look and feel across all Android apps. It includes a theme (including fonts and colors), a set of user interface components (such as button, text, and a range of text fields), icons, and generally defines how an Android app should look, behave and respond to user interactions.

Finally, the Surface is configured to contain a composable function named Greeting which is passed a string value that reads "Android":

```
ComposeDemoTheme {
    // A surface container using the 'background' color from the theme
    Surface(
        modifier = Modifier.fillMaxSize(),
        color = MaterialTheme.colors.background
    ) {
        Greeting("Android")
    }
}
```

Outside of the scope of the MainActivity class, we encounter our first composable function declaration within the activity. The function is named Greeting and is, unsurprisingly, marked as being composable by the @ *Composable* annotation:

```
@Composable
fun Greeting(name: String) {
    Text(text = "Hello $name!")
}
```

The function accepts a String parameter (labeled *name*) and calls the built-in Text composable, passing through a string value containing the word "Hello" concatenated with the name parameter. As will soon become evident as you work through the book, composable functions are the fundamental building blocks for developing Android apps using Compose.

The second composable function declared in the *MainActivity.kt* file reads as follows:

```
@Preview(showBackground = true)
@Composable
fun DefaultPreview() {
    ComposeDemoTheme {
        Greeting("Android")
    }
}
```

Earlier in the chapter, we looked at how the Preview panel allows us to see how the user interface will appear without having to compile and run the app. At first glance, it would be easy to assume that the preview rendering is generated by the code in the *onCreate()* method. In fact, that method only gets called when the app runs on a device or emulator. Previews are generated by preview composable functions. The *@Preview* annotation associated with the function tells Android Studio that this is a preview function and that the content emitted by the function is to be displayed in the Preview panel. As we will see later in the book, a single activity can contain multiple preview composable functions configured to preview specific sections of a user interface using different data values.

In addition, each preview may be configured by passing parameters to the *@Preview* annotation. For example, to view the preview with the rest of the standard Android screen decorations, modify the preview annotation so that it reads as follows:

```
@Preview(showSystemUi = true)
```

Once the preview has been updated, it should now be rendered as shown in Figure 3-13:

Figure 3-13

3.7 Preview updates

One final point worth noting is that the Preview panel is live and will automatically reflect minor changes made to the composable functions that make up a preview. To see this in action, edit the call to the Greeting function in the *DefaultPreview()* preview composable function to change the name from "Android" to "Compose". Note that as you make the change in the code editor, it is reflected in the preview.

More significant changes will require a build and refresh before being reflected in the preview. When this is required, Android Studio will display the following notice at the top of the Preview panel:

The preview is out of date   Build & Refresh (⌥⇧⌘R)

Figure 3-14

Simply click on the *Build & Refresh* link to update the preview for the latest changes.

The Preview panel also includes an interactive mode that allows you to trigger events on the user interface components (for example clicking buttons, moving sliders, scrolling through lists, etc.). Since ComposeDemo contains only an inanimate Text component at this stage, it makes more sense to introduce interactive mode in the next chapter.

3.8 Summary

In this chapter, we have created a new project using Android Studio's *Empty Compose Activity* template and explored some of the code automatically generated for the project. We have also introduced several features of Android Studio designed to make app development with Compose easier. The most useful features, and the places where you will spend most of your time while developing Android apps, are the code editor and Preview panel.

While the default code in the *MainActivity.kt* file provides an interesting example of a basic user interface, it bears no resemblance to the app we want to create. In the next chapter, we will modify and extend the app by removing some of the template code and writing our own composable functions.

4. An Example Compose Project

In the previous chapter, we created a new Compose-based Android Studio project named ComposeDemo and took some time to explore both Android Studio and some of the project code that it generated to get us started. With those basic steps covered, this chapter will use the ComposeDemo project as the basis for a new app. This will involve the creation of new composable functions, introduce the concept of state, and make use of the Preview panel in interactive mode. As with the preceding chapter, key concepts explained in basic terms here will be covered in significantly greater detail in later chapters.

4.1 Getting started

Start Android Studio if it is not already running and open the ComposeDemo project created in the previous chapter. Once the project has loaded, double-click on the *MainActivity.kt* file (located in Project tool window under *app -> java -> <package name>*) to open it in the code editor. If necessary, switch the editor into Split mode so that both the editor and Preview panel are visible.

4.2 Removing the template Code

Within the *MainActivity.kt* file, delete some of the template code so that the file reads as follows:

```
package com.example.composedemo
  .

  .
class MainActivity : ComponentActivity() {
    override fun onCreate(savedInstanceState: Bundle?) {
        super.onCreate(savedInstanceState)
        setContent {
            ComposeDemoTheme {
                Surface(
                    modifier = Modifier.fillMaxSize(),
                    color = MaterialTheme.colors.background
                ) {
                    Greeting("Android")
                }
            }
        }
    }
}


@Composable
fun Greeting(name: String) {
    Text(text = "Hello $name!")
}


@Preview(showSystemUi = true)
```

```
@Composable
fun DefaultPreview() {
    ComposeDemoTheme {
        Greeting("Android")
    }
}
```

4.3 The Composable hierarchy

Before we start to write the composable functions that will make up our user interface, it helps to first visualize the relationships between these components. The ability of one composable to call other composables essentially allows us to build a hierarchy tree of components. Once completed, the composable hierarchy for our ComposeDemo main activity can be represented as shown in Figure 4-1:

Figure 4-1

All of the elements in the above diagram, except for ComponentActivity, are composable functions. Of those functions, the Surface, Column, Spacer, Text, and Slider functions are built-in composables provided by Compose. The DemoScreen, DemoText, and DemoSlider composables, on the other hand, are functions that we will create to provide both structure to the design and the custom functionality we require for our app. The ComposeDemoTheme composable declaration can be found in the *ui.theme -> Theme.kt* file.

4.4 Adding the DemoText composable

We are now going to add a new composable function to the activity to represent the DemoText item in the hierarchy tree. The purpose of this composable is to display a text string using a font size value which adjusts in real-time as the slider is moved. Place the cursor beneath the final closing brace (}) of the MainActivity declaration and add the following function declaration:

```
@Composable
fun DemoText() {
}
```

The @Composable annotation notifies the build system that this is a composable function. When the function is called, the plan is for it to be passed both a text string and the font size at which that text is to be displayed. This means that we need to add some parameters to the function:

```
@Composable
fun DemoText(message: String, fontSize: Float) {

}
```

The next step is to make sure the text is displayed. To achieve this, we will make a call to the built-in Text composable, passing through as parameters the message string, font size and, to make the text more prominent, a bold font weight setting:

```
@Composable
fun DemoText(message: String, fontSize: Float) {
    Text(
        text = message,
        fontSize = fontSize.sp,
        fontWeight = FontWeight.Bold
    )
}
```

Note that after making these changes, the code editor is indicating that "sp" and "FontWeight" are undefined. This is happening because these are defined and implemented in libraries that have not yet been imported into the *MainActivity.kt* file. One way to resolve this is to click on an undefined declaration so that it highlights as shown below, and then press Alt+Enter (Opt+Enter on macOS) on the keyboard to automatically import the missing library:

```
@Composable
fun DemoText(message: String, fontSize: Float) {
    Text(
    ┌─────────────────────────────────────────────────┐
    │ ? androidx.compose.ui.text.font.FontWeight?  ⌥⏎ │
    └─────────────────────────────────────────────────┘
        fontSize = fontSize.sp,
        fontWeight = FontWeight.Bold
    )
}
```

Figure 4-2

Alternatively, the missing import statements may be added manually to the list at the top of the file:

.

.

```
import androidx.compose.ui.text.font.FontWeight
import androidx.compose.ui.unit.sp
```

.

.

In the remainder of this book, all code examples will include any required library import statements.

We have now finished writing our first composable function. Notice that, except for the font weight, all the other properties are passed to the function when it is called (a function that calls another function is generally referred to as the *caller*). This increases the flexibility, and therefore re-usability, of the DemoText composable and is a key goal to keep in mind when writing composable functions.

4.5 Previewing the DemoText composable

At this point, the Preview panel will most likely be displaying a message which reads "No preview found". The reason for this is that our *MainActivity.kt* file does not contain any composable functions prefixed with the @ Preview annotation. Add a preview composable function for DemoText to the *MainActivity.kt* file as follows:

```
@Preview
@Composable
fun DemoTextPreview() {
    DemoText(message = "Welcome to Android", fontSize = 12f)
}
```

After adding the preview composable, the Preview panel should have detected the change and displayed the link to build and refresh the preview rendering. Click the link and wait for the rebuild to complete, at which point the DemoText composable should appear as shown in Figure 4-3:

Figure 4-3

Minor changes made to the code in the *MainActivity.kt* file such as changing values will be instantly reflected in the preview without the need to build and refresh. For example, change the "Welcome to Android" text literal to "Welcome to Compose" and note that the text in the Preview panel changes as you type. Similarly, increasing the font size literal will instantly change the size of the text in the preview. This feature is referred to as Live Edit and can be enabled and disabled using the menu button indicated in Figure 4-4:

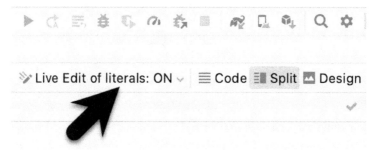

Figure 4-4

4.6 Adding the DemoSlider composable

The DemoSlider composable is a little more complicated than DemoText. It will need to be passed a variable containing the current slider position and an event handler function or lambda to call when the slider is moved by the user so that the new position can be stored and passed to the two Text composables. With these requirements in mind, add the function as follows:

```
.

.

import androidx.compose.foundation.layout.*
import androidx.compose.material.Slider
```

```
import androidx.compose.ui.unit.dp
  .
  .
@Composable
fun DemoSlider(sliderPosition: Float, onPositionChange: (Float) -> Unit ) {
    Slider(
        modifier = Modifier.padding(10.dp),
        valueRange = 20f..40f,
        value = sliderPosition,
        onValueChange = { onPositionChange(it) }
    )
}
```

The DemoSlider declaration contains a single Slider composable which is, in turn, passed four parameters. The first is a Modifier instance configured to add padding space around the slider. Modifier is a Kotlin class built into Compose which allows a wide range of properties to be set on a composable within a single object. Modifiers can also be created and customized in one composable before being passed to other composables where they can be further modified before being applied.

The second value passed to the Slider is a range allowed for the slider value (in this case the slider is limited to values between 20 and 40).

The next parameter sets the value of the slider to the position passed through by the caller. This ensures that each time DemoSlider is recomposed it retains the last position value.

Finally, we set the *onValueChange* parameter of the Slider to call the function or lambda we will be passing to the DemoSlider composable when we call it later. Each time the slider position changes, the call will be made and passed the current value which we can access via the Kotlin *it* keyword. We can further simplify this by assigning just the event handler parameter name (*onPositionChange*) and leaving the compiler to handle the passing of the current value for us:

```
onValueChange = onPositionChange
```

4.7 Adding the DemoScreen composable

The next step in our project is to add the DemoScreen composable. This will contain a variable named *sliderPosition* in which to store the current slider position and the implementation of the *handlePositionChange* event handler to be passed to the DemoSlider. This lambda will be responsible for storing the current position in the *sliderPosition* variable each time it is called with an updated value. Finally, DemoScreen will contain a Column composable configured to display the DemoText, Spacer, DemoSlider and the second, as yet to be added, Text composable in a vertical arrangement.

Start by adding the DemoScreen function as follows:

```
  .
  .
import androidx.compose.runtime.*
  .
  .
@Composable
fun DemoScreen() {
```

```
    var sliderPosition by remember { mutableStateOf(20f) }

    val handlePositionChange = { position : Float ->
        sliderPosition = position
    }
}
```

The *sliderPosition* variable declaration requires some explanation. As we will learn later, the Compose system repeatedly and rapidly *recomposes* user interface layouts in response to data changes. The change of slider position will, therefore, cause DemoScreen to be recomposed along with all of the composables it calls. Consider if we had declared and initialized our *sliderPosition* variable as follows:

```
var sliderPosition = 20f
```

Suppose the user slides the slider to position 21. The *handlePositionChange* event handler is called and stores the new value in the *sliderPosition* variable as follows:

```
val handlePositionChange = { position : Float ->
    sliderPosition = position
}
```

The Compose runtime system detects this data change and recomposes the user interface, including a call to the *DemoScreen* function which will, in turn, reinitialize the *sliderposition* variable to 20 causing the previous value of 21 to be lost. Declaring the *sliderPosition* variable in this way informs Compose that the current value needs to be remembered during recompositions:

```
var sliderPosition by remember { mutableStateOf(20f) }
```

The only remaining work within the DemoScreen implementation is to add a Column containing the required composable functions:

```
.
.
import androidx.compose.ui.Alignment
.
.
@Composable
fun DemoScreen() {

    var sliderPosition by remember { mutableStateOf(20f) }

    val handlePositionChange = { position : Float ->
        sliderPosition = position
    }

    Column(
        horizontalAlignment = Alignment.CenterHorizontally,
        verticalArrangement = Arrangement.Center,
        modifier = Modifier.fillMaxSize()
    ) {

        DemoText(message = "Welcome to Compose", fontSize = sliderPosition)
```

```
        Spacer(modifier = Modifier.height(150.dp))

        DemoSlider(
            sliderPosition = sliderPosition,
            onPositionChange = handlePositionChange
        )

        Text(
            style = MaterialTheme.typography.h2,
            text = sliderPosition.toInt().toString() + "sp"
        )
    }
}
```

Points to note regarding these changes may be summarized as follows:

- When DemoSlider is called, it is passed a reference to our handlePositionChange event handler as the onPositionChange parameter.

- The Column composable accepts parameters that customize layout behavior. In this case, we have configured the column to center its children both horizontally and vertically.

- A Modifier has been passed to the Spacer to place a 150dp vertical space between the DemoText and DemoSlider components.

- The second Text composable is configured to use the h2 (Heading 2) style of the Material theme. The *sliderPosition* value is converted from a Float to an integer so that only whole numbers are displayed and then converted to a string value before being displayed to the user.

4.8 Previewing the DemoScreen composable

To confirm that the DemoScreen layout meets our expectations, we need to add a preview composable to the file. Note that the original DemoTextPreview composable may also be removed at this point:

.

.

```
@Preview(showBackground = true, showSystemUi = true)
@Composable
fun Preview() {
    ComposeDemoTheme {
        DemoScreen()
    }
}

@Preview(showBackground = true, showSystemUi = true)
@Composable
fun DemoTextPreview() {
    SimpleDemoTheme {
        DemoText(message = " Welcome to Compose", 25f)
    }
}
```

Note that we have enabled the *showSystemUi* property of the preview so that we will experience how the app will look when running on an Android device.

After performing a preview rebuild and refresh, the user interface should appear as originally shown in Figure 3-1.

4.9 Testing in interactive mode

At this stage, we know that the user interface layout for our activity looks how we want it to, but we don't know if it will behave as intended. One option is to run the app on an emulator or physical device (topics which are covered in later chapters). A quicker option, however, is to switch the preview panel into interactive mode. This is achieved by clicking on the button indicated in Figure 4-5 below:

Figure 4-5

When clicked, there will be a short delay when interactive mode starts, after which it should be possible to move the slider and watch the two Text components update accordingly:

Figure 4-6

Click the stop button (marked A in Figure 4-7 below) to exit interactive mode. If it appears that the preview needs to be refreshed, simply click on the *Build Refresh* button (B):

Figure 4-7

4.10 Completing the project

The final step is to make sure that the DemoScreen composable is called from within the Surface function located in the *onCreate()* method of the MainActivity class. Locate this method and modify it as follows:

```
.

.

class MainActivity : ComponentActivity() {
    override fun onCreate(savedInstanceState: Bundle?) {
        super.onCreate(savedInstanceState)
        setContent {
            ComposeDemoTheme {
                Surface(
                    modifier = Modifier.fillMaxSize(),
                    color = MaterialTheme.colors.background
                ) {
                    DemoScreen()
                }
            }
        }
    }
}
```

This will ensure that, in addition to appearing in the preview panel, our user interface will also be displayed when the app runs on a device or emulator (a topic that will be covered in later chapters).

4.11 Summary

In this chapter, we have extended our ComposeDemo project to include some additional user interface elements in the form of two Text composables, a Spacer, and a Slider. These components were arranged vertically using a Column composable. We also introduced the concept of mutable state variables and explained how they are used to ensure that the app remembers state when the Compose runtime performs recompositions. The example also demonstrated how to use event handlers to respond to user interaction (in this case the user moving a slider). Finally, we made use of the Preview panel in interactive mode to test the app without the need to compile and run it on an emulator or physical device.

5. Creating an Android Virtual Device (AVD) in Android Studio

Although the Android Studio Preview panel allows us to see the layout we are designing and test basic functionality using interactive mode, it be will necessary to compile and run an entire app to fully test that it works. An Android application may be tested by installing and running it either on a physical device or in an *Android Virtual Device (AVD)* emulator environment. Before an AVD can be used, it must first be created and configured to match the specifications of a particular device model. In this chapter, we will work through the creation of such a virtual device using the Pixel 4 phone as a reference example.

5.1 About Android Virtual Devices

AVDs are essentially emulators that allow Android applications to be tested without the necessity to install the application on a physical Android-based device. An AVD may be configured to emulate a variety of hardware features including options such as screen size, memory capacity, and the presence or otherwise of features such as a camera, GPS navigation support, or an accelerometer. As part of the standard Android Studio installation, several emulator templates are installed allowing AVDs to be configured for a range of different devices. Custom configurations may be created to match any physical Android device by specifying properties such as processor type, memory capacity, and the size and pixel density of the screen.

An AVD session can appear either as a separate window or embedded within the Android Studio window.

New AVDs are created and managed using the Android Virtual Device Manager, which may be used either in command-line mode or with a more user-friendly graphical user interface. To create a new AVD, the first step is to launch the AVD Manager. This can be achieved from within the Android Studio environment by selecting the *Tools -> Device Manager* menu option from within the main window.

Once launched, the manager will appear as a tool window as shown in Figure 5-1:

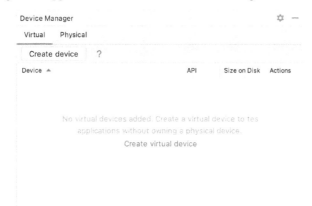

Figure 5-1

To add a new AVD, begin by making sure that the Virtual tab is selected before clicking on the *Create device*

Creating an Android Virtual Device (AVD) in Android Studio

button to open the *Virtual Device Configuration* dialog:

Figure 5-2

Within the dialog, perform the following steps to create a Pixel 4 compatible emulator:

1. From the *Category* panel, select the *Phone* option to display the list of available Android phone AVD templates.

2. Select the *Pixel 4* device option and click *Next*.

3. On the System Image screen, select the latest version of Android. Note that if the system image has not yet been installed a *Download* link will be provided next to the Release Name. Click this link to download and install the system image before selecting it. If the image you need is not listed, click on the *x86 Images* (or *ARM images* if you are running a Mac with Apple Silicon) and *Other images* tabs to view alternative lists.

4. Click *Next* to proceed and enter a descriptive name (for example *Pixel 4 API 32*) into the name field or simply accept the default name.

5. Click *Finish* to create the AVD.

6. With the AVD created, the Device Manager may now be closed. If future modifications to the AVD are necessary, simply re-open the Device Manager, select the AVD from the list, and click on the pencil icon in the Actions column to edit the settings.

5.2 Starting the emulator

To perform a test run of the newly created AVD emulator, simply select the emulator from the Device Manager and click on the launch button (the triangle in the Actions column). The emulator will appear embedded into the main Android Studio window and begin the startup process. The amount of time it takes for the emulator to start will depend on the configuration of both the AVD and the system on which it is running:

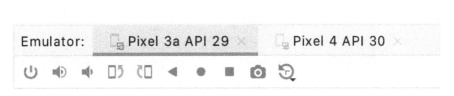

Figure 5-3

To hide and show the emulator tool window, click on the Emulator tool window button (marked A above). Click on the "x" close button next to the tab (B) to exit the emulator. The emulator tool window can accommodate multiple emulator sessions, with each session represented by a tab. Figure 5-4, for example, shows a tool window with two emulator sessions:

Figure 5-4

To switch between sessions, simply click on the corresponding tab.

Although the emulator probably defaulted to appearing in portrait orientation, this and other default options can be changed. Within the Device Manager, select the new Pixel 4 entry and click on the pencil icon in the *Actions* column of the device row. In the configuration screen, locate the *Startup orientation* section and change the orientation setting. Exit and restart the emulator session to see this change take effect. More details on the emulator are covered in the next chapter (*"Using and Configuring the Android Studio AVD Emulator"*).

To save time in the next section of this chapter, leave the emulator running before proceeding.

5.3 Running the application in the AVD

With an AVD emulator configured, the example ComposeDemo application created in the earlier chapter now can be compiled and run. With the ComposeDemo project loaded into Android Studio, make sure that the

Creating an Android Virtual Device (AVD) in Android Studio

newly created Pixel 4 AVD is displayed in the device menu (marked A in Figure 5-5 below), then either click on the run button represented by a green triangle (B), select the *Run -> Run 'app'* menu option or use the Ctrl-R keyboard shortcut:

Figure 5-5

The device menu (A) may be used to select a different AVD instance or physical device as the run target, and also to run the app on multiple devices. The menu also provides access to the Device Manager as well as device connection configuration and troubleshooting options:

Figure 5-6

The app can also be run on the currently selected target by clicking on the icon in the editor gutter next to the preview composable declaration as indicated by the arrow in Figure 5-7:

```
90      @Preview(showBackground = true, showSystemUi = true)
91      @Composable
92      fun Preview() {
93          ComposeDemoTheme {
94              DemoScreen()
95          }
96      }
```

Figure 5-7

Once the application is installed and running, the user interface layout defined by the MainScreen function will appear within the emulator:

Figure 5-8

If the activity does not automatically launch, check to see if the launch icon has appeared among the apps on the emulator. If it has, simply click on it to launch the application. Once the run process begins, the Run tool window will become available. The Run tool window will display diagnostic information as the application package is installed and launched. Figure 5-9 shows the Run tool window output from a successful application launch:

```
Run:    app    app                                                                                                        ✿ —
      08/31 10:37:50: Launching 'app' on Pixel 4 API 30.
      Install successfully finished in 1 s 529 ms.
      $ adb shell am start -n "com.ebookfrenzy.androidsample/com.ebookfrenzy.androidsample.MainActivity" -a android.intent.action.MAIN -c android.intent.category.LAUNCHER
      Connected to process 7477 on device 'emulator-5554'.
      Capturing and displaying logcat messages from application. This behavior can be disabled in the "Logcat output" section of the "Debugger" settings page.
      I/y.androidsampl: The ClassLoaderContext is a special shared library.
      D/NetworkSecurityConfig: No Network Security Config specified, using platform default
      
≣ TODO    🖾 Terminal    ⚒ Build    ⧉ 6: Logcat    ⌢ Profiler    🗄 Database Inspector    ▶ 4: Run                                  ⟲ Event Log    ⧉ Layout Inspector
```

Figure 5-9

If problems are encountered during the launch process, the Run tool window will provide information that will hopefully help to isolate the cause of the problem.

Assuming that the application loads into the emulator and runs as expected, we have safely verified that the Android development environment is correctly installed and configured.

5.4 Running on multiple devices

The run menu shown in Figure 5-6 above includes an option to run the app on multiple emulators and devices in parallel. When selected, this option displays the dialog shown in Figure 5-10 providing a list of both the AVDs configured on the system and any attached physical devices. Enable the checkboxes next to the emulators or devices to be targeted before clicking on the Run button:

Creating an Android Virtual Device (AVD) in Android Studio

Figure 5-10

After the Run button is clicked, Android Studio will launch the app on the selected emulators and devices.

5.5 Stopping a running application

To stop a running application, simply click on the stop button located in the main toolbar as shown in Figure 5-11:

Figure 5-11

An app may also be terminated using the Run tool window. Begin by displaying the *Run* tool window using the window bar button that becomes available when the app is running. Once the Run tool window appears, click the stop button highlighted in Figure 5-12 below:

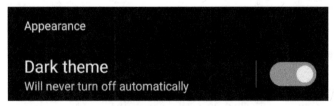

Figure 5-12

5.6 Supporting dark theme

Android 10 introduced the much-awaited dark theme, support for which is enabled by default in Android Studio Compose-based app projects. To test dark theme in the AVD emulator, open the Settings app within the running Android instance in the emulator. Within the Settings app, choose the *Display* category and enable the *Dark theme* option as shown in Figure 5-13 so that the screen background turns black:

Figure 5-13

With dark theme enabled, run the ComposeDemo app and note that it appears using a dark theme including a black background and a purple background color on the button as shown in Figure 5-14:

Figure 5-14

Return to the Settings app and turn off Dark theme mode before continuing.

5.7 Running the emulator in a separate window

So far in this chapter, we have only used the emulator as a tool window embedded within the main Android Studio window. To run the emulator in a separate window, select the *File -> Settings...* menu option (*Android Studio -> Preferences...* on macOS), navigate to *Tools -> Emulator* in the left-hand navigation panel of the preferences dialog, and disable the *Launch in a tool window* option:

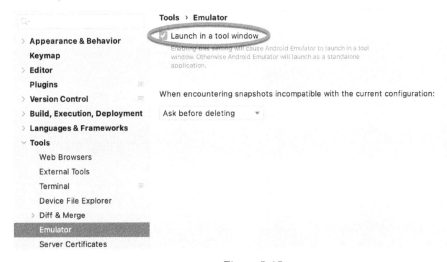

Figure 5-15

With the option disabled, click the Apply button followed by OK to commit the change, then exit the current emulator session by clicking on the close button on the tab marked B in Figure 5-3 above.

Creating an Android Virtual Device (AVD) in Android Studio

Run the sample app once again, at which point the emulator will appear as a separate window as shown below:

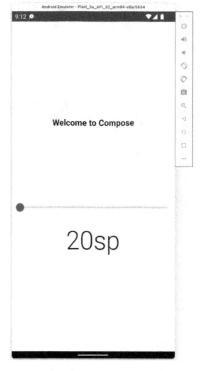

Figure 5-16

The choice of standalone or tool window mode is a matter of personal preference. If you prefer the emulator running in a tool window, return to the settings screen and re-enable the *Launch in a tool window* option. Before committing to standalone mode, however, keep in mind that the emulator tool window may also be detached from the main Android Studio window by clicking on the settings button (represented by the gear icon) in the tool emulator toolbar and selecting the *View Mode -> Float* menu option:

Figure 5-17

5.8 Enabling the device frame

The emulator can be configured to appear with (Figure 5-14) or without the device frame (Figure 5-16). To change the setting, open the Device Manager, select the AVD from the list, and click on the pencil icon in the Actions column to edit the settings. In the settings screen, locate and change the Enable Device Frame option:

Figure 5-18

5.9 AVD command-line creation

As previously discussed, in addition to the graphical user interface it is also possible to create a new AVD directly from the command-line. This is achieved using the *avdmanager* tool in conjunction with some command-line options. Once initiated, the tool will prompt for additional information before creating the new AVD.

The avdmanager tool requires access to the Java Runtime Environment (JRE) to run. If, when attempting to run avdmanager, an error message appears indicating that the 'java' command cannot be found, the command prompt or terminal window within which you are running the command can be configured to use the OpenJDK environment bundled with Android Studio. Begin by identifying the location of the OpenJDK JRE as follows:

1. Launch Android Studio and open the ComposeDemo project created earlier in the book.

2. Select the *File -> Settings...* menu option (*Android Studio -> Preferences...* on macOS).

3. Navigate to the Build, Execution, Deployment section and select the Gradle option listed under the Build Tools category.

4. Click on the *Gradle JDK* setting and make a note of the path for *Android Studio default JDK*:

Figure 5-19

On Windows, execute the following command within the command prompt window from which avdmanager is to be run (where *<path to jre>* is replaced by the path copied from the Project Structure dialog above):

```
set JAVA_HOME=<path to jre>
```

On macOS or Linux, execute the following command:

```
export JAVA_HOME="<path to jre>"
```

If you expect to use the avdmanager tool frequently, follow the environment variable steps for your operating

Creating an Android Virtual Device (AVD) in Android Studio

system outlined in the chapter entitled *"Setting up an Android Studio Development Environment"* to configure JAVA_HOME on a system-wide basis.

Assuming that the system has been configured such that the Android SDK *tools* directory is included in the PATH environment variable, a list of available targets for the new AVD may be obtained by issuing the following command in a terminal or command window:

```
avdmanager list targets
```

The resulting output from the above command will contain a list of Android SDK versions that are available on the system. For example:

```
Available Android targets:
----------
id: 1 or "android-29"
     Name: Android API 29
     Type: Platform
     API level: 29
     Revision: 1
----------
id: 2 or "android-26"
     Name: Android API 26
     Type: Platform
     API level: 26
     Revision: 1
```

The avdmanager tool also allows new AVD instances to be created from the command-line. For example, to create a new AVD named *myAVD* using the target ID for the Android API level 29 device using the x86 ABI, the following command may be used:

```
avdmanager create avd -n myAVD -k "system-images;android-29;google_apis_
playstore;x86"
```

The avdmanager tool will create the new AVD to the specifications required for a basic Android 8 device, also providing the option to create a custom configuration to match the specification of a specific device if required. Once a new AVD has been created from the command-line, it may not show up in the Android Device Manager tool until the *Refresh* button is clicked.

In addition to the creation of new AVDs, several other tasks may be performed from the command-line. For example, a list of currently available AVDs may be obtained using the *list avd* command-line arguments:

```
avdmanager list avd

Available Android Virtual Devices:
    Name: Pixel_XL_API_28_No_Play
  Device: pixel_xl (Google)
    Path: /Users/neilsmyth/.android/avd/Pixel_XL_API_28_No_Play.avd
  Target: Google APIs (Google Inc.)
          Based on: Android API 28 Tag/ABI: google_apis/x86
    Skin: pixel_xl_silver
  Sdcard: 512M
```

Similarly, to delete an existing AVD, simply use the *delete* option as follows:

```
avdmanager delete avd -n <avd name>
```

5.10 Android Virtual Device configuration files

By default, the files associated with an AVD are stored in the *.android/avd* sub-directory of the user's home directory, the structure of which is as follows (where *<avd name>* is replaced by the name assigned to the AVD):

```
<avd name>.avd/config.ini
<avd name>.avd/userdata.img
<avd name>.ini
```

The *config.ini* file contains the device configuration settings such as display dimensions and memory specified during the AVD creation process. These settings may be changed directly within the configuration file and will be adopted by the AVD when it is next invoked.

The *<avd name>.ini* file contains a reference to the target Android SDK and the path to the AVD files. Note that a change to the *image.sysdir* value in the *config.ini* file will also need to be reflected in the *target* value of this file.

5.11 Moving and renaming an Android Virtual Device

The current name or the location of the AVD files may be altered from the command-line using the *avdmanager* tool's *move avd* argument. For example, to rename an AVD named Pixel4 to Pixel4a, the following command may be executed:

```
avdmanager move avd -n Pixel4 -r Pixel4a
```

To physically relocate the files associated with the AVD, the following command syntax should be used:

```
avdmanager move avd -n <avd name> -p <path to new location>
```

For example, to move an AVD from its current file system location to /tmp/Pixel4Test:

```
avdmanager move avd -n Pixel4 -p /tmp/Pixel4Test
```

Note that the destination directory must not already exist before executing the command to move an AVD.

5.12 Summary

A typical application development process follows a cycle of coding, compiling, and running in a test environment. Android applications may be tested on either a physical Android device or using an Android Virtual Device (AVD) emulator. AVDs are created and managed using the Android Studio Device Manager tool which may be used either as a command-line tool or via a graphical user interface. When creating an AVD to simulate a specific Android device model, the virtual device should be configured with a hardware specification matching that of the physical device.

The AVD emulator session may be displayed as a standalone window or embedded into the main Android Studio user interface.

6. Using and Configuring the Android Studio AVD Emulator

Before the next chapter explores testing on physical Android devices, this chapter will take some time to provide an overview of the Android Studio AVD emulator and highlight many of the configuration features that are available to customize the environment in both standalone and tool window modes.

6.1 The emulator environment

When launched in standalone mode, the emulator displays an initial splash screen during the loading process. Once loaded, the main emulator window appears containing a representation of the chosen device type (in the case of Figure 6-1 this is a Pixel 4 device):

Figure 6-1

Positioned along the right-hand edge of the window is the toolbar providing quick access to the emulator controls and configuration options.

6.2 The emulator toolbar options

The emulator toolbar (Figure 6-2) provides access to a range of options relating to the appearance and behavior of the emulator environment.

Figure 6-2

Each button in the toolbar has associated with it a keyboard accelerator which can be identified either by hovering the mouse pointer over the button and waiting for the tooltip to appear or via the help option of the extended controls panel.

Though many of the options contained within the toolbar are self-explanatory, each option will be covered for the sake of completeness:

- **Exit / Minimize** – The uppermost 'x' button in the toolbar exits the emulator session when selected while the '-' option minimizes the entire window.

- **Power** – The Power button simulates the hardware power button on a physical Android device. Clicking and releasing this button will lock the device and turn off the screen. Clicking and holding this button will initiate the device "Power off" request sequence.

- **Volume Up / Down** – Two buttons that control the audio volume of playback within the simulator environment.

- **Rotate Left/Right** – Rotates the emulated device between portrait and landscape orientations.

- **Take Screenshot** – Takes a screenshot of the content currently displayed on the device screen. The captured image is stored at the location specified in the Settings screen of the extended controls panel as outlined later in this chapter.

- **Zoom Mode** – This button toggles in and out of zoom mode, details of which will be covered later in this chapter.

- **Back** – Performs the standard Android "Back" navigation to return to a previous screen.

- **Home** – Displays the device home screen.

- **Overview** – Simulates selection of the standard Android "Overview" navigation which displays the currently running apps on the device.

- **Fold Device** – Simulates the folding and unfolding of a foldable device. This option is only available if the emulator is running a foldable device system image.

- **Extended Controls** – Displays the extended controls panel, allowing for the configuration of options such as simulated location and telephony activity, battery strength, cellular network type, and fingerprint identification.

6.3 Working in zoom mode

The zoom button located in the emulator toolbar switches in and out of zoom mode. When zoom mode is active the toolbar button is depressed and the mouse pointer appears as a magnifying glass when hovering over the device screen. Clicking the left mouse button will cause the display to zoom in relative to the selected point on the screen, with repeated clicking increasing the zoom level. Conversely, clicking the right mouse button decreases the zoom level. Toggling the zoom button off reverts the display to the default size.

Clicking and dragging while in zoom mode will define a rectangular area into which the view will zoom when the mouse button is released.

While in zoom mode the visible area of the screen may be panned using the horizontal and vertical scrollbars located within the emulator window.

6.4 Resizing the emulator window

The size of the emulator window (and the corresponding representation of the device) can be changed at any time by clicking and dragging on any of the corners or sides of the window.

6.5 Extended control options

The extended controls toolbar button displays the panel illustrated in Figure 6-3. By default, the location settings will be displayed. Selecting a different category from the left-hand panel will display the corresponding group of controls:

Figure 6-3

6.5.1 Location

The location controls allow simulated location information to be sent to the emulator in the form of decimal or sexigesimal coordinates. Location information can take the form of a single location, or a sequence of points representing movement of the device, the latter being provided via a file in either GPS Exchange (GPX) or Keyhole Markup Language (KML) format. Alternatively, the integrated Google Maps panel may be used to visually select single points or travel routes.

6.5.2 Displays

In addition to the main display shown within the emulator screen, the Displays option allows additional displays to be added running within the same Android instance. This can be useful for testing apps for dual-screen devices such as the Microsoft Surface Duo. These additional screens can be configured to be any required size and appear within the same emulator window as the main screen.

6.5.3 Cellular

The type of cellular connection being simulated can be changed within the cellular settings screen. Options are available to simulate different network types (CSM, EDGE, HSDPA, etc) in addition to a range of voice and data scenarios such as roaming and denied access.

6.5.4 Battery

A variety of battery state and charging conditions can be simulated on this panel of the extended controls screen, including battery charge level, battery health, and whether the AC charger is currently connected.

6.5.5 Camera

The emulator simulates a 3D scene when the camera is active. This takes the form of the interior of a virtual building through which you can navigate by holding down the Option key (Alt on Windows) while using the mouse pointer and keyboard keys when recording video or before taking a photo within the emulator. This extended configuration option allows different images to be uploaded for display within the virtual environment.

6.5.6 Phone

The phone extended controls provide two very simple but useful simulations within the emulator. The first option allows for the simulation of an incoming call from a designated phone number. This can be of particular use when testing how an app handles high-level interrupts of this nature.

The second option allows the receipt of text messages to be simulated within the emulator session. As in the real world, these messages appear within the Message app and trigger the standard notifications within the emulator.

6.5.7 Directional pad

A directional pad (D-Pad) is an additional set of controls either built into an Android device or connected externally (such as a game controller) that provides directional controls (left, right, up, down). The directional pad settings allow D-Pad interaction to be simulated within the emulator.

6.5.8 Microphone

The microphone settings allow the microphone to be enabled and virtual headset and microphone connections to be simulated. A button is also provided to launch the Voice Assistant on the emulator.

6.5.9 Fingerprint

Many Android devices are now supplied with built-in fingerprint detection hardware. The AVD emulator makes it possible to test fingerprint authentication without the need to test apps on a physical device containing a fingerprint sensor. Details on how to configure fingerprint testing within the emulator will be covered in detail later in this chapter.

6.5.10 Virtual sensors

The virtual sensors option allows the accelerometer and magnetometer to be simulated to emulate the effects of the physical motion of a device such as rotation, movement, and tilting through yaw, pitch and roll settings.

6.5.11 Snapshots

Snapshots contain the state of the currently running AVD session to be saved and rapidly restored making it easy to return the emulator to an exact state. Snapshots are covered in later in this chapter.

6.5.12 Record and playback

Allows the emulator screen and audio to be recorded and saved in either WebM or animated GIF format.

6.5.13 Google Play

If the emulator is running a version of Android with Google Play Services installed, this option displays the current Google Play version and provides the option to update the emulator to the latest version.

6.5.14 Settings

The settings panel provides a small group of configuration options. Use this panel to choose a darker theme for the toolbar and extended controls panel, specify a file system location into which screenshots are to be saved, configure OpenGL support levels, and configure the emulator window to appear on top of other windows on the desktop.

6.5.15 Help

The Help screen contains three sub-panels containing a list of keyboard shortcuts, links to access the emulator online documentation, file bugs and send feedback, and emulator version information.

6.6 Working with snapshots

When an emulator starts for the very first time it performs a *cold boot* much like a physical Android device when it is powered on. This cold boot process can take some time to complete as the operating system loads and all the background processes are started. To avoid the necessity of going through this process every time the emulator is started, the system is configured to automatically save a snapshot (referred to as a *quick-boot snapshot*) of the emulator's current state each time it exits. The next time the emulator is launched, the quick-boot snapshot is loaded into memory and execution resumes from where it left off previously, allowing the emulator to restart in a fraction of the time needed for a cold boot to complete.

The Snapshots screen of the extended controls panel can be used to store additional snapshots at any point during the execution of the emulator. This saves the exact state of the entire emulator allowing the emulator to be restored to the exact point in time that the snapshot was taken. From within the screen, snapshots can be taken using the *Take Snapshot* button (marked A in Figure 6-4). To restore an existing snapshot, select it from the list (B) and click the run button (C) located at the bottom of the screen. Options are also provided to edit (D) the snapshot name and description and to delete (E) the currently selected snapshot:

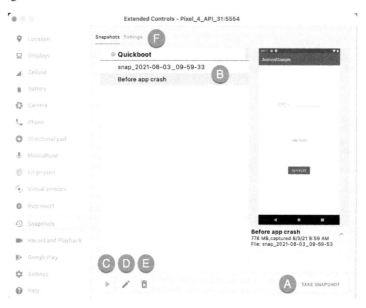

Figure 6-4

The Settings option (F) provides the option to configure the automatic saving of quick-boot snapshots (by default the emulator will ask whether to save the quick boot snapshot each time the emulator exits) and to reload the most recent snapshot. To force an emulator session to perform a cold boot instead of using a previous quick-boot snapshot, open the AVD Manager (*Tools -> AVD Manager*), click on the down arrow in the Actions column for the emulator and select the Cold Boot Now menu option.

Figure 6-5

6.7 Configuring fingerprint emulation

The emulator allows up to 10 simulated fingerprints to be configured and used to test fingerprint authentication within Android apps. To configure simulated fingerprints begin by launching the emulator, opening the Settings app, and selecting the *Security & Location* option.

Within the Security settings screen, select the *Use fingerprint* option. On the resulting information screen click on the *Next* button to proceed to the Fingerprint setup screen. Before fingerprint security can be enabled a backup screen unlocking method (such as a PIN) must be configured. Click on the *Fingerprint + PIN* button and, when prompted, choose not to require the PIN on device startup. Enter and confirm a suitable PIN and complete the PIN entry process by accepting the default notifications option.

Proceed through the remaining screens until the Settings app requests a fingerprint on the sensor. At this point display the extended controls dialog, select the *Fingerprint* category in the left-hand panel and make sure that

Finger 1 is selected in the main settings panel:

Figure 6-6

Click on the *Touch the Sensor* button to simulate Finger 1 touching the fingerprint sensor. The emulator will report the successful addition of the fingerprint:

Figure 6-7

To add additional fingerprints click on the *Add Another* button and select another finger from the extended controls panel menu before clicking on the *Touch the Sensor* button once again.

6.8 The emulator in tool window mode

As outlined in the previous chapter (*"Creating an Android Virtual Device (AVD) in Android Studio"*), Android Studio can be configured to launch the emulator as an embedded tool window so that it does not appear in a separate window. When running in this mode, the same controls available in standalone mode are provided in the toolbar as shown in Figure 6-8:

Figure 6-8

From left to right, these buttons perform the following tasks (details of which match those for standalone mode):

- Power

- Volume Up

- Volume Down

- Rotate Left

- Rotate Right

- Back

- Home

- Overview

- Screenshot

- Snapshots

- Extended Controls

6.9 Summary

Android Studio contains an Android Virtual Device emulator environment designed to make it easier to test applications without the need to run on a physical Android device. This chapter has provided a brief tour of the emulator and highlighted key features that are available to configure and customize the environment to simulate different testing conditions.

Chapter 7

7. A Tour of the Android Studio User Interface

While it is tempting to plunge into running the example application created in the previous chapter, doing so involves using aspects of the Android Studio user interface which are best described in advance.

Android Studio is a powerful and feature-rich development environment that is, to a large extent, intuitive to use. That being said, taking the time now to gain familiarity with the layout and organization of the Android Studio user interface will considerably shorten the learning curve in later chapters of the book. With this in mind, this chapter will provide an initial overview of the various areas and components that make up the Android Studio environment.

7.1 The Welcome screen

The welcome screen (Figure 7-1) is displayed any time that Android Studio is running with no projects currently open (open projects can be closed at any time by selecting the *File -> Close Project* menu option). If Android Studio was previously exited while a project was still open, the tool will bypass the welcome screen next time it is launched, automatically opening the previously active project.

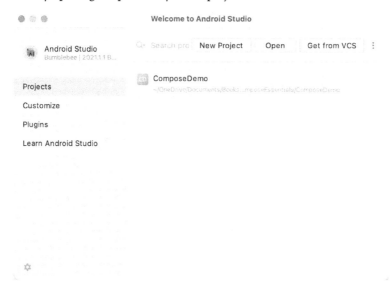

Figure 7-1

In addition to a list of recent projects, the welcome screen provides options for performing tasks such as opening and creating projects along with access to projects currently under version control. In addition, the *Customize* screen provides options to change the theme and font settings used by both the IDE and the editor. Android Studio plugins may be viewed, installed, and managed using the *Plugins* option.

Additional options are available by clicking on the menu button as shown in Figure 7-2:

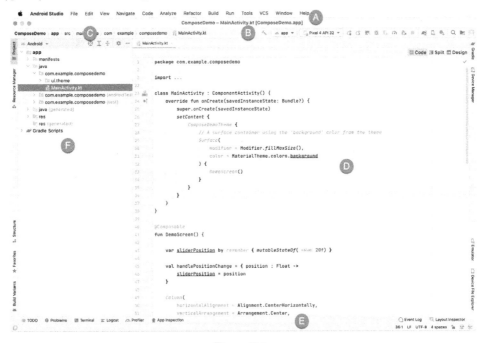

Figure 7-2

7.2 The main window

When a new project is created, or an existing one opened, the Android Studio *main window* will appear. When multiple projects are open simultaneously, each will be assigned its own main window. The precise configuration of the window will vary depending on which tools and panels were displayed the last time the project was open, but will typically resemble that of Figure 7-3.

Figure 7-3

The various elements of the main window can be summarized as follows:

A – Menu Bar – Contains a range of menus for performing tasks within the Android Studio environment.

B – Toolbar – A selection of shortcuts to frequently performed actions. The toolbar buttons provide quick access to a select group of menu bar actions. The toolbar can be customized by right-clicking on the bar and selecting the *Customize Menus and Toolbars…* menu option. If the toolbar is not visible, it can be displayed using the *View -> Appearance -> Toolbar* menu option.

C – Navigation Bar – The navigation bar provides a convenient way to move around the files and folders that make up the project. Clicking on an element in the navigation bar will drop down a menu listing the sub-folders and files at that location ready for selection. Similarly, clicking on a class name displays a menu listing methods contained within that class. Select a method from the list to be taken to the corresponding location within the code editor. Hide and display this bar using the *View -> Appearance -> Navigation Bar* menu option.

D – Editor Window – The editor window displays the content of the file on which the developer is currently working. When multiple files are open, each file is represented by a tab located along the top edge of the editor as shown in Figure 7-4.

Figure 7-4

E – Status Bar – The status bar displays informational messages about the project and the activities of Android Studio together with the tools menu button located in the far left corner. Hovering over items in the status bar will display a description of that field. Many fields are interactive, allowing the user to click to perform tasks or obtain more detailed status information.

F – Project Tool Window – The project tool window provides a hierarchical overview of the project file structure allowing navigation to specific files and folders to be performed. The toolbar can be used to display the project in several different ways. The default setting is the *Android* view which is the mode primarily used in the remainder of this book.

The project tool window is just one of many tool windows available within the Android Studio environment.

7.3 The tool windows

In addition to the project view tool window, Android Studio also includes many other windows which, when enabled, are displayed along the bottom and sides of the main window. The tool window quick access menu can be displayed by hovering the mouse pointer over the button located in the far left-hand corner of the status bar (Figure 7-5) without clicking the mouse button.

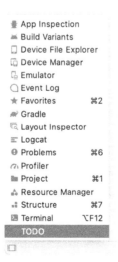

Figure 7-5

Selecting an item from the quick access menu will cause the corresponding tool window to appear within the main window.

Alternatively, a set of *tool window bars* can be displayed by clicking on the quick access menu icon in the status bar. These bars appear along the left, right, and bottom edges of the main window (as indicated by the arrows in

A Tour of the Android Studio User Interface

Figure 7-6) and contain buttons for showing and hiding each of the tool windows. When the tool window bars are displayed, a second click on the button in the status bar will hide them.

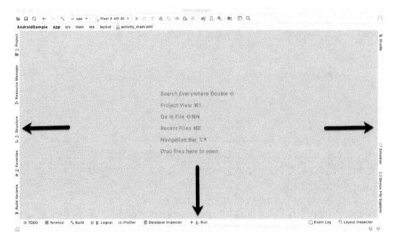

Figure 7-6

Clicking on a button will display the corresponding tool window while a second click will hide the window. Buttons prefixed with a number (for example 1: Project) indicate that the tool window may also be displayed by pressing the Alt key on the keyboard (or the Command key for macOS) together with the corresponding number.

The location of a button in a tool window bar indicates the side of the window against which the window will appear when displayed. These positions can be changed by clicking and dragging the buttons to different locations in other window toolbars.

Each tool window has its own toolbar along the top edge. The buttons within these toolbars vary from one tool to the next, though all tool windows contain a settings option, represented by the cog icon, which allows various aspects of the window to be changed. Figure 7-7 shows the settings menu for the Project tool window. Options are available, for example, to undock a window and to allow it to float outside of the boundaries of the Android Studio main window, and to move and resize the tool panel.

Figure 7-7

All of the windows also include a far-right button on the toolbar providing an additional way to hide the tool window from view. A search of the items within a tool window can be performed simply by giving that window focus by clicking in it and then typing the search term (for example the name of a file in the Project tool window). A search box will appear in the window's toolbar and items matching the search highlighted.

Android Studio offers a wide range of tool windows, the most commonly used of which are as follows:

- **App Inspector** - Provides access to the Database and Background Task inspectors. The Database Inspector allows you to inspect, query, and modify your app's databases while the app is running. The Background Task Inspector allows background worker tasks created using WorkManager to be monitored and managed.

- **Build** - The build tool window displays information about the build process while a project is being compiled and packaged and displays details of any errors encountered.

- **Build Variants** – The build variants tool window provides a quick way to configure different build targets for the current application project (for example different builds for debugging and release versions of the application, or multiple builds to target different device categories).

- **Device File Explorer** – Available via the *View -> Tool Windows -> Device File Explorer* menu, this tool window provides direct access to the filesystem of the currently connected Android device or emulator allowing the filesystem to be browsed and files copied to the local filesystem.

- **Device Manager** - Provides access to the Device Manager tool window where physical Android device connections and emulators may be added, removed, and managed.

- **Emulator** - Contains the AVD emulator if the option has been enabled to run the emulator in a tool window as outlined in the chapter entitled *"Creating an Android Virtual Device (AVD) in Android Studio"*.

- **Event Log** – The event log window displays messages relating to events and activities performed within Android Studio. The successful build of a project, for example, or the fact that an application is now running will be reported within this tool window.

- **Favorites** – A variety of project items can be added to the favorites list. Right-clicking on a file in the project view, for example, provides access to an *Add to Favorites* menu option. Similarly, a method in a source file can be added as a favorite by right-clicking on it in the Structure tool window. Anything added to a Favorites list can be accessed through this Favorites tool window.

- **Gradle** – The Gradle tool window provides a view of the Gradle tasks that make up the project build configuration. The window lists the tasks that are involved in compiling the various elements of the project into an executable application. Right-click on a top-level Gradle task and select the *Open Gradle Config* menu option to load the Gradle build file for the current project into the editor. Gradle will be covered in greater detail later in this book.

- **Layout Inspector** - Provides a visual 3D rendering of the hierarchy of components that make up a user interface layout.

- **Logcat** – The Logcat tool window provides access to the monitoring log output from a running application in addition to options for taking screenshots and videos of the application and stopping and restarting a process.

- **Problems** - A central location in which to view all of the current errors or warnings within the project. Double-clicking on an item in the problem list will take you to the problem file and location.

- **Profiler** – The Android Profiler tool window provides real-time monitoring and analysis tools for identifying performance issues within running apps, including CPU, memory and network usage. This option becomes available when an app is currently running.

- **Project** – The project view provides an overview of the file structure that makes up the project allowing for quick navigation between files. Generally, double-clicking on a file in the project view will cause that file to be loaded into the appropriate editing tool.

- **Resource Manager** - A tool for adding and managing resources and assets such as images, colors, and layout files contained with the project.

- **Run** – The run tool window becomes available when an application is currently running and provides a view of the results of the run together with options to stop or restart a running process. If an application is failing to install and run on a device or emulator, this window will typically provide diagnostic information relating to the problem.

- **Structure** – The structure tool provides a high-level view of the structure of the source file currently displayed in the editor. This information includes a list of items such as classes, methods, and variables in the file. Selecting an item from the structure list will take you to that location in the source file in the editor window.

- **Terminal** – Provides access to a terminal window on the system on which Android Studio is running. On Windows systems, this is the Command Prompt interface, while on Linux and macOS systems this takes the form of a Terminal prompt.

- **TODO** – As the name suggests, this tool provides a place to review items that have yet to be completed on the project. Android Studio compiles this list by scanning the source files that make up the project to look for comments that match specified TODO patterns. These patterns can be reviewed and changed by selecting the *File -> Settings...* menu option (*Android Studio -> Preferences...* on macOS) and navigating to the *TODO* page listed under *Editor*.

7.4 Android Studio keyboard shortcuts

Android Studio includes an abundance of keyboard shortcuts designed to save time when performing common tasks. A full keyboard shortcut keymap listing can be viewed and printed from within the Android Studio project window by selecting the *Help -> Keymap Reference* menu option. You may also list and modify the keyboard shortcuts by selecting the *File -> Settings...* menu option (*Android Studio -> Preferences...* on macOS) and clicking on the Keymap entry as shown in Figure 7-8 below:

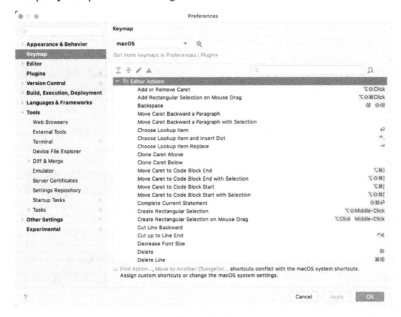

Figure 7-8

7.5 Switcher and recent files navigation

Another useful mechanism for navigating within the Android Studio main window involves the use of the *Switcher*. Accessed via the Ctrl-Tab keyboard shortcut, the switcher appears as a panel listing both the tool windows and currently open files (Figure 7-9).

Figure 7-9

Once displayed, the switcher will remain visible for as long as the Ctrl key remains depressed. Repeatedly tapping the Tab key while holding down the Ctrl key will cycle through the various selection options while releasing the Ctrl key causes the currently highlighted item to be selected and displayed within the main window.

In addition to the switcher, navigation to recently opened files is provided by the Recent Files panel (Figure 7-10). This can be accessed using the Ctrl-E keyboard shortcut (Cmd-E on macOS). Once displayed, either the mouse pointer can be used to select an option or the keyboard arrow keys used to scroll through the file name and tool window options. Pressing the Enter key will select the currently highlighted item.

Figure 7-10

7.6 Changing the Android Studio theme

The overall theme of the Android Studio environment may be changed either from the welcome screen using the *Configure -> Settings* option or via the *File -> Settings...* menu option (*Android Studio -> Preferences...* on macOS) of the main window.

Once the settings dialog is displayed, select the *Appearance & Behavior* option followed by *Appearance* in the left-hand panel and then change the setting of the *Theme* menu before clicking on the *Apply* button. The themes available will depend on the platform but usually include options such as Light, IntelliJ, Windows, High Contrast, and Darcula. Figure 7-11 shows an example of the main window with the Darcula theme selected:

Figure 7-11

To synchronize the Android Studio theme with the operating system light and dark mode setting, enable the *Sync with OS* option and use the drop-down menu to control which theme to use for each mode:

Figure 7-12

7.7 Summary

The primary elements of the Android Studio environment consist of the welcome screen and main window. Each open project is assigned its own main window which, in turn, consists of a menu bar, toolbar, editing and design area, status bar, and a collection of tool windows. Tool windows appear on the sides and bottom edges of the main window and can be accessed either using the quick access menu located in the status bar or via the optional tool window bars.

There are very few actions within Android Studio that cannot be triggered via a keyboard shortcut. A keymap of default keyboard shortcuts can be accessed at any time from within the Android Studio main window.

8. Testing Android Studio Apps on a Physical Android Device

While much can be achieved by testing applications using an Android Virtual Device (AVD), there is no substitute for performing real-world application testing on a physical Android device and there are some Android features that are only available on physical Android devices.

Communication with both AVD instances and connected Android devices is handled by the *Android Debug Bridge (ADB)*. In this chapter, we explain how to configure the adb environment to enable application testing on an Android device with macOS, Windows, and Linux-based systems.

8.1 An overview of the Android Debug Bridge (ADB)

The primary purpose of the ADB is to facilitate interaction between a development system, in this case, Android Studio, and both AVD emulators and Android devices to run and debug applications. ADB allows you to connect to devices either over a WiFi network or directly using a USB cable.

The ADB consists of a client, a server process running in the background on the development system, and a daemon background process running in either AVDs or real Android devices such as phones and tablets.

The ADB client can take a variety of forms. For example, a client is provided in the form of a command-line tool named *adb* located in the Android SDK *platform-tools* sub-directory. Similarly, Android Studio also has a built-in client.

A variety of tasks may be performed using the *adb* command-line tool. For example, a listing of currently active virtual or physical devices may be obtained using the *devices* command-line argument. The following command output indicates the presence of an AVD on the system but no physical devices:

```
$ adb devices
List of devices attached
emulator-5554    device
```

8.2 Enabling USB debugging ADB on Android devices

Before ADB can connect to an Android device, that device must first be configured to allow the connection. On phone and tablet devices running Android 6.0 or later, the steps to achieve this are as follows:

1. Open the Settings app on the device and select the *About tablet* or *About phone* option (on some versions of Android this can be found on the *System* page of the Settings app).

2. On the *About* screen, scroll down to the *Build number* field (Figure 8-1) and tap on it seven times until a message appears indicating that developer mode has been enabled. If the Build number is not listed on the About screen it may be available via the *Software information* option. Alternatively, unfold the Advanced section of the list if available.

Wi-Fi MAC address
02:00:00:44:55:66

Build number
PPP2.180412.012

Figure 8-1

3. Return to the main Settings screen and note the appearance of a new option titled Developer options (on newer versions of Android this option is listed on the System settings screen). Select this option and on the resulting screen, locate the USB debugging option as illustrated in Figure 8-2:

Debugging

USB debugging
Debug mode when USB is connected

Figure 8-2

4. Enable the USB debugging option and tap the Allow button when confirmation is requested.

At this point, the device is now configured to accept debugging connections from adb on the development system over a USB connection. All that remains is to configure the development system to detect the device when it is attached. While this is a relatively straightforward process, the steps involved differ depending on whether the development system is running Windows, macOS, or Linux. Note that the following steps assume that the Android SDK *platform-tools* directory is included in the operating system PATH environment variable as described in the chapter entitled *"Setting up an Android Studio Development Environment"*.

8.2.1 macOS ADB configuration

To configure the ADB environment on a macOS system, connect the device to the computer system using a USB cable, open a terminal window and execute the following command to restart the adb server:

```
$ adb kill-server
$ adb start-server
* daemon not running. starting it now on port 5037 *
* daemon started successfully *
```

Once the server is successfully running, execute the following command to verify that the device has been detected:

```
$ adb devices
List of devices attached
74CE000600000001        offline
```

If the device is listed as *offline*, go to the Android device and check for the presence of the dialog shown in Figure 8-3 seeking permission to *Allow USB debugging*. Enable the checkbox next to the option that reads *Always allow from this computer*, before clicking on *OK*.

Figure 8-3

Repeating the *adb devices* command should now list the device as being available:

```
List of devices attached
015d41d4454bf80c        device
```

If the device is not listed, try logging out and then back into the macOS desktop and, if the problem persists, rebooting the system.

8.2.2 Windows ADB configuration

The first step in configuring a Windows-based development system to connect to an Android device using ADB is to install the appropriate USB drivers on the system. The USB drivers to install will depend on the model of the Android Device. If you have a Google device such as a Pixel phone, then it will be necessary to install and configure the Google USB Driver package on your Windows system. Detailed steps to achieve this are outlined on the following web page:

https://developer.android.com/sdk/win-usb.html

For Android devices not supported by the Google USB driver, it will be necessary to download the drivers provided by the device manufacturer. A listing of drivers together with download and installation information can be obtained online at:

https://developer.android.com/tools/extras/oem-usb.html

With the drivers installed and the device now being recognized as the correct device type, open a Command Prompt window and execute the following command:

```
adb devices
```

This command should output information about the connected device similar to the following:

```
List of devices attached
HT4CTJT01906        offline
```

If the device is listed as *offline* or *unauthorized*, go to the device display and check for the dialog shown in Figure 8-3 seeking permission to *Allow USB debugging*. Enable the checkbox next to the option that reads *Always allow from this computer*, before clicking on *OK*. Repeating the *adb devices* command should now list the device as being ready:

```
List of devices attached
HT4CTJT01906    device
```

If the device is not listed, execute the following commands to restart the ADB server:

```
adb kill-server
adb start-server
```

If the device is still not listed, try executing the following command:

```
android update adb
```

Note that it may also be necessary to reboot the system.

8.2.3 Linux adb configuration

For this chapter, we will once again use Ubuntu Linux as a reference example in terms of configuring adb on Linux to connect to a physical Android device for application testing.

Physical device testing on Ubuntu Linux requires the installation of a package named *android-tools-adb* which, in turn, requires that the Android Studio user be a member of the *plugdev* group. This is the default for user accounts on most Ubuntu versions and can be verified by running the *id* command. If the plugdev group is not listed, run the following command to add your account to the group:

```
sudo usermod -aG plugdev $LOGNAME
```

After the group membership requirement has been met, the *android-tools-adb* package can be installed by executing the following command:

```
sudo apt-get install android-tools-adb
```

Once the above changes have been made, reboot the Ubuntu system. Once the system has restarted, open a Terminal window, start the adb server and check the list of attached devices:

```
$ adb start-server
* daemon not running. starting it now on port 5037 *
* daemon started successfully *
$ adb devices
List of devices attached
015d41d4454bf80c        offline
```

If the device is listed as *offline* or *unauthorized*, go to the Android device and check for the dialog shown in Figure 8-3 seeking permission to *Allow USB debugging*.

8.3 Resolving USB connection issues

If you are unable to successfully connect to the device using the above steps, display the run target menu (Figure 8-4) and select the *Troubleshoot Device Connections* option:

Figure 8-4

The connection assistant will scan for devices and report problems and possible solutions.

8.4 Enabling wireless debugging on Android devices

Follow steps 1 through 3 from section 8.2 above, this time enabling the Wireless Debugging option as shown in Figure 8-5:

Wireless debugging
Debug mode when Wi-Fi is connected

Figure 8-5

Next, tap the above Wireless debugging entry to display the screen shown in Figure 8-6:

Wireless debugging

Use wireless debugging

Device name
sdk_gphone64_arm64

IP address & Port
10.0.2.16:38159

Pair device with QR code
Pair new devices using QR code scanner

Pair device with pairing code
Pair new devices using six digit code

Figure 8-6

If the device you are using has a camera, select *Pair device with QR code*, otherwise select the *Pair device with pairing code* option. Depending on your selection, the Settings app will either start a camera session or display a pairing code as shown in Figure 8-7:

Pair with device
Wi-Fi pairing code
909814
IP address & Port
10.0.2.16:43967

Cancel

Figure 8-7

With an option selected, return to Android Studio and select the *Pair Devices Using WiFi* option from the run target menu as illustrated in Figure 8-8:

Testing Android Studio Apps on a Physical Android Device

Figure 8-8

In the pairing dialog, select either *Pair using QR code* or *Pair using pairing code* depending on your previous selection in the Settings app on the device:

Figure 8-9

Either scan the QR code using the Android device or enter the pairing code displayed on the device screen into the Android Studio dialog (Figure 8-10) to complete the pairing process:

Figure 8-10

If the pairing process fails, try rebooting both the development system and Android device and try again.

8.5 Testing the adb connection

Assuming that the adb configuration has been successful on your chosen development platform, the next step is to try running the test application created in the chapter entitled *"An Example Compose Project"* on the device. Launch Android Studio, open the ComposeDemo project, and verify that the device appears in the device selection menu as highlighted in Figure 8-11:

Figure 8-11

Select the device from the list and click on the run button (the green arrow button located immediately to the right of the device menu) to install and run the app.

8.6 Summary

While the Android Virtual Device emulator provides an excellent testing environment, it is important to keep in mind that there is no real substitute for making sure an application functions correctly on a physical Android device. This, after all, is where the application will be used in the real world.

By default, however, the Android Studio environment is not configured to detect Android devices as a target testing device. It is necessary, therefore, to perform some steps to be able to load applications directly onto an Android device from within the Android Studio development environment either via a USB cable or over a WiFi network. The exact steps to achieve this goal differ depending on the development platform being used. In this chapter, we have covered those steps for Linux, macOS, and Windows-based platforms.

9. The Basics of the Android Studio Code Editor

Developing applications for Android involves a considerable amount of programming work which, by definition, involves typing, reviewing, and modifying lines of code. It should come as no surprise that the majority of a developer's time spent using Android Studio will typically involve editing code within the editor window.

The modern code editor needs to go far beyond the original basics of typing, deleting, cutting, and pasting. Today the usefulness of a code editor is generally gauged by factors such as the amount by which it reduces the typing required by the programmer, ease of navigation through large source code files, and the editor's ability to detect and highlight programming syntax errors in real-time as the code is being written. As will become evident in this chapter, these are just a few of the areas in which the Android Studio editor excels.

While not an exhaustive overview of the features of the Android Studio editor, this chapter aims to provide a guide to the key features of the tool. Experienced programmers will find that some of these features are common to most code editors available today, while a number are unique to this particular editing environment.

9.1 The Android Studio editor

The Android Studio editor appears in the center of the main window when a Java, Kotlin, XML, or other text-based file is selected for editing. Figure 9-1, for example, shows a typical editor session with a Kotlin source code file loaded:

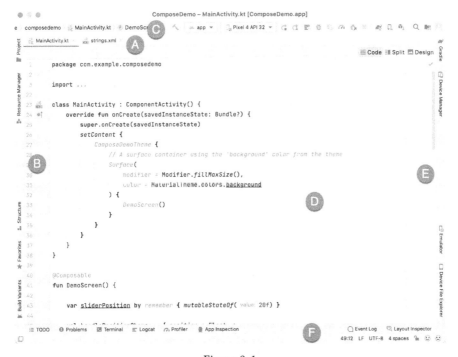

Figure 9-1

The Basics of the Android Studio Code Editor

The elements that comprise the editor window can be summarized as follows:

A – Document Tabs – Android Studio is capable of holding multiple files open for editing at any one time. As each file is opened, it is assigned a document tab displaying the file name in the tab bar located along the top edge of the editor window. A small drop-down menu will appear in the far right-hand corner of the tab bar when there is insufficient room to display all of the tabs. Clicking on this menu will drop down a list of additional open files. A wavy red line underneath a file name in a tab indicates that the code in the file contains one or more errors that need to be addressed before the project can be compiled and run.

Switching between files is simply a matter of clicking on the corresponding tab or using the Alt-Left and Alt-Right keyboard shortcuts. Navigation between files may also be performed using the Switcher mechanism (accessible via the Ctrl-Tab keyboard shortcut).

To detach an editor panel from the Android Studio main window so that it appears in a separate window, click on the tab and drag it to an area on the desktop outside of the main window. To return the editor to the main window, click on the file tab in the separated editor window and drag and drop it onto the original editor tab bar in the main window.

B – The Editor Gutter Area - The gutter area is used by the editor to display informational icons and controls. Some typical items, among others, which appear in this gutter area are debugging breakpoint markers, controls to fold and unfold blocks of code, bookmarks, change markers, and line numbers. Line numbers are switched on by default but may be disabled by right-clicking in the gutter and selecting the Show Line Numbers menu option.

C – Code Structure Location - This bar at the bottom of the editor displays the current position of the cursor as it relates to the overall structure of the code. In the following figure, for example, the bar indicates that the *onCreate()* method is currently being edited and that this method is contained within the MainActivity class.

Figure 9-2

Double-clicking an element within the bar will move the cursor to the corresponding location within the code file. For example, double-clicking on the *onCreate()* entry will move the cursor to the top of that method within the source code. Similarly clicking on the *MainActivity.kt* entry will drop down a list of available code navigation points for selection:

Figure 9-3

D – The Editor Area – This is the main area where the code is displayed, entered, and edited by the user. Later sections of this chapter will cover the key features of the editing area in detail.

E – The Validation and Marker Sidebar – Android Studio incorporates a feature referred to as "on-the-fly code analysis". What this essentially means is that as you are typing code, the editor is analyzing the code to check for warnings and syntax errors. The indicators at the top of the validation sidebar will update in real-time to indicate the number of errors and warnings found as code is added. Clicking on this indicator will display a popup containing a summary of the issues found with the code in the editor as illustrated in Figure 9-4:

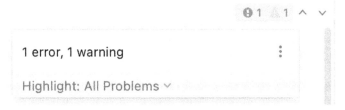

Figure 9-4

The up and down arrows may be used to move between the error locations within the code. A green checkmark indicates that no warnings or errors have been detected.

The sidebar also displays markers at the locations where issues have been detected using the same color-coding. Hovering the mouse pointer over a marker when the line of code is visible in the editor area will display a popup containing a description of the issue:

> Too many arguments for public open fun show(): Unit defined in com.google.android.material.snackbar.Snackbar ⋮
>
> Unresolved reference: nul
>
> Create abstract property 'nul' ⌥⇧⏎   More actions... ⌥⏎

Figure 9-5

Hovering the mouse pointer over a marker for a line of code that is currently scrolled out of the viewing area of the editor will display a "lens" overlay containing the block of code where the problem is located (Figure 9-6) allowing it to be viewed without needing to scroll to that location in the editor:

```
46     override fun onOptionsItemSelected(item: MenuItem): Boolean {
47         // Handle action bar item clicks here. The action bar will
48         // automatically handle clicks on the Home/Up button, so long
49         // as you specify a parent activity in AndroidManifest.xml.
50         return when (item.itemId) {
51             R.id.action_settings -> true
52             else -> super.onOptionsItemSelected(item) |  Unresolved reference: l   Expecting an element
53         }
54     }
55   }
```

Figure 9-6

It is also worth noting that the lens overlay is not limited to warnings and errors in the sidebar. Hovering over any part of the sidebar will result in a lens appearing containing the code present at that location within the source file.

F – The Status Bar – Though the status bar is part of the main window, as opposed to the editor, it does contain some information about the currently active editing session. This information includes the current position of the cursor in terms of lines and characters and the encoding format of the file (UTF-8, ASCII, etc.). Clicking on these values in the status bar allows the corresponding setting to be changed. Clicking on the line number, for example, displays the Go to Line dialog.

Having provided an overview of the elements that comprise the Android Studio editor, the remainder of this chapter will explore the key features of the editing environment in more detail.

9.2 Code mode

The code editor has three modes in which it can be placed using the buttons located in the top right-hand corner of the editor panel. In Figure 9-7 below, for example, Code mode has been selected:

Figure 9-7

When in code mode, only the code editor panel is displayed and the Preview panel is hidden from view. In Split mode, the editor shows the Code and Preview panels side-by-side. In Design mode, only the Preview panel is displayed.

9.3 Splitting the editor window

By default, the editor will display a single panel showing the content of the currently selected file. A particularly useful feature when working simultaneously with multiple source code files is the ability to split the editor into multiple panes. To split the editor, right-click on a file tab within the editor window and select either the Split Vertically or Split Horizontally menu option. Figure 9-8, for example, shows the splitter in action with the editor split into three panels:

Figure 9-8

The orientation of a split panel may be changed at any time by right-clicking on the corresponding tab and selecting the Change Splitter Orientation menu option. Repeat these steps to unsplit a single panel, this time selecting the Unsplit option from the menu. All of the split panels may be removed by right-clicking on any tab and selecting the Unsplit All menu option.

Window splitting may be used to display different files, or to provide multiple windows onto the same file, allowing different areas of the same file to be viewed and edited concurrently.

9.4 Code completion

The Android Studio editor has a considerable amount of built-in knowledge of Kotlin and Compose programming syntax and the classes and methods that make up the Android SDK, as well as knowledge of your codebase. As code is typed, the editor scans what is being typed and, where appropriate, makes suggestions about what might be needed to complete a statement or reference. When a completion suggestion is detected by the editor, a panel will appear containing a list of suggestions. In Figure 9-9, for example, the editor is suggesting possibilities for the beginning of a String declaration:

Figure 9-9

If none of the auto-completion suggestions are correct, simply keep typing and the editor will continue to refine the suggestions where appropriate. To accept the topmost suggestion, simply press the Enter or Tab key on the keyboard. To select a different suggestion, use the arrow keys to move up and down the list, once again using the Enter or Tab key to select the highlighted item.

Completion suggestions can be manually invoked using the Ctrl-Space keyboard sequence. This can be useful when changing a word or declaration in the editor. When the cursor is positioned over a word in the editor, that word will automatically highlight. Pressing Ctrl-Space will display a list of alternate suggestions. To replace the current word with the currently highlighted item in the suggestion list, simply press the Tab key.

In addition to the real-time auto-completion feature, the Android Studio editor also offers a system referred to as Smart Completion. Smart completion is invoked using the Shift-Ctrl-Space keyboard sequence and, when selected, will provide more detailed suggestions based on the current context of the code. Pressing the Shift-Ctrl-Space shortcut sequence a second time will provide more suggestions from a wider range of possibilities.

Code completion can be a matter of personal preference for many programmers. In recognition of this fact, Android Studio provides a high level of control over the auto-completion settings. These can be viewed and modified by selecting the *File -> Settings…* menu option (or *Android Studio -> Preferences…* on macOS) and choosing *Editor -> General -> Code Completion* from the settings panel as shown in Figure 9-10:

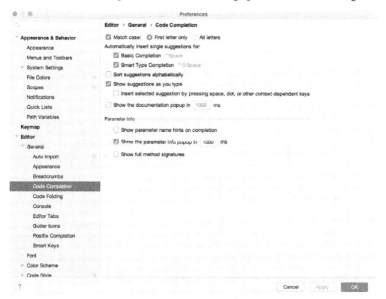

Figure 9-10

9.5 Statement completion

Another form of auto-completion provided by the Android Studio editor is statement completion. This can be used to automatically fill out the parentheses and braces for items such as methods and loop statements. Statement completion is invoked using the Shift-Ctrl-Enter (Shift-Cmd-Enter on macOS) keyboard sequence. Consider for example the following code:

```
fun myMethod()
```

Having typed this code into the editor, triggering statement completion will cause the editor to automatically add the braces to the method:

```
fun myMethod() {


}
```

9.6 Parameter information

It is also possible to ask the editor to provide information about the argument parameters accepted by a method. With the cursor positioned between the brackets of a method call, the Ctrl-P (Cmd-P on macOS) keyboard sequence will display the parameters known to be accepted by that method, with the most likely suggestion highlighted in bold:

Figure 9-11

9.7 Parameter name hints

The code editor may be configured to display parameter name hints within method calls. Figure 9-12, for example, highlights the parameter name hints within the calls to the *make()* and *setAction()* methods of the Snackbar class:

Figure 9-12

The settings for this mode may be configured by selecting the *File -> Settings* menu (*Android Studio -> Preferences* on macOS) option followed by *Editor -> Inlay Hints -> Kotlin* in the left-hand panel. On the resulting screen, select the Parameter Hints item from the list and enable or disable the Show parameter hints option. To adjust the hint settings, click on the *Exclude list...* link and make any necessary adjustments.

9.8 Code generation

In addition to completing code as it is typed the editor can, under certain conditions, also generate code for you. The list of available code generation options shown in Figure 9-13 can be accessed using the Alt-Insert (Cmd-N on macOS) keyboard shortcut when the cursor is at the location in the file where the code is to be generated.

Figure 9-13

For example, consider a situation where we want to be notified when an Activity in our project is about to be destroyed by the operating system. This can be achieved by overriding the *onStop()* lifecycle method of the Activity superclass. To have Android Studio generate a stub method for this, simply select the *Override Methods…* option from the code generation list and select the *onStop()* method from the resulting list of available methods:

Figure 9-14

Having selected the method to override, clicking on OK will generate the stub method at the current cursor location in the Kotlin source file as follows:

```kotlin
override fun onStop() {
    super.onStop()
}
```

9.9 Code folding

Once a source code file reaches a certain size, even the most carefully formatted and well-organized code can become overwhelming and difficult to navigate. Android Studio takes the view that it is not always necessary to have the content of every code block visible at all times. Code navigation can be made easier through the use of the code folding feature of the Android Studio editor. Code folding is controlled using markers appearing in the editor gutter at the beginning and end of each block of code in a source file. Figure 9-15, for example, highlights

The Basics of the Android Studio Code Editor

the start and end markers for code that is not currently folded:

```
71      @Composable
72      fun DemoText(message: String, fontSize: Float) {
73          Text(
74              text = message,
75              fontSize = fontSize.sp,
76              fontWeight = FontWeight.Bold
77          )
78      }
```

Figure 9-15

Clicking on either of these markers will fold the statement such that only the signature line is visible as shown in Figure 9-16:

```
71      @Composable
72      fun DemoText(message: String, fontSize: Float) {...}
79
```

Figure 9-16

To unfold a collapsed section of code, click on the '+' marker in the editor gutter. To see the hidden code without unfolding it, hover the mouse pointer over the "{...}" indicator as shown in Figure 9-17. The editor will then display the lens overlay containing the folded code block:

```
71      @Composable
72      fun DemoText(message: String, fontSize: Float) {..
72      fun DemoText(message: String, fontSize: Float) {
73          Text(
74              text = message,                              nange: (Float) -> Unit ) {
75              fontSize = fontSize.sp,
76              fontWeight = FontWeight.Bold
77          )
78      }
```

Figure 9-17

All of the code blocks in a file may be folded or unfolded using the Ctrl-Shift-Plus and Ctrl-Shift-Minus keyboard sequences.

By default, the Android Studio editor will automatically fold some code when a source file is opened. To configure the conditions under which this happens, select *File -> Settings...* (*Android Studio -> Preferences...* on macOS) and choose the *Editor -> General -> Code Folding* entry in the resulting settings panel (Figure 9-18):

Figure 9-18

9.10 Quick documentation lookup

Context-sensitive Kotlin and Android documentation can be accessed by hovering the cursor over the declaration for which documentation is required. This will display a popup containing the relevant reference documentation for the item. Figure 9-19, for example, shows the documentation for the Android Bundle class.

```
23    class MainActivity : ComponentActivity() {
24        override fun onCreate(savedInstanceState: Bundle?) {
25            super.onCreate(savedInstanceState)
26            setContent {                          Bundle
27                ComposeDemoTheme {               Kotlin ↗  |Java
28                    // A surface container using th
29                    Surface(
30                        modifier = Modifier.fillMax    public final class Bundle
31                        color = MaterialTheme.color    extends BaseBundle ↗  implements Cloneable ↗ , Parcelable ↗
32                    ) {                                A mapping from String keys to various Parcelable ↗  values.
33                        DemoScreen()                   See also:
34                    }                                  • PersistableBundle ↗
35                }                                      ≣ < Android API 32 Platform >
36            }                                          `Bundle` on developer.android.com ↗
```

Figure 9-19

Once displayed, the documentation popup can be moved around the screen as needed.

9.11 Code reformatting

In general, the Android Studio editor will automatically format code in terms of indenting, spacing, and nesting of statements and code blocks as they are added. In situations where lines of code need to be reformatted (a common occurrence, for example, when cutting and pasting sample code from a website), the editor provides a source code reformatting feature which, when selected, will automatically reformat code to match the prevailing code style.

To reformat source code, press the Ctrl-Alt-L (Cmd-Opt-L on macOS) keyboard shortcut sequence. To display the Reformat File dialog (Figure 9-20) use the Ctrl-Alt-Shift-L (Cmd-Opt-Shift-L on macOS). This dialog provides the option to reformat only the currently selected code, the entire source file currently active in the editor, or only code that has changed as the result of a source code control update.

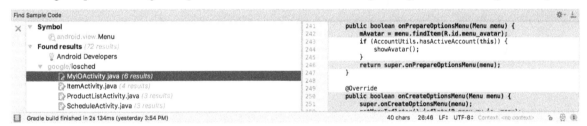

Figure 9-20

The full range of code style preferences can be changed from within the project settings dialog. Select the *File -> Settings* menu option (*Android Studio -> Preferences...* on macOS) and choose Code Style in the left-hand panel to access a list of supported programming and markup languages. Selecting a language will provide access to a vast array of formatting style options, all of which may be modified from the Android Studio default to match your preferred code style. To configure the settings for the Rearrange code option in the above dialog, for example, unfold the Code Style section, select Kotlin and, from the Kotlin settings, select the Arrangement tab.

9.12 Finding sample code

The Android Studio editor provides a way to access sample code relating to the currently highlighted entry within the code listing. This feature can be useful for learning how a particular Android class or method is used. To find sample code, highlight a method or class name in the editor, right-click on it and select the *Find Sample Code* menu option. The Find Sample Code panel (Figure 9-21) will appear beneath the editor with a list of matching samples. Selecting a sample from the list will load the corresponding code into the right-hand panel:

Figure 9-21

9.13 Live templates

As you write Android code you will find that there are common constructs that are used frequently. For example, a common requirement is to display a popup message to the user using the Android Toast class. Live templates are a collection of common code constructs that can be entered into the editor by typing the initial characters followed by a special key (set to the Tab key by default) to insert template code. To experience this in action, type toast in the code editor followed by the Tab key, and Android Studio will insert the following code at the cursor position ready for editing:

```
Toast.makeText(, "", Toast.LENGTH_SHORT).show()
```

To list and edit existing templates, change the special key, or add your own templates, open the Preferences dialog and select Live Templates from the Editor section of the left-hand navigation panel:

Figure 9-22

Add, remove, duplicate or reset templates using the buttons marked A in Figure 9-22 above. To modify a template, select it from the list (B) and change the settings in the panel marked C.

9.14 Summary

The Android Studio editor goes to great length to reduce the amount of typing needed to write code and to make that code easier to read and navigate. In this chapter, we have covered many of the key editor features including code completion, code generation, editor window splitting, code folding, reformatting, documentation lookup, and live templates.

10. An Overview of the Android Architecture

So far in this book, steps have been taken to set up an environment suitable for the development of Android applications using Android Studio. An initial step has also been taken into the process of application development through the creation of an Android Studio project.

Before delving further into the practical matters of Android application development, however, it is important to gain an understanding of some of the more abstract concepts of both the Android SDK and Android development in general. Gaining a clear understanding of these concepts now will provide a sound foundation on which to build further knowledge.

10.1 The Android software stack

Android is structured in the form of a software stack comprising applications, an operating system, run-time environment, middleware, services, and libraries. This architecture can, perhaps, best be represented visually as outlined in Figure 10-1. Each layer of the stack, and the corresponding elements within each layer, are tightly integrated and carefully tuned to provide the optimal application development and execution environment for mobile devices. In the rest of this chapter, we will explore the different layers of the Android stack, starting at the bottom with the Linux Kernel.

Figure 10-1

10.2 The Linux kernel

Positioned at the bottom of the Android software stack, the Linux Kernel provides a level of abstraction between the device hardware and the upper layers of the Android software stack. The kernel provides preemptive multitasking, low-level core system services such as memory, process, and power management in addition to providing a network stack and device drivers for hardware such as the device display, WiFi, and audio.

The original Linux kernel was developed in 1991 by Linus Torvalds and was combined with a set of tools, utilities, and compilers developed by Richard Stallman at the Free Software Foundation to create a full operating system referred to as GNU/Linux. Various Linux distributions have been derived from these basic underpinnings such as Ubuntu and Red Hat Enterprise Linux.

It is important to note, however, that Android uses only the Linux kernel. That said, it is worth noting that the Linux kernel was originally developed for use in traditional computers in the form of desktops and servers. In fact, Linux is now most widely deployed in mission-critical enterprise server environments. It is a testament to both the power of today's mobile devices and the efficiency and performance of the Linux kernel that we find this software at the heart of the Android software stack.

10.3 Android runtime – ART

When an Android app is built within Android Studio it is compiled into an intermediate bytecode format (referred to as DEX format). When the application is subsequently loaded onto the device, the Android Runtime (ART) uses a process referred to as Ahead-of-Time (AOT) compilation to translate the bytecode down to the native instructions required by the device processor. This format is known as Executable and Linkable Format (ELF).

Each time the application is subsequently launched, the ELF executable version is run, resulting in faster application performance and improved battery life.

This contrasts with the Just-in-Time (JIT) compilation approach used in older Android implementations whereby the bytecode was translated within a virtual machine (VM) each time the application was launched.

10.4 Android libraries

In addition to a set of standard Java development libraries (providing support for such general-purpose tasks as string handling, networking, and file manipulation), the Android development environment also includes the Android Libraries. These are a set of Java and Kotlin-based libraries that are specific to Android development. Examples of libraries in this category include the application framework libraries in addition to those that facilitate user interface building, graphics drawing, and database access.

10.4.1 C/C++ libraries

The Android runtime core libraries outlined in the preceding section are Java-based and provide the primary APIs for developers writing Android applications. It is important to note, however, that the core libraries do not perform much of the actual work and are, in fact, essentially Java "wrappers" around a set of C/C++-based libraries. When making calls, for example, to the *android.opengl* library to draw 3D graphics on the device display, the library ultimately makes calls to the *OpenGL ES* C++ library which, in turn, works with the underlying Linux kernel to perform the drawing tasks.

C/C++ libraries are included to fulfill a wide and diverse range of functions including 2D and 3D graphics drawing, Secure Sockets Layer (SSL) communication, SQLite database management, audio, and video playback, bitmap and vector font rendering, display subsystem, and graphic layer management and an implementation of the standard C system library (libc).

In practice, the typical Android application developer will access these libraries solely through the Java-based

Android core library APIs. If direct access to these libraries is needed, this can be achieved using the Android Native Development Kit (NDK), the purpose of which is to call the native methods of non-Java or Kotlin programming languages (such as C and C++) from within Java code using the Java Native Interface (JNI).

10.5 Application framework

The Application Framework is a set of services that collectively form the environment in which Android applications run and are managed. This framework implements the concept that Android applications are constructed from reusable, interchangeable, and replaceable components. This concept is taken a step further in that an application is also able to *publish* its capabilities along with any corresponding data so that they can be found and reused by other applications.

The Android framework includes the following key services:

- **Activity Manager** – Controls all aspects of the application lifecycle and activity stack.

- **Content Providers** – Allows applications to publish and share data with other applications.

- **Resource Manager** – Provides access to non-code embedded resources such as strings, color settings, and user interface layouts.

- **Notifications Manager** – Allows applications to display alerts and notifications to the user.

- **View System** – An extensible set of views used to create application user interfaces.

- **Package Manager** – The system by which applications can find out information about other applications currently installed on the device.

- **Telephony Manager** – Provides information to the application about the telephony services available on the device such as status and subscriber information.

- **Location Manager** – Provides access to the location services allowing an application to receive updates about location changes.

10.6 Applications

Located at the top of the Android software stack are the applications. These comprise both the native applications provided with the particular Android implementation (for example web browser and email applications) and the third-party applications installed by the user after purchasing the device.

10.7 Summary

A good Android development knowledge foundation requires an understanding of the overall architecture of Android. Android is implemented in the form of a software stack architecture consisting of a Linux kernel, a runtime environment and corresponding libraries, an application framework, and a set of applications. Applications are predominantly written in Java or Kotlin and compiled down to bytecode format within the Android Studio build environment. When the application is subsequently installed on a device, this bytecode is compiled down by the Android Runtime (ART) to the native format used by the CPU. The key goals of the Android architecture are performance and efficiency, both in application execution and in the implementation of reuse in application design.

Chapter 11

11. An Introduction to Kotlin

Android development is performed primarily using Android Studio which is, in turn, based on the IntelliJ IDEA development environment created by a company named JetBrains. Before the release of Android Studio 3.0, all Android apps were written using Android Studio and the Java programming language (with some occasional C++ code when needed).

Since the introduction of Android Studio 3.0, however, developers now have the option of creating Android apps using another programming language called Kotlin. Although detailed coverage of all features of this language is beyond the scope of this book (entire books can and have been written covering solely Kotlin), the objective of this and the following six chapters is to provide enough information to begin programming in Kotlin and quickly get up to speed developing Android apps using this programming language.

11.1 What is Kotlin?

Named after an island located in the Baltic Sea, Kotlin is a programming language created by JetBrains and follows Java in the tradition of naming programming languages after islands. Kotlin code is intended to be easier to understand and write and also safer than many other programming languages. The language, compiler, and related tools are all open source and available for free under the Apache 2 license.

The primary goals of the Kotlin language are to make code both concise and safe. Code is generally considered concise when it can be easily read and understood. Conciseness also plays a role when writing code, allowing code to be written more quickly and with greater efficiency. In terms of safety, Kotlin includes several features that improve the chances that potential problems will be identified when the code is being written instead of causing runtime crashes.

A third objective in the design and implementation of Kotlin involves interoperability with Java.

11.2 Kotlin and Java

Originally introduced by Sun Microsystems in 1995 Java is still by far the most popular programming language in use today. Until the introduction of Kotlin, it is quite likely that every Android app available on the market was written in Java. Since acquiring the Android operating system, Google has invested heavily in tuning and optimizing compilation and runtime environments for running Java-based code on Android devices.

Rather than try to re-invent the wheel, Kotlin is designed to both integrate with and work alongside Java. When Kotlin code is compiled it generates the same bytecode as that generated by the Java compiler enabling projects to be built using a combination of Java and Kotlin code. This compatibility also allows existing Java frameworks and libraries to be used seamlessly from within Kotlin code and also for Kotlin code to be called from within Java.

Kotlin's creators also acknowledged that while there were ways to improve on existing languages, there are many features of Java that did not need to be changed. Consequently, those familiar with programming in Java will find many of these skills to be transferable to Kotlin-based development. Programmers with Swift programming experience will also find much that is familiar when learning Kotlin.

11.3 Converting from Java to Kotlin

Given the high level of interoperability between Kotlin and Java, it is not essential to convert existing Java code to Kotlin since these two languages will comfortably co-exist within the same project. That being said, Java code can be converted to Kotlin from within Android Studio using a built-in Java to Kotlin converter. To convert an entire Java source file to Kotlin, load the file into the Android Studio code editor and select the *Code -> Convert Java File to Kotlin File* menu option. Alternatively, blocks of Java code may be converted to Kotlin by cutting the code and pasting it into an existing Kotlin file within the Android Studio code editor. Note when performing Java to Kotlin conversions that the Java code will not always convert to the best possible Kotlin code and that time should be taken to review and tidy up the code after conversion.

11.4 Kotlin and Android Studio

Support for Kotlin is provided within Android Studio via the Kotlin Plug-in which is integrated by default into Android Studio 3.0 or later.

11.5 Experimenting with Kotlin

When learning a new programming language, it is often useful to be able to enter and execute snippets of code. One of the best ways to do this with Kotlin is to use the Kotlin Playground (Figure 11-1) located at *https://play. kotlinlang.org*:

Figure 11-1

In addition to providing an environment in which Kotlin code may be quickly entered and executed, the playground also includes a set of examples and tutorials demonstrating key Kotlin features in action.

Try out some Kotlin code by opening a browser window, navigating to the playground, and entering the following into the main code panel:

```
fun main(args: Array<String>) {

    println("Welcome to Kotlin")

    for (i in 1..8) {
        println("i = $i")
    }
```

```
}
```

After entering the code, click on the Run button and note the output in the console panel:

```
Welcome to Kotlin
i = 1
i = 2
i = 3
i = 4
i = 5
i = 6
i = 7
i = 8
```

Figure 11-2

11.6 Semi-colons in Kotlin

Unlike programming languages such as Java and C++, Kotlin does not require semi-colons at the end of each statement or expression line. The following, therefore, is valid Kotlin code:

```
val mynumber = 10
println(mynumber)
```

Semi-colons are only required when multiple statements appear on the same line:

```
val mynumber = 10; println(mynumber)
```

11.7 Summary

For the first time since the Android operating system was introduced, developers now have an alternative to writing apps in Java code. Kotlin is a programming language developed by JetBrains, the company that created the development environment on which Android Studio is based. Kotlin is intended to make code safer and easier to understand and write. Kotlin is also highly compatible with Java, allowing Java and Kotlin code to co-exist within the same projects. This interoperability ensures that most of the standard Java and Java-based Android libraries and frameworks are available for use when developing using Kotlin.

Kotlin support for Android Studio is provided via a plug-in bundled with Android Studio 3.0 or later. This plug-in also provides a converter to translate Java code to Kotlin.

When learning Kotlin, the online playground provides a useful environment for quickly trying out Kotlin code.

12. Kotlin Data Types, Variables and Nullability

Both this and the following few chapters are intended to introduce the basics of the Kotlin programming language. This chapter will focus on the various data types available for use within Kotlin code. This will also include an explanation of constants, variables, type casting and Kotlin's handling of null values.

As outlined in the previous chapter, entitled *"An Introduction to Kotlin"* a useful way to experiment with the language is to use the Kotlin online playground environment. Before starting this chapter, therefore, open a browser window, navigate to *https://play.kotlinlang.org* and use the playground to try out the code in both this and the other Kotlin introductory chapters that follow.

12.1 Kotlin data types

When we look at the different types of software that run on computer systems and mobile devices, from financial applications to graphics intensive games, it is easy to forget that computers are really just binary machines. Binary systems work in terms of 0 and 1, true or false, set and unset. All the data sitting in RAM, stored on disk drives and flowing through circuit boards and buses are nothing more than sequences of 1s and 0s. Each 1 or 0 is referred to as a bit and bits are grouped together in blocks of 8, each group being referred to as a byte. When people talk about 32-bit and 64-bit computer systems they are talking about the number of bits that can be handled simultaneously by the CPU bus. A 64-bit CPU, for example, is able to handle data in 64-bit blocks, resulting in faster performance than a 32-bit based system.

Humans, of course, don't think in binary. We work with decimal numbers, letters and words. For a human to easily ('easily' being a relative term in this context) program a computer, some middle ground between human and computer thinking is needed. This is where programming languages such as Kotlin come into play. Programming languages allow humans to express instructions to a computer in terms and structures we understand, and then compile that down to a format that can be executed by a CPU.

One of the fundamentals of any program involves data, and programming languages such as Kotlin define a set of *data types* that allow us to work with data in a format we understand when programming. For example, if we want to store a number in a Kotlin program we could do so with syntax similar to the following:

```
val mynumber = 10
```

In the above example, we have created a variable named *mynumber* and then assigned to it the value of 10. When we compile the source code down to the machine code used by the CPU, the number 10 is seen by the computer in binary as:

```
1010
```

Similarly, we can express a letter, the visual representation of a digit ('0' through to '9') or punctuation mark (referred to in computer terminology as *characters*) using the following syntax:

```
val myletter = 'c'
```

Once again, this is understandable by a human programmer, but gets compiled down to a binary sequence for the CPU to understand. In this case, the letter 'c' is represented by the decimal number 99 using the ASCII table (an internationally recognized standard that assigns numeric values to human readable characters). When converted to binary, it is stored as:

```
10101100011
```

Now that we have a basic understanding of the concept of data types and why they are necessary we can take a closer look at some of the more commonly used data types supported by Kotlin.

12.1.1 Integer data types

Kotlin integer data types are used to store whole numbers (in other words a number with no decimal places). All integers in Kotlin are signed (in other words capable of storing positive, negative and zero values).

Kotlin provides support for 8, 16, 32 and 64 bit integers (represented by the Byte, Short, Int and Long types respectively).

12.1.2 Floating point data types

The Kotlin floating-point data types are able to store values containing decimal places. For example, 4353.1223 would be stored in a floating-point data type. Kotlin provides two floating-point data types in the form of Float and Double. Which type to use depends on the size of value to be stored and the level of precision required. The Double type can be used to store up to 64-bit floating-point numbers. The Float data type, on the other hand, is limited to 32-bit floating-point numbers.

12.1.3 Boolean data type

Kotlin, like other languages, includes a data type for the purpose of handling true or false (1 or 0) conditions. Two Boolean constant values (*true* and *false*) are provided by Kotlin specifically for working with Boolean data types.

12.1.4 Character data type

The Kotlin Char data type is used to store a single character of rendered text such as a letter, numerical digit, punctuation mark or symbol. Internally characters in Kotlin are stored in the form of 16-bit Unicode grapheme clusters. A grapheme cluster is made of two or more Unicode code points that are combined to represent a single visible character.

The following lines assign a variety of different characters to Character type variables:

```
val myChar1 = 'f'
val myChar2 = ':'
val myChar3 = 'X'
```

Characters may also be referenced using Unicode code points. The following example assigns the 'X' character to a variable using Unicode:

```
val myChar4 = '\u0058'
```

Note the use of single quotes when assigning a character to a variable. This indicates to Kotlin that this is a Char data type as opposed to double quotes which indicate a String data type.

12.1.5 String data type

The String data type is a sequence of characters that typically make up a word or sentence. In addition to providing a storage mechanism, the String data type also includes a range of string manipulation features allowing strings to be searched, matched, concatenated and modified. Double quotes are used to surround single line strings during assignment, for example:

```
val message = "You have 10 new messages."
```

Alternatively, a multi-line string may be declared using triple quotes

```
val message = """You have 10 new messages,
                            5 old messages
             and 6 spam messages."""
```

The leading spaces on each line of a multi-line string can be removed by making a call to the *trimMargin()* function of the String data type:

```
val message = """You have 10 new messages,
                            5 old messages
             and 6 spam messages.""".trimMargin()
```

Strings can also be constructed using combinations of strings, variables, constants, expressions, and function calls using a concept referred to as string interpolation. For example, the following code creates a new string from a variety of different sources using string interpolation before outputting it to the console:

```
val username = "John"
val inboxCount = 25
val maxcount = 100
val message = "$username has $inboxCount messages. Message capacity remaining is
${maxcount - inboxCount} messages"

println(message)
```

When executed, the code will output the following message:

```
John has 25 messages. Message capacity remaining is 75 messages.
```

12.1.6 Escape sequences

In addition to the standard set of characters outlined above, there is also a range of special characters (also referred to as escape characters) available for specifying items such as a new line, tab or a specific Unicode value within a string. These special characters are identified by prefixing the character with a backslash (a concept referred to as escaping). For example, the following assigns a new line to the variable named newline:

```
var newline = '\n'
```

In essence, any character that is preceded by a backslash is considered to be a special character and is treated accordingly. This raises the question as to what to do if you actually want a backslash character. This is achieved by escaping the backslash itself:

```
var backslash = '\\'
```

The complete list of special characters supported by Kotlin is as follows:

- \n - New line

- \r - Carriage return

- \t - Horizontal tab

- \\ - Backslash

- \" - Double quote (used when placing a double quote into a string declaration)

- \' - Single quote (used when placing a single quote into a string declaration)

- \$ - Used when a character sequence containing a $ is misinterpreted as a variable in a string template.

- \unnnn – Double byte Unicode scalar where nnnn is replaced by four hexadecimal digits representing the

Unicode character.

12.2 Mutable variables

Variables are essentially locations in computer memory reserved for storing the data used by an application. Each variable is given a name by the programmer and assigned a value. The name assigned to the variable may then be used in the Kotlin code to access the value assigned to that variable. This access can involve either reading the value of the variable or, in the case of *mutable variables*, changing the value.

12.3 Immutable variables

Often referred to as a *constant,* an immutable variable is similar to a mutable variable in that it provides a named location in memory to store a data value. Immutable variables differ in one significant way in that once a value has been assigned it cannot subsequently be changed.

Immutable variables are particularly useful if there is a value which is used repeatedly throughout the application code. Rather than use the value each time, it makes the code easier to read if the value is first assigned to a constant which is then referenced in the code. For example, it might not be clear to someone reading your Kotlin code why you used the value 5 in an expression. If, instead of the value 5, you use an immutable variable named *interestRate* the purpose of the value becomes much clearer. Immutable values also have the advantage that if the programmer needs to change a widely used value, it only needs to be changed once in the constant declaration and not each time it is referenced.

12.4 Declaring mutable and immutable variables

Mutable variables are declared using the *var* keyword and may be initialized with a value at creation time. For example:

```
var userCount = 10
```

If the variable is declared without an initial value, the type of the variable must also be declared (a topic which will be covered in more detail in the next section of this chapter). The following, for example, is a typical declaration where the variable is initialized after it has been declared:

```
var userCount: Int
userCount = 42
```

Immutable variables are declared using the *val* keyword.

```
val maxUserCount = 20
```

As with mutable variables, the type must also be specified when declaring the variable without initializing it:

```
val maxUserCount: Int
maxUserCount = 20
```

When writing Kotlin code, immutable variables should always be used in preference to mutable variables whenever possible.

12.5 Data types are objects

All of the above data types are objects, each of which provides a range of functions and properties that may be used to perform a variety of different type specific tasks. These functions and properties are accessed using so-called dot notation. Dot notation involves accessing a function or property of an object by specifying the variable name followed by a dot followed in turn by the name of the property to be accessed or function to be called.

A string variable, for example, can be converted to uppercase via a call to the *toUpperCase()* function of the String class:

```
val myString = "The quick brown fox"
val uppercase = myString.toUpperCase()
```

Similarly, the length of a string is available by accessing the length property:

```
val length = myString.length
```

Functions are also available within the String class to perform tasks such as comparisons and checking for the presence of a specific word. The following code, for example, will return a *true* Boolean value since the word "fox" appears within the string assigned to the *myString* variable:

```
val result = myString.contains("fox")
```

All of the number data types include functions for performing tasks such as converting from one data type to another such as converting an Int to a Float:

```
val myInt = 10
val myFloat = myInt.toFloat()
```

A detailed overview of all of the properties and functions provided by the Kotlin data type classes is beyond the scope of this book (there are hundreds). An exhaustive list for all data types can, however, be found within the Kotlin reference documentation available online at:

https://kotlinlang.org/api/latest/jvm/stdlib/kotlin/

12.6 Type annotations and type inference

Kotlin is categorized as a statically typed programming language. This essentially means that once the data type of a variable has been identified, that variable cannot subsequently be used to store data of any other type without inducing a compilation error. This contrasts to loosely typed programming languages where a variable, once declared, can subsequently be used to store other data types.

There are two ways in which the type of a variable will be identified. One approach is to use a type annotation at the point the variable is declared in the code. This is achieved by placing a colon after the variable name followed by the type declaration. The following line of code, for example, declares a variable named userCount as being of type Int:

```
val userCount: Int = 10
```

In the absence of a type annotation in a declaration, the Kotlin compiler uses a technique referred to as *type inference* to identify the type of the variable. When relying on type inference, the compiler looks to see what type of value is being assigned to the variable at the point that it is initialized and uses that as the type. Consider, for example, the following variable declarations:

```
var signalStrength = 2.231
val companyName = "My Company"
```

During compilation of the above lines of code, Kotlin will infer that the *signalStrength* variable is of type Double (type inference in Kotlin defaults to Double for all floating-point numbers) and that the companyName constant is of type String.

When a constant is declared without a type annotation it must be assigned a value at the point of declaration:

```
val bookTitle = "Android Studio Development Essentials"
```

If a type annotation is used when the constant is declared, however, the value can be assigned later in the code. For example:

```
val iosBookType = false
val bookTitle: String
```

```
if (iosBookType) {
        bookTitle = "iOS App Development Essentials"
} else {
        bookTitle = "Android Studio Development Essentials"
}
```

12.7 Nullable type

Kotlin nullable types are a concept that does not exist in most other programming languages (with the exception of the *optional* type in Swift). The purpose of nullable types is to provide a safe and consistent approach to handling situations where a variable may have a null value assigned to it. In other words, the objective is to avoid the common problem of code crashing with the null pointer exception errors that occur when code encounters a null value where one was not expected.

By default, a variable in Kotlin cannot have a null value assigned to it. Consider, for example, the following code:

```
val username: String = null
```

An attempt to compile the above code will result in a compilation error similar to the following:

```
Error: Null cannot be a value of a non-null string type String
```

If a variable is required to be able to store a null value, it must be specifically declared as a nullable type by placing a question mark (?) after the type declaration:

```
val username: String? = null
```

The *username* variable can now have a null value assigned to it without triggering a compiler error. Once a variable has been declared as nullable, a range of restrictions are then imposed on that variable by the compiler to prevent it being used in situations where it might cause a null pointer exception to occur. A nullable variable, cannot, for example, be assigned to a variable of non-null type as is the case in the following code:

```
val username: String? = null
val firstname: String = username
```

The above code will elicit the following error when encountered by the compiler:

```
Error: Type mismatch: inferred type is String? but String was expected
```

The only way that the assignment will be permitted is if some code is added to check that the value assigned to the nullable variable is non-null:

```
val username: String? = null

if (username != null) {
        val firstname: String = username
}
```

In the above case, the assignment will only take place if the username variable references a non-null value.

12.8 The safe call operator

A nullable variable also cannot be used to call a function or to access a property in the usual way. Earlier in this chapter, the *toUpperCase()* function was called on a String object. Given the possibility that this could cause a function to be called on a null reference, the following code will be disallowed by the compiler:

```
val username: String? = null
val uppercase = username.toUpperCase()
```

The exact error message generated by the compiler in this situation reads as follows:

```
Error: (Only safe (?.) or non-null asserted (!!.) calls are allowed on a nullable
receiver of type String?
```

In this instance, the compiler is essentially refusing to allow the function call to be made because no attempt has been made to verify that the variable is non-null. One way around this is to add some code to verify that something other than null value has been assigned to the variable before making the function call:

```
if (username != null) {
        val uppercase = username.toUpperCase()
}
```

A much more efficient way to achieve this same verification, however, is to call the function using the *safe call operator* (represented by *?.*) as follows:

```
val uppercase = username?.toUpperCase()
```

In the above example, if the username variable is null, the *toUpperCase()* function will not be called and execution will proceed at the next line of code. If, on the other hand, a non-null value is assigned the *toUpperCase()* function will be called and the result assigned to the *uppercase* variable.

In addition to function calls, the safe call operator may also be used when accessing properties:

```
val uppercase = username?.length
```

12.9 Not-null assertion

The *not-null assertion* removes all of the compiler restrictions from a nullable type, allowing it to be used in the same ways as a non-null type, even if it has been assigned a null value. This assertion is implemented using double exclamation marks after the variable name, for example:

```
val username: String? = null
val length = username!!.length
```

The above code will now compile, but will crash with the following exception at runtime since an attempt is being made to call a function on a non existent object:

```
Exception in thread "main" kotlin.KotlinNullPointerException
```

Clearly, this causes the very issue that nullable types are designed to avoid. Use of the not-null assertion is generally discouraged and should only be used in situations where you are certain that the value will not be null.

12.10 Nullable types and the let function

Earlier in this chapter, we looked at how the safe call operator can be used when making a call to a function belonging to a nullable type. This technique makes it easier to check if a value is null without having to write an *if* statement every time the variable is accessed. A similar problem occurs when passing a nullable type as an argument to a function which is expecting a non-null parameter. As an example, consider the *times()* function of the Int data type. When called on an Int object and passed another integer value as an argument, the function multiplies the two values and returns the result. When the following code is executed, for example, the value of 200 will be displayed within the console:

```
val firstNumber = 10
val secondNumber = 20

val result = firstNumber.times(secondNumber)
print(result)
```

The above example works because the secondNumber variable is a non-null type. A problem, however, occurs if the secondNumber variable is declared as being of nullable type:

```
val firstNumber = 10
val secondNumber: Int? = 20

val result = firstNumber.times(secondNumber)
print(result)
```

Now the compilation will fail with the following error message because a nullable type is being passed to a function that is expecting a non-null parameter:

```
Error: Type mismatch: inferred type is Int? but Int was expected
```

A possible solution to this problem is to simply write an *if* statement to verify that the value assigned to the variable is non-null before making the call to the function:

```
val firstNumber = 10
val secondNumber: Int? = 20

if (secondNumber != null) {
    val result = firstNumber.times(secondNumber)
    print(result)
}
```

A more convenient approach to addressing the issue, however, involves use of the *let* function. When called on a nullable type object, the let function converts the nullable type to a non-null variable named *it* which may then be referenced within a lambda statement.

```
secondNumber?.let {
    val result = firstNumber.times(it)
    print(result)
}
```

Note the use of the safe call operator when calling the *let* function on secondVariable in the above example. This ensures that the function is only called when the variable is assigned a non-null value.

12.11 Late initialization (lateinit)

As previously outlined, non-null types need to be initialized when they are declared. This can be inconvenient if the value to be assigned to the non-null variable will not be known until later in the code execution. One way around this is to declare the variable using the *lateinit* modifier. This modifier designates that a value will be initialized with a value later. This has the advantage that a non-null type can be declared before it is initialized, with the disadvantage that the programmer is responsible for ensuring that the initialization has been performed before attempting to access the variable. Consider the following variable declaration:

```
var myName: String
```

Clearly, this is invalid since the variable is a non-null type but has not been assigned a value. Suppose, however, that the value to be assigned to the variable will not be known until later in the program execution. In this case, the lateinit modifier can be used as follows:

```
lateinit var myName: String
```

With the variable declared in this way, the value can be assigned later, for example:

```
myName = "John Smith"
print("My Name is " + myName)
```

Of course, if the variable is accessed before it is initialized, the code will fail with an exception:

```
lateinit var myName: String

print("My Name is " + myName)
```

```
Exception in thread "main" kotlin.UninitializedPropertyAccessException: lateinit
property myName has not been initialized
```

To verify whether a lateinit variable has been initialized, check the *isInitialized* property on the variable. To do this, we need to access the properties of the variable by prefixing the name with the ':' operator:

```
if (::myName.isInitialized) {
    print("My Name is " + myName)
}
```

12.12 The Elvis operator

The Kotlin Elvis operator can be used in conjunction with nullable types to define a default value that is to be returned if a value or expression result is null. The Elvis operator (?:) is used to separate two expressions. If the expression on the left does not resolve to a null value that value is returned, otherwise the result of the rightmost expression is returned. This can be thought of as a quick alternative to writing an if-else statement to check for a null value. Consider the following code:

```
if (myString != null) {
    return myString
} else {
    return "String is null"
}
```

The same result can be achieved with less coding using the Elvis operator as follows:

```
return myString ?: "String is null"
```

12.13 Type casting and type checking

When compiling Kotlin code, the compiler can typically infer the type of an object. Situations will occur, however, where the compiler is unable to identify the specific type. This is often the case when a value type is ambiguous or an unspecified object is returned from a function call. In this situation it may be necessary to let the compiler know the type of object that your code is expecting or to write code that checks whether the object is of a particular type.

Letting the compiler know the type of object that is expected is known as *type casting* and is achieved within Kotlin code using the *as* cast operator. The following code, for example, lets the compiler know that the result returned from the *getSystemService()* method needs to be treated as a KeyguardManager object:

```
val keyMgr = getSystemService(Context.KEYGUARD_SERVICE) as KeyguardManager
```

The Kotlin language includes both safe and unsafe cast operators. The above cast is an unsafe cast and will cause the app to throw an exception if the cast cannot be performed. A safe cast, on the other hand, uses the *as?* operator and returns null if the cast cannot be performed:

```
val keyMgr = getSystemService(Context.KEYGUARD_SERVICE) as? KeyguardManager
```

A type check can be performed to verify that an object conforms to a specific type using the *is* operator, for example:

```
if (keyMgr is KeyguardManager) {
```

```
        // It is a KeyguardManager object
}
```

12.14 Summary

This chapter has begun the introduction to Kotlin by exploring data types together with an overview of how to declare variables. The chapter has also introduced concepts such as nullable types, type casting and type checking and the Elvis operator, each of which is an integral part of Kotlin programming and designed specifically to make code writing less prone to error.

13. Kotlin Operators and Expressions

So far we have looked at using variables and constants in Kotlin and also described the different data types. Being able to create variables is only part of the story, however. The next step is to learn how to use these variables in Kotlin code. The primary method for working with data is in the form of *expressions*.

13.1 Expression syntax in Kotlin

The most basic expression consists of an *operator*, two *operands*, and an *assignment*. The following is an example of an expression:

```
val myresult = 1 + 2
```

In the above example, the (+) operator is used to add two operands (1 and 2) together. The *assignment operator* (=) subsequently assigns the result of the addition to a variable named *myresult*. The operands could just have easily been variables (or a mixture of values and variables) instead of the actual numerical values used in the example.

In the remainder of this chapter, we will look at the basic types of operators available in Kotlin.

13.2 The Basic assignment operator

We have already looked at the most basic of assignment operators, the = operator. This assignment operator simply assigns the result of an expression to a variable. In essence, the = assignment operator takes two operands. The left-hand operand is the variable to which a value is to be assigned and the right-hand operand is the value to be assigned. The right-hand operand is, more often than not, an expression that performs some type of arithmetic or logical evaluation or a call to a function, the result of which will be assigned to the variable. The following examples are all valid uses of the assignment operator:

```
var x: Int // Declare a mutable Int variable
val y = 10 // Declare and initialize an immutable Int variable

x = 10 // Assign a value to x
x = x + y // Assign the result of x + y to x
x = y // Assign the value of y to x
```

13.3 Kotlin arithmetic operators

Kotlin provides a range of operators for creating mathematical expressions. These operators primarily fall into the category of *binary operators* in that they take two operands. The exception is the *unary negative operator* (-) which serves to indicate that a value is negative rather than positive. This contrasts with the *subtraction operator* (-) which takes two operands (i.e. one value to be subtracted from another). For example:

```
var x = -10 // Unary - operator used to assign -10 to variable x
x = x - 5 // Subtraction operator. Subtracts 5 from x
```

The following table lists the primary Kotlin arithmetic operators:

Operator	Description
-(unary)	Negates the value of a variable or expression
*	Multiplication

/	Division
+	Addition
-	Subtraction
%	Remainder/Modulo

Table 13-1

Note that multiple operators may be used in a single expression.

For example:

```
x = y * 10 + z - 5 / 4
```

13.4 Augmented assignment operators

In an earlier section, we looked at the basic assignment operator (=). Kotlin provides several operators designed to combine an assignment with a mathematical or logical operation. These are primarily of use when performing an evaluation where the result is to be stored in one of the operands. For example, one might write an expression as follows:

```
x = x + y
```

The above expression adds the value contained in variable x to the value contained in variable y and stores the result in variable x. This can be simplified using the addition augmented assignment operator:

```
x += y
```

The above expression performs the same task as $x = x + y$ but saves the programmer some typing.

Numerous augmented assignment operators are available in Kotlin. The most frequently used of which are outlined in the following table:

Operator	Description
x += y	Add x to y and place result in x
x -= y	Subtract y from x and place result in x
x *= y	Multiply x by y and place result in x
x /= y	Divide x by y and place result in x
x %= y	Perform Modulo on x and y and place result in x

Table 13-2

13.5 Increment and decrement operators

Another useful shortcut can be achieved using the Kotlin increment and decrement operators (also referred to as unary operators because they operate on a single operand). Consider the code fragment below:

```
x = x + 1 // Increase value of variable x by 1
x = x - 1 // Decrease value of variable x by 1
```

These expressions increment and decrement the value of x by 1. Instead of using this approach, however, it is quicker to use the ++ and -- operators. The following examples perform the same tasks as the examples above:

```
x++ // Increment x by 1
x-- // Decrement x by 1
```

These operators can be placed either before or after the variable name. If the operator is placed before the variable name, the increment or decrement operation is performed before any other operations are performed on the variable. For example, in the following code, x is incremented before it is assigned to y, leaving y with a value of 10:

```
var x = 9
val y = ++x
```

In the next example, however, the value of x (9) is assigned to variable y before the decrement is performed. After the expression is evaluated the value of y will be 9 and the value of x will be 8.

```
var x = 9
val y = x--
```

13.6 Equality operators

Kotlin also includes a set of logical operators useful for performing comparisons. These operators all return a Boolean result depending on the result of the comparison. These operators are *binary operators* in that they work with two operands.

Equality operators are most frequently used in constructing program control flow logic. For example an *if* statement may be constructed based on whether one value matches another:

```
if (x == y) {
      // Perform task
}
```

The result of a comparison may also be stored in a Boolean variable. For example, the following code will result in a *true* value being stored in the variable result:

```
var result: Boolean
val x = 10
val y = 20

result = x < y
```

Clearly 10 is less than 20, resulting in a *true* evaluation of the $x < y$ expression. The following table lists the full set of Kotlin comparison operators:

Operator	Description
x == y	Returns true if x is equal to y
x > y	Returns true if x is greater than y
x >= y	Returns true if x is greater than or equal to y
x < y	Returns true if x is less than y
x <= y	Returns true if x is less than or equal to y
x != y	Returns true if x is not equal to y

Table 13-3

13.7 Boolean logical operators

Kotlin also provides a set of so-called logical operators designed to return Boolean *true* or *false* values. These operators both return Boolean results and take Boolean values as operands. The key operators are NOT (!), AND (&&), and OR (||).

The NOT (!) operator simply inverts the current value of a Boolean variable or the result of an expression. For example, if a variable named *flag* is currently true, prefixing the variable with a '!' character will invert the value to false:

```
val flag = true // variable is true
```

```
val secondFlag = !flag // secondFlag set to false
```

The OR (||) operator returns true if one of its two operands evaluates to true, otherwise, it returns false. For example, the following code evaluates to true because at least one of the expressions on either side of the OR operator is true:

```
if ((10 < 20) || (20 < 10)) {
        print("Expression is true")
}
```

The AND (&&) operator returns true only if both operands evaluate to be true. The following example will return false because only one of the two operand expressions evaluates to true:

```
if ((10 < 20) && (20 < 10)) {
        print("Expression is true")
}
```

13.8 Range operator

Kotlin includes a useful operator that allows a range of values to be declared. As will be seen in later chapters, this operator is invaluable when working with looping in program logic.

The syntax for the range operator is as follows:

```
x..y
```

This operator represents the range of numbers starting at x and ending at y where both x and y are included within the range (referred to as a closed range). The range operator 5..8, for example, specifies the numbers 5, 6, 7, and 8.

13.9 Bitwise operators

As previously discussed, computer processors work in binary. These are essentially streams of ones and zeros, each one referred to as a bit. Bits are formed into groups of 8 to form bytes. As such, it is not surprising that we, as programmers, will occasionally end up working at this level in our code. To facilitate this requirement, Kotlin provides a range of *bit operators*.

Those familiar with bitwise operators in other languages such as C, C++, C#, Objective-C, and Java will find nothing new in this area of the Kotlin language syntax. For those unfamiliar with binary numbers, now may be a good time to seek out reference materials on the subject to understand how ones and zeros are formed into bytes to form numbers. Other authors have done a much better job of describing the subject than we can do within the scope of this book.

For this exercise, we will be working with the binary representation of two numbers. First, the decimal number 171 is represented in binary as:

```
10101011
```

Second, the number 3 is represented by the following binary sequence:

```
00000011
```

Now that we have two binary numbers with which to work, we can begin to look at the Kotlin bitwise operators:

13.9.1 Bitwise Inversion

The Bitwise inversion (also referred to as NOT) is performed using the *inv()* operation and has the effect of inverting all of the bits in a number. In other words, all the zeros become ones and all the ones become zeros. Taking our example 3 number, a Bitwise NOT operation has the following result:

```
00000011 NOT
```

```
========
11111100
```

The following Kotlin code, therefore, results in a value of -4:

```
val y = 3
val z = y.inv()

print("Result is $z")
```

13.9.2 Bitwise AND

The Bitwise AND is performed using the *and()* operation. It makes a bit-by-bit comparison of two numbers. Any corresponding position in the binary sequence of each number where both bits are 1 results in a 1 appearing in the same position of the resulting number. If either bit position contains a 0 then a zero appears in the result. Taking our two example numbers, this would appear as follows:

```
10101011 AND
00000011
========
00000011
```

As we can see, the only locations where both numbers have 1s are the last two positions. If we perform this in Kotlin code, therefore, we should find that the result is 3 (00000011):

```
val x = 171
val y = 3
val z = x.and(y)

print("Result is $z")
```

13.9.3 Bitwise OR

The bitwise OR also performs a bit-by-bit comparison of two binary sequences. Unlike the AND operation, the OR places a 1 in the result if there is a 1 in the first or second operand. Using our example numbers, the result will be as follows:

```
10101011 OR
00000011
========
10101011
```

If we perform this operation in Kotlin using the *or()* operation the result will be 171:

```
val x = 171
val y = 3
val z = x.or(y)

print("Result is $z")
```

13.9.4 Bitwise XOR

The bitwise XOR (commonly referred to as *exclusive OR* and performed using the *xor()* operation) performs a similar task to the OR operation except that a 1 is placed in the result if one or other corresponding bit positions in the two numbers is 1. If both positions are a 1 or a 0 then the corresponding bit in the result is set to a 0. For example:

```
10101011 XOR
```

```
00000011
========
10101000
```

The result, in this case, is 10101000 which converts to 168 in decimal. To verify this we can, once again, try some Kotlin code:

```
val x = 171
val y = 3
val z = x.xor(y)

print("Result is $z")
```

When executed, we get the following output from print:

```
Result is 168
```

13.9.5 Bitwise left shift

The bitwise left shift moves each bit in a binary number a specified number of positions to the left. Shifting an integer one position to the left has the effect of doubling the value.

As the bits are shifted to the left, zeros are placed in the vacated rightmost (low order) positions. Note also that once the leftmost (high order) bits are shifted beyond the size of the variable containing the value, those high order bits are discarded:

```
10101011 Left Shift one bit
========
101010110
```

In Kotlin the bitwise left shift operator is performed using the *shl()* operation, passing through the number of bit positions to be shifted. For example, to shift left by 1 bit:

```
val x = 171
val z = x.shl(1)

print("Result is $z")
```

When compiled and executed, the above code will display a message stating that the result is 342 which, when converted to binary, equates to 101010110.

13.9.6 Bitwise right shift

A bitwise right shift is, as you might expect, the same as a left except that the shift takes place in the opposite direction. Shifting an integer one position to the right has the effect of halving the value.

Note that since we are shifting to the right there is no opportunity to retain the lowermost bits regardless of the data type used to contain the result. As a result, the low order bits are discarded. Whether or not the vacated high order bit positions are replaced with zeros or ones depends on whether the *sign bit* used to indicate positive and negative numbers is set or not.

```
10101011 Right Shift one bit
========
01010101
```

The bitwise right shift is performed using the *shr()* operation passing through the shift count:

```
val x = 171
```

```
val z = x.shr(1)
```

```
print("Result is $z")
```

When executed, the above code will report the result of the shift as being 85, which equates to binary 01010101.

13.10 Summary

Operators and expressions provide the underlying mechanism by which variables and constants are manipulated and evaluated within Kotlin code. This can take the simplest of forms whereby two numbers are added using the addition operator in an expression and the result stored in a variable using the assignment operator. Operators fall into a range of categories, details of which have been covered in this chapter.

14. Kotlin Control flow

Regardless of the programming language used, application development is largely an exercise in applying logic, and much of the art of programming involves writing code that makes decisions based on one or more criteria. Such decisions define which code gets executed, how many times it is executed, and, conversely, which code gets bypassed when the program is running. This is often referred to as *control flow* since it controls the *flow* of program execution. Control flow typically falls into the categories of *looping control* (how often code is executed) and *conditional control flow* (whether or not code is executed). This chapter is intended to provide an introductory overview of both types of control flow in Kotlin.

14.1 Looping control flow

This chapter will begin by looking at control flow in the form of loops. Loops are essentially sequences of Kotlin statements that are to be executed repeatedly until a specified condition is met. The first looping statement we will explore is the *for* loop.

14.1.1 The Kotlin *for-in* Statement

The for-in loop is used to iterate over a sequence of items contained in a collection or number range.

The syntax of the for-in loop is as follows:

```
for variable name in collection or range {
        // code to be executed
}
```

In this syntax, *variable name* is the name to be used for a variable that will contain the current item from the collection or range through which the loop is iterating. The code in the body of the loop will typically use this name as a reference to the current item in the loop cycle. The *collection* or *range* references the item through which the loop is iterating. This could, for example, be an array of string values, a range operator, or even a string of characters.

Consider, for example, the following for-in loop construct:

```
for (index in 1..5) {
  println("Value of index is $index")
}
```

The loop begins by stating that the current item is to be assigned to a constant named *index*. The statement then declares a closed range operator to indicate that the for loop is to iterate through a range of numbers, starting at 1 and ending at 5. The body of the loop simply prints out a message to the console indicating the current value assigned to the *index* constant, resulting in the following output:

```
Value of index is 1
Value of index is 2
Value of index is 3
Value of index is 4
Value of index is 5
```

The for-in loop is of particular benefit when working with collections such as arrays. In fact, the for-in loop can be used to iterate through any object that contains more than one item. The following loop, for example, outputs each of the characters in the specified string:

```
for (index in "Hello") {
  println("Value of index is $index")
}
```

The operation of a for-in loop may be configured using the *downTo* and *until* functions. The downTo function causes the for loop to work backward through the specified collection until the specified number is reached. The following for loop counts backward from 100 until the number 90 is reached:

```
for (index in 100 downTo 90) {
  print("$index.. ")
}
```

When executed, the above loop will generate the following output:

```
100.. 99.. 98.. 97.. 96.. 95.. 94.. 93.. 92.. 91.. 90..
```

The until function operates in much the same way with the exception that counting starts from the bottom of the collection range and works up until (but not including) the specified endpoint (a concept referred to as a half-closed range):

```
for (index in 1 until 10) {
  print("$index.. ")
}
```

The output from the above code will range from the start value of 1 through to 9:

```
1.. 2.. 3.. 4.. 5.. 6.. 7.. 8.. 9..
```

The increment used on each iteration through the loop may also be defined using the step function as follows:

```
for (index in 0 until 100 step 10) {
  print("$index.. ")
}
```

The above code will result in the following console output:

```
0.. 10.. 20.. 30.. 40.. 50.. 60.. 70.. 80.. 90..
```

14.1.2 The *while* loop

The Kotlin *for* loop described previously works well when it is known in advance how many times a particular task needs to be repeated in a program. There will, however, be instances where code needs to be repeated until a certain condition is met, with no way of knowing in advance how many repetitions are going to be needed to meet that criterion. To address this need, Kotlin includes the *while* loop.

Essentially, the while loop repeats a set of tasks while a specified condition is met. The *while* loop syntax is defined as follows:

```
while condition {
        // Kotlin statements go here
}
```

In the above syntax, *condition* is an expression that will return either *true* or *false* and the // *Kotlin statements go here* comment represents the code to be executed while the condition expression is true. For example:

```
var myCount = 0

while  (myCount < 100) {
```

```
    myCount++
    println(myCount)
}
```

In the above example, the *while* expression will evaluate whether the *myCount* variable is less than 100. If it is already greater than 100, the code in the braces is skipped and the loop exits without performing any tasks.

If, on the other hand, *myCount* is not greater than 100 the code in the braces is executed and the loop returns to the while statement and repeats the evaluation of *myCount*. This process repeats until the value of *myCount* is greater than 100, at which point the loop exits.

14.1.3 The *do ... while* loop

It is often helpful to think of the *do ... while* loop as an inverted while loop. The *while* loop evaluates an expression before executing the code contained in the body of the loop. If the expression evaluates to *false* on the first check then the code is not executed. The *do ... while* loop, on the other hand, is provided for situations where you know that the code contained in the body of the loop will *always* need to be executed at least once. For example, you may want to keep stepping through the items in an array until a specific item is found. You know that you have to at least check the first item in the array to have any hope of finding the entry you need. The syntax for the *do ... while* loop is as follows:

```
do {
        // Kotlin statements here
} while conditional expression
```

In the *do ... while* example below the loop will continue until the value of a variable named i equals 0:

```
var i = 10

do {
    i--
    println(i)
} while (i > 0)
```

14.1.4 Breaking from Loops

Having created a loop, it is possible that under certain conditions you might want to break out of the loop before the completion criteria have been met (particularly if you have created an infinite loop). One such example might involve continually checking for activity on a network socket. Once activity has been detected it will most likely be necessary to break out of the monitoring loop and perform some other task.

To break out of a loop, Kotlin provides the *break* statement which breaks out of the current loop and resumes execution at the code directly after the loop. For example:

```
var j = 10

for (i in 0..100)
{
    j += j

    if (j > 100) {
        break
    }
```

```
    println("j = $j")
}
```

In the above example, the loop will continue to execute until the value of j exceeds 100 at which point the loop will exit and execution will continue with the next line of code after the loop.

14.1.5 The *continue* statement

The *continue* statement causes all remaining code statements in a loop to be skipped, and execution to be returned to the top of the loop. In the following example, the *println* function is only called when the value of variable *i* is an even number:

```
var i = 1

while (i < 20)
{
        i += 1

        if (i % 2 != 0) {
            continue
        }

        println("i = $i")
}
```

The *continue* statement in the above example will cause the *println* call to be skipped unless the value of *i* can be divided by 2 with no remainder. If the *continue* statement is triggered, execution will skip to the top of the while loop and the statements in the body of the loop will be repeated (until the value of *i* exceeds 19).

14.1.6 Break and continue labels

Kotlin expressions may be assigned a label by preceding the expression with a label name followed by the @ sign. This label may then be referenced when using break and continue statements to designate where execution is to resume. This is particularly useful when breaking out of nested loops. The following code contains a for loop nested within another for loop. The inner loop contains a break statement which is executed when the value of j reaches 10:

```
for (i in 1..100) {

    println("Outer loop i = $i")

    for (j in 1..100) {
        println("Inner loop j = $j")
        if (j == 10) break
    }

}
```

As currently implemented, the break statement will exit the inner for loop but execution will resume at the top of the outer for loop. Suppose, however, that the break statement is required to also exit the outer loop. This can be achieved by assigning a label to the outer loop and referencing that label with the break statement as follows:

```
outerloop@ for (i in 1..100) {
```

```
    println("Outer loop i = $i")

    for (j in 1..100) {

        println("Inner loop j = $j")

        if (j == 10) break@outerloop
    }
}
```

Now when the value assigned to variable j reaches 10 the break statement will break out of both loops and resume execution at the line of code immediately following the outer loop.

14.2 Conditional control flow

In the previous chapter, we looked at how to use logical expressions in Kotlin to determine whether something is *true* or *false*. Since programming is largely an exercise in applying logic, much of the art of programming involves writing code that makes decisions based on one or more criteria. Such decisions define which code gets executed and, conversely, which code gets bypassed when the program is executing.

14.2.1 Using the *if* expressions

The *if* expression is perhaps the most basic of control flow options available to the Kotlin programmer. Programmers who are familiar with C, Swift, C++, or Java will immediately be comfortable using Kotlin if statements, although there are some subtle differences.

The basic syntax of the Kotlin *if* expression is as follows:

```
if (boolean expression) {
    // Kotlin code to be performed when expression evaluates to true
}
```

Unlike some other programming languages, it is important to note that the braces are optional in Kotlin if only one line of code is associated with the *if* expression. In fact, in this scenario, the statement is often placed on the same line as the if expression.

Essentially if the *Boolean expression* evaluates to *true* then the code in the body of the statement is executed. If, on the other hand, the expression evaluates to *false* the code in the body of the statement is skipped.

For example, if a decision needs to be made depending on whether one value is greater than another, we would write code similar to the following:

```
val x = 10

if (x > 9) println("x is greater than 9!")
```

Clearly, x is indeed greater than 9 causing the message to appear in the console panel.

At this point, it is important to notice that we have been referring to the if expression instead of the if statement. The reason for this is that unlike the if statement in other programming languages, the Kotlin if returns a result. This allows if constructs to be used within expressions. As an example, a typical if expression to identify the largest of two numbers and assign the result to a variable might read as follows:

```
if (x > y)
    largest = x
else
```

```
    largest = y
```

The same result can be achieved using the *if* statement within an expression using the following syntax:

```
variable = if (condition) return_val_1 else return_val_2
```

The original example can, therefore be re-written as follows:

```
val largest = if (x > y) x else y
```

The technique is not limited to returning the values contained within the condition. The following example is also a valid use of if in an expression, in this case assigning a string value to the variable:

```
val largest = if (x > y) "x is greatest" else "y is greatest"
println(largest)
```

For those familiar with programming languages such as Java, this feature allows code constructs similar to ternary statements to be implemented in Kotlin.

14.2.2 Using *if ... else ...* expressions

The next variation of the *if* expression allows us to also specify some code to perform if the expression in the if expression evaluates to *false*. The syntax for this construct is as follows:

```
if (boolean expression) {
    // Code to be executed if expression is true
} else {
    // Code to be executed if expression is false
}
```

The braces are, once again, optional if only one line of code is to be executed.

Using the above syntax, we can now extend our previous example to display a different message if the comparison expression evaluates to be *false*:

```
val x = 10

if (x > 9) println("x is greater than 9!")
    else println("x is less than 9!")
```

In this case, the second println statement will execute if the value of x was less than 9.

14.2.3 Using *if ... else if ...* Expressions

So far we have looked at *if* statements that make decisions based on the result of a single logical expression. Sometimes it becomes necessary to make decisions based on several different criteria. For this purpose, we can use the *if ... else if ...* construct, an example of which is as follows:

```
var x = 9

if (x == 10) println("x is 10")
        else if (x == 9) println("x is 9")
            else if (x == 8) println("x is 8")
                else println("x is less than 8")
}
```

14.2.4 Using the *when* statement

The Kotlin *when* statement provides a cleaner alternative to the *if ... else if ...* construct and uses the following syntax:

```
when (value) {
      match1 -> // code to be executed on match
      match2 -> // code to be executed on match
         .

         .

      else -> // default code to executed if no match
}
```

Using this syntax, the previous *if ... else if ...* construct can be rewritten to use the *when* statement:

```
when (x) {
    10 -> println ("x is 10")
    9 -> println("x is 9")
    8 -> println("x is 8")
    else ->  println("x is less than 8")
}
```

The *when* statement is similar to the *switch* statement found in many other programming languages.

14.3 Summary

The term *control flow* is used to describe the logic that dictates the execution path that is taken through the source code of an application as it runs. This chapter has looked at the two types of control flow provided by Kotlin (looping and conditional) and explored the various Kotlin constructs that are available to implement both forms of control flow logic.

15. An Overview of Kotlin Functions and Lambdas

Kotlin functions and lambdas are a vital part of writing well-structured and efficient code and provide a way to organize programs while avoiding code repetition. In this chapter, we will look at how functions and lambdas are declared and used within Kotlin.

15.1 What is a function?

A function is a named block of code that can be called upon to perform a specific task. It can be provided data on which to perform the task and is capable of returning results to the code that called it. For example, if a particular arithmetic calculation needs to be performed in a Kotlin program, the code to perform the arithmetic can be placed in a function. The function can be programmed to accept the values on which the arithmetic is to be performed (referred to as parameters) and to return the result of the calculation. At any point in the program code where the calculation is required, the function is simply called, parameter values passed through as arguments and the result returned.

The terms parameter and argument are often used interchangeably when discussing functions. There is, however, a subtle difference. The values that a function can accept when it is called are referred to as parameters. At the point that the function is called and passed those values, however, they are referred to as arguments.

15.2 How to declare a Kotlin function

A Kotlin function is declared using the following syntax:

```
fun <function name> (<para name>: <para type>, <para name>: <para type>, ... ):
<return type> {
        // Function code
}
```

This combination of function name, parameters, and return type is referred to as the function *signature* or *type*. Explanations of the various fields of the function declaration are as follows:

- fun – The prefix keyword used to notify the Kotlin compiler that this is a function.

- <function name> - The name assigned to the function. This is the name by which the function will be referenced when it is called from within the application code.

- <para name> - The name by which the parameter is to be referenced in the function code.

- <para type> - The type of the corresponding parameter.

- <return type> - The data type of the result returned by the function. If the function does not return a result then no return type is specified.

- Function code - The code of the function that does the work.

As an example, the following function takes no parameters, returns no result, and simply displays a message:

```
fun sayHello() {
```

```
    println("Hello")
}
```

The following sample function, on the other hand, takes an integer and a string as parameters and returns a string result:

```
fun buildMessageFor(name: String, count: Int): String {
    return("$name, you are customer number $count")
}
```

15.3 Calling a Kotlin function

Once declared, functions are called using the following syntax:

```
<function name> (<arg1>, <arg2>, ... )
```

Each argument passed through to a function must match the parameters the function is configured to accept. For example, to call a function named sayHello that takes no parameters and returns no value, we would write the following code:

```
sayHello()
```

In the case of a message that accepts parameters, the function could be called as follows:

```
buildMessageFor("John", 10)
```

15.4 Single expression functions

When a function contains a single expression, it is not necessary to include the braces around the expression. All that is required is an equals sign (=) after the function declaration followed by the expression. The following function contains a single expression declared in the usual way:

```
fun multiply(x: Int, y: Int): Int {
    return x * y
}
```

Below is the same function expressed as a single line expression:

```
fun multiply(x: Int, y: Int): Int = x * y
```

When using single-line expressions, the return type may be omitted in situations where the compiler can infer the type returned by the expression making for even more compact code:

```
fun multiply(x: Int, y: Int) = x * y
```

15.5 Local functions

A local function is a function that is embedded within another function. In addition, a local function has access to all of the variables contained within the enclosing function:

```
fun main(args: Array<String>) {

    val name = "John"
    val count = 5

    fun displayString() {
        for (index in 0..count) {
            println(name)
        }
    }
}
```

```
        displayString()
}
```

15.6 Handling return values

To call a function named buildMessage that takes two parameters and returns a result, on the other hand, we might write the following code:

```
val message = buildMessageFor("John", 10)
```

To improve code readability, the parameter names may also be specified when making the function call:

```
val message = buildMessageFor(name = "John", count = 10)
```

In the above examples, we have created a new variable called message and then used the assignment operator (=) to store the result returned by the function.

15.7 Declaring default function parameters

Kotlin provides the ability to designate a default parameter value to be used if the value is not provided as an argument when the function is called. This simply involves assigning the default value to the parameter when the function is declared.

To see default parameters in action the buildMessageFor function will be modified so that the string "Customer" is used as a default if a customer name is not passed through as an argument. Similarly, the *count* parameter is declared with a default value of 0:

```
fun buildMessageFor(name: String = "Customer", count: Int = 0): String {
        return("$name, you are customer number $count")
}
```

When parameter names are used when making the function call, any parameters for which defaults have been specified may be omitted. The following function call, for example, omits the customer name argument but still compiles because the parameter name has been specified for the second argument:

```
val message = buildMessageFor(count = 10)
```

If parameter names are not used within the function call, however, only the trailing arguments may be omitted:

```
val message = buildMessageFor("John") // Valid
val message = buildMessageFor(10) // Invalid
```

15.8 Variable number of function parameters

It is not always possible to know in advance the number of parameters a function will need to accept when it is called within the application code. Kotlin handles this possibility through the use of the *vararg* keyword to indicate that the function accepts an arbitrary number of parameters of a specified data type. Within the body of the function, the parameters are made available in the form of an array object. The following function, for example, takes as parameters a variable number of String values and then outputs them to the console panel:

```
fun displayStrings(vararg strings: String)
{
    for (string in strings) {
        println(string)
    }
}

displayStrings("one", "two", "three", "four")
```

Kotlin does not permit multiple vararg parameters within a function and any single parameters supported by the function must be declared before the vararg declaration:

```
fun displayStrings(name: String, vararg strings: String)
{
    for (string in strings) {
        println(string)
    }
}
```

15.9 Lambda expressions

Having covered the basics of functions in Kotlin it is now time to look at the concept of lambda expressions. Essentially, lambdas are self-contained blocks of code. The following code, for example, declares a lambda, assigns it to a variable named sayHello, and then calls the function via the lambda reference:

```
val sayHello = { println("Hello") }
sayHello()
```

Lambda expressions may also be configured to accept parameters and return results. The syntax for this is as follows:

```
{<para name>: <para type>, <para name> <para type>, ... ->
        // Lambda expression here
}
```

The following lambda expression, for example, accepts two integer parameters and returns an integer result:

```
val multiply = { val1: Int, val2: Int -> val1 * val2 }
val result = multiply(10, 20)
```

Note that the above lambda examples have assigned the lambda code block to a variable. This is also possible when working with functions. Of course, the following syntax will execute the function and assign the result of that execution to a variable, instead of assigning the function itself to the variable:

```
val myvar = myfunction()
```

To assign a function reference to a variable, simply remove the parentheses and prefix the function name with double colons (::) as follows. The function may then be called simply by referencing the variable name:

```
val myvar = ::myfunction
myvar()
```

A lambda block may be executed directly by placing parentheses at the end of the expression including any arguments. The following lambda directly executes the multiplication lambda expression multiplying 10 by 20.

```
val result = { val1: Int, val2: Int -> val1 * val2 }(10, 20)
```

The last expression within a lambda serves as the expression's return value (hence the value of 200 being assigned to the result variable in the above multiplication examples). In fact, unlike functions, lambdas do not support the *return* statement. In the absence of an expression that returns a result (such as an arithmetic or comparison expression), simply declaring the value as the last item in the lambda will cause that value to be returned. The following lambda returns the Boolean true value after printing a message:

```
val result = { println("Hello"); true }()
```

Similarly, the following lambda simply returns a string literal:

```
val nextmessage = { println("Hello"); "Goodbye" }()
```

A particularly useful feature of lambdas and the ability to create function references is that they can be both passed to functions as arguments and returned as results. This concept, however, requires an understanding of function types and higher-order functions.

15.10 Higher-order functions

On the surface, lambdas and function references do not seem to be particularly compelling features. The possibilities that these features offer become more apparent, however, when we consider that lambdas and function references have the same capabilities as many other data types. In particular, these may be passed through as arguments to another function, or even returned as a result from a function.

A function that is capable of receiving a function or lambda as an argument, or returning one as a result is referred to as a *higher-order function*.

Before we look at what is, essentially, the ability to plug one function into another, it is first necessary to explore the concept of *function types*. The type of a function is dictated by a combination of the parameters it accepts and the type of result it returns. A function that accepts an Int and a Double as parameters and returns a String result for example is considered to have the following function type:

```
(Int, Double) -> String
```

To accept a function as a parameter, the receiving function simply declares the type of function it can accept.

As an example, we will begin by declaring two unit conversion functions:

```
fun inchesToFeet (inches: Double): Double {
    return inches * 0.0833333
}


fun inchesToYards (inches: Double): Double {
    return inches * 0.0277778
}
```

The example now needs an additional function, the purpose of which is to perform a unit conversion and print the result in the console panel. This function needs to be as general-purpose as possible, capable of performing a variety of different measurement unit conversions. To demonstrate functions as parameters, this new function will take as a parameter a function type that matches both the inchesToFeet and inchesToYards functions together with a value to be converted. Since the type of these functions is equivalent to (Double) -> Double, our general-purpose function can be written as follows:

```
fun outputConversion(converterFunc: (Double) -> Double, value: Double) {
    val result = converterFunc(value)
    println("Result of conversion is $result")
}
```

When the outputConversion function is called, it will need to be passed a function matching the declared type. That function will be called to perform the conversion and the result displayed in the console panel. This means that the same function can be called to convert inches to both feet and yards, simply by "plugging in" the appropriate converter function as a parameter, keeping in mind that it is the function reference that is being passed as an argument:

```
outputConversion(::inchesToFeet, 22.45)
outputConversion(::inchesToYards, 22.45)
```

Functions can also be returned as a data type simply by declaring the type of the function as the return type. The following function is configured to return either our inchesToFeet or inchesToYards function type (in other words a function that accepts and returns a Double value) based on the value of a Boolean parameter:

```
fun decideFunction(feet: Boolean): (Double) -> Double
{
    if (feet) {
        return ::inchesToFeet
    } else {
        return ::inchesToYards
    }
}
```

When called, the function will return a function reference which can then be used to perform the conversion:

```
val converter = decideFunction(true)
val result = converter(22.4)
println(result)
```

15.11 Summary

Functions and lambda expressions are self-contained blocks of code that can be called upon to perform a specific task and provide a mechanism for structuring code and promoting reuse. This chapter has introduced the basic concepts of function and lambda declaration and implementation in addition to the use of higher-order functions that allow lambdas and functions to be passed as arguments and returned as results.

Chapter 16

16. The Basics of Object-Oriented Programming in Kotlin

Kotlin provides extensive support for developing object-oriented applications. The subject area of object-oriented programming is, however, large. As such, a detailed overview of object-oriented software development is beyond the scope of this book. Instead, we will introduce the basic concepts involved in object-oriented programming and then move on to explaining the concept as it relates to Kotlin application development.

16.1 What is an object?

Objects (also referred to as instances) are self-contained modules of functionality that can be easily used and re-used as the building blocks for a software application.

Objects consist of data variables (called properties) and functions (called methods) that can be accessed and called on the object or instance to perform tasks and are collectively referred to as class members.

16.2 What is a class?

Much as a blueprint or architect's drawing defines what an item or a building will look like once it has been constructed, a class defines what an object will look like when it is created. It defines, for example, what the methods will do and what the properties will be.

16.3 Declaring a Kotlin class

Before an object can be instantiated, we first need to define the class 'blueprint' for the object. In this chapter, we will create a bank account class to demonstrate the basic concepts of Kotlin object-oriented programming.

In declaring a new Kotlin class we specify an optional parent class from which the new class is derived and also define the properties and methods that the class will contain. The basic syntax for a new class is as follows:

```
class NewClassName: ParentClass {
    // Properties
    // Methods
}
```

The Properties section of the declaration defines the variables and constants that are to be contained within the class. These are declared in the same way that any other variable would be declared in Kotlin.

The Methods sections define the methods that are available to be called on the class and instances of the class. These are essentially functions specific to the class that perform a particular operation when called upon and will be described in greater detail later in this chapter.

To create an example outline for our BankAccount class, we would use the following:

```
class BankAccount {


}
```

Now that we have the outline syntax for our class, the next step is to add some properties to it.

16.4 Adding properties to a class

A key goal of object-oriented programming is a concept referred to as data encapsulation. The idea behind data encapsulation is that data should be stored within classes and accessed only through methods defined in that class. Data encapsulated in a class are referred to as properties or instance variables.

Instances of our BankAccount class will be required to store some data, specifically a bank account number and the balance currently held within the account. Properties are declared in the same way any other variables are declared in Kotlin. We can, therefore, add these variables as follows:

```kotlin
class BankAccount {
    var accountBalance: Double = 0.0
    var accountNumber: Int = 0
}
```

Having defined our properties, we can now move on to defining the methods of the class that will allow us to work with our properties while staying true to the data encapsulation model.

16.5 Defining methods

The methods of a class are essentially code routines that can be called upon to perform specific tasks within the context of that class.

Methods are declared within the opening and closing braces of the class to which they belong and are declared using the standard Kotlin function declaration syntax.

For example, the declaration of a method to display the account balance in our example might read as follows:

```kotlin
class BankAccount {
    var accountBalance: Double = 0.0
    var accountNumber: Int = 0

    fun displayBalance()
    {
        println("Number $accountNumber")
        println("Current balance is $accountBalance")
    }
}
```

16.6 Declaring and initializing a class instance

So far all we have done is define the blueprint for our class. To do anything with this class, we need to create instances of it. The first step in this process is to declare a variable to store a reference to the instance when it is created. We do this as follows:

```kotlin
val account1: BankAccount = BankAccount()
```

When executed, an instance of our BankAccount class will have been created and will be accessible via the account1 variable. Of course, the Kotlin compiler will be able to use inference here, making the type declaration optional:

```kotlin
val account1 = BankAccount()
```

16.7 Primary and secondary constructors

A class will often need to perform some initialization tasks at the point of creation. These tasks can be implemented using constructors within the class. In the case of the BankAccount class, it would be useful to be able to initialize the account number and balance properties with values when a new class instance is created. To achieve this, a *secondary constructor* can be declared within the class header as follows:

```kotlin
class BankAccount {

    var accountBalance: Double = 0.0
    var accountNumber: Int = 0

    constructor(number: Int, balance: Double) {
        accountNumber =  number
        accountBalance = balance
    }
    .
    .
    .
}
```

When creating an instance of the class, it will now be necessary to provide initialization values for the account number and balance properties as follows:

```kotlin
val account1: BankAccount = BankAccount(456456234, 342.98)
```

A class can contain multiple secondary constructors allowing instances of the class to be initiated with different value sets. The following variation of the BankAccount class includes an additional secondary constructor for use when initializing an instance with the customer's last name in addition to the corresponding account number and balance:

```kotlin
class BankAccount {

    var accountBalance: Double = 0.0
    var accountNumber: Int = 0
    var lastName: String = ""

    constructor(number: Int,
                balance: Double) {
        accountNumber =  number
        accountBalance = balance
    }

    constructor(number: Int,
                balance: Double,
                name: String ) {
        accountNumber =  number
        accountBalance = balance
        lastName = name
    }
    .
    .
    .
}
```

Instances of the BankAccount may now also be created as follows:

```
val account1: BankAccount = BankAccount(456456234, 342.98, "Smith")
```

It is also possible to use a *primary constructor* to perform basic initialization tasks. The primary constructor for a class is declared within the class header as follows:

```
class BankAccount (val accountNumber: Int, var accountBalance: Double) {

    .

    .

    fun displayBalance()
    {
        println("Number $accountNumber")
        println("Current balance is $accountBalance")
    }
}
```

Note that now both properties have been declared in the primary constructor, it is no longer necessary to also declare the variables within the body of the class. Since the account number will now not change after an instance of the class has been created, this property is declared as being immutable using the *val* keyword.

Although a class may only contain one primary constructor, Kotlin allows multiple secondary constructors to be declared in addition to the primary constructor. In the following class declaration the constructor that handles the account number and balance is declared as the primary constructor while the variation that also accepts the user's last name is declared as a secondary constructor:

```
class BankAccount (val accountNumber: Int, var accountBalance: Double) {

    var lastName: String = ""

    constructor(accountNumber: Int,
                accountBalance: Double,
                name: String ) : this(accountNumber, accountBalance) {

        lastName = name
    }

    .

    .

}
```

In the above example, two key points need to be noted. First, since the lastName property is referenced by a secondary constructor, the variable is not handled automatically by the primary constructor and must be declared within the body of the class and initialized within the constructor.

```
var lastName: String = ""

    .

    .

lastName = name
```

Second, although the accountNumber and accountBalance properties are accepted as parameters to the secondary constructor, the variable declarations are still handled by the primary constructor and do not need to be declared. To associate the references to these properties in the secondary constructor with the primary constructor, however, they must be linked back to the primary constructor using the *this* keyword:

```
... this(accountNumber, accountBalance)...
```

16.8 Initializer blocks

In addition to the primary and secondary constructors, a class may also contain *initializer blocks* which are called after the constructors. Since a primary constructor cannot contain any code, these methods are a particularly useful location for adding code to perform initialization tasks when an instance of the class is created. Initializer blocks are declared using the *init* keyword with the initialization code enclosed in braces:

```
class BankAccount (val accountNumber: Int, var accountBalance: Double) {


    init {
        // Initialization code goes here
    }
.
.
.
}
```

16.9 Calling methods and accessing properties

Now is probably a good time to recap what we have done so far in this chapter. We have now created a new Kotlin class named BankAccount. Within this new class, we declared primary and secondary constructors to accept and initialize account number, balance, and customer name properties. In the preceding sections, we also covered the steps necessary to create and initialize an instance of our new class. The next step is to learn how to call the instance methods and access the properties we built into our class. This is most easily achieved using dot notation.

Dot notation involves accessing a property, or calling a method by specifying a class instance followed by a dot followed in turn by the name of the property or method:

```
classInstance.propertyname
classInstance.methodname()
```

For example, to get the current value of our accountBalance instance variable:

```
val balance1 = account1.accountBalance
```

Dot notation can also be used to set values of instance properties:

```
account1.accountBalance = 6789.98
```

The same technique is used to call methods on a class instance. For example, to call the displayBalance method on an instance of the BankAccount class:

```
account1.displayBalance()
```

16.10 Custom accessors

When accessing the accountBalance property in the previous section, the code is making use of property accessors that are provided automatically by Kotlin. In addition to these default accessors, it is also possible to implement *custom accessors* that allow calculations or other logic to be performed before the property is returned or set.

Custom accessors are implemented by creating getter and optional corresponding setter methods containing the code to perform any tasks before returning the property. Consider, for example, that the BankAcccount class might need an additional property to contain the current balance less any recent banking fees. Rather than use a standard accessor, it makes more sense to use a custom accessor that calculates this value on request. The modified BankAccount class might now read as follows:

```
class BankAccount (val accountNumber: Int, var accountBalance: Double) {
```

```
    val fees: Double = 25.00

    val balanceLessFees: Double
        get() {
            return accountBalance - fees
        }

    fun displayBalance()
    {
        println("Number $accountNumber")
        println("Current balance is $accountBalance")
    }
}
```

The above code adds a getter that returns a computed property based on the current balance minus a fee amount. An optional setter could also be declared in much the same way to set the balance value less fees:

```
val fees: Double = 25.00

var balanceLessFees: Double
    get() {
        return accountBalance - fees
    }
    set(value) {
        accountBalance = value - fees
    }
    .
    .
    .
}
```

The new setter takes as a parameter a Double value from which it deducts the fee value before assigning the result to the current balance property. Even though these are custom accessors, they are accessed in the same way as stored properties using dot-notation. The following code gets the current balance less the fees value before setting the property to a new value:

```
val balance1 = account1.balanceLessFees
account1.balanceLessFees = 12123.12
```

16.11 Nested and inner classes

Kotlin allows one class to be nested within another class. In the following code, for example, ClassB is nested inside ClassA:

```
class ClassA {
    class ClassB {
    }
}
```

In the above example, ClassB does not have access to any of the properties within the outer class. If access is required, the nested class must be declared using the *inner* directive. In the example below ClassB now has access to the myProperty variable belonging to ClassA:

```kotlin
class ClassA {
        var myProperty: Int = 10

    inner class ClassB {
                val result = 20 + myProperty
    }
}
```

16.12 Companion objects

A Kotlin class can also contain a companion object. A companion object contains methods and variables that are common to all instances of the class. In addition to being accessible via class instances, these properties are also accessible at the class level (in other words without the need to create an instance of the class).

The syntax for declaring a companion object within a class is as follows:

```kotlin
class ClassName: ParentClass {
    // Properties
    // Methods

    companion object {
        // properties
        // methods
    }
}
```

To experience a companion object example in action, enter the following into the Kotlin online playground at https://try.kotl.in:

```kotlin
class MyClass {

    fun showCount() {
        println("counter = " + counter)
    }

    companion object {
        var counter = 1

        fun counterUp() {
            counter += 1
        }
    }
}

fun main(args: Array<String>) {
    println(MyClass.counter)
}
```

The class contains a companion object consisting of a counter variable and a method to increment that variable. The class also contains a method to display the current counter value. The *main()* method simply displays the current value of the counter variable, but does so by calling the method on the class itself instead of a class

The Basics of Object-Oriented Programming in Kotlin

instance:

```
println(MyClass.counter)
```

Modify the *main()* method to also increment the counter, displaying the current value both before and after:

```
fun main(args: Array<String>) {
    println(MyClass.counter)
    MyClass.counterUp()
    println(MyClass.counter)
}
```

Run the code and verify that the following output appears in the console:

```
1
2
```

Next, add some code to create an instance of MyClass before making a call to the *showCount()* method:

```
fun main(args: Array<String>) {
    println(MyClass.counter)
    MyClass.counterUp()
    println(MyClass.counter)

    val instanceA = MyClass()
    instanceA.showCount()
}
```

When executed, the following output will appear in the console:

```
1
2
counter = 2
```

Clearly, the class has access to the variables and methods contained within the companion object.

Another useful aspect of companion objects is that all instances of the containing class see the same companion object, including current variable values. To see this in action, create a second instance of MyClass and call the *showCount()* method on that instance:

```
fun main(args: Array<String>) {
    println(MyClass.counter)
    MyClass.counterUp()
    println(MyClass.counter)

    val instanceA = MyClass()
    instanceA.showCount()

    val instanceB = MyClass()
    instanceB.showCount()
}
```

When run, the code will produce the following console output:

```
1
2
```

```
counter = 2
counter = 2
```

Note that both instances return the incremented value of 2, showing that the two class instances are sharing the same companion object data.

16.13 Summary

Object-oriented programming languages such as Kotlin encourage the creation of classes to promote code reuse and the encapsulation of data within class instances. This chapter has covered the basic concepts of classes and instances within Kotlin together with an overview of primary and secondary constructors, initializer blocks, properties, methods, companion objects, and custom accessors.

17. An Introduction to Kotlin Inheritance and Subclassing

In *"The Basics of Object-Oriented Programming in Kotlin"* we covered the basic concepts of object-oriented programming and worked through an example of creating and working with a new class using Kotlin. In that example, our new class was not specifically derived from a base class (though in practice, all Kotlin classes are ultimately derived from the *Any* class). In this chapter, we will provide an introduction to the concepts of subclassing, inheritance, and extensions in Kotlin.

17.1 Inheritance, classes, and subclasses

The concept of inheritance brings something of a real-world view to programming. It allows a class to be defined that has a certain set of characteristics (such as methods and properties) and then other classes to be created which are derived from that class. The derived class inherits all of the features of the parent class and typically then adds some features of its own. In fact, all classes in Kotlin are ultimately subclasses of the Any superclass which provides the basic foundation on which all classes are based.

By deriving classes, we create what is often referred to as a class hierarchy. The class at the top of the hierarchy is known as the base class or root class and the derived classes as subclasses or child classes. Any number of subclasses may be derived from a class. The class from which a subclass is derived is called the parent class or superclass.

Classes need not only be derived from a root class. For example, a subclass can also inherit from another subclass with the potential to create large and complex class hierarchies.

In Kotlin a subclass can only be derived from a single direct parent class. This is a concept referred to as single inheritance.

17.2 Subclassing syntax

As a safety measure designed to make Kotlin code less prone to error, before a subclass can be derived from a parent class, the parent class must be declared as open. This is achieved by placing the *open* keyword within the class header:

```
open class MyParentClass {
    var myProperty: Int = 0
}
```

With a simple class of this type, the subclass can be created as follows:

```
class MySubClass : MyParentClass() {


}
```

For classes containing primary or secondary constructors, the rules for creating a subclass are slightly more complicated. Consider the following parent class which contains a primary constructor:

```
open class MyParentClass(var myProperty: Int) {
```

```
}
```

To create a subclass of this class, the subclass declaration references any base class parameters while also initializing the parent class using the following syntax:

```
class MySubClass(myProperty: Int) : MyParentClass(myProperty) {


}
```

If, on the other hand, the parent class contains one or more secondary constructors, the constructors must also be implemented within the subclass declaration and include a call to the secondary constructors of the parent class, passing through as arguments the values passed to the subclass secondary constructor. When working with subclasses, the parent class can be referenced using the *super* keyword. A parent class with a secondary constructor might read as follows:

```
open class MyParentClass {
    var myProperty: Int = 0

    constructor(number: Int) {
        myProperty = number
    }
}
```

The code for the corresponding subclass would need to be implemented as follows:

```
class MySubClass : MyParentClass {
    constructor(number: Int) : super(number)
}
```

If additional tasks need to be performed within the constructor of the subclass, this can be placed within curly braces after the constructor declaration:

```
class MySubClass : MyParentClass {

    constructor(number: Int) : super(number) {
        // Subclass constructor code here
    }
}
```

17.3 A Kotlin inheritance example

As with most programming concepts, the subject of inheritance in Kotlin is perhaps best illustrated with an example. In *"The Basics of Object-Oriented Programming in Kotlin"* we created a class named BankAccount designed to hold a bank account number and corresponding current balance. The BankAccount class contained both properties and methods. A simplified declaration for this class is reproduced below and will be used for the basis of the subclassing example in this chapter:

```
class BankAccount {

    var accountNumber = 0
    var accountBalance = 0.0

    constructor(number: Int, balance: Double) {
        accountNumber = number
```

```
        accountBalance = balance
    }

    open fun displayBalance()
    {
        println("Number $accountNumber")
        println("Current balance is $accountBalance")
    }
}
```

Though this is a somewhat rudimentary class, it does everything necessary if all you need it to do is store an account number and account balance. Suppose, however, that in addition to the BankAccount class you also needed a class to be used for savings accounts. A savings account will still need to hold an account number and a current balance and methods will still be needed to access that data. One option would be to create an entirely new class, one that duplicates all of the functionality of the BankAccount class together with the new features required by a savings account. A more efficient approach, however, would be to create a new class that is a subclass of the BankAccount class. The new class will then inherit all the features of the BankAccount class but can then be extended to add the additional functionality required by a savings account. Before a subclass of the BankAccount class can be created, the declaration needs to be modified to declare the class as open:

open class BankAccount {

To create a subclass of BankAccount that we will call SavingsAccount, we simply declare the new class, this time specifying BankAccount as the parent class and add code to call the constructor on the parent class:

```
class SavingsAccount : BankAccount {
    constructor(accountNumber: Int, accountBalance: Double) :
        super(accountNumber, accountBalance)
}
```

Note that although we have yet to add any properties or methods, the class has inherited all the methods and properties of the parent BankAccount class. We could, therefore, create an instance of the SavingsAccount class and set variables and call methods in the same way we did with the BankAccount class in previous examples. That said, we haven't achieved anything unless we take steps to extend the class.

17.4 Extending the functionality of a subclass

So far we have been able to create a subclass that contains all the functionality of the parent class. For this exercise to make sense, however, we now need to extend the subclass so that it has the features we need to make it useful for storing savings account information. To do this, we simply add the properties and methods that provide the new functionality, just as we would for any other class we might wish to create:

```
class SavingsAccount : BankAccount {
        var interestRate: Double = 0.0

    constructor(accountNumber: Int, accountBalance: Double) :
                    super(accountNumber, accountBalance)


    fun calculateInterest(): Double
    {
        return interestRate * accountBalance
    }
}
```

}

17.5 Overriding inherited methods

When using inheritance it is not unusual to find a method in the parent class that almost does what you need, but requires modification to provide the precise functionality you require. That being said, it is also possible you'll inherit a method with a name that describes exactly what you want to do, but it does not come close to doing what you need. One option in this scenario would be to ignore the inherited method and write a new method with an entirely new name. A better option is to override the inherited method and write a new version of it in the subclass.

Before proceeding with an example, three rules that must be obeyed when overriding a method. First, the overriding method in the subclass must accept the same number and type of parameters as the overridden method in the parent class. Second, the new method must have the same return type as the parent method. Finally, the original method in the parent class must be declared as open before the compiler will allow it to be overridden.

In our BankAccount class, we have a method named displayBalance that displays the bank account number and current balance held by an instance of the class. In our SavingsAccount subclass, we might also want to output the current interest rate assigned to the account. To achieve this, we simply declare a new version of the displayBalance method in our SavingsAccount subclass, prefixed with the *override* keyword:

```
class SavingsAccount : BankAccount {
    var interestRate: Double = 0.0

    constructor(accountNumber: Int, accountBalance: Double) :
            super(accountNumber, accountBalance)

    fun calculateInterest(): Double
    {
        return interestRate * accountBalance
    }

    override fun displayBalance()
    {
        println("Number $accountNumber")
        println("Current balance is $accountBalance")
        println("Prevailing interest rate is $interestRate")
    }
}
```

Before this code will compile, the displayBalance method in the BankAccount class must be declared as open:

```
open fun displayBalance()
{
    println("Number $accountNumber")
    println("Current balance is $accountBalance")
}
```

It is also possible to make a call to the overridden method in the superclass from within a subclass. The displayBalance method of the superclass could, for example, be called to display the account number and balance, before the interest rate is displayed, thereby eliminating further code duplication:

```
override fun displayBalance()
{
    super.displayBalance()
    println("Prevailing interest rate is $interestRate")
}
```

17.6 Adding a custom secondary constructor

As the SavingsAccount class currently stands, it makes a call to the secondary constructor from the parent BankAccount class which was implemented as follows:

```
constructor(accountNumber: Int, accountBalance: Double) :
            super(accountNumber, accountBalance)
```

Clearly this constructor takes the necessary steps to initialize both the account number and balance properties of the class. The SavingsAccount class, however, contains an additional property in the form of the interest rate variable. The SavingsAccount class, therefore, needs its own constructor to ensure that the interestRate property is initialized when instances of the class are created. Modify the SavingsAccount class one last time to add an additional secondary constructor allowing the interest rate to also be specified when class instances are initialized:

```
class SavingsAccount : BankAccount {

    var interestRate: Double = 0.0

    constructor(accountNumber: Int, accountBalance: Double) :
                super(accountNumber, accountBalance)

    constructor(accountNumber: Int, accountBalance: Double, rate: Double) :
                    super(accountNumber, accountBalance) {
        interestRate = rate
    }
    .
    .
    .
}
```

17.7 Using the SavingsAccount class

Now that we have completed work on our SavingsAccount class, the class can be used in some example code in much the same way as the parent BankAccount class:

```
val savings1 = SavingsAccount(12311, 600.00, 0.07)

println(savings1.calculateInterest())
savings1.displayBalance()
```

17.8 Summary

Inheritance extends the concept of object re-use in object oriented programming by allowing new classes to be derived from existing classes, with those new classes subsequently extended to add new functionality. When an existing class provides some, but not all, of the functionality required by the programmer, inheritance allows that class to be used as the basis for a new subclass. The new subclass will inherit all the capabilities of the parent class, but may then be extended to add the missing functionality.

18. An Overview of Compose

Now that Android Studio has been installed and the basics of the Kotlin programing language covered, it is time to start introducing Jetpack Compose.

Jetpack Compose is an entirely new approach to developing apps for all of Google's operating system platforms. The basic goals of Compose are to make app development easier, faster, and less prone to the types of bugs that typically appear when developing software projects. These elements have been combined with Compose-specific additions to Android Studio that allow Compose projects to be tested in near real-time using an interactive preview of the app during the development process.

Many of the advantages of Compose originate from the fact that it is both *declarative* and *data-driven*, topics which will be explained in this chapter.

The discussion in this chapter is intended as a high-level overview of Compose and does not cover the practical aspects of implementation within a project. Implementation and practical examples will be covered in detail in the remainder of the book.

18.1 Development before Compose

To understand the meaning and advantages of the Compose declarative syntax, it helps to understand how user interface layouts were designed before the introduction of Compose. Previously, Android apps were still built entirely using Android Studio together with a collection of associated frameworks that make up the Android Development Kit.

To aid in the design of the user interface layouts that make up the screens of an app, Android Studio includes a tool called the Layout Editor. The Layout Editor is a powerful tool that allows XML files to be created which contain the individual components that make up a screen of an app.

The user interface layout of a screen is designed within the Layout Editor by dragging components (such as buttons, text, text fields, and sliders) from a widget palette to the desired location on the layout canvas. Selecting a component in a scene provides access to a range of property panels where the attributes of the components can be changed.

The layout behavior of the screen (in other words how it reacts to different device screen sizes and changes to device orientation between portrait and landscape) is defined by configuring a range of constraints that dictate how each component is positioned and sized in relation to both the containing window and the other components in the layout.

Finally, any components that need to respond to user events (such as a button tap or slider motion) are connected to methods in the app source code where the event is handled.

At various points during this development process, it is necessary to compile and run the app on a simulator or device to test that everything is working as expected.

18.2 Compose declarative syntax

Compose introduces a declarative syntax that provides an entirely different way of implementing user interface layouts and behavior from the Layout Editor approach. Instead of manually designing the intricate details of the layout and appearance of components that make up a scene, Compose allows the scenes to be described using a simple and intuitive syntax. In other words, Compose allows layouts to be created by declaring how the user interface should appear without having to worry about the complexity of how the layout is built.

This essentially involves declaring the components to be included in the layout, stating the kind of layout manager in which they are to be contained (column, row, box, list, etc.), and using modifiers to set attributes such as the text on a button, the foreground color of a label, or the handler to be called in the event of a tap gesture. Having made these declarations, all the intricate and complicated details of how to position, constrain and render the layout are handled automatically by Compose.

Compose declarations are structured hierarchically, which also makes it easy to create complex views by composing together small, re-usable custom sub-views.

While a layout is being declared and tested, Android Studio provides a preview canvas that changes in real-time to reflect the appearance of the layout. Android Studio also includes an *interactive preview* mode which allows the app to be launched within the preview canvas and fully tested without the need to build and run on a simulator or device.

Coverage of the Compose declaration syntax begins with the chapter entitled *"Composable Functions Overview"*.

18.3 Compose is data-driven

When we say that Compose is data-driven, this is not to say that it is no longer necessary to handle events generated by the user (in other words the interaction between the user and the app user interface). It is still necessary, for example, to know when the user taps a button or moves a slider and to react in some app-specific way. Being data-driven relates more to the relationship between the underlying app data and the user interface and logic of the app.

Before the introduction of Compose, an Android app would contain code responsible for checking the current values of data within the app. If data was likely to change over time, code had to be written to ensure that the user interface always reflected the latest state of the data (perhaps by writing code to frequently check for changes to the data, or by providing a refresh option for the user to request a data update). Similar challenges arise when keeping the user interface state consistent and making sure issues like toggle button settings are stored appropriately. Requirements such as these can become increasingly complex when multiple areas of an app depend on the same data sources.

Compose addresses this complexity by providing a system that is based on *state*. Data that is stored as state ensures that any changes to that data are automatically reflected in the user interface without the need to write any additional code to detect the change. Any user interface component that accesses a state is essentially *subscribed* to that state. When the state is changed anywhere in the app code, any subscriber components to that data will be destroyed and recreated to reflect the data change in a process called *recomposition*. This ensures that when any state on which the user interfaces is dependent changes, all components that rely on that data will automatically update to reflect the latest state.

State and recomposition will be covered in the chapter entitled *"An Overview of Compose State and Recomposition"*.

18.4 Summary

Jetpack introduces a different approach to app development than that offered by the Android Studio Layout Editor. Rather than directly implement the way in which a user interface is to be rendered, Compose allows the user interface to be declared in descriptive terms and then does all the work of deciding the best way to perform the rendering when the app runs.

Compose is also data-driven in that data changes drive the behavior and appearance of the app. This is achieved through states and recomposition.

This chapter has provided a very high-level view of Jetpack Compose. The remainder of this book will explore Compose in greater depth.

19. Composable Functions Overview

Composable functions are the building blocks used to create user interfaces for Android apps when developing with Jetpack Compose. In the ComposeDemo project created earlier in the book, we made use of both the built-in compose functions provided with Compose and also created our own functions. In this chapter, we will explore composable functions in more detail, including topics such as stateful and stateless functions, function syntax, and the difference between foundation and material composables.

19.1 What is a composable function?

Composable functions (also referred to as *composables* or *components*) are special Kotlin functions that are used to create user interfaces when working with Compose. A composable function is differentiated from regular Kotlin functions in code using the @Composable annotation.

When a composable is called, it is typically passed some data and a set of properties that define how the corresponding section of the user interface is to behave and appear when rendered to the user in the running app. In essence, composable functions transform data into user interface elements. Composables do not return values in the traditional sense of the Kotlin function, but instead, *emit* user interface elements to the Compose runtime system for rendering.

Composable functions can call other composables to create a hierarchy of components as demonstrated in the ComposeDemo project. While a composable function may also call standard Kotlin functions, standard functions may not call composable functions.

A typical Compose-based user interface will be comprised of a combination of built-in and custom-built composables.

19.2 Stateful vs. stateless composables

Composable functions are categorized as being either *stateful* or *stateless*. State, in the context of Compose, is defined as being any value that can change during the execution of an app. For example, a slider position value, the string entered into a text field, or the current setting of a check box are all forms of state.

As we saw in the ComposeDemo project, a composable function can store a state value which defines in some way how the composable function, or those that it calls appear or behave. This is achieved using the *remember* keyword and the *mutableStateOf* function. Our DemoScreen composable, for example, stored the current slider position as state using this technique:

```
@Composable
fun DemoScreen() {

    var sliderPosition by remember { mutableStateOf(20f) }

    .
    .

}
```

Because the DemoScreen contains state, it is considered to be a stateful composable. Now consider the DemoSlider composable which reads as follows:

```
@Composable
```

Composable Functions Overview

```
fun DemoSlider(sliderPosition: Float, onPositionChange : (Float) -> Unit ) {
    Slider(
        modifier = Modifier.padding(10.dp),
        valueRange = 20f..40f,
        value = sliderPosition,
        onValueChange = onPositionChange
    )
}
```

Although this composable is passed and makes use of the state value stored by the DemoScreen, it does not itself store any state value. DemoSlider is, therefore, considered to be a stateless composable function.

The topic of state will be covered in greater detail in the chapter entitled *"An Overview of Compose State and Recomposition"*.

19.3 Composable function syntax

Composable functions, as we already know, are declared using the @Composable annotation and are written in much the same way as a standard Kotlin function. We can, for example, declare a composable function that does nothing as follows:

```
@Composable
fun MyFunction() {
}
```

We can also call other composables from within the function:

```
@Composable
fun MyFunction() {
    Text("Hello")
}
```

Composables may also be implemented to accept parameters. The following function accepts text, font weight, and color parameters and passes them to the built-in Text composable. The fragment also includes a preview composable to demonstrate how the CustomText function might be called:

```
@Composable
fun CustomText(text: String, fontWeight: FontWeight, color: Color) {
    Text(text = text, fontWeight = fontWeight, color = color)
}


@Preview(showBackground = true)
@Composable
fun DefaultPreview() {
    CustomText(text = "Hello Compose", fontWeight = FontWeight.Bold,
                        color = Color.Magenta)
}
```

When previewed, magenta-colored bold text reading "Hello Compose" will be rendered in the preview panel.

Just about any Kotlin logic code may be included in the body of a composable function. The following composable, for example, displays different text within a Column depending on the setting of a built-in Switch composable:

```
@Composable
```

```
fun CustomSwitch() {

    val checked = remember { mutableStateOf(true) }

    Column {
        Switch(
            checked = checked.value,
            onCheckedChange = { checked.value = it }
        )
        if (checked.value) {
            Text("Switch is On")
        } else {
            Text("Switch is Off")
        }
    }
}
```

In the above example, we have declared a state value named *checked* initialized to true and then constructed a Column containing a Switch composable. The state of the Switch is based on the value of *checked* and a lambda assigned as the *onCheckedChanged* event handler. This lambda sets the *checked* state to the current Switch setting. Finally, an *if* statement is used to decide which of two Text composables are displayed depending on the current value of the *checked* state. When run, the text displayed will alternate between "Switch is on" and "Switch is off":

Figure 19-1

Similarly, we could use looping syntax to iterate through the items in a list and display them in a Column separated by instances of the Divider composable:

```
@Composable
fun CustomList(items: List<String>) {
    Column {
        for (item in items) {
            Text(item)
            Divider(color = Color.Black)
        }
    }
}
```

The following composable could be used to preview the above function:

```
@Preview(showBackground = true)
@Composable
fun DefaultPreview() {
```

```
    MyApplicationTheme {
        CustomList(listOf("One", "Two", "Three", "Four", "Five", "Six"))
    }
}
```

Once built and refreshed, the composable will appear in the Preview panel as shown in Figure 19-2 below:

DefaultPreview

One
———————————
Two
———————————
Three
———————————
Four
———————————
Five
———————————
Six
———————————

Figure 19-2

19.4 Foundation and Material composables

When developing apps with Compose we do so using a mixture of our own composable functions (for example the CustomText and CustomList composables created earlier in the chapter) combined with a set of ready to use components provided by the Compose development kit (such as the Text, Button, Column and Slider composables).

The composables bundled with Compose fall into three categories, referred to as *Layout, Foundation,* and *Material Design* components.

Layout components provide a way to define both how components are positioned on the screen, and how those components behave in relation to each other. The following are all layout composables:

• Box

• BoxWithConstraints

• Column

• ConstraintLayout

• Row

Foundation components are a set of minimal components that provide basic user interface functionality. While these components do not, by default, impose a specific style or theme, they can be customized to provide any look and behavior you need for your app. The following lists the set of Foundation components:

• BaseTextField

• Canvas

• Image

• LazyColumn

• LazyRow

- Shape

- Text

The Material Design components, on the other hand, have been designed so that they match Google's Material theme guidelines and include the following composables:

- AlertDialog

- Button

- Card

- CircularProgressIndicator

- DropdownMenu

- Checkbox

- FloatingActionButton

- LinearProgressIndicator

- ModalDrawer

- RadioButton

- Scaffold

- Slider

- Snackbar

- Switch

- TextField

- TopAppBar

- BottomNavigation

When choosing components, it is important to note that the Foundation and Material Design components are not mutually exclusive. You will inevitably use components from both categories in your design since the Material Design category has components for which there is no Foundation equivalent and vice versa.

19.5 Summary

In this chapter, we have looked at composable functions and explored how they are used to construct Android-based user interfaces. Composable functions are declared using the @Composable annotation and use the same syntax as standard Kotlin functions, including the passing and handling of parameters. Unlike standard Kotlin functions, composable functions do not return values. Instead, they *emit* user interface units to be rendered by the Compose runtime. A composable function can be either *stateful* or *stateless* depending on whether the function stores a state value. The built-in composables are categorized as either Layout, Foundation, or Material Design components. The Material Design components conform with the Material style and theme guidelines provided by Google to encourage consistent UI design.

One type of composable we have not yet introduced is the Slot API composable, a topic that will be covered later in the chapter entitled *"An Overview of Compose Slot APIs"*.

20. An Overview of Compose State and Recomposition

State is the cornerstone of how the Compose system is implemented. As such, a clear understanding of state is an essential step in becoming a proficient Compose developer. In this chapter, we will explore and demonstrate the basic concepts of state and explain the meaning of related terms such as *recomposition*, *unidirectional data flow*, and *state hoisting*. The chapter will also cover saving and restoring state through *configuration changes*.

20.1 The basics of state

In declarative languages such as Compose, *state* is generally referred to as "a value that can change over time". At first glance, this sounds much like any other data in an app. A standard Kotlin variable, for example, is by definition designed to store a value that can change at any time during execution. State, however, differs from a standard variable in two significant ways.

First, the value assigned to a state variable in a composable function needs to be remembered. In other words, each time a composable function containing state (a *stateful function*) is called, it must remember any state values from the last time it was invoked. This is different from a standard variable which would be re-initialized each time a call is made to the function in which it is declared.

The second key difference is that a change to any state variable has far reaching implications for the entire hierarchy tree of composable functions that make up a user interface. To understand why this is the case, we now need to talk about recomposition.

20.2 Introducing recomposition

When developing with Compose, we build apps by creating hierarchies of composable functions. As previously discussed, a composable function can be thought of as taking data and using that data to generate sections of a user interface layout. These elements are then rendered on the screen by the Compose runtime system. In most cases, the data passed from one composable function to another will have been declared as a state variable in a parent function. This means that any change of state value in a parent composable will need to be reflected in any child composables to which the state has been passed. Compose addresses this by performing an operation referred to as *recomposition*.

Recomposition occurs whenever a state value changes within a hierarchy of composable functions. As soon as Compose detects a state change, it works through all of the composable functions in the activity and recomposes any functions affected by the state value change. Recomposing simply means that the function gets called again and passed the new state value.

Recomposing the entire composable tree for a user interface each time a state value changes would be a highly inefficient approach to rendering and updating a user interface. Compose avoids this overhead using a technique called *intelligent recomposition* that involves only recomposing those functions directly affected by the state change. In other words, only functions that read the state value will be recomposed when the value changes.

20.3 Creating the StateExample project

Launch Android Studio and select the New Project option from the welcome screen. Within the resulting new project dialog, choose the *Empty Compose Activity* template before clicking on the Next button.

Enter *StateExample* into the Name field and specify *com.example.stateexample* as the package name. Before clicking on the Finish button, change the Minimum API level setting to API 26: Android 8.0 (Oreo). On completion of the project creation process, the StateExample project should be listed in the Project tool window located along the left-hand edge of the Android Studio main window.

20.4 Declaring state in a composable

The first step in declaring a state value is to wrap it in a MutableState object. MutableState is a Compose class which is referred to as an *observable type*. Any function that reads a state value is said to have *subscribed* to that observable state. As a result, any changes to the state value will trigger the recomposition of all subscribed functions.

Within Android Studio, open the *MainActivity.kt* file, delete the Greeting composable and modify the class so that it reads as follows:

```kotlin
package com.example.stateexample
.
.
.
class MainActivity : ComponentActivity() {
    override fun onCreate(savedInstanceState: Bundle?) {
        super.onCreate(savedInstanceState)
        setContent {
            StateExampleTheme {
                Surface(color = MaterialTheme.colors.background) {
                    DemoScreen()
                }
            }
        }
    }
}


@Composable
fun DemoScreen() {
    MyTextField()
}


@Composable
fun MyTextField() {

}


@Preview(showBackground = true)
@Composable
fun DefaultPreview() {
    StateExampleTheme {
```

```
        DemoScreen()
    }
}
```

The objective here is to implement MyTextField as a stateful composable function containing a state variable and an event handler that changes the state based on the user's keyboard input. The result is a text field in which the characters appear as they are typed.

MutableState instances are created by making a call to the *mutableStateOf()* runtime function, passing through the initial state value. The following, for example, creates a MutableState instance initialized with an empty String value:

```
var textState = { mutableStateOf("") }
```

This provides an observable state which will trigger a recomposition of all subscribed functions when the contained value is changed. The above declaration is, however, missing a key element. As previously discussed, state must be remembered through recompositions. As currently implemented, the state will be reinitialized to an empty string each time the function in which it is declared is recomposed. To retain the current state value, we need to use the *remember* keyword:

```
var myState = remember { mutableStateOf("") }
```

Remaining within the *MainActivity.kt* file, add some imports and modify the MyTextField composable as follows:

```
.

.

import androidx.compose.material.*
import androidx.compose.runtime.mutableStateOf
import androidx.compose.runtime.remember
import androidx.compose.foundation.layout.Column

.

.

@Composable
fun MyTextField() {

    var textState = remember { mutableStateOf("") }

    val onTextChange = { text : String ->
        textState.value = text
    }

    TextField(
        value = textState.value,
        onValueChange = onTextChange
    )
}
```

Test the code using the Preview panel in interactive mode and confirm that keyboard input appears in the TextField as it is typed. Note that at the time of writing, keyboard input within the preview was not working. If you encounter a similar problem, run the app on an emulator or physical device to test.

When looking at Compose code examples, you may see MutableState objects declared in different ways. When

An Overview of Compose State and Recomposition

using the above format, it is necessary to read and set the *value* property of the MutableState instance. For example, the event handler to update the state reads as follows:

```
val onTextChange = { text: String ->
    textState.value = text
}
```

Similarly, the current state value is assigned to the TextField as follows:

```
TextField(
    value = textState.value,
    onValueChange = onValueChange
)
```

A more common and concise approach to declaring state is to use Kotlin property delegates via the *by* keyword as follows (note that two additional libraries need to be imported when using property delegates):

```
.
.
import androidx.compose.runtime.getValue
import androidx.compose.runtime.setValue
.
.
@Composable
fun MyTextField() {

    var textState by remember { mutableStateOf("") }
.
.
```

We can now access the state value without needing to directly reference the MutableState *value* property within the event handler:

```
val onTextChange = { text: String ->
    textState = text
}
```

This also makes reading the current value more concise:

```
TextField(
    value = textState,
    onValueChange = onTextChange
)
```

A third technique separates the access to a MutableState object into a *value* and a *setter function* as follows:

```
var (textValue, setText) = remember { mutableStateOf("") }
```

When changing the value assigned to the state we now do so by calling the *setText* setter, passing through the new value:

```
val onTextChange = { text: String ->
    setText(text)
}
```

The state value is now accessed by referencing *textValue*:

```
TextField(
    value = textValue,
    onValueChange = onValueChange
)
```

In most cases, the use of the *by* keyword and property delegates is the most commonly used technique because it results in cleaner code. Before continuing with the chapter, revert the example to use the *by* keyword.

20.5 Unidirectional data flow

Unidirectional data flow is an approach to app development whereby state stored in a composable should not be directly changed by any child composable functions. Consider, for example, a composable function named FunctionA containing a state value in the form of a Boolean value. This composable calls another composable function named FunctionB that contains a Switch component. The objective is for the switch to update the state value each time the switch position is changed by the user. In this situation, adherence to unidirectional data flow prohibits FunctionB from directly changing the state value.

Instead, FunctionA would declare an event handler (typically in the form of a lambda) and pass it as a parameter to the child composable along with the state value. The Switch within FunctionB would then be configured to call the event handler each time the switch position changes, passing it the current setting value. The event handler in FunctionA will then update the state with the new value.

Make the following changes to the *MainActivity.kt* file to implement FunctionA and FunctionB together with a corresponding modification to the preview composable:

```
@Composable
fun FunctionA() {

    var switchState by remember { mutableStateOf(true) }

    val onSwitchChange = { value : Boolean ->
        switchState = value
    }

    FunctionB(
        switchState = switchState,
        onSwitchChange = onSwitchChange
    )
}


@Composable
fun FunctionB(switchState: Boolean, onSwitchChange : (Boolean) -> Unit ) {
    Switch(
        checked = switchState,
        onCheckedChange = onSwitchChange
    )
}


@Preview(showBackground = true)
@Composable
```

An Overview of Compose State and Recomposition

```
fun DefaultPreview() {
    StateExampleTheme {
        Column {
            DemoScreen()
            FunctionA()
        }
    }
}
```

Preview the app using interactive mode and verify that clicking the switch changes the slider position between on and off states.

We can now use this example to break down the state process into the following individual steps which occur when FunctionA is called:

1. The *switchState* state variable is initialized with a true value.

2. The *onSwitchChange* event handler is declared to accept a Boolean parameter which it assigns to *switchState* when called.

3. FunctionB is called and passed both *switchState* and a reference to the *onSwitchChange* event handler.

4. FunctionB calls the built-in Switch component and configures it to display the state assigned to *switchState*. The Switch component is also configured to call the *onSwitchChange* event handler when the user changes the switch setting.

5. Compose renders the Switch component on the screen.

The above sequence explains how the Switch component gets rendered on the screen when the app first launches. We can now explore the sequence of events that occur when the user slides the switch to the "off" position:

1. The switch is moved to the "off" position.

2. The Switch component calls the *onSwitchChange* event handler passing through the current switch position value (in this case *false*).

3. The *onSwitchChange* lambda declared in FunctionA assigns the new value to *switchState*.

4. Compose detects that the *switchState* state value has changed and initiates a recomposition.

5. Compose identifies that FunctionB contains code that reads the value of *switchState* and therefore needs to be recomposed.

6. Compose calls FunctionB with the latest state value and the reference to the event handler.

7. FunctionB calls the Switch composable and configures it with the state and event handler.

8. Compose renders the Switch on the screen, this time with the switch in the "off" position.

The key point to note about this process is that the value assigned to *switchState* is only changed from within FunctionA and never directly updated by FunctionB. The Switch setting is not moved from the "on" position to the "off" position directly by FunctionB. Instead, the state is changed by calling upwards to the event handler located in FunctionA, and allowing recomposition to regenerate the Switch with the new position setting.

As a general rule, data is passed down through a composable hierarchy tree while events are called upwards to handlers in ancestor components as illustrated in Figure 20-1:

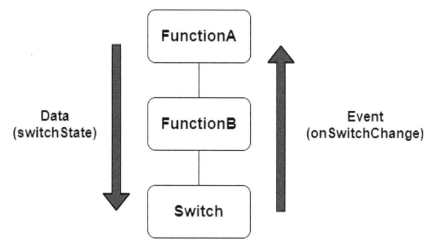

Figure 20-1

20.6 State hoisting

If you look up the word "hoist" in a dictionary it will likely be defined as the act of raising or lifting something. The term *state hoisting* has a similar meaning in that it involves moving state from a child composable up to the calling (parent) composable or a higher ancestor. When the child composable is called by the parent, it is passed the state along with an event handler. When an event occurs in the child composable that requires an update to the state, a call is made to the event handler passing through the new value as outlined earlier in the chapter. This has the advantage of making the child composable stateless and, therefore, easier to reuse. It also allows the state to be passed down to other child composables later in the app development process.

Consider our MyTextField example from earlier in the chapter:

```
@Composable
fun DemoScreen() {
    MyTextField()
}


@Composable
fun MyTextField() {

    var textState by remember { mutableStateOf("") }

    val onTextChange = { text : String ->
        textState = text
    }

    TextField(
        value = textState,
        onValueChange = onTextChange
    )

}
```

The self-contained nature of the MyTextField composable means that it is not a particularly useful component. One issue is that the text entered by the user is not accessible to the calling function and, therefore, cannot be passed to any sibling functions. It is also not possible to pass a different state and event handler through to the function, thereby limiting its re-usability.

To make the function more useful we need to hoist the state into the parent DemoScreen function as follows:

```
@Composable
fun DemoScreen() {

    var textState by remember { mutableStateOf("") }

    val onTextChange = { text : String ->
        textState = text
    }

    MyTextField(text = textState, onTextChange = onTextChange)
}


@Composable
fun MyTextField(text: String, onTextChange : (String) -> Unit) {

    var textState by remember { mutableStateOf("") }

    val onTextChange = { text : String ->
        textState = text
    }

    TextField(
        value = text,
        onValueChange = onTextChange
    )
}
```

With the state hoisted to the parent function, MyTextField is now a stateless, reusable composable which can be called and passed any state and event handler. Also, the text entered by the user is now accessible by the parent function and may be passed down to other composables if necessary.

State hoisting is not limited to moving to the immediate parent of a composable. State can be raised any number of levels upward within the composable hierarchy and subsequently passed down through as many layers of children as needed (within reason). This will often be necessary when multiple children need access to the same state. In such a situation, the state will need to be hoisted up to an ancestor that is common to both children.

In Figure 20-2 below, for example, both NameField and NameText need access to *textState*. The only way to make the state available to both composables is to hoist it up to the MainScreen function since this is the only ancestor both composables have in common:

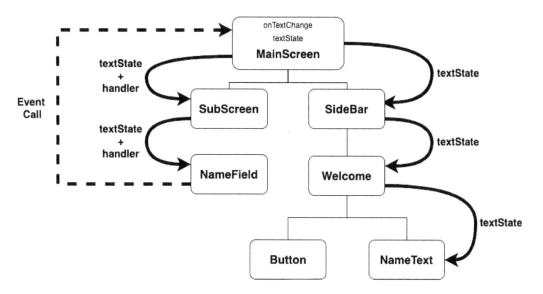

Figure 20-2

The solid arrows indicate the path of *textState* as it is passed down through the hierarchy to the NameField and NameText functions (in the case of the NameField, a reference to the event handler is also passed down), while the dotted line represents the calls from NameField function to an event handler declared in MainScreen as the text changes.

Note that if you find yourself passing state down through an excessive number of child layers, it may be worth looking at *CompositionLocalProvider*, a topic covered in the chapter entitled *"An Introduction to Composition Local"*.

When adding state to a function, take some time to decide whether hoisting state to the caller (or higher) might make for a more re-usable and flexible composable. While situations will arise where state is only needed to be used locally in a composable, in most cases it probably makes sense to hoist the state up to an ancestor.

20.7 Saving state through configuration changes

We now know that the *remember* keyword can be used to save state values through recompositions. This technique does not, however, retain state between *configuration changes*. A configuration change generally occurs when some aspect of the device changes in a way that alters the appearance of an activity (such as rotating the orientation of the device between portrait and landscape or changing a system-wide font setting).

Changes such as these will cause the entire activity to be destroyed and recreated. The reasoning behind this is that such changes affect resources such as the layout of the user interface and simply destroying and recreating impacted activities is the quickest way for an activity to respond to the configuration change. The result is a newly initialized activity with no memory of any previous state values.

To experience the effect of a configuration change, run the StateExample app on an emulator or device and, once running, enter some text so that it appears in the TextField before changing the orientation from portrait to landscape. When using the emulator, device rotation may be simulated using the rotation button located in the emulator toolbar. To complete the rotation on Android 11 or older, it may also be necessary to tap on the rotation button. This appears in the toolbar of the device or emulator screen as shown in Figure 20-3:

Figure 20-3

Before performing the rotation on Android 12 or later, you may need to enter the Settings app, select the Display category and enable the *Auto-rotate screen* option.

Note that after rotation, the TextField is now blank and the text entered has been lost. In situations where state needs to be retained through configuration changes, Compose provides the *rememberSaveable* keyword. When *rememberSaveable* is used, the state will be retained not only through recompositions, but also configuration changes. Modify the *textState* declaration to use *rememberSaveable* as follows:

```
.
.
import androidx.compose.runtime.saveable.rememberSaveable
.
.
@Composable
fun DemoScreen() {

    var textState by rememberSaveable { mutableStateOf("") }
.
.
```

Build and run the app once again, enter some text and perform another rotation. Note that the text is now preserved following the configuration change.

20.8 Summary

When developing apps with Compose it is vital to have a clear understanding of how state and recomposition work together to make sure that the user interface is always up to date. In this chapter, we have explored state and described how state values are declared, updated, and passed between composable functions. You should also have a better understanding of recomposition and how it is triggered in response to state changes.

We also introduced the concept of unidirectional data flow and explained how data flows down through the compose hierarchy while data changes are made by making calls upward to event handlers declared within ancestor stateful functions.

An important goal when writing composable functions is to maximize reusability. This can be achieved, in part, by hoisting state out of a composable up to the calling parent or a higher function in the compose hierarchy.

Finally, the chapter described configuration changes and explained how such changes result in the destruction and recreation of entire activities. Ordinarily, state is not retained through configuration changes unless specifically configured to do so using the *rememberSaveable* keyword.

Chapter 21

21. An Introduction to Composition Local

We already know from previous chapters that user interfaces are built in Compose by constructing hierarchies of composable functions. We also know that Compose is state-driven and that state should generally be declared in the highest possible node of the composable tree (a concept referred to as state hoisting) and passed down through the hierarchy to the descendant composables where it is needed. While this works well for most situations, it can become cumbersome if the state needs to be passed down through multiple levels within the hierarchy. A solution to this problem exists in the form of CompositionLocal, which is the subject of this chapter.

21.1 Understanding CompositionLocal

In simple terms, CompositionLocal provides a way to make state declared higher in the composable hierarchy tree available to functions lower in the tree without having to pass it through every composable between the point where it is declared and the function where it is used. Consider, for example, the following hierarchy diagram:

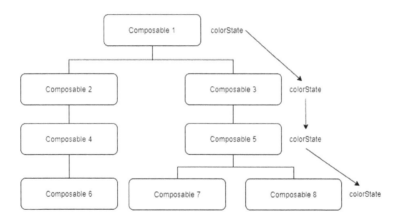

Figure 21-1

In the hierarchy, a state named *colorState* is declared in Composable1 but is only used in Composable8. Although the state is not needed in either Composable3 or Composable5, *colorState* still needs to be passed down through those functions to reach Composable8. The deeper the tree becomes, the more levels through which the state needs to be passed to reach the function where it is used.

A solution to this problem is to use CompositionLocal. CompositionLocal allows us to declare the data at the highest necessary node in the tree and then access it in descendants without having to pass it through the intervening children as shown in Figure 21-2:

157

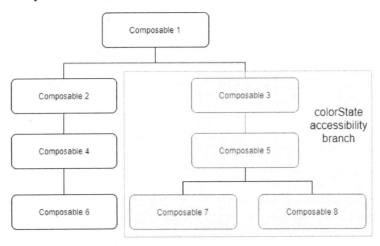

Figure 21-2

CompositionLocal has the added advantage of only making the data available to the branch of the tree below the point at which it is assigned a value. In other words, if the state were assigned a value when calling composable3 it will be accessible within composable numbers 3, 5, 7, and 8, but not to composables 1, 2, 4, or 6. This allows state to be kept local to specific branches of the composable tree, and also for different sub-branches to have different values assigned to the same CompositionLocal state. Composable5 could, for example, have a different color assigned to *colorState* from that assigned when Composable7 is called.

21.2 Using CompositionLocal

Declaring state using CompositionLocal starts with the creation of a ProvidableCompositionLocal instance which can be obtained via a call to either the *compositionLocalOf()* or *staticCompositionLocalOf()* function. In each case the function accepts a lambda defining a default value to be assigned to the state in the absence of a specific assignment, for example:

```
val LocalColor = compositionLocalOf { Color.Red }
val LocalColor = staticCompositionLocalOf { Color.Red }
```

The *staticCompositionLocalOf()* function is recommended for storing state values that are unlikely to change very often. The reason for this is that any changes to the state value will cause the entire tree beneath where the value is assigned to be recomposed. The *compositionLocalOf()* function, on the other hand, will only cause recomposition to be performed on composables where the current state is accessed. This function should be used when dealing with states that change frequently.

The next step is to assign a value to the ProvidableCompositionLocal instance and wrap the call to the immediate descendant child composable in a CompositionLocalProvider call:

```
val color = Color.Blue

CompositionLocalProvider(LocalColor provides color) {
    Composable5()
}
```

Any descendants of Composition5 will now be able to access the CompositionLocal state via the current property of the ProviderCompositionLocal instance, for example:

```
val background = LocalColor.current
```

In the rest of this chapter, we will build a project that mirrors the hierarchy illustrated in Figure 21-1 to show

CompositionLocal in action.

21.3 Creating the CompLocalDemo project

Launch Android Studio and create a new *Empty Compose Activity* project named CompLocalDemo, specifying *com.example.complocaldemo* as the package name, and selecting a minimum API level of API 26: Android 8.0 (Oreo). Within the *MainActivity.kt* file, delete the Greeting function and add a new empty composable named Composable1:

```
@Composable
fun Composable1() {


}
```

Next, edit the *onCreateActivity()* method and DefaultPreview function to call Composable1 instead of Greeting.

21.4 Designing the layout

Within the *MainActivity.kt* file, implement the composable hierarchy as follows:

```
.
.
import androidx.compose.foundation.background
import androidx.compose.foundation.isSystemInDarkTheme
import androidx.compose.foundation.layout.Column
import androidx.compose.runtime.CompositionLocalProvider
import androidx.compose.runtime.staticCompositionLocalOf
import androidx.compose.ui.graphics.Color
.
.

@Composable
fun Composable1() {
    Column {
        Composable2()
        Composable3()
    }
}

@Composable
fun Composable2() {
    Composable4()
}

@Composable
fun Composable3() {
    Composable5()
}

@Composable
fun Composable4() {
```

```
    Composable6()
}


@Composable
fun Composable5() {
    Composable7()
    Composable8()
}


@Composable
fun Composable6() {
    Text("Composable 6")
}


@Composable
fun Composable7() {


}


@Composable
fun Composable8() {
    Text("Composable 8")
}
```

21.5 Adding the CompositionLocal state

The objective for this project is to declare a color state that can be changed depending on whether the device is in light or dark mode, and use that to control the background color of the text component in Composable8. Since this is a value that will not change regularly, we can use the *staticCompositionLocalOf()* function. Remaining within the *MainActivity.kt* file, add the following line above the Composable1 declaration:

```
.

.

val LocalColor = staticCompositionLocalOf { Color(0xFFffdbcf) }

@Composable
fun Composable1() {
    Column {

.

.
```

Next, a call to *isSystemInDarkTheme()* needs to be added, and the result used to assign a different color to the LocalColor state. We also need to call Composable3 from within the context of the CompositionLocal provider:

```
@Composable
fun Composable1() {


    var color = if (isSystemInDarkTheme()) {
        Color(0xFFa08d87)
```

```
    } else {
        Color(0xFFffdbcf)
    }

    Column {
        Composable2()

        CompositionLocalProvider(LocalColor provides color) {
            Composable3()
        }
    }
}
```

21.6 Accessing the CompositionLocal state

The final task before testing the code is to assign the color state to the Text component in Composable8 as follows:

```
@Composable
fun Composable8() {
    Text("Composable 8", modifier = Modifier.background(LocalColor.current))
}
```

21.7 Testing the design

To test the activity code in both light and dark modes, add a new Preview composable to *MainActivity.kt* with uiMode set to UI_NIGHT_MODE_YES:

```
.
.
import android.content.res.Configuration.UI_MODE_NIGHT_YES
.
.
@Preview(showBackground = true, uiMode = UI_MODE_NIGHT_YES)
@Composable
fun DarkPreview() {
    CompLocalDemoTheme {
        Composable1()
    }
}
```

After refreshing the Preview panel, both the default and dark preview should appear, each using a different color as the background for the Text component in Composable8:

Figure 21-3

We can also modify the code so that composables 3, 5, 7, and 8 all have a different color setting. All this requires is calling each composable from within a CompositionLocalProvider with a different color assignment:

```
.
.
@Composable
fun Composable3() {

    Text("Composable 3", modifier = Modifier.background(LocalColor.current))

    CompositionLocalProvider(LocalColor provides Color.Red) {
        Composable5()
    }
}
.
.
@Composable
fun Composable5() {

    Text("Composable 5", modifier = Modifier.background(LocalColor.current))

    CompositionLocalProvider(LocalColor provides Color.Green) {
        Composable7()
    }

    CompositionLocalProvider(LocalColor provides Color.Yellow) {
        Composable8()
    }
}
.
.
```

```
@Composable
fun Composable7() {
    Text("Composable 7", modifier = Modifier.background(LocalColor.current))
}
.
.
.
```

Now when the Preview panel is refreshed, all four components will have a different color, all based on the same LocalColor state:

Figure 21-4

As one final step, try to access the LocalColor state from Composable6:

```
@Composable
fun Composable6() {
    Text("Composable 6", modifier = Modifier.background(LocalColor.current))
}
```

On refreshing the preview the Text component for Compsoable6 will appear using the default color assigned to LocalColor. This is because Composable6 is in a different branch of the tree and does not have access to the current LocalColor setting.

21.8 Summary

This chapter has introduced CompositionLocal and demonstrated how it can be used to declare state that is accessible to composables lower down in the layout hierarchy without having to be passed from one child to another. State declared in this way is local to the branch of the hierarchy tree in which a value is assigned.

22. An Overview of Compose Slot APIs

Now that we have a better idea of what composable functions are and how to create them, it is time to explore composables that provide a *slot API*. In this chapter, we will explain what a slot API is, what it is used for and how you can include slots in your own composable functions. We will also explore some of the built-in composables that provide slot API support.

22.1 Understanding slot APIs

As we already know, composable functions can include calls to one or more other composable functions. This usually means that the content of a composable is predefined in terms of which other composables it calls and, therefore, the content it displays. Consider the following function consisting of a Column and three Text components:

```
@Composable
fun SlotDemo() {
    Column {
        Text("Top Text")
        Text("Middle Text")
        Text("Bottom Text")
    }
}
```

The function could be modified to pass in parameters that specify the text to be displayed or even the color and font size of that text. Regardless of the changes we make, however, the function is still restricted to displaying a column containing three Text components:

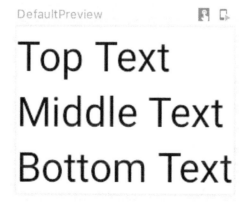

Figure 22-1

Suppose, however, that we need to display three items in a column, but do not know what composable will take up the middle position until just before the composable is called. In its current form, there is no way to display anything but the declared Text component in the middle position. The solution to this problem is to open up the middle composable as a *slot* into which any other composable may be placed when the function is called. This is referred to as providing a *slot API* for the composable. API is an abbreviation of Application Programming Interface and, in this context, implies that we are adding a programming interface to our composable that allows the caller to specify the composable to appear within a slot. In fact, a composable function can provide multiple slots to the caller. In the above function, for example, all of the Text components could be declared as slots if required.

22.2 Declaring a slot API

It can be helpful to think of a slot API composable as a user interface template in which one or more elements are left blank. These missing pieces are then passed as parameters when the composable is called and included when the user interface is rendered by the Compose runtime system.

The first step in adding slots to a composable is to specify that it accepts a slot as a parameter. This is essentially a case of declaring that a composable accepts other composables as parameters. In the case of our example SlotDemo composable, we would modify the function signature as follows:

```
@Composable
fun SlotDemo(middleContent: @Composable () -> Unit) {
    .
    .
```

When the SlotDemo composable is called, it will now need to be passed a composable function. Note that the function is declared as returning a *Unit* object. Unit is a Kotlin type used to indicate that a function does not return any value. Unit can be considered to be the Kotlin equivalent of *void* in other languages. The parameter has been assigned a label of "middleContent", though this could be any valid label name that helps to describe the slot and allows us to reference it within the body of the function.

The only remaining change to this composable is to substitute the middleContent component into the Column declaration as follows:

```
@Composable
fun SlotDemo(middleContent: @Composable () -> Unit) {
    Column {
        Text("Top Text")
        middleContent()
        Text("Bottom Text")
    }
}
```

We have now successfully declared a slot API for our SlotDemo composable.

22.3 Calling slot API composables

The next step is to learn how to make use of the slot API configured into our SlotDemo composable. This simply involves passing a composable through as a parameter when making the SlotDemo function call. Suppose, for example, that we need the following composable to appear in the middleContent slot:

```
@Composable
fun ButtonDemo() {
    Button(onClick = { }) {
        Text("Click Me")
    }
}
```

We can now call our SlotDemo composable function as follows:

```
SlotDemo(middleContent = { ButtonDemo() })
```

While this syntax works, it can quickly become cluttered if the composable has more than one slot to be filled. A cleaner syntax reads as follows:

```
SlotDemo {
    ButtonDemo()
}
```

Regardless of the syntax used, the design will be rendered as shown below in Figure 22-2:

Figure 22-2

A slot API is not, of course, limited to a single slot. The SlotDemo example could be composed entirely of slots as follows:

```
@Composable
fun SlotDemo(
    topContent: @Composable () -> Unit,
    middleContent: @Composable () -> Unit,
    bottomContent: @Composable () -> Unit) {
    Column {
        topContent()
        middleContent()
        bottomContent()
    }
}
```

With these changes made, the call to SlotDemo could be structured as follows:

```
SlotDemo(
    topContent = { Text("Top Text") },
    middleContent = { ButtonDemo() },
    bottomContent = { Text("Bottom Text") }
)
```

As with the single slot, this can be abbreviated for clarity:

```
SlotDemo(
```

```
    { Text("Top Text") },
    { ButtonDemo() },
    { Text("Bottom Text") }
)
```

22.4 Summary

In this chapter, we have introduced the concept of slot APIs and demonstrated how they can be added to composable functions. By implementing a slot API, the content of a composable function can be specified dynamically at the point that it is called. This contrasts with the static content of a typical composable where the content is defined at the point the function is written and cannot subsequently be changed. A composable with a slot API is essentially a user interface template containing one or more slots into which other composables can be inserted at runtime.

With the basics of slot APIs covered in this chapter, the next chapter will create a project that puts this theory into practice.

Chapter 23

23. A Compose Slot API Tutorial

In this chapter, we will be creating a project within Android Studio to practice the use of slot APIs to build flexible and dynamic composable functions. This will include writing a composable function with two slots and calling that function with different content composables based on selections made by the user.

23.1 About the project

Once the project is completed, it will consist of a title, progress indicator, and two checkboxes. The checkboxes will be used to control whether the title is represented as text or graphics, and also whether a circular or linear progress indicator is displayed. Both the title and progress indicator will be declared as slots which will be filled with either a Text or Image composable for the title or, in the case of the progress indicator, a LinearProgressIndicator or CircularProgressIndicator component.

23.2 Creating the SlotApiDemo project

Launch Android Studio and select the New Project option from the welcome screen. Within the New Project dialog, choose the *Empty Compose Activity* template before clicking on the Next button.

Enter *SlotApiDemo* into the Name field and specify *com.example.slotapidemo* as the package name. Before clicking on the Finish button, change the Minimum API level setting to API 26: Android 8.0 (Oreo). Once the project has been created, the SlotApiDemo project should be listed in the Project tool window located along the left-hand edge of the Android Studio main window.

23.3 Preparing the MainActivity class file

Android Studio should have automatically loaded the *MainActivity.kt* file into the code editor. If it has not, locate it in the Project tool window (*app -> java -> com.example.slotapidemo -> MainActivity.kt*) and double-click on it to load it into the editor. Once loaded, modify the file to remove the template code as follows:

```
package com.example.slotapidemo
 .
 .
class MainActivity : ComponentActivity() {
    override fun onCreate(savedInstanceState: Bundle?) {
        super.onCreate(savedInstanceState)
        setContent {
            SlotApiDemoTheme {
                Surface(
                    modifier = Modifier.fillMaxSize(),
                    color = MaterialTheme.colors.background
                ) {
                    Greeting("Android")
                }
            }
        }
    }
}
```

```
}

@Composable
fun Greeting(name: String) {
      Text(text = "Hello $name!")
}

@Preview(showBackground = true)
@Composable
fun DefaultPreview() {
      SlotApiDemoTheme {
            Greeting("Android")
      }
}
```

23.4 Creating the MainScreen composable

Edit the *onCreate* method of the MainActivity class to call a composable named *MainScreen* from within the Surface component:

```
override fun onCreate(savedInstanceState: Bundle?) {
    super.onCreate(savedInstanceState)
    setContent {
        SlotDemoTheme {
            Surface(
                modifier = Modifier.fillMaxSize(),
                color = MaterialTheme.colors.background
            ) {
                MainScreen()
            }
        }
    }
}
```

MainScreen will contain the state and event handlers for the two Checkbox components, so start adding this composable now, making sure to place it after the closing brace (}) of the MainActivity class declaration:

```
package com.example.slotapidemo

.

.

import androidx.compose.runtime.*
import androidx.compose.material.*
import androidx.compose.foundation.layout.*

.

.

@Composable
fun MainScreen() {

    var linearSelected by remember { mutableStateOf(true) }
```

170

```
    var imageSelected by remember { mutableStateOf(true) }

    val onLinearClick = { value : Boolean ->
        linearSelected = value
    }

    val onTitleClick = { value : Boolean ->
        imageSelected = value
    }
}
```

Here we have declared two state variables, one for each of the two Checkbox components, and initialized them to *true*. Next, event handlers have been declared to allow the state of each variable to be changed when the user toggles the Checkbox settings. Later in the project, MainScreen will be modified to call a second composable named ScreenContent.

23.5 Adding the ScreenContent composable

When it is called by the MainScreen function, the ScreenContent composable will need to be passed the state variables and event handlers and can initially be declared as follows:

```
package com.example.slotapidemo
.
.
import androidx.compose.ui.Alignment
import androidx.compose.ui.unit.dp
.
.
@Composable
fun ScreenContent(
    linearSelected: Boolean,
    imageSelected: Boolean,
    onTitleClick: (Boolean) -> Unit,
    onLinearClick: (Boolean) -> Unit) {

    Column(
        modifier = Modifier.fillMaxSize(),
        horizontalAlignment = Alignment.CenterHorizontally,
        verticalArrangement = Arrangement.SpaceBetween
    ) {

    }
}
```

As the name suggests, the ScreenContent composable is going to be responsible for displaying the screen content including the title, progress indicator, and checkboxes. In preparation for this content, we have made a call to the Column composable and configured it to center its children along the horizontal axis. The SpaceBetween arrangement property has also been set. This tells the column to space its children evenly but not to include spacing before the first or after the last child.

One of the child composables which will be called by ScreenContent will be responsible for rendering the two Checkbox components. While these could be added directly within the Column composable, a better approach is to place them in a separate composable which can be called from within ScreenContent.

23.6 Creating the Checkbox composable

The composable containing the checkboxes will consist of a Row component containing two Checkbox instances. In addition, Text composables will be positioned to the left of each Checkbox with a Spacer separating the two Text/Checkbox pairs.

When it is called, the Checkboxes composable will need to be passed the two state variables which will be used to make sure the checkboxes display the current state. Also passed will be references to the *onLinearClick* and *onTitleClick* event handlers which will be assigned to the *onCheckChange* properties of the two Checkbox components.

Remaining within the *MainActivity.kt* file, add the CheckBoxes composable so that it reads as follows:

```
.

.

import androidx.compose.foundation.layout.Row

.

.

@Composable
fun CheckBoxes(
    linearSelected: Boolean,
    imageSelected: Boolean,
    onTitleClick: (Boolean) -> Unit,
    onLinearClick: (Boolean) -> Unit
) {
    Row(Modifier.padding(20.dp)) {

        Checkbox(
            checked = imageSelected,
            onCheckedChange = onTitleClick
        )
        Text("Image Title")
        Spacer(Modifier.width(20.dp))
        Checkbox(checked = linearSelected,
            onCheckedChange = onLinearClick
        )
        Text("Linear Progress")
    }
}
```

If you would like to preview the composable before proceeding, add the following preview declaration before clicking on the *Build & Refresh* link in the Preview panel:

```
@Preview
@Composable
fun DemoPreview() {
    CheckBoxes(
```

```
        linearSelected = true,
        imageSelected = true,
        onTitleClick = { /*TODO*/ },
        onLinearClick = { /*TODO*/})
}
```

When calling the CheckBoxes composable in the above preview function we are setting the two state properties to true and assigning stub lambdas that do nothing as the event callbacks.

Once the preview has been refreshed, the layout should match that shown in Figure 23-1 below:

Figure 23-1

23.7 Implementing the ScreenContent slot API

Now that we have added the composable containing the two checkboxes, we can call it from within the Column contained within ScreenContent. Since both the state variables and event handlers were already passed into ScreenContent, we can simply pass these to the Checkboxes composable when we call it. Locate the ScreenContent composable and modify it as follows:

```
@Composable
fun ScreenContent(
    linearSelected: Boolean,
    imageSelected: Boolean,
    onTitleClick: (Boolean) -> Unit,
    onLinearClick: (Boolean) -> Unit) {

    Column(
        modifier = Modifier.fillMaxSize(),
        horizontalAlignment = Alignment.CenterHorizontally,
        verticalArrangement = Arrangement.SpaceBetween
    ) {
        CheckBoxes(linearSelected, imageSelected, onTitleClick, onLinearClick)
    }
}
```

In addition to the row of checkboxes, ScreenContent also needs slots for the title and progress indicator. These will be named *titleContent* and *progressContent* and need to be added as parameters and referenced as children of the Column:

```
@Composable
fun ScreenContent(
    linearSelected: Boolean,
    imageSelected: Boolean,
    onTitleClick: (Boolean) -> Unit,
```

```
    onLinearClick: (Boolean) -> Unit,
    titleContent: @Composable () -> Unit,
    progressContent: @Composable () -> Unit) {

    Column(
        modifier = Modifier.fillMaxSize(),
        horizontalAlignment = Alignment.CenterHorizontally,
        verticalArrangement = Arrangement.SpaceBetween
    ) {
        titleContent()
        progressContent()
        CheckBoxes(linearSelected, imageSelected, onTitleClick, onLinearClick)

    }

}
```

All that remains is to add some code to the MainScreen declaration so that different composables are provided for the slots based on the current values of the *linearSelected* and *imageSelected* state variables. Before taking that step, however, we need to add one more composable to display an image in the title slot.

23.8 Adding an Image drawable resource

For this example, we will use one of the built-in vector drawings included with the Android SDK. To select a drawing and add it to the project, begin by locating the *drawable* folder in the Project tool window (*app -> res -> drawable*) and right-click on it. In the resulting menu (Figure 23-2) select the *New -> Vector Asset* menu option:

Figure 23-2

Once the menu option has been selected, Android Studio will display the Asset Studio dialog shown in Figure 23-3 below:

Figure 23-3

Within the dialog, click on the image to the right of the Clip Art label as indicated by the arrow in the above figure to display a list of available icons. In the search box, enter "cloud" and select the "Cloud Download" icon as shown in Figure 23-4 below:

Figure 23-4

Click on the OK button to select the drawing and return to the Asset Studio dialog. Increase the size of the image to 150dp x 150dp before clicking the Next button. On the subsequent screen, click on Finish to save the file in the default location.

While it was possible to change the color of the image in the Asset Studio dialog, the color selector only allows us to specify colors by RGB value. Instead, we want to use a named color from the project theme. Within the Project tool window, find and open the *Theme.kt* file located under *app -> com.example.slotapidemo -> ui.theme*. This file contains color settings for both light and dark color palettes. In this example, the plan is to use the *primaryVariant* color setting which, in both palettes, is set to a color named Purple700:

```
primaryVariant = Purple700
```

Having chosen a color from the theme, double-click on the *ic_baseline_cloud_download_24.xml* vector asset file in the Project tool window to load it into the code editor and modify the android:tint property as follows:

```
<vector android:height="150dp" android:tint="@color/purple_700"
    android:viewportHeight="24" android:viewportWidth="24"
    android:width="150dp" xmlns:android="http://schemas.android.com/apk/res/
android">
    <path android:fillColor="@android:color/white" android:pathData="M19.35,10.0
4C18.67,6.59 15.64,4 12,4 9.11,4 6.6,5.64 5.35,8.04 2.34,8.36 0,10.91 0,14c0,3.31
2.69,6 6,6h13c2.76,0 5,-2.24 5,-5 0,-2.64 -2.05,-4.78 -4.65,-4.96zM17,13l-5,5
-5,-5h3V9h4v4h3z"/>
</vector>
```

23.9 Writing the TitleImage composable

Now that we have an image to display for the title, the next step is to write a composable to display the image. To make this composable as reusable as possible we will design it so that it is passed the image resource to be displayed:

.

.

```
import androidx.compose.foundation.Image
```

```
import androidx.compose.ui.res.painterResource
.
.
.
@Composable
fun TitleImage(drawing: Int) {
    Image(
        painter = painterResource(drawing),
        contentDescription = "title image"
    )
}
```

The Image component provides several ways to render graphics depending on which parameters are used when it is called. Since we are using a resource image, the component makes a call to the *painterResource* method to render the image.

23.10 Completing the MainScreen composable

Now that all of the child composables have been added and the state variable and event handlers implemented, it is time to complete work on the MainScreen declaration. Specifically, code needs to be added to this composable so that different content is displayed in the two ScreenContent slots depending on the current checkbox selections.

Locate the MainScreen composable in the *MainActivity.kt* file and add code to call the ScreenContent function as follows:

```
@Composable
fun MainScreen() {

    var linearSelected by remember { mutableStateOf(true) }
    var imageSelected by remember { mutableStateOf(true) }

    val onLinearClick = { value : Boolean ->
        linearSelected = value
    }

    val onTitleClick = { value : Boolean ->
        imageSelected = value
    }

    ScreenContent(
        linearSelected = linearSelected,
        imageSelected = imageSelected,
        onLinearClick = onLinearClick,
        onTitleClick = onTitleClick,
        titleContent = {
            if (imageSelected) {

                TitleImage(drawing = R.drawable.ic_baseline_cloud_download_24)
```

```
        } else {
            Text("Downloading", style = MaterialTheme.typography.h3,
                modifier = Modifier.padding(30.dp))
        }
    },
    progressContent = {
        if (linearSelected) {
            LinearProgressIndicator(Modifier.height(40.dp))
        } else {
            CircularProgressIndicator(Modifier.size(200.dp),
                strokeWidth = 18.dp)
        }
    }
)
}
```

The ScreenContent call begins by passing through the state variables and event handlers which will subsequently be passed down to the two Checkbox instances:

```
ScreenContent(
    linearSelected = linearSelected,
    imageSelected = imageSelected,
    onLinearClick = onLinearClick,
    onTitleClick = onTitleClick,
```

The next parameter deals with the *titleContent* slot and uses an *if* statement to pass through either a TitleImage or Text component depending on the current value of the *imageSelected* state:

```
titleContent = {
    if (imageSelected) {

        TitleImage(drawing = R.drawable.ic_baseline_cloud_download_24)

    } else {
        Text("Downloading", style = MaterialTheme.typography.h3,
            modifier = Modifier.padding(30.dp))
    }
},
```

Finally, either a linear or circular progress indicator is used to fill ScreenContent's *progressContent* slot based on the current value of the *linearSelected* state:

```
progressContent = {
    if (linearSelected) {
        LinearProgressIndicator(Modifier.height(40.dp))
    } else {
        CircularProgressIndicator(Modifier.size(200.dp), strokeWidth = 18.dp)
    }
}
```

Note that we haven't passed a progress value through to either of the progress indicators. This will cause the components to enter *indeterminate progress* mode which will cause them to show a continually cycling indicator.

23.11 Previewing the project

With these changes complete, the project is now ready to preview. Locate the DemoPreview composable added earlier in the chapter and modify it so that it calls MainScreen instead of the Checkboxes composable and to add the system UI to the preview:

```
@Preview(showSystemUi = true)
@Composable
fun DemoPreview() {
    MainScreen()
}
```

Once a rebuild has been performed, the Preview panel should resemble that shown in Figure 23-5:

Figure 23-5

To test that the project works, start interactive mode by clicking on the button indicated in Figure 23-6:

Figure 23-6

Once interactive mode has started, experiment with different combinations of checkbox settings to confirm that the slot API for the ScreenContent composable is performing as expected. Figure 23-7, for example, shows the rendering with both checkboxes disabled:

Figure 23-7

23.12 Summary

In this chapter, we have demonstrated the use of a slot API to insert different content into a composable at the point that it is called during runtime. Incidentally, we also passed state variables and event handler references down through multiple levels of composable functions and explored how to use Android Studio's Asset Studio to select and configure built-in vector drawable assets. Finally, we also made use of the built-in Image component to render an image within a user interface layout.

Chapter 24

24. Using Modifiers in Compose

In this chapter, we will introduce Compose modifiers and explain how they can be used to customize the appearance and behavior of composables. Topics covered will include an overview of modifiers and an introduction to the Modifier object. The chapter will also explain how to create and use modifiers, and how to add modifier support to your own composables.

24.1 An overview of modifiers

Many composables accept one or more parameters that define their appearance and behavior within the running app. We can, for example, specify the font size and weight of a Text composable by passing through parameters as follows:

```
@Composable
fun DemoScreen() {
    Text(
        "My Vacation",
        fontSize = 40.sp,
        fontWeight = FontWeight.Bold
    )
}
```

In addition to parameters of this type, most built-in composables also accept an optional *modifier* parameter which allows additional aspects of the composable to be configured. Unlike parameters, which are generally specific to the type of composable (a font setting would have no meaning to a Column component for example), modifiers are more general in that they can be applied to any composable.

The foundation for building modifiers is the Modifier object. Modifier is a built-in Compose object designed to store configuration settings that can be applied to composables. The Modifier object provides a wide selection of methods that can be called upon to configure properties such as borders, padding, background, size requirements, event handlers, and gestures to name just a few. Once declared, a Modifier can be passed to other composables and used to change appearance and behavior.

In the remainder of this chapter, we will explore the key concepts of modifiers and demonstrate their use within an example project.

24.2 Creating the ModifierDemo project

Launch Android Studio and select the New Project option from the welcome screen. Within the new project dialog, choose the *Empty Compose Activity* template before clicking on the Next button.

Enter *ModifierDemo* into the Name field and specify *com.example.modifierdemo* as the package name. Before clicking on the Finish button, change the Minimum API level setting to API 26: Android 8.0 (Oreo). Once the project has been created, the project files should be listed in the Project tool window located along the left-hand edge of the Android Studio main window.

Load the *MainActivity.kt* file into the code editor and delete the Greeting composable before making the following changes:

```
package com.example.modifierdemo
```

.

.

```
import androidx.compose.ui.graphics.Color
import androidx.compose.ui.unit.sp
import androidx.compose.ui.text.font.FontWeight
```

.

.

```
class MainActivity : ComponentActivity() {
    override fun onCreate(savedInstanceState: Bundle?) {
        super.onCreate(savedInstanceState)
        setContent {
            ModifierDemoTheme {
                Surface(color = MaterialTheme.colors.background) {
                    DemoScreen()
                }
            }
        }
    }
}


@Composable
fun DemoScreen() {
    Text(
        "Hello Compose",
        fontSize = 40.sp,
        fontWeight = FontWeight.Bold
    )
}

@Preview(showBackground = true)
@Composable
fun DefaultPreview() {
    ModifierDemoTheme {
        DemoScreen()
    }
}
```

24.3 Creating a modifier

The first step in learning to work with modifiers is to create one. To begin with, we can create a modifier without any configuration settings as follows:

```
val modifier = Modifier
```

This essentially gives us a blank modifier containing no configuration settings. To configure the modifier, we need to call methods on it. For example, the modifier can be configured to add 10dp of padding on all four sides of any composable to which it is applied:

```
val modifier = Modifier.padding(all = 10.dp)
```

Method calls on a Modifier instance may be *chained* together to apply multiple configuration settings in a single operation. The following addition to the modifier will draw a black, 2dp wide border around a composable:

```
val modifier = Modifier
    .padding(all = 10.dp)
    .border(width = 2.dp, color = Color.Black)
```

Once a modifier has been created it can be passed to any composable which accepts a modifier parameter. Edit the DemoScreen function so that it reads as follows to pass our modifier to the Text composable:

```
.
.
import androidx.compose.foundation.border
import androidx.compose.foundation.layout.padding
import androidx.compose.ui.unit.dp
.
.
@Composable
fun DemoScreen() {

    val modifier = Modifier
        .border(width = 2.dp, color = Color.Black)
        .padding(all = 10.dp)

    Text(
        "Hello Compose",
        modifier = modifier,
        fontSize = 40.sp,
        fontWeight = FontWeight.Bold
    )
}
```

When the layout is previewed it should appear as illustrated in Figure 24-1:

Figure 24-1

As we can see from the preview, the padding and border have been applied to the text. Clearly, the Text composable has been implemented such that it accepts a modifier as a parameter. If a composable accepts a modifier it will always be the first optional parameter in the parameter list. This has the added benefit of allowing the modifier to be passed without declaring the argument name. The following, therefore, is syntactically correct:

```
Text(
    "Hello Compose",
    modifier,
    fontSize = 40.sp,
```

```
        fontWeight = FontWeight.Bold
)
```

24.4 Modifier ordering

The order in which modifiers are chained is of great significance to the resulting output. In the above example, the border was applied first followed by the padding. This has the result of the border appearing outside the padding. To place the border inside the padding, the order of the modifiers needs to be swapped as follows:

```
val modifier = Modifier
    .padding(all = 10.dp)
    .border(width = 2.dp, color = Color.Black)
```

When previewed, the Text composable will appear as shown in Figure 24-2 below:

Figure 24-2

If you don't see the expected effects when working with chained modifiers, keep in mind this may be because of the order in which they are being applied to the component.

24.5 Adding modifier support to a composable

So far in this chapter, we have shown how to create a modifier and use it with a built-in composable. When developing your own composables it is important to consider whether modifier support should be included to make the function more configurable.

When adding modifier support to a composable the first rule is that the parameter should be named "modifier" and must be the first optional parameter in the function's parameter list. As an example, we can add a new composable named CustomImage to our project which accepts as parameters the image resource to display and a modifier. Edit the *MainActivity.kt* file and add this composable so that it reads as follows:

```
.

.

import androidx.compose.foundation.Image
import androidx.compose.ui.res.painterResource

.

.

@Composable
fun CustomImage(image: Int) {
    Image(
        painter = painterResource(image),
        contentDescription = null
    )
}
```

As currently declared, the function only accepts one parameter in the form of the image resource. The next step is to add the modifier parameter:

```
@Composable
```

```
fun CustomImage(image: Int, modifier: Modifier) {
    Image(
        painter = painterResource(image),
        contentDescription = null
    )
}
```

It is important to remember that the modifier parameter must be optional so that the function can be called without one. This means that we need to specify an empty Modifier instance as the default for the parameter:

```
@Composable
fun CustomImage(image: Int, modifier: Modifier = Modifier) {
.
.
```

Finally, we need to make sure that the modifier is applied to the Image composable, keeping in mind that it will be the first optional parameter:

```
@Composable
fun CustomImage(image: Int, modifier: Modifier = Modifier) {
    Image(
        painter = painterResource(image),
        contentDescription = null,
        modifier
    )
}
```

Now that we have created a new composable with modifier support we are almost ready to call it from the DemoScreen function. First, however, we need to add an image resource to the project. The image is named *vacation.jpg* and can be found in the *images* folder of the sample code archive which can be downloaded from the following web page:

https://www.ebookfrenzy.com/retail/compose/index.php

Within Android Studio, display the Resource Manager tool window (*View -> Tool Windows -> Resource Manager*). Locate the *vacation.png* image in the file system navigator for your operating system and drag and drop it onto the Resource Manager tool window. In the resulting dialog, click Next followed by the Import button to add the image to the project. The image should now appear in the Resource Manager as shown in Figure 24-3 below:

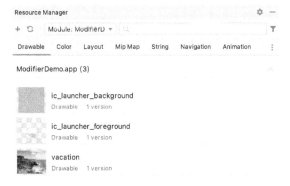

Figure 24-3

Using Modifiers in Compose

The image will also appear in the *res -> drawables* section of the Project tool window:

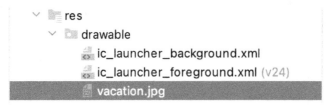

Figure 24-4

Next, modify the DemoScreen composable to include a call to the CustomImage component:

.

.

```
import androidx.compose.ui.Alignment
import androidx.compose.foundation.layout.*

.

.

@Composable
fun DemoScreen() {

    val modifier = Modifier
        .border(width = 2.dp, color = Color.Black)
        .padding(all = 10.dp)

    Column(
        Modifier.padding(20.dp),
        horizontalAlignment = Alignment.CenterHorizontally,
        verticalArrangement = Arrangement.Center
    ) {
        Text(
            "Hello Compose",
            modifier = modifier,
            fontSize = 40.sp,
            fontWeight = FontWeight.Bold
        )
        Spacer(Modifier.height(16.dp))
        CustomImage(R.drawable.vacation)
    }
}
```

Refresh and build the preview and verify that the layout matches that shown in Figure 24-5 below:

Figure 24-5

At this point, the Image component is using the default Modifier instance that we declared in the CustomImage function signature. To change this we need to construct a custom modifier and pass it through to CustomImage to modify the appearance on the image resource when it is displayed:

```
.
.
import androidx.compose.foundation.shape.RoundedCornerShape
import androidx.compose.ui.draw.clip
.
.
Spacer(Modifier.height(16.dp))
CustomImage(R.drawable.vacation,
    Modifier
        .padding(16.dp)
        .width(270.dp)
        .clip(shape = RoundedCornerShape(30.dp))
)
.
.
```

The preview should now display the image with padding, fixed width, and rounded corners:

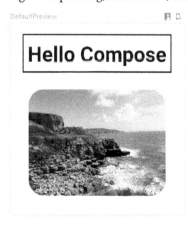

Figure 24-6

24.6 Common built-in modifiers

A list of the full set of Modifier methods is beyond the scope of this book (there are currently over 100). For a detailed and complete list of methods, refer to the Compose documentation at the following URL:

https://developer.android.com/reference/kotlin/androidx/compose/ui/Modifier

The following is a selection of some of the more commonly used functions:

- **background** - Draws a solid colored shape behind the composable.
- **clickable** - Specifies a handler to be called when the composable is clicked. Also causes a ripple effect when the click is performed.
- **clip** - Clips the composable content to a specified shape.
- **fillMaxHeight** - The composable will be sized to fit the maximum height permitted by its parent.
- **fillMaxSize** - The composable will be sized to fit the maximum height and width permitted by its parent.
- **fillMaxWidth** - The composable will be sized to fit the maximum width permitted by its parent.
- **layout** - Used when implementing custom layout behavior, a topic covered in the chapter entitled *"Building Custom Layouts"*.
- **offset** - Positions the composable the specified distance from its current position along the x and y-axis.
- **padding** - Adds space around a composable. Parameters can be used to apply spacing to all four sides or to specify different padding for each side.
- **rotate** - Rotates the composable on its center point by a specified number of degrees.
- **scale** - Increase or reduce the size of the composable by the specified scale factor.
- **scrollable** - Enables scrolling for a composable that extends beyond the viewable area of the layout in which it is contained.
- **size** - Used to specify the height and width of a composable. In the absence of a size setting, the composable will be sized to accommodate its content (referred to as *wrapping*).

24.7 Combining modifiers

When working with Compose, situations may arise where you have two or more Modifier objects, all of which need to be applied to the same composable. For this situation, Compose allows modifiers to be combined using the *then* keyword. The syntax for using this is as follows:

```
val combinedModifier = firstModifier.then(secondModifier).then(thirdModifier) ...
```

The result will be a modifier that contains the configurations of all specified modifiers. To see this in action, modify the *MainActivity.kt* file to add a second modifier for use with the Text composable:

```
.
.
.
val modifier = Modifier
    .border(width = 2.dp, color = Color.Black)
    .padding(all = 10.dp)

val secondModifier = Modifier.height(100.dp)
```

.

.

Next, change the Text call to combine both modifiers:

```
Text(
    "Hello Compose",
    modifier.then(secondModifier),
    fontSize = 40.sp,
    fontWeight = FontWeight.Bold
)
```

The Text composable should now appear in the preview panel with a height of 100dp in addition to the original font, border, and padding settings.

24.8 Summary

Modifiers are created using instances of the Compose Modifier object and are passed as parameters to composables to change appearance and behavior. A modifier is configured by calling methods on the Modifier object to define settings such as size, padding, rotation, and background color. Most of the built-in composables provided with the Compose system will accept a modifier as a parameter. It is also possible (and recommended) to add modifier support to your own composable functions. If a composable function accepts a modifier, it will always be the second optional parameter in the function's parameter list. Multiple modifier instances may be combined using the *then* keyword before being applied to a component.

25. Composing Layouts with Row and Column

User interface design is largely a matter of selecting the appropriate interface components, deciding how those views will be positioned on the screen, and then implementing navigation between the different screens of the app.

As is to be expected, Compose includes a wide range of user interface components for use when developing an app. Compose also provides a set of layout composables to define both how the user interface is organized and how the layout responds to factors such as changes in screen orientation and size.

This chapter will introduce the Row and Column composables included with Compose and explain how these can be used to create user interface designs with relative ease.

25.1 Creating the RowColDemo project

Launch Android Studio and select the New Project option from the welcome screen. Within the resulting new project dialog, choose the *Empty Compose Activity* template before clicking on the Next button.

Enter *RowColDemo* into the Name field and specify *com.example.rowcoldemo* as the package name. Before clicking on the Finish button, change the Minimum API level setting to API 26: Android 8.0 (Oreo).

Within the *MainActivity.kt* file, delete the Greeting function and add a new empty composable named MainScreen:

```
@Composable
fun MainScreen() {

}
```

Next, edit the *onCreateActivity()* method and DefaultPreview function to call MainScreen instead of Greeting. As we work through the examples in this chapter, row and column-based layouts will be built using instances of a custom component named TextCell which displays text within a black border with a small amount of padding to provide space between adjoining components. Before proceeding, add this function to the *MainActivity.kt* file as follows:

.
.

```
import androidx.compose.foundation.border
import androidx.compose.foundation.layout.padding
import androidx.compose.foundation.layout.*
import androidx.compose.ui.graphics.Color
import androidx.compose.ui.text.font.FontWeight
import androidx.compose.ui.text.style.TextAlign
import androidx.compose.ui.unit.dp
import androidx.compose.ui.unit.sp
```

.

.

```
@Composable
fun TextCell(text: String, modifier: Modifier = Modifier) {

    val cellModifier = Modifier
        .padding(4.dp)
        .size(100.dp, 100.dp)
        .border(width = 4.dp, color = Color.Black)

    Text(text = text, cellModifier.then(modifier),
            fontSize = 70.sp,
            fontWeight = FontWeight.Bold,
            textAlign = TextAlign.Center)
}
```

25.2 Row composable

The Row composable, as the name suggests, lays out its children horizontally on the screen. For example, add a simple Row composable to the MainScreen function as follows:

.

.

```
@Composable
fun MainScreen() {
    Row {
        TextCell("1")
        TextCell("2")
        TextCell("3")
    }
}
```

When rendered, the Row declared above will appear as illustrated in Figure 25-1 below:

Figure 25-1

25.3 Column composable

The Column composable performs the same purpose as the Row with the exception that its children are arranged vertically. The following example places the same three composables within a Column:

.

.

```
@Composable
fun MainScreen() {
    Column {
        TextCell("1")
```

```
        TextCell("2")
        TextCell("3")
    }
}
```

The rendered output from the code will appear as shown in Figure 25-2:

Figure 25-2

25.4 Combining Row and Column composables

Row and Column composables can, of course, be embedded within each other to create table style layouts. Try, for example, the following composition containing a mixture of embedded Row and Column layouts:

```
@Composable
fun MainScreen() {
    Column {
        Row {
            Column {
                TextCell("1")
                TextCell("2")
                TextCell("3")
            }

            Column {
                TextCell("4")
                TextCell("5")
                TextCell("6")
            }

            Column {
                TextCell("7")
                TextCell("8")
            }
        }

        Row {
            TextCell("9")
            TextCell("10")
```

```
            TextCell("11")
        }
    }
}
```

Figure 25-3 illustrates the layout generated by the above code:

Figure 25-3

Using this technique, Row and Column layouts may be embedded within each other to achieve just about any level of layout complexity.

25.5 Layout alignment

Both the Row and Column composables will occupy an area of space within the user interface layout depending on child elements, other composables, and any size-related modifiers that may have been applied. By default, the group of child elements within a Row or Column will be aligned with the top left-hand corner of the content area (assuming the app is running on a device configured with a left-to-right reading locale). We can see this effect if we increase the size of our original example Row composable:

```
@Composable
fun MainScreen() {
    Row(modifier = Modifier.size(width = 400.dp, height = 200.dp)) {
        TextCell("1")
        TextCell("2")
        TextCell("3")
    }
}
```

Before making this change, the Row was *wrapping* its children (in other words sizing itself to match the content). Now that the Row is larger than the content we can see that the default alignment has placed the children in the top left-hand corner of the Row component:

Figure 25-4

This default alignment in the vertical axis may be changed by passing through a new value using the *verticalAlignment* parameter of the Row composable. For example, to position the children in the vertical center of the available space, the *Alignment.CenterVertically* value would be passed to the Row as follows:

```
.
.
.
import androidx.compose.ui.Alignment
.
.
.
@Composable
fun MainScreen() {
    Row(verticalAlignment = Alignment.CenterVertically,
        modifier = Modifier.size(width = 400.dp, height = 200.dp)) {
        TextCell("1")
        TextCell("2")
        TextCell("3")
    }
}
```

This will cause the content to be positioned in the vertical center of the Row's area as illustrated below:

Figure 25-5

The following is a list of alignment values accepted by the Row vertical alignment parameter:

- **Alignment.Top** - Aligns the content at the top of the Row content area.

- **Alignment.CenterVertically** - Positions the content in the vertical center of the Row content area.

- **Alignment.Bottom** - Aligns the content at the bottom of the Row content area.

When working with the Column composable, the *horizontalAlignment* parameter is used to configure alignment along the horizontal axis. Acceptable values are as follows:

Composing Layouts with Row and Column

- **Alignment.Start** - Aligns the content at the horizontal start of the Column content area.

- **Alignment.CenterHorizontally** - Positions the content in the horizontal center of the Column content area

- **Alignment.End** - Aligns the content at the horizontal end of the Column content area.

In the following example, the Column's children have been aligned with the end of the Column content area:

.

.

```
@Composable
fun MainScreen() {
    Column(horizontalAlignment = Alignment.End,
            modifier = Modifier.width(250.dp)) {
        TextCell("1")
        TextCell("2")
        TextCell("3")
    }
}
```

When rendered, the resulting column will appear as shown in Figure 25-6:

Figure 25-6

When working with alignment it is worth remembering that it works on the opposite axis to the flow of the containing composable. For example, while the Row organizes children horizontally, alignment operates on the vertical axis. Conversely, alignment operates on the horizontal axis for the Column composable while children are arranged vertically. The reason for emphasizing this point will become evident when we introduce arrangements.

25.6 Layout arrangement positioning

Unlike the alignment settings, arrangement controls child positioning along the same axis as the container (i.e. horizontally for Rows and vertically for Columns). Arrangement values are set on Row and Column instances using the *horizontalArrangement* and *verticalArrangement* parameters respectively. Arrangement properties can be categorized as influencing either position or child spacing.

The following positional settings are available for the Row component via the *horizontalArrangement* parameter:

- **Arrangement.Start** - Aligns the content at the horizontal start of the Row content area.

- **Arrangement.Center** - Positions the content in the horizontal center of the Row content area.

- **Arrangement.End** - Aligns the content at the horizontal end of the Row content area.

The above settings can be visualized as shown in Figure 25-7:

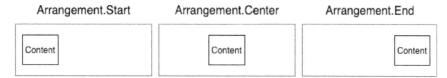

Figure 25-7

The Column composable, on the other hand, accepts the following values for the *verticalArrangement* parameter:

- **Arrangement.Top** - Aligns the content at the top of the Column content area.

- **Arrangement.Center** - Positions the content in the vertical center of the Column content area.

- **Arrangement.Bottom** - Aligns the content at the bottom of the Column content area.

Figure 25-8 illustrates these *verticalArrangement* settings:

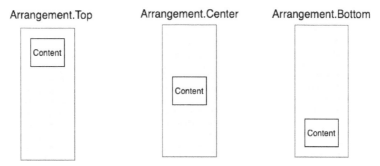

Figure 25-8

Using our example once again, the following change moves the child elements to the end of the Row content area:

```
Row(horizontalArrangement = Arrangement.End,
        modifier = Modifier.size(width = 400.dp, height = 200.dp)) {
        TextCell("1")
        TextCell("2")
        TextCell("3")
}
```

The above code will generate the following user interface layout:

Figure 25-9

Similarly, the following positions child elements at the bottom of the containing Column:

Composing Layouts with Row and Column

```
Column(verticalArrangement = Arrangement.Bottom,
            modifier = Modifier.height(400.dp)) {
    TextCell("1")
    TextCell("2")
    TextCell("3")
}
```

The above composable will render within the Preview panel as illustrated in Figure 25-10 below:

Figure 25-10

25.7 Layout arrangement spacing

Arrangement spacing controls how the child components in a Row or Column are spaced across the content area. These settings are still defined using the *horizontalArrangement* and *verticalArrangement* parameters, but require one of the following values:

- **Arrangement.SpaceEvenly** - Children are spaced equally, including space before the first and after the last child.

- **Arrangement.SpaceBetween** - Children are spaced equally, with no space allocation before the first and after the last child.

- **Arrangement.SpaceAround** - Children are spaced equally, including half spacing before the first and after the last child.

In the following declaration, the children of a Row are positioned using the SpaceEvenly setting:

```
Row(horizontalArrangement = Arrangement.SpaceEvenly,
                modifier = Modifier.width(1000.dp)) {
        TextCell("1")
        TextCell("2")
        TextCell("3")
}
```

The above code gives us the following layout with equal gaps at the beginning and end of the row and between each child:

Figure 25-11

Figure 25-12, on the other hand, shows the same row configured with the SpaceBetween setting. Note that the row has no leading or trailing spacing:

Figure 25-12

Finally, Figure 25-13 shows the effect of applying the SpaceAround setting which adds full spacing between children and half the spacing on the leading and trailing ends:

Figure 25-13

25.8 Row and Column scope modifiers

The children of a Row or Column are said to be within the *scope* of the parent. These two scopes (RowScope and ColumnScope) provide a set of additional modifier functions that can be applied to change the behavior and appearance of individual children within a Row or Column. The Android Studio code editor provides a visual indicator when children are within a scope. In Figure 25-14, for example, the editor indicates that the RowScope modifier functions are available to the three child composables:

```
@Composable
fun MainScreen() {

    Row() {  this: RowScope
                TextCell( text: "1")
                TextCell( text: "2")
                TextCell( text: "3")
    }
}
```

Figure 25-14

When working with the Column composable, a similar ColumnScope indicator will appear.

ColumnScope includes the following modifiers for controlling the position of child components:

- **Modifier.align()** - Allows the child to be aligned horizontally using *Alignment.CenterHorizontally*, *Alignment. Start*, and *Alignment.End* values.

- **Modifier.alignBy()** - Aligns a child horizontally with other siblings on which the *alignBy()* modifier has also been applied.

- **Modifier.weight()** - Sets the height of the child relative to the weight values assigned to its siblings.

Composing Layouts with Row and Column

RowScope provides the following additional modifier functions to Row children:

- **Modifier.align()** - Allows the child to be aligned vertically using *Alignment.CenterVertically*, *Alignment.Top*, and *Alignment.Bottom* values.

- **Modifier.alignBy()** - Aligns a child with other siblings on which the alignBy() modifier has also been applied. Alignment may be performed by baseline or using custom alignment line configurations.

- **Modifier.alignByBaseline()** - Aligns the baseline of a child with any siblings that have also been configured by either the *alignBy()* or *alignByBaseline()* modifier.

- **Modifier.paddingFrom()** - Allows padding to be added to the alignment line of a child.

- **Modifier.weight()** - Sets the width of the child relative to the weight values assigned to its siblings.

The following Row declaration, for example, sets different alignments on each of the three TextCell children:

```
Row(modifier = Modifier.height(300.dp)) {
    TextCell("1", Modifier.align(Alignment.Top))
    TextCell("2", Modifier.align(Alignment.CenterVertically))
    TextCell("3", Modifier.align(Alignment.Bottom))
}
```

When previewed, this will generate a layout resembling Figure 25-15:

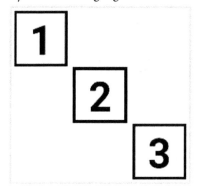

Figure 25-15

The baseline alignment options are especially useful for aligning text content with differing font sizes. Consider, for example, the following Row configuration:

```
Row {
  Text(
      text = "Large Text",
      fontSize = 40.sp,
      fontWeight = FontWeight.Bold
  )
  Text(
      text = "Small Text",
      fontSize = 32.sp,
      fontWeight = FontWeight.Bold
  )
}
```

This code consists of a Row containing two Text composables, each using a different font size resulting in the following layout:

Large TextSmall Text

Figure 25-16

The Row has aligned the two Text composables along their top edges causing the text content to be out of alignment relative to the text baselines. To resolve this problem we can apply the *alignByBaseline()* modifier to both children as follows:

```
Row {
    Text(
      text = "Large Text",
      Modifier.alignByBaseline(),
      fontSize = 40.sp,
      fontWeight = FontWeight.Bold
    )
    Text(
      text = "Small Text",
      Modifier.alignByBaseline(),
      fontSize = 32.sp,
      fontWeight = FontWeight.Bold,
    )
}
```

Now when the layout is rendered, the baselines of the two Text composables will be aligned as illustrated in Figure 25-17:

Large TextSmall Text

Figure 25-17

As an alternative, the *alignByBaseline()* modifier may be replaced by a call to the *alignBy()* function, passing through FirstBaseline as the alignment parameter:

```
Modifier.alignBy(FirstBaseline)
```

When working with multi-line text, passing LastBaseline through to the *alignBy()* modifier function will cause appropriately configured sibling components to align with the baseline of the last line of text:

```
.
.
.
import androidx.compose.ui.layout.LastBaseline
.
.
.
@Composable
fun MainScreen() {
    Row {
```

```
Text(
    text = "Large Text\nMore Text",
    Modifier.alignBy(LastBaseline),
    fontSize = 40.sp,
    fontWeight = FontWeight.Bold
)
Text(
    text = "Small Text",
    Modifier.alignByBaseline(),
    fontSize = 32.sp,
    fontWeight = FontWeight.Bold,
)
    }
}
```

Now when the layout appears the baseline of the text content of the second child will align with the baseline of the last line of text in the first child:

Large Text
More Text Small Text

Figure 25-18

Using the FirstBaseline in the above example would, of course, align the baseline of the small text composable with the baseline of the first line of text in the multi-line component:

Large TextSmall Text
More Text

Figure 25-19

In the examples we have looked at so far we have specified the baseline as the alignment line for both children. If we need the alignment to be offset for a child, we can do so using the *paddingFrom()* modifier. The following example adds an additional 80dp vertical offset to the first baseline alignment position of the small text composable:

```
@Composable
fun MainScreen() {
    Row {
        Text(
            text = "Large Text\nMore Text",
            Modifier.alignBy(FirstBaseline),
            fontSize = 40.sp,
            fontWeight = FontWeight.Bold
```

```
    )
    Text(
        text = "Small Text",
        modifier = Modifier.paddingFrom(
            alignmentLine = FirstBaseline, before = 80.dp, after = 0.dp),
        fontSize = 32.sp,
        fontWeight = FontWeight.Bold
    )
}
}
```

When rendered, the above layout will appear as shown in Figure 25-20:

Figure 25-20

25.9 Scope modifier weights

The RowScope weight modifier allows the width of each child to be specified relative to its siblings. This works by assigning each child a weight percentage (between 0.0 and 1.0). Two children assigned a weight of 0.5, for example, would each occupy half of the available space. Modify the MainScreen function one last time as follows to demonstrate the use of the weight modifier:

```
@Composable
fun MainScreen() {
    Row {
        TextCell("1", Modifier.weight(weight = 0.2f, fill = true))
        TextCell("2", Modifier.weight(weight = 0.4f, fill = true))
        TextCell("3", Modifier.weight(weight = 0.3f, fill = true))
    }
}
```

Rebuild and refresh the preview panel, at which point the layout should resemble that shown in Figure 25-21 below:

Figure 25-21

Siblings that do not have a weight modifier applied will appear at their preferred size leaving the weighted children to share the remaining space.

ColumnScope also provides *align()*, *alignBy()*, and *weight()* modifiers, though these all operate on the horizontal axis. Unlike RowScope, there is no concept of baselines when working with ColumnScope.

25.10 Summary

The Compose Row and Column components provide an easy way to layout child composables in horizontal and vertical arrangements. When embedded within each other, the Row and Column allow table style layouts of any level of complexity to be created. Both layout components include options for customizing the alignment, spacing, and positioning of children. Scope modifiers allow the positioning, and sizing behavior of individual children to be defined, including aligning and sizing children relative to each other.

26. Box Layouts in Compose

Now that we have an understanding of the Compose Row and Column composables, we will move on to look at the third layout type provided by Compose in the form of the Box component. This chapter will introduce the Box layout and explore some of the key parameters and modifiers that are available when designing user interface layouts.

26.1 An introduction to the Box composable

Unlike the Row and Column which organize children in a horizontal row or vertical column, the Box layout stacks its children on top of each other. The stacking order is defined by the order in which the children are called within the Box declaration, with the first child positioned at the bottom of the stack. As with the Row and Column layouts, Box is provided with several parameters and modifiers that can be used to customize the layout.

26.2 Creating the BoxLayout project

Begin by launching Android Studio and, if necessary, closing any currently open projects using the *File -> Close Project* menu option so that the Welcome screen appears.

Select the New Project option from the welcome screen and, when the new project dialog appears, choose the *Empty Compose Activity* template before clicking on the Next button.

Enter *BoxLayout* into the Name field and specify *com.example.boxlayout* as the package name. Before clicking on the Finish button, change the Minimum API level setting to API 26: Android 8.0 (Oreo). On completion of the project creation process, the BoxLayout project should be listed in the Project tool window located along the left-hand edge of the Android Studio main window.

Within the *MainActivity.kt* file, delete the Greeting function and add a new empty composable named MainScreen:

```
@Composable
fun MainScreen() {


}
```

Next, change the *onCreateActivity()* method and DefaultPreview function to call MainScreen instead of Greeting.

26.3 Adding the TextCell composable

In this chapter, we will once again use our TextCell composable, though to best demonstrate the features of the Box layout, we will modify the declaration slightly so that it can be passed an optional font size when called. Remaining within the *MainActivity.kt* file, add this composable function so that it reads as follows:

.
.

```
import androidx.compose.foundation.border
import androidx.compose.foundation.layout.padding
import androidx.compose.ui.graphics.Color
import androidx.compose.ui.text.font.FontWeight
```

Box Layouts in Compose

```
import androidx.compose.ui.text.style.TextAlign
import androidx.compose.ui.unit.dp
import androidx.compose.ui.unit.sp
.
.

@Composable
fun TextCell(text: String, modifier: Modifier = Modifier,  fontSize: Int = 150 ) {

    val cellModifier = Modifier
        .padding(4.dp)
        .border(width = 5.dp, color = Color.Black)

    Text(
        text = text, cellModifier.then(modifier),
        fontSize = fontSize.sp,
        fontWeight = FontWeight.Bold,
        textAlign = TextAlign.Center
    )
}
```

26.4 Adding a Box layout

Next, modify the MainScreen function to include a Box layout with three TextCell children:

```
.
.

import androidx.compose.foundation.layout.Box
import androidx.compose.foundation.layout.size

.
.

@Composable
fun MainScreen() {
    Box {
        val height = 200.dp
        val width = 200.dp

        TextCell("1", Modifier.size(width = width, height = height))
        TextCell("2", Modifier.size(width = width, height = height))
        TextCell("3", Modifier.size(width = width, height = height))
    }
}
```

After modifying the function, update the Preview panel to reflect these latest changes. Once the layout appears it should resemble Figure 26-1:

Figure 26-1

The transparent nature of the Text composable allows us to see that the three children have, indeed, been stacked directly on top of each other. While this transparency is useful to show that the children have been stacked, this isn't the behavior we are looking for in this example. To give the TextCell an opaque background, we need to call the Text composable from within a Surface component. To achieve this, edit the TextCell function so that it now reads as follows:

```
@Composable
fun TextCell(text: String, modifier: Modifier = Modifier,  fontSize: Int = 150 ) {
.
.

    Surface {
        Text(
            text = text, cellModifier.then(modifier),
            fontSize = fontSize.sp,
            fontWeight = FontWeight.Bold,
            textAlign = TextAlign.Center
        )
    }
}
```

When the preview is updated, only the last composable to be called by the Box will be visible because it is the uppermost child of the stack.

26.5 Box alignment

The Box composable includes support for an alignment parameter to customize the positioning of the group of children within the content area of the box. The parameter is named *contentAlignment* and may be set to any one of the following values:

- **Alignment.TopStart**
- **Alignment.TopCenter**
- **Alignment.TopEnd**
- **Alignment.CenterStart**
- **Alignment.Center**
- **Alignment.CenterEnd**
- **Alignment.BottomCenter**
- **Alignment.BottomEnd**
- **Alignment.BottomStart**

Box Layouts in Compose

The diagram in Figure 26-2 illustrates the positioning of the Box content for each of the above settings:

Figure 26-2

To try out some of these alignments options, edit the Box declaration in the MainScreen function both to increase its size and to add a *contentAlignment* parameter:

```
.
.
import androidx.compose.ui.Alignment
.
.
@Composable
fun MainScreen() {
.
.
    Box(contentAlignment = Alignment.CenterEnd,
            modifier = Modifier.size(400.dp, 400.dp)) {
        val height = 200.dp
        val width = 200.dp
        TextCell("1", Modifier.size(width = width, height = height))
        TextCell("2", Modifier.size(width = width, height = height))
        TextCell("3", Modifier.size(width = width, height = height))
    }
}
```

Refresh the preview and verify that the Box content now appears at the CenterEnd position within the Box content area:

Figure 26-3

26.6 BoxScope modifiers

In the chapter entitled *"Composing Layouts with Row and Column"*, we introduced ColumnScope and RowScope and explored how these provide additional modifiers that can be applied individually to child components. In the case of the Box layout, the following BoxScope modifiers are available to be applied to child composables:

- **align()** - Aligns the child within the Box content area using the specified Alignment value.

- **matchParentSize()** - Sizes the child on which the modifier is applied to match the size of the parent Box.

The set of Alignment values accepted by the align modifier is the same as those listed above for Box alignment. The following changes to the MainScreen function demonstrate the *align()* modifier in action:

```
@Composable
fun MainScreen() {

.

.

    Box(modifier = Modifier.size(height = 90.dp, width = 290.dp)) {
        Text("TopStart", Modifier.align(Alignment.TopStart))
        Text("TopCenter", Modifier.align(Alignment.TopCenter))
        Text("TopEnd", Modifier.align(Alignment.TopEnd))

        Text("CenterStart", Modifier.align(Alignment.CenterStart))
        Text("Center", Modifier.align(Alignment.Center))
        Text(text = "CenterEnd", Modifier.align(Alignment.CenterEnd))

        Text("BottomStart", Modifier.align(Alignment.BottomStart))
        Text("BottomCenter", Modifier.align(Alignment.BottomCenter))
        Text("BottomEnd", Modifier.align(Alignment.BottomEnd))
    }
}
```

When previewed, the above Box layout will appear as shown in Figure 26-4 below:

TopStart	TopCenter	TopEnd
CenterStart	Center	CenterEnd
BottomStart	BottomCenter	BottomEnd

Figure 26-4

26.7 Using the clip() modifier

The compose *clip()* modifier allows composables to be rendered to conform to specific shapes. Though not specific to Box, the Box component provides perhaps the best example of clipping shapes. To define the shape of a composable, the *clip()* modifier is called and passed a Shape value which can be RectangleShape, CircleShape, RoundedCornerShape, or CutCornerShape.

The following code, for example, draws a Box clipped to appear as a circle:

.

.

```
import androidx.compose.foundation.background
import androidx.compose.ui.draw.clip
import androidx.compose.foundation.shape.CircleShape
```

.

.

```
Box(Modifier.size(200.dp).clip(CircleShape).background(Color.Blue))
```

.

.

When rendered, the Box will appear as shown in Figure 26-5:

Figure 26-5

To draw a composable with rounded corners call RoundedCornerShape, passing through the radius for each corner. If a single radius value is provided it will be applied to all four corners:

.

.

```
import androidx.compose.foundation.shape.RoundedCornerShape
```

.

.

```
Box(Modifier.size(200.dp).clip(RoundedCornerShape(30.dp)).background(Color.Blue))
```

The above composable will appear as shown below:

Figure 26-6

As an alternative to rounded corners, composables may also be rendered with cut corners. In this case,

CutCornerShape is passed the cut length for the corners. Once again different values may be specified for each corner, or all corners cut equally with a single length parameter:

.

.

```
import androidx.compose.foundation.shape.CutCornerShape
```

.

.

```
Box(Modifier.size(200.dp).clip(CutCornerShape(30.dp)).background(Color.Blue))
```

.

.

The following figure shows the Box rendered by the above code:

Figure 26-7

26.8 Summary

The Compose Box layout positions all of its children on top of each other in a stack arrangement with the first child positioned at the bottom of the stack. By default, this stack will be positioned in the top left-hand corner of the content area, though this can be changed using the *contentAlignment* parameter when calling the Box composable.

Direct children of a Box layout have access to additional modifiers via RowScope. These modifiers allow individual children to be positioned independently within the Box content using a collection of nine pre-defined position settings.

27. Custom Layout Modifiers

Although the Box, Row, and Column composables provide a great deal of flexibility in terms of layout design, situations will inevitably arise where you have a specific layout requirement that cannot be achieved using the built-in layout components. Fortunately, Compose includes several more advanced layout options. In this chapter, we will explore one of these in the form of custom layout modifiers.

27.1 Compose layout basics

Before exploring custom layouts, it will be helpful to first understand the basics of how user interface elements are positioned in a Compose-based user interface. As we already know, user interface layouts are created by writing composable functions which generate UI elements that are, in turn, rendered on the screen. Composables call other composables creating a UI hierarchy tree consisting of parent and child relationships. Each child can have its own children, and so on.

As the app executes, the composable hierarchy is rapidly and continually recomposed in response to changes in state. Each time a parent composable is called, it is responsible for controlling the size and positioning of all of its children. The position of the child is defined using x and y coordinates relative to the position of the parent. In terms of size, the parent imposes *constraints* that define the maximum and minimum allowable height and width dimensions of the child.

Depending on configuration, the size of a parent can either be fixed (for example using the *size()* modifier) or calculated based on the size and positioning of its children.

The built-in Box, Row, and Column components all contain logic that measures each child and calculates how to position each to create the corresponding row, column, or stack positioning. The same techniques used behind the scenes by these built-in layouts are also available to you to create your own custom layouts.

27.2 Custom layouts

Custom layouts are quite straightforward to implement and fall into two categories. In its most basic form, a custom layout can be implemented as a *layout modifier* which can be applied to a single user interface element (something similar to the standard *padding()* modifier). Alternatively, a new Layout composable can be written which applies to all the children of a composable (the technique used by the Box, Column, and Row composables).

In the rest of this chapter, we will explore the custom layout modifier approach to custom layout development. Since experimentation is a good way to understand custom layouts, each step of this introduction to custom layout modifiers will be demonstrated using an example project. Feel free to modify the examples in this chapter and observe how the changes affect the resulting user interface layout.

27.3 Creating the LayoutModifier project

Launch Android Studio and select the New Project option from the welcome screen. Within the resulting new project dialog, choose the *Empty Compose Activity* template before clicking on the Next button.

Enter *LayoutModifier* into the Name field and specify *com.example.LayoutModifier* as the package name. Before clicking on the Finish button, change the Minimum API level setting to API 26: Android 8.0 (Oreo).

Within the *MainActivity.kt* file, delete the Greeting function and add a new empty composable named MainScreen:

Custom Layout Modifiers

```
@Composable
fun MainScreen() {


}
```

Next, edit the *onCreateActivity()* method and DefaultPreview function to call MainScreen instead of Greeting.

27.4 Adding the ColorBox composable

The child elements in most of these examples in this chapter will be represented by colored boxes. Although the Box component is primarily intended as a way to stack children on top of each other, an empty Box is also a simple and effective way to draw rectangles on the screen. Since we will be drawing multiple boxes, it makes sense to add a reusable composable for this purpose. Add the following ColorBox composable function to the *MainActivity.kt* file:

.
.

```
import androidx.compose.foundation.background
import androidx.compose.foundation.layout.*
import androidx.compose.ui.graphics.Color
import androidx.compose.ui.unit.dp
import androidx.compose.ui.layout.layout
```

.
.

```
@Composable
fun ColorBox(modifier: Modifier) {
    Box(Modifier.padding(1.dp).size(width = 50.dp, height = 10.dp).then(modifier))
}
```

Next, modify the MainScreen composable function to include a Box with a ColorBox child:

```
@Composable
fun MainScreen() {
    Box(modifier = Modifier.size(120.dp, 80.dp)) {
        ColorBox(
            Modifier.background(Color.Blue)
        )
    }
}
```

When the layout is previewed, it will appear as shown in Figure 27-1 below:

Figure 27-1

214

27.5 Creating a custom layout modifier

The Box layout in the above example has positioned the ColorBox element in the top left-hand corner of its content area. This is the default position for the child of a Box layout in absence of alignment parameters or modifiers to the contrary.

We can now create a simple custom layout modifier that can be applied to the ColorBox to move it to a new position within the parent Box.

Custom layout modifiers are written using the following standard syntax:

```
fun Modifier.<custom layout name> (
    // Optional parameters here
) = layout { measurable, constraints ->
    // Code to adjust position and size of element
}
```

The layout's trailing lambda is passed two parameters named *measurable* and *constraints* respectively. The measurable parameter is the child element on which the modifier was called, while the constraints parameter contains the maximum and minimum width and height values allowed for the child.

For this example, we want to be able to specify a new x and y position for the child relative to the default position assigned to it by the parent. Before we do that, we to clarify what is meant by *default position*.

27.6 Understanding default position

In the example created so far, the default position is the top left-hand corner of the Box's content area which equates to x and y coordinates 0, 0. The second child of a Row layout, on the other hand, would be positioned at entirely different default x and y coordinates within the context of the parent.

The layout modifier is not concerned about the default position of the child within the context of the parent. Instead, it is only interested in calculating where the child will be positioned *relative to the default position*. In other words, the modifier will calculate the new position relative to 0, 0, and return the new offset coordinates. The parent will then apply the offset to the actual coordinates to move the child to the custom position.

A parent might, for example, calculate the default x and y coordinates of a child are 50, 70. A custom layout modifier will calculate the new position relative to 0, 0 and return the new offset (perhaps 20, 10). The parent will then apply the offset to the actual position (in this case 50, 70) to move the child to the custom position at 70, 80.

27.7 Completing the layout modifier

The next step in implementing our modifier is to allow new coordinate offsets to be passed through when it is called. Begin implementing the modifier, which we will name *exampleLayout* within the *MainActivity.kt* file so that it reads as follows:

```
fun Modifier.exampleLayout(
        x: Int,
        y: Int
) = layout { measurable, constraints ->

}
```

When the modifier lays out the child it will need to know the child's measurements to make sure it conforms to the constraints passed to the lambda. These values are obtained by calling the *measure()* method of the *measurable* instance, passing through the *constraints* object. This call will return a Placeable instance containing height and width values. We can also call methods on the Placeable instance to specify the new position of the element within its parent content area. Start by adding code to the modifier to perform this measurement as follows:

```
fun Modifier.exampleLayout(
    x: Int,
    y: Int
) = layout { measurable, constraints ->
    val placeable = measurable.measure(constraints)
}
```

When developing custom layouts an important rule to remember is that a child must only be measured once each time the modifier is called. This rule, referred to as *single-pass measurement*, is required to ensure that the user interface tree hierarchies are rendered quickly and efficiently.

Next, we need to call a method named *layout()*, passing through the height and width values from the placeable value. We also need to pass a trailing lambda to the *layout()* method containing the code to position the child:

```
fun Modifier.exampleLayout(
    x: Int,
    y: Int
) = layout { measurable, constraints ->
    val placeable = measurable.measure(constraints)

    layout(placeable.width, placeable.height) {
        placeable.placeRelative(x, y)
    }
}
```

Within the lambda, the child element is positioned via a call to the *placeRelative()* method of the Placeable object, using the new x and y coordinates that were passed to the modifier.

27.8 Using a custom modifier

Now that we have created the custom modifier, it is ready to be applied to a child composable, in this case, our ColorBox component. Locate and edit the MainScreen composable and modify the ColorBox call to apply the *exampleLayout()* modifier:

```
@Composable
fun MainScreen() {
    Box(Modifier.size(120.dp, 80.dp)) {
        ColorBox(
            Modifier
                .exampleLayout(90, 50)
                .background(Color.Blue)
        )
    }
}
```

When the layout is now rendered in the preview panel, the position of the ColorBox element will be adjusted to match the x and y coordinates passed to the *exampleLayout* modifier:

Figure 27-2

27.9 Working with alignment lines

When adjusting the position of the child composable in the above example, the top left-hand corner of the ColorBox was moved to a specific x and y coordinate. It could also be said that the box was positioned based on the intersection of two alignment lines which correspond to the left and top sides of the rectangle as illustrated in Figure 27-3:

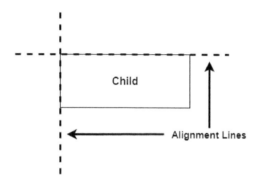

Figure 27-3

Given that we have access to the height and width measurements of the child element, we can set positioning based on any horizontal or vertical alignment line (or a combination of both). We could, for example, position the child based on a vertical alignment line located midway along its length as visualized below:

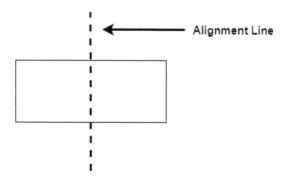

Figure 27-4

In fact, we could make the position of our hypothetical alignment line configurable by passing it through as a parameter to the layout modifier. To demonstrate this concept, modify the exampleLayout modifier code as follows:

.

Custom Layout Modifiers

```
import kotlin.math.roundToInt


fun Modifier.exampleLayout(
    fraction: Float
) = layout { measurable, constraints ->
    val placeable = measurable.measure(constraints)

    val x = -(placeable.width * fraction).roundToInt()

    layout(placeable.width, placeable.height) {
        placeable.placeRelative(x = x, y = 0)
    }
}
```

These changes require some explanation. To begin with, the modifier is no longer passed x and y coordinates. Instead, the new position will be calculated relative to the default coordinates defined by the parent (which will be 0, 0). Also, the modifier now accepts a floating-point parameter representing the position of the vertical alignment line as a percentage of the width of the child. The x coordinate is then calculated as follows:

```
val x = -(placeable.width * fraction).roundToInt()
```

This calculation takes the width of the child from the placeable object and multiplies it by the fraction parameter value. Because this results in a floating-point result, it is rounded to an integer so that it can be used as a coordinate value in the call to *placeRelative()*. Finally, since a move of the alignment line to the right is equivalent to moving the child to the left, the x value is inverted into a negative value. The child is then placed at the new coordinates. Note that since the vertical positioning is unchanged, the y value is set to 0.

Perhaps the best way to see this modifier in action is to apply it to the children of a Column layout. With this in mind, modify the MainScreen composable as follows:

```
import androidx.compose.ui.Alignment


@Composable
fun MainScreen() {
    Box(contentAlignment = Alignment.Center,
            modifier = Modifier.size(120.dp, 80.dp)) {
        Column {
            ColorBox(
                Modifier.exampleLayout(0f).background(Color.Blue)
            )
            ColorBox(
                Modifier.exampleLayout(0.25f).background(Color.Green)
            )
            ColorBox(
                Modifier.exampleLayout(0.5f).background(Color.Yellow)
```

```
        )
        ColorBox(
            Modifier.exampleLayout(0.25f).background(Color.Red)
        )
        ColorBox(
            Modifier.exampleLayout(0.0f).background(Color.Magenta)
        )
    }
  }
}
```

The above layout will appear in the Preview panel as shown in Figure 27-5. Note that the dotted line has been superimposed to indicate the position of the alignment line for each child:

Figure 27-5

27.10 Working with baselines

We already know from working with the Row and Column layouts in the chapter entitled *"Composing Layouts with Row and Column"* that a Text composable can be aligned relative to its text content baselines. The FirstBaseline and LastBaseline alignment lines correspond to the bottom edge of the first and last lines of text content contained within a Text component respectively.

When writing custom layout modifiers, these baselines can be accessed via the Placeable object and used as reference points for customizing child positioning. For example:

```
val placeable = measurable.measure(constraints)

val firstBaseline = placeable[FirstBaseLine]
val lastBaseline = placeable[LastBaseline]
```

Since not all composables support baseline alignment, the code in the layout modifier should check that the child it has been passed supports this type of alignment. This can be achieved by checking that the alignment does not equate to *AlignmentLine.Unspecified*, for example:

```
if placeable[FirstBaseline] == AlignmentLine.Unspecified {
    // child passed to modifier does not support FirstBaseline alignment
}
```

27.11 Summary

While much can be achieved using the built-in Row, Column, and Box layouts in combination with the corresponding scope modifiers, there will often be instances where a child element will need to be positioned in a way that is not supported using the standard options. This challenge can be addressed by creating a custom layout modifier which can then be applied to any child element as needed. A custom layout modifier is passed a set of constraints indicating size restrictions and the child element to be positioned. The child can then be measured (an action that must only be performed once within a layout modifier) and calculations performed to customize the size and position of the child within the content area of the parent. Positioning may also be customized based on baseline alignment when supported by the child element.

Chapter 28

28. Building Custom Layouts

So far in this book, we have introduced the Box, Column, and Row layout components provided with Compose and shown how these are used to layout child elements in an organized way. We have also covered the creation and use of custom layout modifiers and explored how these can be used to modify the position of individual child elements within a parent layout. In this chapter, we will cover the creation of your own custom layout components.

28.1 An overview of custom layouts

Custom layouts in Compose allow you to design your own layout components with full control over how all of the child elements are sized and positioned. The techniques covered in this chapter are the same as those used by Google to create the built-in Compose Row, Column, and Box layouts. Custom layouts also share some similarities with custom content modifiers. A custom layout can be thought of as a way to apply a custom layout modifier to multiple children.

Custom layouts are declared using the Compose *Layout* composable function, the sole purpose of which is to provide a way to measure and position multiple children.

28.2 Custom layout syntax

Most custom layout declarations will begin with the same standard structure. The following code, for example, declares a custom layout which doesn't make any changes to the layout properties of its children and serves as a template from which to build your own custom layouts:

```
@Composable
fun DoNothingLayout(
    modifier: Modifier = Modifier,
    content: @Composable () -> Unit
) {
    Layout(
        modifier = modifier,
        content = content
    ) { measurables, constraints ->
        val placeables = measurables.map { measurable ->
            // Measure each children
            measurable.measure(constraints)
        }

        layout(constraints.maxWidth, constraints.maxHeight) {
            placeables.forEach { placeable ->
                placeable.placeRelative(x = 0, y = 0)
            }
        }
    }
}
```

Building Custom Layouts

As we can see, the layout is declared as a composable function named DoNothingLayout. This function accepts both a modifier and the content to be displayed via a slot API:

```
@Composable
fun DoNothingLayout (
    modifier: Modifier = Modifier,
    content: @Composable () -> Unit
) {
    .

    .
```

The custom layout composable may also be designed to accept additional parameters which can then be used when calculating child layout properties.

The function then makes a call to the Compose *Layout()* composable which accepts a trailing lambda. This lambda is passed two parameters named *measurables* and *constraints* respectively. The measurables parameter contains all of the child elements contained within the content, while the constraints parameter contains the maximum and minimum width and height values allowed for the children:

```
    .

    .

    Layout (
        modifier = modifier,
        content = content
    ) { measurables, constraints ->
        .

        .
```

Next, the children are measured and those measurements mapped to a list of Placeable objects:

```
    .

    .

        val placeables = measurables.map { measurable ->
            // Measure each child
            measurable.measure(constraints)
        }
    .

    .
```

The *map* method used above executes the code within the trailing lambda on each child element in the measurables object which, in turn, measures each child. The result is a list of Placeable instances (one for each child) which is then assigned to a variable named *placeables*.

Finally, the *layout()* function (this is the same function that was used for custom layout modifiers in the previous chapter) is called and passed the maximum height and width values allowed by the parent. The trailing lambda then iterates through each child in the *placeables* variable and positions it relative to the default position designated by the parent.

28.3 Using a custom layout

Once a custom layout has been created, it can be called in much the same way as the standard Compose layouts. Our example layout could, therefore be called as follows:

```
DoNothingLayout(Modifier.padding(8.dp)) {
    Text("Text Line 1")
    Text("Text Line 2")
    Text("Text Line 3")
    Text("Text Line 4")
}
```

Since the custom layout doesn't reposition any child elements, the above code would result in the four Text composables being stacked in top of each other. In the remainder of this chapter we will create a project containing a custom layout that lays out its children.

28.4 Creating the CustomLayout project

Launch Android Studio and select the New Project option from the welcome screen. Within the resulting new project dialog, choose the *Empty Compose Activity* template before clicking on the Next button.

Enter *CustomLayout* into the Name field and specify *com.example.customlayout* as the package name. Before clicking on the Finish button, change the Minimum API level setting to API 26: Android 8.0 (Oreo). On completion of the project creation process, the CustomLayout project should be listed in the Project tool window located along the left-hand edge of the Android Studio main window.

Within the *MainActivity.kt* file, delete the Greeting function and add a new empty composable named MainScreen:

```
@Composable
fun MainScreen() {


}
```

Next, edit the *onCreateActivity()* method and DefaultPreview function to call MainScreen instead of Greeting.

28.5 Creating the CascadeLayout composable

The custom layout will be named CascadeLayout, the purpose of which is to layout its children in a column with each child indented by the width of the preceding child. An optional parameter will also be implemented to allow the spacing between the child elements to be configured.

Edit the *MainActivity.kt* file and begin by implementing the basic template of the CascadeLayout composable so that it reads as follows:

```
.

.

import androidx.compose.ui.layout.Layout

.

.

@Composable
fun CascadeLayout(
    modifier: Modifier = Modifier,
    content: @Composable () -> Unit
) {
    Layout(
        modifier = modifier,
        content = content
```

```
) { measurables, constraints ->
    layout(constraints.maxWidth, constraints.maxHeight) {
        val placeables = measurables.map { measurable ->
        measurable.measure(constraints)
    }


    placeables.forEach { placeable ->


    }
  }
 }
}
```

Next, the spacing parameter needs to be added. To make this optional, we will provide this parameter with a zero default value. Also, since the amount by which a child is to be indented will increase each time a child is added to the column, we need to add a variable in which to track the latest indent. Similarly, the y coordinate will also need to be retained so that each child appears below the preceding child:

```
@Composable
fun CascadeLayout(
    modifier: Modifier = Modifier,
    spacing: Int = 0,
    content: @Composable () -> Unit
) {
    Layout(
        modifier = modifier,
        content = content
    ) { measurables, constraints ->
        var indent = 0

.

.

        layout(constraints.maxWidth, constraints.maxHeight) {
            var yCoord = 0

.

.
```

Finally, code needs to be added to the *forEach* loop to calculate the positions of each child:

```
.

.

        layout(constraints.maxWidth, constraints.maxHeight) {
            var yCoord = 0

            placeables.forEach { placeable ->
                placeable.placeRelative(x = indent, y = yCoord)
                indent += placeable.width + spacing
                yCoord += placeable.height + spacing
            }
        }
```

.

.

The first child will be positioned at coordinates 0, 0 so we simply use the zero initialized *indent* and *yCoord* values:

```
placeable.placeRelative(x = indent, y = yCoord)
```

Next, we increase the indent value by the width of the current child, plus the optional spacing value. The yCoord value is also increased by the height of the current child, once again adding the optional spacing:

```
indent += placeable.width + spacing
yCoord += placeable.height + spacing
```

With the indent and y coordinate variable updated, the *forEach* loop iterates to the next child, repeating the process until all the children have been positioned.

28.6 Using the CascadeLayout composable

We are now ready to try out our new custom layout. The layout is designed to work with children of varying sizes, so the test will involve Box layouts of differing widths and heights. We will also pass a spacing value to the layout when it is called.

Locate the MainScreen composable within the *MainActivity.kt* file and add a call to our new custom layout as follows:

.

.

```
import androidx.compose.foundation.background
import androidx.compose.foundation.layout.Box
import androidx.compose.foundation.layout.size
import androidx.compose.ui.graphics.Color
import androidx.compose.ui.unit.dp
```

.

.

```
@Composable
fun MainScreen() {

    Box {
        CascadeLayout(spacing = 20) {
            Box(modifier = Modifier.size(60.dp).background(Color.Blue))
            Box(modifier = Modifier.size(80.dp, 40.dp).background(Color.Red))
            Box(modifier = Modifier.size(90.dp, 100.dp).background(Color.Cyan))
            Box(modifier = Modifier.size(50.dp).background(Color.Magenta))
            Box(modifier = Modifier.size(70.dp).background(Color.Green))
        }
    }
}
```

Preview the layout and verify that it appears as shown in Figure 28-1:

Figure 28-1

28.7 Summary

Custom layout support in Compose allows you to create your own layouts which operate at the same syntactic level as the built-in Row, Column and Box layouts. These custom layouts are created using a standard template mechanism built around the Compose Layout function. This function is passed a measurables object containing all children of the layout together with a set of constraints providing the maximum and minimum size values permitted by the parent. The individual children are then extracted from the measurables object and placed at specific coordinates within the layout content area to meet the custom layout requirements. In this chapter, we created a custom layout that positions its children in a cascading column layout. In practice, this technique can be used to design custom layouts of just about any level of complexity.

29. A Guide to ConstraintLayout in Compose

As we have seen in the preceding chapters, Compose provides several layout components to design user interfaces in addition to the ability to create custom layouts and modifiers. While these will meet most layout needs, there may still be situations where more detailed control over the positioning and sizing of composables may be required. Before the introduction of Jetpack Compose this capability was provided by the ConstraintLayout manager which is also available from within Compose.

This chapter will outline the basic concepts of ConstraintLayout while the next chapter will provide a detailed overview of how constraint-based layouts can be created using ConstraintLayout within Compose.

29.1 An introduction to ConstraintLayout

Introduced as part of the Android 7 SDK, ConstraintLayout provides a simple, expressive and flexible layout system designed to ease the creation of responsive user interface layouts. ConstraintLayout is of particular use when developing user interface layouts that need to adapt automatically to different screen sizes and changes in device orientation.

29.2 How ConstraintLayout works

In common with all other layouts, ConstraintLayout is responsible for managing the positioning and sizing behavior of its child components. It does this based on the constraint connections that are set on each child.

To fully understand and use ConstraintLayout, it is important to gain an appreciation of the following key concepts:

- Constraints
- Margins
- Opposing Constraints
- Constraint Bias
- Chains
- Chain Styles
- Guidelines
- Barriers

29.2.1 Constraints

Constraints are essentially sets of rules that dictate how a composable is aligned and distanced in relation to other composables, the sides of the containing ConstraintLayout parent, and special elements called *guidelines* and *barriers*. Constraints also dictate how the user interface layout of an activity will respond to changes in device orientation, or when displayed on devices of differing screen sizes. To be adequately configured, a composable must have sufficient constraint connections such that its position can be resolved by the ConstraintLayout layout engine in both the horizontal and vertical planes.

29.2.2 Margins

A margin is a form of constraint that specifies a fixed distance. Consider a Button component that needs to be positioned near the top right-hand corner of the device screen. This might be achieved by implementing margin constraints from the top and right-hand edges of the Button connected to the corresponding sides of the parent ConstraintLayout as illustrated in Figure 29-1:

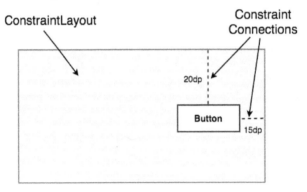

Figure 29-1

As indicated in the above diagram, each of these constraint connections has associated with it a margin value dictating the fixed distances of the Button from two sides of the parent layout. Under this configuration, regardless of screen size or the device orientation, the Button will always be positioned 20 and 15 device-independent pixels (dp) from the top and right-hand edges of the parent ConstraintLayout respectively as specified by the two constraint connections.

While the above configuration will be acceptable for some situations, it does not provide any flexibility in terms of allowing the ConstraintLayout layout engine to adapt the position of the button to respond to device rotation and to support screens of different sizes. To add this responsiveness to the layout it is necessary to implement opposing constraints.

29.2.3 Opposing constraints

Two constraints operating along the same axis on a single composable are referred to as *opposing constraints*. In other words, a component with constraints on both its left and right-hand sides is considered to have horizontally opposing constraints. Figure 29-2, for example, illustrates the addition of both horizontally and vertically opposing constraints to the previous layout:

Figure 29-2

The key point to understand here is that once opposing constraints are implemented on a particular axis, the positioning of the composable becomes percentage rather than coordinate-based. Instead of being fixed at 20dp from the top of the layout, for example, the widget is now positioned at a point 30% from the top of the layout. In different orientations and when running on larger or smaller screens, the Button will always be in the same location relative to the dimensions of the parent layout.

It is now important to understand that the layout outlined in Figure 29-2 has been implemented using not only opposing constraints but also by applying *constraint bias*.

29.2.4 Constraint bias

It has now been established that a component in a ConstraintLayout can potentially be subject to opposing constraint connections. By default, opposing constraints are equal, resulting in the corresponding widget being centered along the axis of opposition. Figure 29-3, for example, shows a button centered within the containing ConstraintLayout using opposing horizontal and vertical constraints:

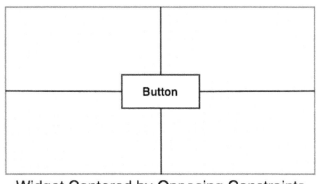

Widget Centered by Opposing Constraints

Figure 29-3

To allow for the adjustment of component position in the case of opposing constraints, the ConstraintLayout implements a feature known as *constraint bias*. Constraint bias allows the positioning of a composable along the axis of opposition to be biased by a specified percentage in favor of one constraint. Figure 29-4, for example, shows the previous constraint layout with a 75% horizontal bias and 10% vertical bias:

Widget Offset using Constraint Bias

Figure 29-4

The next chapter, entitled *"Working with ConstraintLayout in Compose"*, will cover these concepts in greater detail and explain how these features have been integrated into Compose. In the meantime, however, a few more areas of the ConstraintLayout class need to be covered.

29.2.5 Chains

ConstraintLayout chains provide a way for the layout behavior of two or more composables to be defined as a group. Chains can be declared in either the vertical or horizontal axis and configured to define how the components in the chain are spaced and sized.

Although Compose provides a helper to ease the creation of chains, it is worth noting that behind the scenes, composables are chained when connected by bi-directional constraints. Figure 29-5, for example, illustrates three Buttons chained in this way:

Figure 29-5

The first element in the chain is the *chain head* which translates to the top item in a vertical chain or, in the case of a horizontal chain, the left-most item. The layout behavior of the entire chain is primarily configured by setting attributes on the chain head component.

29.2.6 Chain styles

The layout behavior of a ConstraintLayout chain is dictated by the *chain style* setting applied to the chain head composable. The ConstraintLayout class currently supports the following chain layout styles:

- **Spread Chain** – The composables contained within the chain are distributed evenly across the available space. This is the default behavior for chains.

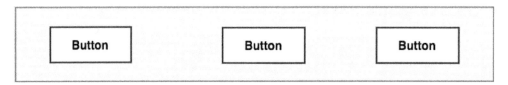

Figure 29-6

- **Spread Inside Chain** – The composables contained within the chain are spread evenly between the chain head and the last widget in the chain. The head and last composables are not included in the distribution of spacing.

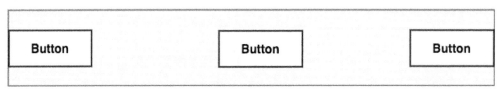

Figure 29-7

- **Weighted Chain** – Allows the space taken up by each composable in the chain to be defined via weighting properties.

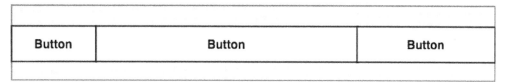

Figure 29-8

- **Packed Chain** – The composables that make up the chain are packed together without any spacing. A bias may be applied to control the horizontal or vertical positioning of the chain in relation to the parent container.

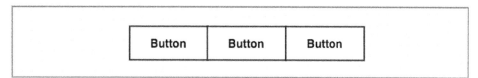

Figure 29-9

29.3 Configuring dimensions

Controlling the dimensions of a composable is a key element of the user interface design process. The ConstraintLayout provides five options that can be set on individual components to manage sizing behavior. These settings are configured individually for height and width dimensions:

- **Dimension.preferredWrapContent** - The size of the composable is dictated by the content it contains (i.e. text or graphics) subject to prevailing constraints.

- **Dimension.wrapContent** - The size of the composable is dictated by the content it contains regardless of prevailing constraints.

- **Dimension.fillToConstraints** - Allows the composable to be sized to fill the space allowed by the prevailing constraints.

- **Dimension.preferredValue** - The composable is fixed to specified dimensions subject to the prevailing constraints.

- **Dimension.value** - The composable is fixed to specified dimensions regardless of the prevailing constraints.

29.4 Guideline helper

Guidelines are special elements available within the ConstraintLayout that provide an additional target to which constraints may be connected. Multiple guidelines may be added to a ConstraintLayout instance which may, in turn, be configured in horizontal or vertical orientations. Once added, constraint connections may be established from Composables in the layout to the guidelines. This is particularly useful when multiple composables need to be aligned along an axis. In Figure 29-10, for example, three Buttons contained within a ConstraintLayout are constrained along a vertical guideline:

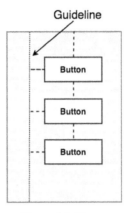

Figure 29-10

29.5 Barrier helper

Rather like guidelines, barriers are virtual views that can be used to constrain composables within a layout. As with guidelines, a barrier can be vertical or horizontal and one or more composables may be constrained to it (to avoid confusion, these will be referred to as *constrained components*). Unlike guidelines where the guideline remains at a fixed position within the layout, however, the position of a barrier is defined by a set of so-called *reference components*. Barriers were introduced to address an issue that occurs with some frequency involving overlapping components. Consider, for example, the layout illustrated in Figure 29-11 below:

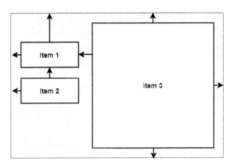

Figure 29-11

The key point to note about the above layout is that the width of Item 3 is set to *fillToConstraints* mode, and the left-hand edge of the view is connected to the right-hand edge of Item 1. As currently implemented, an increase in width of Item 1 will have the desired effect of reducing the width of Item 3:

Figure 29-12

A problem arises, however, if Item 2 increases in width instead of Item 1:

Figure 29-13

Because Item 3 is only constrained by Item 1, it does not resize to accommodate the increase in width of Item 2 causing the components to overlap.

A solution to this problem is to add a vertical barrier and assign Items 1 and 2 as the barrier's *reference components* so that they control the barrier position. The left-hand edge of Item 3 will then be constrained in relation to the barrier, making it a *constrained component*.

Now when either Item 1 or Item 2 increase in width, the barrier will move to accommodate the widest of the two components, causing the width of Item 3 to change in relation to the new barrier position:

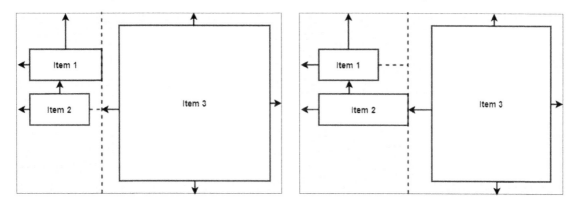

Figure 29-14

When working with barriers there is no limit to the number of reference views and constrained components that can be associated with a single barrier.

29.6 Summary

ConstraintLayout is a layout manager introduced with Android 7 and is now available for use within Compose layouts. It is designed to ease the creation of flexible layouts that adapt to the size and orientation of the many Android devices now on the market. ConstraintLayout uses constraints to control the alignment and positioning of components in relation both to each other and to the parent ConstraintLayout instance, guidelines, and barriers. ConstraintLayout provides an alternative when desired layout behavior cannot be achieved using the standard Compose layout techniques.

30. Working with ConstraintLayout in Compose

In the previous chapter, we introduced ConstraintLayout and explained how the key features of this layout manager can be used to create complex and responsive user interface designs. This chapter will describe how ConstraintLayout is used within Compose layouts while providing example implementations of the various ConstraintLayout features which you can combine to design your layouts.

30.1 Calling ConstraintLayout

ConstraintLayout is provided in the form of a composable in the same way as all other layouts in Compose and can be called as follows:

```
ConstraintLayout {
    // Children here
}
```

As with other layout composables, ConstraintLayout also accepts a Modifier parameter, for example:

```
ConstraintLayout(Modifier.size(width = 200.dp, height = 300.dp)
                     .background(Color.Green)) {
    // Children here
}
```

30.2 Generating references

In the absence of any constraints, a composable child of a ConstraintLayout will be positioned in the top left-hand corner of the content area (assuming the app is running in a left-to-right, top to bottom locale). Composables that are to be constrained must be assigned a reference before constraints can be applied. This is a two-step process consisting of generating the references, and then assigning them to composables before constraints are applied. A single reference can be generated via a call to the *createRef()* function and the result assigned to a constant:

```
val text1 = createRef()
```

Alternatively, multiple references may be created in a single step by calling *createRefs()* as follows:

```
val (button, text1, text2) = createRefs()
```

30.3 Assigning a reference to a composable

Once references have been generated, they are applied to individual composables using the *constrainAs()* modifier function. The following code, for example, assigns the *text1* reference to a Text component:

```
ConstraintLayout {
    val text1 = createRef()

    Text("Hello", modifier = Modifier.constrainAs(text1) {
        // Constraints here
    })
```

As we can see in the above code, the *constrainAs()* modifier has a trailing lambda in which the constraints are added.

30.4 Adding constraints

The most common form of constraint is one between one side of a composable and one side of either the parent ConstraintLayout, or another composable. Constraints of this type are declared within the *constrainAs()* trailing lambda via calls to the *linkTo()* function. There are different ways to call *linkTo()* depending on the nature of the constraints being created. The following code, for example, constrains the top and bottom edges of a Text component to the top and bottom of the parent ConstraintLayout instance, both with a 16dp margin:

```
Text("Hello", modifier = Modifier.constrainAs(text1) {
    top.linkTo(parent.top, margin = 16.dp)
    bottom.linkTo(parent.bottom, margin = 16.dp)
})
```

The *linkTo()* function may also be passed multiple constraints as parameters. In the following example, the start and end sides of the Text component are constrained to components named button1 and button2, while the top and bottom edges are constrained to the top and bottom of the parent with a bias of 0.8:

```
Text("Hello", modifier = Modifier.constrainAs(mytext) {
    linkTo(parent.top, parent.bottom, bias = 0.8f)
    linkTo(button1.end, button2.start)
})
```

In addition to applying constraints using the *linkTo()* function, a component can be centered horizontally and vertically relative to another component or the parent:

```
Text("text1", modifier = Modifier.constrainAs(text1) {
    centerVerticallyTo(text2)
    centerHorizontallyTo(parent)
})
```

In the above example, *text1* will be positioned on the vertical axis to align with the vertical center of *text2* and at the horizontal center of the ConstraintLayout parent.

The *centerAround()* function can be used to center a component horizontally or vertically relative to a side of another component. In the following example, *text1* is centered horizontally relative to the end of *text2*, and vertically relative to the top edge of *text4*:

```
Text("text1", modifier = Modifier.constrainAs(text1) {
    centerAround(text2.end)
    centerAround(text4.top)
})
```

In the remainder of this chapter, we will create a new project and work through some examples of using ConstraintLayout in Compose.

30.5 Creating the ConstraintLayout project

Launch Android Studio and select the New Project option from the welcome screen. In the new project dialog, choose the *Empty Compose Activity* template before clicking on the Next button.

Enter *ConstraintLayout* into the Name field and specify *com.example.constraintlayout* as the package name. Before clicking on the Finish button, change the Minimum API level setting to API 26: Android 8.0 (Oreo). Within the

MainActivity.kt file, delete the Greeting function and add a new empty composable named MainScreen:

```
@Composable
fun MainScreen() {


}
```

Next, edit the *onCreateActivity()* method and DefaultPreview function to call MainScreen instead of Greeting.

30.6 Adding the ConstraintLayout library

Support for ConstraintLayout in Compose is contained in a separate library that is not included in new projects by default. Before starting to work with ConstraintLayout, we need to add this library to the project build configuration. Within the Project tool window, navigate to the Gradle Scripts folder and open the *build.gradle (Module: ConstraintLayout)* file for editing. Once the file is loaded into the editor, locate the *dependencies* section and add an implementation line for the Compose ConstraintLayout library as follows:

```
dependencies {
    .

    .

    implementation "androidx.constraintlayout:constraintlayout-compose:1.0.0"

    .

    .
```

Note that a more recent version of the library may have been released since this book was published. If the line is highlighted in yellow, hover the mouse pointer over the line and wait for a popup message to appear containing the latest version number. Update the implementation directive to reflect this newer library version.

30.7 Adding a custom button composable

When working through the examples in this chapter, we will be applying constraints to Button composables of various sizes. To make the code easier to read, we need to create a custom button composable to which we can pass the text content and a modifier. Within the *MainActivity.kt* file, add this composable so that it reads as follows:

```
.

.

import androidx.compose.material.Button
import androidx.constraintlayout.compose.ConstraintLayout

.

.

@Composable
fun MyButton(text: String, modifier: Modifier = Modifier) {
    Button(
        onClick = { },
        modifier = modifier
    ) {
        Text(text)
    }
}
```

With these initial steps completed, we can start to experiment with the various features of ConstraintLayout.

30.8 Basic constraints

Begin by adding a ConstraintLayout to the MainScreen function together with a set of references that will be used throughout the remainder of this chapter:

```
.

.

import androidx.compose.foundation.layout.size
import androidx.compose.ui.unit.dp

.

.

@Composable
fun MainScreen() {
    ConstraintLayout(Modifier.size(width = 200.dp, height = 200.dp)) {
        val (button1, button2, button3) = createRefs()


    }
}
```

Next, add a single MyButton call to the layout and use the *constrainAs()* modifier to assign it the *button1* reference:

```
@Composable
fun MainScreen() {
    ConstraintLayout(Modifier.size(width = 200.dp, height = 200.dp)) {
        val (button1, button2, button3) = createRefs()

        MyButton(text = "Button1", Modifier.constrainAs(button1)
        {

        })
    }
}
```

The above layout will appear in the Preview panel with the button positioned in the top left-hand corner of the ConstraintLayout content area. We can move the position of the button by constraining it to the sides of the parent layout. The following changes constrain the top and start edges of the button to the corresponding sides of the ConstraintLayout parent with margins of 60dp and 30dp respectively:

```
.

.

MyButton(text = "Button1", Modifier.constrainAs(button1)
{
    top.linkTo(parent.top, margin = 60.dp)
    start.linkTo(parent.start, margin = 30.dp)
})

.

.
```

Refresh the preview and verify that the button has moved to the location specified by the constraints. Note also that hovering over the preview causes annotations to appear indicating the constraints that have been applied to the layout as shown in Figure 30-1:

Figure 30-1

30.9 Opposing constraints

The previous example demonstrated how to constrain a composable to a fixed position within the parent using constraints with margins. In this section, we will begin to look at opposing constraints. An opposing constraint is created when both sides along the same axis of a composable are constrained. The following changes, for example, apply opposing constraints on button1 along the horizontal axis:

```
MyButton(text = "Button1", Modifier.constrainAs(button1)
{
    top.linkTo(parent.top, margin = 60.dp)
    start.linkTo(parent.start)
    end.linkTo(parent.end)
})
```

The opposing constraints have the effect of horizontally centering the component within the ConstraintLayout resulting in the preview shown in Figure 30-2:

Figure 30-2

Note that opposing constraints are designated by the jagged spring-like connecting lines between the button and parent. Opposing constraints may be declared more concisely passing through the constraints as parameters to the *linkTo()* function as follows:

```
MyButton(text = "Button1", Modifier.constrainAs(button1)
{
    top.linkTo(parent.top, margin = 60.dp)
    linkTo(parent.start, parent.end)
})
```

If the goal is simply to use opposing constraints to center the component within the parent, the same result can more easily be achieved as follows:

```
centerVerticallyTo(parent)
centerHorizontallyTo(parent)
```

So far, all of the constraints we have looked at have involved links between a composable and the parent. Constraints can, of course, also be applied between components, for example:

```
MyButton(text = "Button1", Modifier.constrainAs(button1)
{
    centerHorizontallyTo(parent)
    top.linkTo(parent.top)
    bottom.linkTo(button2.top)
})

MyButton(text = "Button2", Modifier.constrainAs(button2)
{
    centerHorizontallyTo(parent)
    top.linkTo(button1.bottom)
    bottom.linkTo(parent.bottom)
})
```

The above code will render in the preview panel as shown in Figure 30-3 below:

Figure 30-3

30.10 Constraint bias

In the previous chapter, the concept of using bias settings to favor one opposing constraint over another was outlined. In the absence of other settings, opposing constraints will always center a component between the elements to which it is constrained. Applying bias allows the positioning of the constrained composable to be moved relative to the available space. The original button1 constraints from earlier in the chapter can, for example, be modified to include bias as follows:

```
MyButton(text = "Button1", Modifier.constrainAs(button1)
{
```

```
    top.linkTo(parent.top, margin = 60.dp)
    linkTo(parent.start, parent.end, bias = 0.75f)
})
```

When previewed, button1 will be positioned at 75% of the width of the parent as illustrated in Figure 30-4:

Figure 30-4

30.11 Constraint margins

Constraints can be used in conjunction with margins to implement fixed gaps between a component and another element (such as another composable, a guideline, barrier, or the side of the parent layout). Consider the following example from earlier in the chapter:

```
MyButton(text = "Button1", Modifier.constrainAs(button1)
{
    top.linkTo(parent.top, margin = 60.dp)
    linkTo(parent.start, parent.end)
})
```

This code gives us the layout illustrated in Figure 30-2 above. As currently configured, horizontal constraints run to the left and right edges of the parent ConstraintLayout. As such, button1 has opposing horizontal constraints indicating that the ConstraintLayout layout engine has some discretion in terms of the actual positioning of the component at runtime. This allows the layout some flexibility to accommodate different screen sizes and device orientations. The horizontal bias setting is also able to control the position of the component right up to the right-hand side of the layout. Figure 30-5, for example, shows the same button with 100% horizontal bias applied:

Figure 30-5

ConstraintLayout margins appear at the end of constraint connections and represent a fixed gap into which the button cannot be moved even when adjusting bias or in response to layout changes elsewhere in the user interface. In the following code, the right-hand constraint now includes a 30dp margin into which the component cannot be moved even though the bias is still set at 100%:

```
MyButton(text = "Button1", Modifier.constrainAs(button1)
{
    top.linkTo(parent.top, margin = 60.dp)
    linkTo(parent.start, parent.end, endMargin = 30.dp, bias = 1.0f)
})
```

Figure 30-6

This margin would also be preserved if the width of the parent reduced (such as occurs when a device is rotated between landscape and portrait orientation), or if a component to the left, to which button1 was constrained, were to grow in size.

Even without a bias setting, margins will have an impact on the positioning of a component. The following code, for example, sets margins of different widths on the start and end constraints of button1:

```
MyButton(text = "Button1", Modifier.constrainAs(button1)
{
    top.linkTo(parent.top, margin = 60.dp)
    linkTo(parent.start, parent.end, startMargin = 30.dp, endMargin = 50.dp)
})
```

This results in the button being offset relative to the margins as shown in Figure 30-7:

Figure 30-7

30.12 The importance of opposing constraints and bias

As discussed in the previous chapter, opposing constraints, margins, and bias form the cornerstone of responsive layout design in Android when using the ConstraintLayout. When a composable is constrained without opposing constraint connections, those constraints are essentially margin constraints. This is indicated visually within the Preview panel by solid straight lines accompanied by margin measurements as shown in Figure 30-8.

Figure 30-8

The above constraints essentially fix the button at that position. The result of this is that if the device is rotated to landscape orientation, the button will no longer be visible since the vertical constraint pushes it beyond the top edge of the device screen (as is the case in Figure 30-9). A similar problem will arise if the app is run on a device with a smaller screen than that used during the design process.

Figure 30-9

When opposing constraints are implemented, the constraint connection is represented by the spring-like jagged line (the spring metaphor is intended to indicate that the position of the component is not fixed to absolute x and y coordinates):

Figure 30-10

In the above layout, vertical and horizontal bias settings have been configured such that the button will always be positioned 90% of the distance from the bottom and 35% from the left-hand edge of the parent layout. When rotated, therefore, the button is still visible and positioned in the same location relative to the dimensions of the screen:

Figure 30-11

When designing a responsive and adaptable user interface layout, it is important to take into consideration both bias and opposing constraints when manually designing a user interface layout and making corrections to automatically created constraints.

30.13 Creating chains

A chain constraint may be created between two or more components by calling either *createHorizontalChain()* or *createVerticalChain()*, passing through the component references as parameters. The following code, for example, creates a horizontal chain between three buttons:

```
ConstraintLayout(Modifier.size(width = 400.dp, height = 100.dp)) {
    val (button1, button2, button3) = createRefs()

    createHorizontalChain(button1, button2, button3)

    MyButton(text = "Button1", Modifier.constrainAs(button1) {
        centerVerticallyTo(parent)
    })

    MyButton(text = "Button2", Modifier.constrainAs(button2) {
        centerVerticallyTo(parent)
    })

    MyButton(text = "Button3", Modifier.constrainAs(button3) {
        centerVerticallyTo(parent)
    })
}
```

When previewed, the buttons will be positioned as shown in Figure 30-12 below:

Figure 30-12

As outlined in *"A Guide to ConstraintLayout in Compose"*, a chain may be arranged using Packed, Spread, or SpreadInside styles. Modify the *createHorizontalChain()* function call to change the style from the default (Spread) to SpreadInside as follows:

```
.
.
import androidx.constraintlayout.compose.ChainStyle
.
.
@Composable
fun MainScreen() {
    ConstraintLayout(Modifier.size(width = 400.dp, height = 100.dp)) {
        val (button1, button2, button3) = createRefs()

        createHorizontalChain(button1, button2, button3,
```

```
        chainStyle = ChainStyle.SpreadInside)
```

.

.

The buttons will now be arranged as shown below:

Figure 30-13

30.14 Working with guidelines

ConstraintLayout guidelines provide a horizontal or vertical anchor line to which composables may be contained. This is particularly useful when a group of components needs to be aligned relative to a specific axis line. A guideline position can be declared as a percentage of either the height or width of the parent or positioned at a specific offset from a side. The following, for example, creates a guideline that is parallel to the starting edge of the parent (in other words a vertical line) positioned 25% of the way across the parent content area:

```
createGuidelineFromStart(fraction = .25f)
```

Similarly, the following function call creates a horizontal guideline positioned 60dp above the bottom edge of the parent:

```
createGuidelineFromBottom(offset = 60.dp)
```

Replace the code in the MainScreen function with the following code to create a vertical guideline to which the three buttons are constrained:

```
ConstraintLayout(Modifier.size(width = 400.dp, height = 220.dp)) {
    val (button1, button2, button3) = createRefs()

    val guide = createGuidelineFromStart(fraction = .60f)

    MyButton(text = "Button1", Modifier.constrainAs(button1) {
        top.linkTo(parent.top, margin = 30.dp)
        end.linkTo(guide, margin = 30.dp)
    })

    MyButton(text = "Button2", Modifier.constrainAs(button2) {
        top.linkTo(button1.bottom, margin = 20.dp)
        start.linkTo(guide, margin = 40.dp)
    })

    MyButton(text = "Button3", Modifier.constrainAs(button3) {
        top.linkTo(button2.bottom, margin = 40.dp)
        end.linkTo(guide, margin = 20.dp)
    })
}
```

This layout should appear as illustrated in Figure 30-14 below when rendered in the Preview panel:

Figure 30-14

30.15 Working with barriers

ConstraintLayout barriers are created relative to a specific side of one or more components using the following functions:

- createStartBarrier()

- createEndBarrier()

- createTopBarrier()

- createBottomBarrier()

Each function is passed a list of components to which the barrier is to be assigned together with an optional margin and returns a barrier reference to which other components may be constrained, for example:

```
val barrier = createEndBarrier(button1, button2, margin = 30.dp)
```

The above statement will create a vertical barrier (start and end barriers are vertical while top and bottom are horizontal) positioned 30dp from the end of button1 and button2. If button1 and button2 are of different widths the barrier will be 30dp from the end of the widest component at any given time.

To demonstrate ConstraintLayout barriers, we will begin by recreating the layout illustrated in Figure 29-11 in the previous chapter. Begin by modifying the MainScreen function so that it reads as follows:

```
.
.
import androidx.compose.foundation.layout.width
import androidx.constraintlayout.compose.Dimension
.
.
@Composable
fun MainScreen() {
    ConstraintLayout(Modifier.size(width = 350.dp, height = 220.dp)) {
        val (button1, button2, button3) = createRefs()
```

```
    MyButton(text = "Button1", Modifier.width(100.dp).constrainAs(button1) {
        top.linkTo(parent.top, margin = 30.dp)
        start.linkTo(parent.start, margin = 8.dp)
    })

    MyButton(text = "Button2", Modifier.width(100.dp).constrainAs(button2) {
        top.linkTo(button1.bottom, margin = 20.dp)
        start.linkTo(parent.start, margin = 8.dp)
    })

    MyButton(text = "Button3", Modifier.constrainAs(button3) {
        linkTo(parent.top, parent.bottom,
                topMargin = 8.dp, bottomMargin = 8.dp)
        linkTo(button1.end, parent.end, startMargin = 30.dp,
                                        endMargin = 8.dp)
    })
    }
}
```

The button3 component needs to be sized to fill the maximum available space allowed by its constraints. Not only will this ensure that the button fills the available height, but also allows the width to adjust in response to changes in the size of button1 and button2. To achieve this, the width and height dimension constraints of button3 need to be changed to *fillConstraints*. Modify the button3 declaration to add these dimension constraints as follows:

```
MyButton(text = "Button3", Modifier.constrainAs(button3) {
    linkTo(parent.top, parent.bottom, topMargin = 8.dp, bottomMargin = 8.dp)
    linkTo(button1.end, parent.end, startMargin = 30.dp, endMargin = 8.dp)
    width = Dimension.fillToConstraints
    height = Dimension.fillToConstraints
})
```

In the Preview panel, the layout should appear as shown in Figure 30-15:

Figure 30-15

Next, we need to check if the layout is already providing the required behavior by increasing the width of button1 as follows:

```
MyButton(text = "Button1", Modifier.width(150.dp).constrainAs(button1) {
```

Note the width dimension of button3 has reduced as required as expected:

Figure 30-16

Now return the width of button1 to 100dp, then increase the width of button2 to 150dp. This time the width of button3 has not been reduced, causing an overlap with button2:

Figure 30-17

Clearly, this does not meet our layout specifications. This is happening because button3 is only constrained by button1 and is not affected by changes to button2. To resolve this shortcoming, we need to create a barrier positioned at the end of button1 and button2. Instead of constraining the start edge of button3 against the end of button1 we will, instead, constrain the start of the button against the barrier:

```
@Composable
fun MainScreen() {
    ConstraintLayout(Modifier.size(width = 350.dp, height = 220.dp)) {
        val (button1, button2, button3) = createRefs()

        val barrier = createEndBarrier(button1, button2)

        .
        .

        MyButton(text = "Button3", Modifier.constrainAs(button3) {
            linkTo(parent.top, parent.bottom,
                topMargin = 8.dp, bottomMargin = 8.dp)
            linkTo(button1.end, parent.end, startMargin = 30.dp,
                endMargin = 8.dp)
            start.linkTo(barrier, margin = 30.dp)
            width = Dimension.fillToConstraints
```

```
        height = Dimension.fillToConstraints
    })
  }
}
```

With these changes made, button3 will resize regardless of whether it is button1 or button2 which increases in width. As either width changes, the barrier to which button3 is constrained will move proportionally, thereby reducing the width of button3:

Figure 30-18

30.16 Decoupling constraints with constraint sets

So far in this chapter, all of the constraints have been declared within modifiers applied to individual composables. Compose also allows constraints to be declared separately in the form of *constraint sets*. These *decoupled constraints* can then be passed to the ConstraintLayout and applied to composable children.

Decoupled constraints allow you to create sets of constraints that can be reused without having to duplicate modifier declarations. These constraint sets also provide flexibility in terms of passing different sets of constraints depending on other criteria. A layout might, for example, use different constraint sets depending on screen size or device orientation.

To demonstrate constraint sets, modify the MainScreen function as follows:

```
@Composable
fun MainScreen() {
    ConstraintLayout(Modifier.size(width = 200.dp, height = 200.dp)) {
        val button1 = createRef()

        MyButton(text = "Button1", Modifier.size(200.dp).constrainAs(button1) {
            linkTo(parent.top, parent.bottom, topMargin = 8.dp,
                                                bottomMargin = 8.dp)
            linkTo(parent.start, parent.end, startMargin = 8.dp,
                                                endMargin = 8.dp)
            width = Dimension.fillToConstraints
            height = Dimension.fillToConstraints
        })
    }
}
```

This layout displays a button that is allowed to fill the available size allowed by the constraints applied to it:

Figure 30-19

We will now decouple these constraints into a separate constraint set. To make the constraint set more useful, we will allow the margin value to be passed as an argument. Remaining within the *MainActivity.kt* file, declare the constraint set as follows:

.

.

```
import androidx.compose.ui.unit.Dp
import androidx.constraintlayout.compose.ConstraintSet
```

.

.

```
private fun myConstraintSet(margin: Dp): ConstraintSet {
    return ConstraintSet {
        val button1 = createRefFor("button1")

        constrain(button1) {
            linkTo(parent.top, parent.bottom, topMargin = margin,
                                    bottomMargin = margin)
            linkTo(parent.start, parent.end, startMargin = margin,
                                    endMargin = margin)
            width = Dimension.fillToConstraints
            height = Dimension.fillToConstraints
        }
    }
}
```

The above code declares a new function that accepts a margin value and returns a ConstraintSet object. Next, a call is made to the *createRefFor()* function to generate a reference for whichever composable the constraint set is applied to. Next, the constraint set is created by calling the *constrain()* function passing through the reference and declaring the constraints in the trailing lambda.

With the constraint set created, it can be passed to the ConstraintLayout and applied to button1. This involves creating an instance of the constraint set, passing it through to the ConstraintLayout instance, and using the *layout()* modifier function to associate the constraint set reference with the button1 composable. Modify the MainScreen function to apply these changes:

Working with ConstraintLayout in Compose

```
@Composable
fun MainScreen() {

    ConstraintLayout(constraints, Modifier.size(width = 200.dp, height = 200.dp))
    {
        val button1 = createRef()
        val constraints = myConstraintSet(margin = 8.dp)

        MyButton(text = "Button1", Modifier.size(200.dp).layoutId("button1"))

    }
}
```

Preview the layout to verify that it still appears as expected.

30.17 Summary

ConstraintLayout provides a flexible way to implement complex user interface layouts that respond well to dynamic changes such as screen orientation rotation and changes in the size of components included in a layout. Before a composable can be constrained it must first be associated with a ConstraintLayout reference. The most basic of constraints involves attaching or linking the sides of a component to either the parent container or the side of another component. These links can be applied either with or without margins. Components may be centered by applying opposing constraints or offset by applying bias. The chapter also demonstrated the use of chains, barriers, and guidelines to influence the positioning behavior of multiple components and explored the use of constraint sets to create reusable sets of constraints that can be passed through to ConstraintLayout instances.

31. Working with IntrinsicSize in Compose

As we already know from the previous chapters, one of the ways that Compose can render user interface layouts quickly and efficiently is by limiting each composable to being measured only once during a recomposition operation. Situations sometimes arise, however, where a parent composable needs to know size information about its children before they are measured as part of the recomposition. You might, for example, need the width of a Column to match that of its widest child. Although a parent cannot measure its children, size information may be obtained without breaking the "measure once" rule by making use of *intrinsic measurements*.

31.1 Intrinsic measurements

A parent composable can obtain sizing information about its children by accessing the *Max* and *Min* values of the Compose IntrinsicSize enumeration. IntrinsicSize provides the parent with information about the maximum or minimum possible width or height of its widest or tallest child. This allows the parent to make sizing decisions based on the sizing needs of its children. The following code, for example, sets the height of a Row composable based on intrinsic size information:

```
Row(modifier = modifier.height(IntrinsicSize.Min)) {
.
.
}
```

When this composable is rendered, the height of the Row will be set to the minimum possible height needed to display its tallest child. Similarly, the following code configures the width of a Column to the maximum possible width of its widest child:

```
Column(modifier = modifier.width(IntrinsicSize.Max)) {
.
.
}
```

In the absence of modifiers to the contrary, a layout composable such as a Row or Column will typically be sized to occupy all of the space made available to it by its parent. By making use of IntrinsicSize, these composables can instead be sized to match the space requirements of their children. As we will see in the following example project, this becomes particularly useful when one or more children are subject to dynamic size changes.

31.2 Max. vs Min. Intrinsic Size measurements

The IntrinsicSize enumeration provides access to both maximum and minimum measurements. The difference between these two values needs some explanation. All visible composables need space on the device display in which to render their content, and many can adapt to changes in the amount of space available. This concept is, perhaps, best described using the Text composable as an example. A Text composable displaying a single line of text has a maximum width equivalent to the length of text it is displaying. This equates to the IntrinsicSize *Max* value:

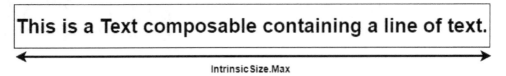

Figure 31-1

The Text component is, however, also able to display multi-line text. This means that the same line of text could potentially be placed on multiple lines, considerably reducing the width required to display the content. Assuming there are no restrictions on height, the minimum width required by a Text composable could be as narrow as the length of the longest word in the text string. This value equates to the IntrinsicSize *Min* value:

Figure 31-2

As indicated in the above diagram, this example IntrinsicSize.Min value assumes that no height constraints have been applied to the Text component. In the presence of a height restriction, Compose would arrive at a different minimum intrinsic width measurement:

Figure 31-3

31.3 About the example project

When the project is complete it will consist of a Text composable, colored rectangular Box and custom TextField. The objective is for the text entered into the TextField to appear in the Text component. As text is typed, the width of the Box, which will be positioned directly beneath the Text component, will adjust so that it matches the width of the displayed text.

This will be achieved by placing the Text and Box components within a Column, the width of which will be defined using the IntrinsicSize measurements of its children.

31.4 Creating the IntrinsicSizeDemo project

Launch Android Studio and select the New Project option from the welcome screen. Within the new project dialog, choose the *Empty Compose Activity* template and click on the Next button.

Enter *IntrinsicSizeDemo* into the Name field and specify *com.example.intrinsicsizedemo* as the package name. Before clicking on the Finish button, change the Minimum API level setting to API 26: Android 8.0 (Oreo). Within the *MainActivity.kt* file, delete the Greeting function and add a new empty composable named MainScreen:

```
@Composable
fun MainScreen() {


}
```

Next, edit the *onCreateActivity()* method and DefaultPreview function to call MainScreen instead of Greeting.

31.5 Creating the custom text field

The custom text field will need to accept as parameters the state variable used to store the current text and an event handler reference to be called for each user keystroke. Remaining within the *MainActivity.kt* file, add a new composable with these features named MyTextField:

```
.
.
import androidx.compose.material.TextField
.
.
@Composable
fun MyTextField(text: String, onTextChange : (String) -> Unit) {

    TextField(
        value = text,
        onValueChange = onTextChange
    )
}
```

Before moving on to the next step, take this opportunity to add the text state variable and event handler to the MainScreen function as follows:

```
.
.
import androidx.compose.runtime.*
.
.
@Composable
fun MainScreen() {

    var textState by remember { mutableStateOf("") }

    val onTextChange = { text : String ->
        textState = text
```

```
    }

    .

    .

}
```

31.6 Adding the Text and Box components

A Column now needs to be added to the MainScreen function containing both the Text and Box components. Continue editing the *MainActivity.kt* file to add these composables:

.

.

```
import androidx.compose.foundation.background
import androidx.compose.foundation.layout.*
import androidx.compose.ui.graphics.Color
import androidx.compose.ui.unit.dp


    .

    .

@Composable
fun MainScreen() {

    var textState by remember { mutableStateOf("") }

    val onTextChange = { text : String ->
        textState = text
    }

    Column {
        Text(
            modifier = Modifier
                .padding(start = 4.dp),
            text = textState
        )

        Box(Modifier.height(10.dp).fillMaxWidth().background(Color.Blue))
    }
}
```

Note that the Box is configured to use the full width of the parent Column. Later we will use the intrinsic width measurement to make sure the Column is only wide enough to contain the Text composable.

31.7 Adding the top-level Column

The final step before we perform an initial test is to embed the Column added above within another Column together with the custom text field as outlined below. Since this is the top-most Column in the component hierarchy, we will refer to it as the "top-level" column:

```
@Composable
fun MainScreen() {
```

```
var textState by remember { mutableStateOf("") }

val onTextChange = { text : String ->
    textState = text
}

Column(Modifier.width(200.dp).padding(5.dp)) {
    Column {
        Text(
            modifier = Modifier
                .padding(start = 4.dp),
            text = textState
        )
        Box(Modifier.height(10.dp).fillMaxWidth().background(Color.Blue))
    }
    MyTextField(text = textState, onTextChange = onTextChange)
}
}
```

31.8 Testing the project

Using either an emulator or device, run the app and enter some text into the TextField as shown in Figure 31-4:

Figure 31-4

Note that text appears in the Text composable as it is typed, but that the Box extends to the width of the top-level Column instead of matching the text width.

31.9 Applying IntrinsicSize.Max measurements

All that is required to resolve the current problem is to configure the Column containing the Text and Box so that its width is based on the maximum intrinsic size measurement of its children. Modify the Column declaration so that it now reads as follows:

.

.

```
Column(Modifier.width(200.dp).padding(5.dp)) {
    Column(Modifier.width(IntrinsicSize.Max)){
```

.

.

Test the app again, and verify that the width of the Box now matches the text width as it is typed. In fact, even as text is deleted, the Box width updates accordingly. This is because the width of the parent Column is changing on each recomposition as characters are typed or deleted.

Figure 31-5

31.10 Applying IntrinsicSize.Min measurements

Now that we have seen the effect of the minimum IntrinsicSize measurement on the Column parent, we are ready to explore the use of the minimum measurement. Edit the Column declaration so that it now uses IntrinsicSize. Min as follows:

```
.
.
.

Column(Modifier.width(200.dp).padding(5.dp)) {
    Column(Modifier.width(IntrinsicSize.Min)) {

.
.
.
```

Test the app once again, this time entering a longer sentence into the text field as shown in Figure 31-6 below:

Figure 31-6

With this change implemented, the minimum Column width matches that of the line displaying the longest word (in this case the line that reads "containing").

31.11 Summary

To maximize rendering speeds, Compose prohibits a composable from being measured more than once during recomposition. This can be problematic if a parent needs to make sizing decisions before its children have been measured. All composables have a minimum and maximum size at which they can comfortably render their content without that content being clipped or obscured. IntrinsicSize allows a parent to scan its children and identify the minimum and maximum height and width values of its widest and tallest child, and to use that information to configure its own dimensions.

32. An Overview of Lists and Grids in Compose

It is a common requirement when designing user interface layouts to present information in either scrollable list or grid configurations. For basic list requirements, the Row and Column components can be re-purposed to provide vertical and horizontal lists of child composables. Extremely large lists, however, are likely to cause degraded performance if rendered using the standard Row and Column composables. For lists containing large numbers of items, Compose provides the LazyColumn and LazyRow composables. Similarly, grid-based layouts can be presented using the LazyVerticalGrid composable.

This chapter will introduce the basics of list and grid creation and management in Compose in preparation for the tutorials in subsequent chapters.

32.1 Standard vs. lazy lists

Part of the popularity of lists is that they provide an effective way to present large amounts of items in a scrollable format. Each item in a list is represented by a composable which may, itself, contain descendant composables. When a list is created using the Row or Column component, all of the items it contains are also created at initialization, regardless of how many are visible at any given time. While this does not necessarily pose a problem for smaller lists, it can be an issue for lists containing many items.

Consider, for example, a list that is required to display 1000 photo images. It can be assumed with a reasonable degree of certainty that only a small percentage of items will be visible to the user at any one time. If the application was permitted to create each of the 1000 items in advance, however, the device would very quickly run into memory and performance limitations.

When working with longer lists, the recommended course of action is to use LazyColumn, LazyRow, and LazyVerticalGrid. These components only create those items that are visible to the user. As the user scrolls, items that move out of the viewable area are destroyed to free up resources while those entering view are created just in time to be displayed. This allows lists of potentially infinite length to be displayed with no performance degradation.

Since there are differences in approach and features when working with Row and Column compared to the lazy equivalents, this chapter will provide an overview of both types.

32.2 Working with Column and Row lists

Although lacking some of the features and performance advantages of the LazyColumn and LazyRow, the Row and Column composables provide a good option for displaying shorter, basic lists of items. Lists are declared in much the same way as regular rows and columns with the exception that each list item is usually generated programmatically. The following declaration, for example, uses the Column component to create a vertical list containing 100 instances of a composable named MyListItem:

```
Column {
    repeat(100) {
        MyListItem()
    }
}
```

```
}
```

Similarly, the following example creates a horizontal list containing the same items:

```
Row {
    repeat(100) {
        MyListItem()
    }
}
```

The MyListItem composable can be anything from a single Text composable to a complex layout containing multiple composables.

32.3 Creating lazy lists

Lazy lists are created using the LazyColumn and LazyRow composables. These layouts place children within a LazyListScope block which provides additional features for managing and customizing the list items. For example, individual items may be added to a lazy list via calls to the *item()* function of the LazyListScope:

```
LazyColumn {
    item {
        MyListItem()
    }
}
```

Alternatively, multiple items may be added in a single statement by calling the *items()* function:

```
LazyColumn {
    items(1000) { index ->
        Text("This is item $index");
    }
}
```

LazyListScope also provides the *itemsIndexed()* function which associates the item content with an index value, for example:

```
val colorNamesList = listOf("Red", "Green", "Blue", "Indigo")

LazyColumn {
    itemsIndexed(colorNamesList) { index, item ->
        Text("$index = $item")
    }
}
```

When rendered, the above lazy column will appear as shown in Figure 32-1 below:

0 = Red
1 = Green
2 = Blue
3 = Indigo

Figure 32-1

Lazy lists also support the addition of headers to groups of items in a list using the *stickyHeader()* function. This topic will be covered in more detail later in the chapter.

32.4 Enabling scrolling with ScrollState

While the above Column and Row list examples will display a list of items, only those that fit into the viewable screen area will be accessible to the user. This is because lists are not scrollable by default. To make Row and Column-based lists scrollable, some additional steps are needed. LazyList and LazyRow, on the other hand, support scrolling by default.

The first step in enabling list scrolling when working with Row and Column-based lists is to create a ScrollState instance. This is a special state object designed to allow Row and Column parents to remember the current scroll position through recompositions. A ScrollState instance is generated via a call to the *rememberScrollState()* function, for example:

```
val scrollState = rememberScrollState()
```

Once created, the scroll state is passed as a parameter to the Column or Row composable using the *verticalScroll()* and *horizontalScroll()* modifiers. In the following example, vertical scrolling is being enabled in a Column list:

```
Column(Modifier.verticalScroll(scrollState)) {
    repeat(100) {
        MyListItem()
    }
}
```

Similarly, the following code enables horizontal scrolling on a LazyRow list:

```
Row(Modifier.horizontalScroll(scrollState)) {
    repeat(1000) {
        MyListItem()
    }
}
```

32.5 Programmatic scrolling

We generally think of scrolling as being something a user performs through dragging or swiping gestures on the device screen. It is also important to know how to change the current scroll position from within code. An app screen might, for example, contain buttons which can be tapped to scroll to the start and end of a list. The steps to implement this behavior differ between Row and Columns lists and the lazy list equivalents.

When working with Row and Column lists, programmatic scrolling can be performed by calling the following functions on the ScrollState instance:

- **animateScrollTo(value: Int)** - Scrolls smoothly to the specified pixel position in the list using animation.

- **scrollTo(value: Int)** - Scrolls instantly to the specified pixel position.

Note that the value parameters in the above function represent the list position in pixels instead of referencing a specific item number. It is safe to assume that the start of the list is represented by pixel position 0, but the pixel position representing the end of the list may be less obvious. Fortunately, the maximum scroll position can be identified by accessing the *maxValue* property of the scroll state instance:

```
val maxScrollPosition = scrollState.maxValue
```

To programmatically scroll LazyColumn and LazyRow lists, functions need to be called on a LazyListState instance which can be obtained via a call to the *rememberLazyListState()* function as follows:

An Overview of Lists and Grids in Compose

```
val listState = rememberLazyListState()
```

Once the list state has been obtained, it must be applied to the LazyRow or LazyColumn declaration as follows:

```
.

.

LazyColumn(
    state = listState,
{

.

.
```

Scrolling can then be performed via calls to the following functions on the list state instance:

- **animateScrollToItem(index: Int)** - Scrolls smoothly to the specified list item (where 0 is the first item).

- **scrollToItem(index: Int)** - Scrolls instantly to the specified list item (where 0 is the first item).

In this case, the scrolling position is referenced by the index of the item instead of pixel position.

One complication is that all four of the above scroll functions are *coroutine* functions. Coroutines are a feature of Kotlin that allows blocks of code to execute asynchronously without blocking the thread from which they are launched (in this case the *main thread* which is responsible for making sure the app remains responsive to the user). Coroutines can be implemented without having to worry about building complex implementations or directly managing multiple threads. Because of the way they are implemented, coroutines are much more efficient and less resource-intensive than using traditional multi-threading options. Coroutines also make for code that is much easier to write, understand and maintain since it allows code to be written sequentially without having to write callbacks to handle thread-related events and results.

Although a relatively recent addition to Kotlin, there is nothing new or innovative about coroutines. Coroutines in one form or another have existed in programming languages since the 1960s and are based on a model known as Communicating Sequential Processes (CSP). In fact, Kotlin still uses multi-threading behind the scenes, though it does so highly efficiently.

A problem with threads is that they are a finite resource expensive in terms of CPU capabilities and system overhead. In the background, a lot of work is involved in creating, scheduling, and destroying a thread. Although modern CPUs can run large numbers of threads, the actual number of threads that can be run in parallel at any one time is limited by the number of CPU cores (though newer CPUs have 8 cores, most Android devices contain CPUs with 4 cores). When more threads are required than there are CPU cores, the system has to perform thread scheduling to decide how the execution of these threads is to be shared between the available cores.

To avoid these overheads, instead of starting a new thread for each coroutine and then destroying it when the coroutine exits, Kotlin maintains a pool of active threads and manages how coroutines are assigned to those threads. When an active coroutine is suspended it is saved by the Kotlin runtime and another coroutine resumed to take its place. When the coroutine is resumed, it is simply restored to an existing unoccupied thread within the pool to continue executing until it either completes or is suspended. Using this approach, a limited number of threads are used efficiently to execute asynchronous tasks with the potential to perform large numbers of concurrent tasks without the inherent performance degenerations that would occur using standard multi-threading.

One of the key requirements of coroutine functions is that they must be launched from within a *coroutine scope*.

As with ScrollState and LazyListState, we need access to a CoroutineScope instance that will be remembered through recompositions. This requires a call to the *rememberCoroutineScope()* function as follows:

```
val coroutineScope = rememberCoroutineScope()
```

Once we have a coroutine scope, we can use it to launch the scroll functions. The following code, for example, declares a Button component configured to launch the *animateScrollTo()* function within the coroutine scope. In this case, the button will cause the list to scroll to the end position when clicked:

```
.
.
.

Button(onClick = {
    coroutineScope.launch {
        scrollState.animateScrollTo(scrollState.maxValue)
    }
.
.
}
```

32.6 Sticky headers

Sticky headers is a feature only available within lazy lists that allows list items to be grouped under a corresponding header. Sticky headers are created using the LazyListScope *stickyHeader()* function.

The headers are referred to as being sticky because they remain visible on the screen while the current group is scrolling. Once a group scrolls from view, the header for the next group takes its place. Figure 32-2, for example, shows a list with sticky headers. Note that although the Apple group is scrolled partially out of view, the header remains in position at the top of the screen:

Figure 32-2

When working with sticky headers, the list content must be stored in an Array or List which has been mapped using the Kotlin *groupBy()* function. The *groupBy()* function accepts a lambda which is used to define the *selector* which defines how data is to be grouped. This selector then serves as the key to access the elements of each group. Consider, for example, the following list which contains mobile phone models:

```
val phones = listOf("Apple iPhone 12", "Google Pixel 4", "Google Pixel 6",
    "Samsung Galaxy 6s", "Apple iPhone 7", "OnePlus 7", "OnePlus 9 Pro",
        "Apple iPhone 13", "Samsung Galaxy Z Flip", "Google Pixel 4a",
            "Apple iPhone 8")
```

Now suppose that we want to group the phone models by manufacturer. To do this we would use the first word of each string (in other words, the text before the first space character) as the selector when calling *groupBy()* to map the list:

```
val groupedPhones = phones.groupBy { it.substringBefore(' ') }
```

Once the phones have been grouped by manufacturer, we can use the *forEach* statement to create a sticky header for each manufacture name, and display the phones in the corresponding group as list items:

```
groupedPhones.forEach { (manufacturer, models) ->
    stickyHeader {
        Text(
            text = manufacturer,
            color = Color.White,
            modifier = Modifier
                .background(Color.Gray)
                .padding(5.dp)
                .fillMaxWidth()
        )
    }

    items(models) { model ->
        MyListItem(model)
    }
}
```

In the above *forEach* lambda, *manufacturer* represents the selector key (for example "Apple") and *models* an array containing the items in the corresponding manufacturer group ("Apple iPhone 12", "Apple iPhone 7", and so on for the Apple selector):

```
groupedPhones.forEach { (manufacturer, models) ->
```

The selector key is then used as the text for the sticky header, and the *models* list is passed to the *items()* function to display all the group elements, in this case using a custom composable named MyListItem for each item:

```
items(models) { model ->
    MyListItem(model)
}
```

When rendered, the above code will display the list shown in Figure 32-2 above.

32.7 Responding to scroll position

Both LazyRow and LazyColumn allow actions to be performed when a list scrolls to a specified item position. This can be particularly useful for displaying a "scroll to top" button that appears only when the user scrolls towards the end of the list.

The behavior is implemented by accessing the *firstVisibleItemIndex* property of the LazyListState instance which contains the index of the item that is currently the first visible item in the list. For example, if the user scrolls a LazyColumn list such that the third item in the list is currently the topmost visible item, *firstVisibleItemIndex* will contain a value of 2 (since indexes start counting at 0). The following code, for example, could be used to display a "scroll to top" button when the first visible item index exceeds 8:

```
val firstVisible = listState.firstVisibleItemIndex

if (firstVisible > 8) {
    // Display scroll to top button
}
```

32.8 Creating a lazy grid

Grid layouts may be created using the LazyVerticalGrid composable. The appearance of the grid is controlled by the *cells* parameter that can be set to either *adaptive* or *fixed* mode. In adaptive mode, the grid will calculate the number of rows and columns that will fit into the available space, with even spacing between items and subject to a minimum specified cell size. Fixed mode, on the other hand, is passed the number of rows to be displayed and sizes each column width equally to fill the width of the available space.

The following code, for example, declares a grid containing 30 cells, each with a minimum width of 60dp:

```
LazyVerticalGrid(
    cells = GridCells.Adaptive(minSize = 60.dp),
    state = rememberLazyListState(),
    contentPadding = PaddingValues(10.dp)
) {
        items(30) { index ->
            Card(backgroundColor = Color.Blue,
                modifier = Modifier.padding(5.dp).fillMaxSize()) {
                Text(
                    "$index",
                    fontSize = 35.sp,
                    color = Color.White,
                    textAlign = TextAlign.Center)
            }
        }
}
```

When called, the LazyVerticalGrid composable will fit as many items as possible into each row without making the column width greater than 60dp as illustrated in the figure below:

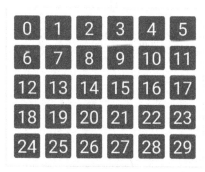

Figure 32-3

The following code organizes items in a grid containing three columns:

An Overview of Lists and Grids in Compose

```
LazyVerticalGrid(
    cells = GridCells.Fixed(3),
    state = rememberLazyListState(),
    contentPadding = PaddingValues(10.dp)
) {

        items(15) { index ->
            Card(backgroundColor = Color.Blue,
                modifier = Modifier.padding(5.dp).fillMaxSize()) {
                Text(
                    "$index",
                    fontSize = 35.sp,
                    color = Color.White,
                    textAlign = TextAlign.Center)

            }
        }

}
```

The layout from the above code will appear as illustrated in Figure 32-4 below:

Figure 32-4

Both the above grid examples used a Card composable containing a Text component for each cell item. The Card component provides a surface into which to group content and actions relating to a single content topic and is often used as the basis for list items. Although we provided a Text composable as the child, the content in a card can be any composable, including containers such as Row, Column, and Box layouts. A key feature of Card is the ability to create a shadow effect by specifying an elevation:

```
Card(
    modifier = Modifier
        .fillMaxWidth()
        .padding(15.dp),
    elevation = 10.dp
) {
    Column(horizontalAlignment = Alignment.CenterHorizontally,
        modifier = Modifier.padding(15.dp)
```

```
) {
    Text("Jetpack Compose", fontSize = 30.sp)
    Text("Card Example", fontSize = 20.sp)
    }
}
```

When rendered, the above Card component will appear as shown in Figure 32-5:

Jetpack Compose
Card Example

Figure 32-5

32.9 Summary

Lists in Compose may be created using either standard or lazy list components. The lazy components have the advantage that they can present large amounts of content without impacting the performance of the app or the device on which it is running. This is achieved by creating list items only when they become visible and destroying them as they scroll out of view. Lists can be presented in row, column, and grid formats and can be static or scrollable. It is also possible to programmatically scroll lists to specific positions and to trigger events based on the current scroll position.

33. A Compose Row and Column List Tutorial

In this chapter, we will create a project that makes use of the Column and Row components to display items in a list format. In addition to creating the list, the tutorial will also enable scrolling and provide a demonstration of programmatic scrolling.

33.1 Creating the ListDemo project

Launch Android Studio and select the New Project option from the welcome screen. In the new project dialog, choose the *Empty Compose Activity* template before clicking on the Next button.

Enter *ListDemo* into the Name field and specify *com.example.listdemo* as the package name. Before clicking on the Finish button, change the Minimum API level setting to API 26: Android 8.0 (Oreo). Within the *MainActivity.kt* file, delete the Greeting function and add a new empty composable named MainScreen:

```
@Composable
fun MainScreen() {


}
```

Next, edit the *onCreateActivity()* method and DefaultPreview function to call MainScreen instead of Greeting.

33.2 Creating a Column-based list

We will start this tutorial by creating a basic list layout using the Column composable to display a scrollable list of Text component items. Start by modifying the *MainActivity.kt* file as follows to add and call a new composable named *ColumnList*:

```
.
.
import androidx.compose.foundation.layout.Column
import androidx.compose.foundation.layout.padding
import androidx.compose.ui.unit.dp
.
.
@Composable
fun MainScreen() {
    ColumnList()
}

@Composable
fun ColumnList() {
    Column {
        repeat(500) {
```

```
            Text("List Item $it",
            style = MaterialTheme.typography.h4,
            modifier = Modifier.padding(5.dp))
        }
    }
}
```

The code within the ColumnList composable creates a Column containing a list of 500 Text components. The Text component is customized using the "Heading 4" Material typographical style and a padding modifier. Each Text instance displays a string including the current item number.

To best view the layout, modify the Preview composable to display the system UI:

```
@Preview(showBackground = true, showSystemUi = true)
@Composable
fun DefaultPreview() {
    ListDemoTheme {
        MainScreen()
    }
}
```

Once these changes have been made, the preview should be rendered as follows:

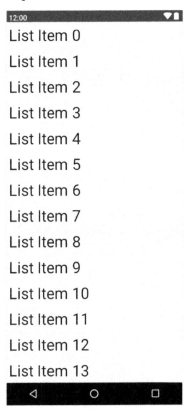

Figure 33-1

Start interactive mode in the Preview panel and note that it is not possible to scroll the list to view the items currently outside the bounds of the screen viewing area. To resolve this we need to enable vertical scrolling support on the Column component.

33.3 Enabling list scrolling

The first requirement when enabling scrolling support within a Column is a ScrollState state instance which can be obtained via a call to the *rememberScrollState()* function. Once the state has been obtained, it needs to be passed to the Column via the *verticalScroll()* modifier:

```
.

.

import androidx.compose.foundation.rememberScrollState
import androidx.compose.foundation.verticalScroll

.

.

@Composable
fun ColumnList() {

    val scrollState = rememberScrollState()

    Column(Modifier.verticalScroll(scrollState)) {
        repeat(500) {
            Text("List Item $it",
                style = MaterialTheme.typography.h4,
                modifier = Modifier.padding(5.dp))
        }
    }
}
```

After adding scrolling support, refresh the interactive preview, then click and drag the list up and down to verify that vertical scrolling is now working.

33.4 Manual scrolling

The next step in this tutorial is to add some buttons to the layout that can be used to instantly scroll to the top and bottom of the list. As previously discussed, the list scroll position can be controlled from within code by making calls to methods of the ScrollState instance, specifying the target list position. Since these are coroutine functions, we also need to obtain a coroutine scope within which to initiate the scrolling action. We create coroutine scope instances via a call to the *rememberCoroutineScope()* function.

Locate the ColumnList function in the *MainActivity.kt* file and modify it so that the list column is embedded in a new Column which also contains two Buttons arranged using a Row component:

```
.

.

import androidx.compose.foundation.layout.Row
import androidx.compose.material.Button
import androidx.compose.runtime.rememberCoroutineScope

.

.

@Composable
```

A Compose Row and Column List Tutorial

```
fun ColumnList() {

    val scrollState = rememberScrollState()
    val coroutineScope = rememberCoroutineScope()

    Column {

        Row {
            Button(onClick = {

            },
                modifier = Modifier.weight(0.5f)
                .padding(2.dp)) {
                Text("Top")
            }

            Button(onClick = {

            },
                modifier = Modifier.weight(0.5f)
                .padding(2.dp)) {
                Text("End")
            }
        }

        Column(Modifier.verticalScroll(scrollState)) {
            repeat(500) {
                Text(
                    "List Item $it",
                    style = MaterialTheme.typography.h4,
                    modifier = Modifier.padding(5.dp)
                )
            }
        }
    }
}
```

All that remains is to create a coroutine scope instance and then use it to perform the scrolling within the Button onClick actions:

.

.

```
import kotlinx.coroutines.launch
```

.

.

```
Row {
    Button(onClick = {
```

272

```
        coroutineScope.launch {
            scrollState.animateScrollTo(0)
        }
    },
        modifier = Modifier.weight(0.5f)
        .padding(2.dp)) {
        Text("Top")
    }

    Button(onClick = {
        coroutineScope.launch {
            scrollState.animateScrollTo(scrollState.maxValue)
        }
    },
        modifier = Modifier.weight(0.5f)
        .padding(2.dp)) {
        Text("End")
    }
}
```

Instead of scrolling instantly to the top and bottom of the list, we have used animated scrolling. Since the target list position is specified by pixel position, the code uses 0 as the top target. To find the end position of the list, the code accesses the *maxValue* property of the ScrollState instance and passes it to the *animateScrollTo()* function.

Preview the app in interactive mode, or run it on a device or emulator and test that the two buttons scroll to the top and bottom of the list as expected. Figure 33-2, for example, shows the list after the End button has been clicked:

Figure 33-2

33.5 A Row list example

In addition to vertical Column-based lists we can, of course, also use the Row composable to create horizontal lists. To try out a horizontally scrolling Row list, add the following composable to the *MainActivity.kt* file and modify the MainScreen function to call it instead of ColumnList:

```
.
.
import androidx.compose.foundation.horizontalScroll
.
.
@Composable
fun MainScreen() {
    RowList()
}

@Composable
fun RowList() {

    val scrollState = rememberScrollState()

    Row(Modifier.horizontalScroll(scrollState)) {
        repeat(50) {
            Text(" $it ",
                style = MaterialTheme.typography.h1,
                modifier = Modifier.padding(5.dp))
        }
    }
}
```

Preview the list in interactive mode and click and drag the list sideways to test horizontal scrolling as shown in Figure 33-3 below:

Figure 33-3

33.6 Summary

In this chapter, we have used the Row and Column components to create vertical and horizontal lists. In both cases, scrolling was enabled to allow us to move through the list items using drag motions. In the case of the vertical list, buttons were added and configured to scroll directly to the top and bottom of the list when clicked. This involved launching the *animateScrollTo()* method of the ScrollState instance from within a coroutine scope.

34. A Compose Lazy List Tutorial

Although the creation of lists using the standard compose Row and Column layout composables was covered in the previous chapter, in most situations you will be more likely to make use of the LazyColumn and LazyRow components. Not only do these provide a more efficient way to display long lists of items, but the lazy composables also include additional features such as sticky headers and responding to changes in scroll position.

This chapter will create a project which demonstrates some of the key features of both the LazyColumn and LazyRow components. In the next chapter, entitled *"Lazy List Sticky Headers and Scroll Detection"*, the project will be extended to include support for sticky headers and scroll position detection.

34.1 Creating the LazyListDemo project

Launch Android Studio and select the New Project option from the welcome screen. When the new project dialog appears, choose the *Empty Compose Activity* template before clicking on the Next button.

Enter *LazyListDemo* into the Name field and specify *com.example.lazylistdemo* as the package name. Before clicking on the Finish button, change the Minimum API level setting to API 26: Android 8.0 (Oreo). Within the *MainActivity.kt* file, delete the Greeting function and add a new empty composable named MainScreen:

```
@Composable
fun MainScreen() {


}
```

Next, edit the *onCreateActivity()* method and DefaultPreview function to call MainScreen instead of Greeting.

34.2 Adding list data to the project

Before designing the list we first need some data to provide the list item content. For this example, we will use an XML resource file containing the list items and read it into an array. The XML resource file for this project is included with the source code samples download within the *XML* folder. If you have not already done so, the sample code can be downloaded from the following web page:

https://www.ebookfrenzy.com/retail/compose/index.php

Once the sample code has been unpacked, use the file system navigator for your operating system (i.e. Finder on macOS or Windows Explorer in Windows), locate the *car_list.xml* file in the XML folder, and copy it. Return to Android Studio, right-click on the *app -> res > values* folder in the Project tool window, and select Paste from the resulting menu as shown in Figure 34-1:

A Compose Lazy List Tutorial

Figure 34-1

Finally, click the OK button in the "Copy" dialog to add the file to the project resources, making sure to keep the "Open in editor" option enabled:

Figure 34-2

Once the file has been added and loaded into the editor, it should read as follows:

```xml
<?xml version="1.0" encoding="utf-8"?>
<resources>
    <string-array name="car_array">
        <item>Buick Century</item>
        <item>Buick LaSabre</item>
        <item>Buick Roadmaster</item>
        <item>Buick Special Riviera</item>
        <item>Cadillac Couple De Ville</item>
        <item>Cadillac Eldorado</item>
        <item>Cadillac Fleetwood</item>
        <item>Cadillac Series 62</item>
        <item>Cadillac Seville</item>
        <item>Ford Fairlane</item>
        <item>Ford Galaxie 500</item>
        <item>Ford Mustang</item>
        <item>Ford Thunderbird</item>
        <item>GMC Le Mans</item>
        <item>Plymouth Fury</item>
        <item>Plymouth GTX</item>
        <item>Plymouth Roadrunner</item>
```

```
        </string-array>
</resources>
```

Note that the data is declared as being of type *string-array* and given the resource name *car_array*. This is the name by which the data will be referenced when it is read from the file.

34.3 Reading the XML data

Now that the XML file has been added to the project it needs to be parsed and read into an array. This array will, in turn, provide the data in a format that can be used by the LazyColumn component. To achieve this, we will be using the *getStringArray()* method of the Android *resources* instance. Since the data needs to be initialized when the main activity is created, we can perform this task within the *onCreate()* method. Some changes are also required to pass the array through to our MainScreen function and to provide some sample data for the Preview composable.

Edit the *MainActivity.kt* file and modify it so that it reads as follows:

```
.
.
class MainActivity : ComponentActivity() {

    private var itemArray: Array<String>? = null

    override fun onCreate(savedInstanceState: Bundle?) {

        itemArray = resources.getStringArray(R.array.car_array)

        super.onCreate(savedInstanceState)
        setContent {
            LazyListDemoTheme {
                Surface(
                    modifier = Modifier.fillMaxSize(),
                    color = MaterialTheme.colors.background
                ) {
                    MainScreen(itemArray = itemArray as Array<out String>)
                }
            }
        }
    }
}

@Composable
fun MainScreen(itemArray: Array<out String>) {

}

@Preview(showBackground = true)
@Composable
fun DefaultPreview() {
```

```
val itemArray: Array<String> = arrayOf("Cadillac Eldorado",
                                "Ford Fairlane", "Plymouth Fury")


LazyListDemoTheme {
    MainScreen(itemArray = itemArray)
}
}
```

34.4 Handling image loading

The project now has access to a list of cars with each item containing the car manufacturer and model. In addition to this text content, each list item will also display an image containing the manufacturer's logo. These logos are hosted on a web server and will need to be downloaded and rendered within an Image composable. There are many factors to take into consideration when downloading and displaying images within an app. For example, the images need to be downloaded asynchronously so that the app execution is not interrupted. The download process should also be able to recover from connectivity issues, and should also handle downsampling of the images to minimize memory usage. Instead of writing all the code to perform these tasks, this project will use an existing image loading library called Coil to automatically perform these tasks. If you would like to learn more about Coil, information can be found at the following URL:

https://coil-kt.github.io/coil/

To add Coil support to the project, open the module-level *build.gradle* file (located in the Project tool window under *Gradle Scripts -> build.gradle (Module: LazyListDemo.app)*), locate the *dependencies* section, and add the Coil library:

```
dependencies {
.

.

    implementation('io.coil-kt:coil-compose:1.3.2')
.

.

}
```

After the library has been added, a warning bar (Figure 34-3) will appear indicating that the project needs to be re-synchronized to include the change:

Figure 34-3

Click on the *Sync Now* link and wait while the synchronization process completes.

The next step is to add a composable function to download an image and display it using the Image component. The naming convention for the image files is *<manufacturer>_logo.png* where *<manufacturer>* is replaced by the manufacturer name (Ford, Cadillac, etc.). Since each car string begins with the manufacturer name, we can construct the image name for each car entry by combining the first word of the string with "_logo.png". Within the *MainActivity.kt* file, begin writing the ImageLoader composable function:

```
@Composable
```

```
fun ImageLoader(item: String) {

    val url = "https://www.ebookfrenzy.com/book_examples/car_logos/" + item.
substringBefore(" ") + "_logo.png"
}
```

While constructing the full image URL, the code calls the Kotlin *subStringBefore()* method on the item string to obtain the text before the first space character.

With the path to the image obtained, code now needs to be added to create an Image component rendered with the image:

.
.

```
import androidx.compose.foundation.Image
import androidx.compose.foundation.layout.*
import androidx.compose.ui.layout.ContentScale
import androidx.compose.ui.unit.dp
import coil.compose.rememberImagePainter

.

.

@Composable
fun ImageLoader(item: String) {

    val url = "https://www.ebookfrenzy.com/book_examples/car_logos/" + item.
                            substringBefore(" ") + "_logo.png"

    Image(
        painter = rememberImagePainter(url),
        contentDescription = "car image",
        contentScale = ContentScale.Fit,
        modifier = Modifier.size(75.dp)
    )
}
```

The above code creates an Image and requests an image painter via a call to the Coil *rememberImagePainter()* function, passing through the image URL. The image is scaled to fit the size of the Image component, the height and width of which is restricted via a modifier to 75dp.

As the logo images will be downloaded, the project manifest needs to be updated to add Internet access permission. Within the Project tool window, open the *app -> manifests -> AndroidManifest.xml* file and add the Internet permission element as follows:

```
<?xml version="1.0" encoding="utf-8"?>
<manifest xmlns:android="http://schemas.android.com/apk/res/android"
    package="com.example.lazylistdemo">

    <uses-permission android:name="android.permission.INTERNET" />
```

.
.

At the time of writing, the Compose Preview panel did not support the rendering of images using Coil. To test that the ImageLoader works, make the following addition to the MainScreen function:

```
@Composable
fun MainScreen(itemArray: Array<out String>) {
    ImageLoader("Plymouth GTX")
}
```

With the change made, run the app on an emulator or device where the Plymouth logo should appear as illustrated in Figure 34-4:

Figure 34-4

34.5 Designing the list item composable

At this point in the tutorial, we have an array of list items and a mechanism for loading images. The next requirement is a composable to display each item within the list. This will consist of a Row containing an ImageLoader and a Text component displaying the list item string. To provide more customization options such as elevation effects and rounded corners, the Row will be placed within a Card component. Add the MyListItem function to the *MainActivity.kt* file so that it reads as follows:

```
.
.
import androidx.compose.foundation.shape.RoundedCornerShape
import androidx.compose.material.Card
import androidx.compose.ui.Alignment
.
.
@Composable
fun MyListItem(item: String) {
    Card(
        Modifier
            .padding(8.dp)
            .fillMaxWidth(),
        shape = RoundedCornerShape(10.dp),
        elevation = 5.dp) {

        Row(verticalAlignment = Alignment.CenterVertically) {
            ImageLoader(item)
            Spacer(modifier = Modifier.width(8.dp))
            Text(
```

```
            text = item,
            style = MaterialTheme.typography.h6,
            modifier = Modifier.padding(8.dp)
        )
    }
}
}
```

Modify the MainScreen function to call the MyListItem composable as follows before testing the app on a device or emulator:

```
@Composable
fun MainScreen(itemArray: Array<out String>) {
    MyListItem("Buick Roadmaster")
}
```

Once the app is running, the list item should appear as illustrated in Figure 34-5. Note that this time the ImageLoader function has loaded the Buick logo to match the car description:

Figure 34-5

34.6 Building the lazy list

With the preparation work complete, the project is ready for the addition of the LazyColumn component.

.

.

```
import androidx.compose.foundation.lazy.LazyColumn
import androidx.compose.foundation.lazy.items
```

.

.

```
@Composable
fun MainScreen(itemArray: Array<out String>) {
    LazyColumn {
        items(itemArray) { model ->
            MyListItem(item = model)
        }
    }
}
```

All this code does is call the LazyColumn composable and use the *items()* function of the LazyListScope to iterate through each element of the itemArray, passing each through to the MyListItem function.

34.7 Testing the project

Compile and run the project once again and verify that a scrollable list resembling that shown in Figure 34-6 below appears on the device or emulator screen:

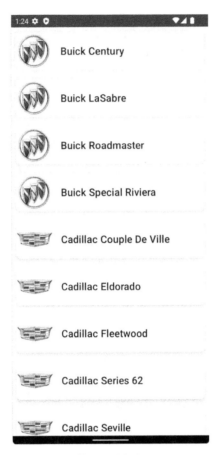

Figure 34-6

34.8 Making list items clickable

It is common for the items in a list to do something when clicked. For example, selecting an item for the list might perform an action or even navigate to another screen. The final step in this chapter is to make the items in the list clickable. For this example, we will configure the list items to display a toast message to the user containing the text content of the item. Created using the Android Toast class, toast messages are small notifications that appear on the screen without interrupting the currently visible activity.

Within the MainScreen function, we need to declare an event handler to be called when the user clicks on a list item. This handler will be passed the text of the current item which it will display within a toast message. Locate the MainScreen function in the *MainActivity.kt* file and modify it as follows:

```
.
.
import android.widget.Toast
import androidx.compose.ui.platform.LocalContext
import androidx.compose.foundation.*
.
.
@Composable
fun MainScreen(itemArray: Array<out String>) {
```

```
        val context = LocalContext.current

        val onListItemClick = { text : String ->

            Toast.makeText(
                context,
                text,
                Toast.LENGTH_SHORT
            ).show()
        }

        LazyColumn {
            items(itemArray) { model ->
                MyListItem(item = model)
            }
        }
}
```

Next, both the MyListItem function and how it is called need to be updated to pass through a reference to the event handler:

```
@Composable
fun MainScreen(itemArray: Array<out String>) {

.

.

    LazyColumn {
        items(itemArray) { model ->
            MyListItem(item = model, onItemClick = onListItemClick)
        }
    }
}


@Composable
fun MyListItem(item: String, onItemClick: (String) -> Unit) {

.

.

}
```

The last task before testing this new behavior is to add a clickable modifier to the Card component within MyListItem. This needs to call the onListItemClick handler, passing it the current item:

```
@Composable
fun MyListItem(item: String, onItemClick: (String) -> Unit) {

    Card(
        Modifier
            .padding(8.dp)
```

```
            .fillMaxWidth()
            .clickable { onItemClick(item) },
        shape = RoundedCornerShape(10.dp),
        elevation = 5.dp) {
.

.
```

Compile and run the app and test that clicking on an item displays the toast message containing the text of the selected item:

Figure 34-7

34.9 Summary

This chapter began by exploring the use of an XML resource for storing data and demonstrated how to read that data into an array during activity initialization. We then introduced the Coil image loading library and explained how it can be used to download and display images over an Internet connection with minimal coding. Next, the tutorial created a scrollable list based on the XML data, making use of the LazyColumn layout composable and the Card component. Finally, code was added to make each item in the list respond to click events.

Although we now have a running example of a Compose lazy list, the project created so far does not yet take advantage of other features of the Compose lazy list components such as sticky headers and scroll position detection. The next chapter, entitled "Lazy List Sticky Headers and Scroll Detection", will extend the LazyListDemo project to add these features.

35. Lazy List Sticky Headers and Scroll Detection

In the previous chapter, we created a project that makes use of the LazyColumn layout to display a list of Card components containing images and text. The project also implemented clickable list items which display a message when tapped.

This chapter will extend the project both to include sticky header support and to use scroll detection to display a "go to top" button when the user has scrolled a specific distance through the list, both of which were introduced in the chapter entitled *"An Overview of Lists and Grids in Compose"*.

35.1 Grouping the list item data

As currently implemented, the LazyColumn list is populated directly from an array of string values. The goal is now to group those items by manufacturer, with each group preceded in the list by a sticky header displaying the manufacturer's name.

The first step in adding sticky header support is to call the *groupBy()* method on the itemList array, passing through the first word of each item string (i.e. the manufacturer name) as the group selector value. Edit the *MainActivity.kt* file, locate the MainScreen function and modify it as follows to group the items into a mapped list:

```
@Composable
fun MainScreen(itemArray: Array<out String>) {

    val context = LocalContext.current
    val groupedItems = itemArray.groupBy { it.substringBefore(' ') }
    .
    .
}
```

35.2 Displaying the headers and items

Now that the list items have been grouped, the body of the LazyColumn needs to be modified. In terms of logic, this will require an outer loop that iterates through each of the manufacturer names, displaying the corresponding sticky header. The inner loop will display the items for each manufacturer. Within the MainScreen function, start by embedding the existing *items()* loop within a *forEach* loop on the *groupedItems* object:

```
@Composable
fun MainScreen(itemArray: Array<out String>) {
    .
    .
    LazyColumn {
        groupedItems.forEach { (manufacturer, models) ->
            items(itemArray) { model ->
                MyListItem(item = model, onItemClick = onListItemClick)
            }
```

```
            }
        }
```
.

.

On each loop iteration, the *forEach* statement will call the trailing lambda, passing through the current selector value (manufacturer) and the items (models). Instead of displaying items from the ungrouped *itemArray*, the *items()* call now needs to be passed the *models* parameter:

```
items(models) { model ->
    MyListItem(item = model, onItemClick = onListItemClick)
}
```

Before we add sticky headers, compile and run the app to confirm that all the items still appear in the list as before.

35.3 Adding sticky headers

For each manufacturer group, we now need to display the header. This involves a call to the LazyListScope stickyHeader function. Although the content of the header can be any combination of composables, an appropriately configured Text component is usually more than adequate for most requirements:

.

.


```
import androidx.compose.ui.graphics.Color
```
.

.


```
LazyColumn() {

    groupedItems.forEach { (manufacturer, models) ->

        stickyHeader {
            Text(
                text = manufacturer,
                color = Color.White,
                modifier = Modifier
                    .background(Color.Gray)
                    .padding(5.dp)
                    .fillMaxWidth()
            )
        }

        items(models) { model ->
            MyListItem(item = model, onItemClick = onListItemClick)
        }
    }
}
```

If the code editor reports that stickyHeader is an experimental feature, mark the MainScreen function using the *ExperimentalFoundationApi* annotation as follows:

```
@OptIn(ExperimentalFoundationApi::class)
```

```
@Composable
fun MainScreen(itemArray: Array<out String>) {

.

.
```

After building and running the app, it should now appear as shown in Figure 35-1 with the manufacturer name appearing in the headers above each group:

Figure 35-1

35.4 Reacting to scroll position

In this, the final step of the LazyListDemo tutorial, the project will be modified to make use of scroll position detection. Once these changes have been made, scrolling beyond the item in list position 4 will display a button that, when clicked, returns the user to the top of the list.

The button will appear at the bottom of the screen and needs to be placed outside of the LazyColumn so that it does not scroll out of view. To achieve this, we first need to place the LazyColumn declaration within a Box component. Within *MainActivity.kt*, edit the MainScreen function so that it reads as follows:

```
@Composable
fun MainScreen(itemArray: Array<out String>) {

    val context = LocalContext.current
    val groupedItems = itemArray.groupBy { it.substringBefore(' ') }
```

```
   .
   .

     Box {
         LazyColumn() {

             groupedItems.forEach { (manufacturer, models) ->

   .

   .

         }

   .

   .

}
```

Next, we need to request a LazyListState instance and pass it to the LazyColumn. Now is also a good opportunity to obtain the coroutine scope which will be needed to perform the scroll when the button is clicked.

```
   .
   .

import androidx.compose.foundation.lazy.rememberLazyListState
import androidx.compose.runtime.rememberCoroutineScope

   .

   .

@Composable
fun MainScreen(itemArray: Array<out String>) {

    val listState = rememberLazyListState()
    val coroutineScope = rememberCoroutineScope()

   .

   .

    Box {
        LazyColumn(
            state = listState,
            contentPadding = PaddingValues(bottom = 40.dp)
        ) {

            groupedItems.forEach { (manufacturer, models) ->

   .

   .
```

In addition to applying the list state to the LazyColumn, the above changes also add padding to the bottom of the list. This will ensure that when the bottom of the list is reached there will be enough space for the button.

The visibility of the button will be controlled by a Boolean variable which we will name *displayButton*. The value of this variable will be derived using the *firstVisibleItemIndex* property of the list state:

```
@Composable
fun MainScreen(itemArray: Array<out String>) {

    val listState = rememberLazyListState()
```

```
val coroutineScope = rememberCoroutineScope()
val displayButton = listState.firstVisibleItemIndex > 5
.
.
```

In the above declaration, the *displayButton* variable will be false unless the index of the first visible list item is greater than 5.

35.5 Adding the scroll button

Now that code has been added to detect the list scroll position, the button needs to be added. This will be called within the Box component and will be represented by the OutlinedButton composable. The OutlinedButton is one of the Material Design components and allows buttons to be drawn with an outline border with other effects such as border stroke patterns and rounded corners.

Add an OutlinedButton inside the Box declaration and immediately after the LazyColumn:

```
.
.
import androidx.compose.material.*

import kotlinx.coroutines.launch
.
.

    Box {
        LazyColumn(
            state = listState
        ) {
.
.

                items(models) { model ->
                    MyListItem(item = model, onItemClick = onListItemClick)
                }
            }
        }

        OutlinedButton(
            onClick = {
                coroutineScope.launch {
                    listState.scrollToItem(0)
                }
            },
            border = BorderStroke(1.dp, Color.Gray),
            shape = RoundedCornerShape(50),
            colors = ButtonDefaults.outlinedButtonColors(
                            contentColor = Color.DarkGray),
            modifier = Modifier.padding(5.dp)
        ) {
            Text( text = "Top" )
```

```
            }
        }
    .
    .
```

Next, we need to control the position and visibility of the button so that it appears at the bottom center of the screen and is only visible when *displayButton* is true. This can be achieved by calling the OutlinedButton function from within an AnimatedVisibility composable, the purpose of which is to animate the hiding and showing of its child components (a topic covered in the chapter entitled *"Compose Visibility Animation"*). Make the following change to base the visibility of the OutlinedButton on the *displayButton* variable and to position it using CenterBottom alignment:

```
.
.
import androidx.compose.animation.AnimatedVisibility
.

        AnimatedVisibility(visible = displayButton,
                Modifier.align(Alignment.BottomCenter)) {
            OutlinedButton(
                onClick = {
                    coroutineScope.launch {
                        listState.scrollToItem(0)
                    }
                },
                border = BorderStroke(1.dp, Color.Gray),
                shape = RoundedCornerShape(40),
                colors = ButtonDefaults.outlinedButtonColors(
                                contentColor = Color.DarkGray),
                modifier = Modifier.padding(5.dp)
            ) {
                Text(text = "Top")
            }
        }
    .
    .
```

If the editor reports that the AnimatedVisibility composable is experimental, add the *ExperimentalAnimationApi* annotation to the Mainscreen function before proceeding:

```
@OptIn(ExperimentalFoundationApi::class, androidx.compose.animation.ExperimentalA
nimationApi::class)
@Composable
fun MainScreen(itemArray: Array<out String>) {
    .
    .
```

35.6 Testing the finished app

Compile and run the app one last time and, once running, scroll down the list until the button appears. Continue scrolling until the bottom of the list to check that enough bottom padding was added to the LazyColumn so that there is no overlap with the button as shown in Figure 35-2 below:

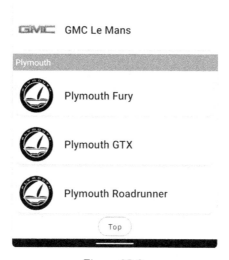

Figure 35-2

Click on the Top button to return to the top of the list.

35.7 Summary

This chapter completed the LazyListDemo project by adding support for sticky headers and scroll position detection. The tutorial also introduced the Material Theme OutlinedButton and the use of lazy list content padding.

Chapter 36

36. Compose Visibility Animation

For adding animation effects to user interfaces, Jetpack Compose includes the Animation API. The Animation API consists of classes and functions that provide a wide range of animation options that can be added to your apps with relative ease. In this chapter, we will explore the use of animation when hiding and showing user interface components including the use of cross fading when replacing one component with another. The next chapter, entitled *"Compose State-Driven Animation"*, will cover topics such as animating motion, rotation, and color changes, in addition to combining multiple animations into a single transition.

Throughout this chapter, each animation technique will be demonstrated within an example project.

36.1 Creating the AnimateVisibility project

Launch Android Studio and create a new *Empty Compose Activity* project named AnimateVisibility, specifying *com.example.animatevisibility* as the package name, and selecting a minimum API level of API 26: Android 8.0 (Oreo). Within the *MainActivity.kt* file, delete the Greeting function and add a new empty composable named MainScreen:

```
@Composable
fun MainScreen() {


}
```

Next, edit the *onCreateActivity()* method and DefaultPreview function to call MainScreen instead of Greeting. Also, enable the system UI option on the preview composable:

```
@Preview(showBackground = true, showSystemUi = true)
@Composable
fun DefaultPreview() {
    AnimateVisibilityTheme {
        MainScreen()
    }
}
```

36.2 Animating visibility

Perhaps the simplest form of animation involves animating the appearance and disappearance of a composable. Instead of a component instantly appearing and disappearing, a variety of animated effects can be applied using the AnimatedVisibility composable. For example, user interface elements can be made to gradually fade in and out of view, slide into and out of position horizontally or vertically, or show and hide by expanding and shrinking.

The minimum requirement for calling AnimatedVisibility is a Boolean state variable parameter to control whether or not its child composables are to be visible. Before exploring the capabilities of AnimatedVisibility, it first helps to experience the hiding and showing of a composable without animation.

When the following layout design is complete, two buttons will be used to show and hide content using animation. Before designing the screen layout, add a new composable named CustomButton to the *MainActivity.kt* file as follows:

Compose Visibility Animation

.

.

```
import androidx.compose.material.*
import androidx.compose.ui.graphics.Color
```

.

.

```
@Composable
fun CustomButton(text: String, targetState: Boolean,
        onClick: (Boolean) -> Unit, bgColor: Color = Color.Blue) {

    Button(
        onClick = { onClick(targetState) },
        colors= ButtonDefaults.buttonColors(backgroundColor = bgColor,
                        contentColor = Color.White)) {
        Text(text)
    }
}
```

The composable is passed the text to be displayed on the button and both an onClick handler and the new state value to be passed to the handler when the button is clicked. The button also accepts an optional background color which defaults to blue.

Next, locate the MainScreen function and modify it as follows:

.

.

```
import androidx.compose.foundation.background
import androidx.compose.foundation.layout.*
import androidx.compose.ui.unit.dp
import androidx.compose.ui.Alignment
import androidx.compose.runtime.*
```

.

.

```
@Composable
fun MainScreen() {

    var boxVisible by remember { mutableStateOf(true) }

    val onClick = { newState : Boolean ->
        boxVisible = newState
    }

    Column(
        Modifier.padding(20.dp),
        horizontalAlignment = Alignment.CenterHorizontally
    ) {
        Row(
```

```
            Modifier.fillMaxWidth(),
            horizontalArrangement = Arrangement.SpaceEvenly
        ) {
            CustomButton(text = "Show", targetState = true, onClick = onClick)
            CustomButton(text = "Hide", targetState = false, onClick = onClick)
        }

        Spacer(modifier = Modifier.height(20.dp))

        if (boxVisible) {
            Box(modifier = Modifier
                .size(height = 200.dp, width = 200.dp)
                .background(Color.Blue))
        }
    }
}
```

In summary, this code begins by declaring a Boolean state variable named *boxVisible* with an initial true value and an onClick event handler to be passed to instances of the CustomButton composable. The purpose of the handler is to change the *boxVisible* state based on button selection.

Column and Row composables are then used to display two CustomButton composables and a blue Box. The buttons are passed the text to be displayed, the new setting for the *boxVisible* state, and a reference to the onClick handler. When a button is clicked, it calls the handler and passes it the new state value. Finally, an *if* statement is used to control whether the Box composable is included as a child of the Column based on the value of *boxVisible*.

When previewed in interactive mode, or tested on a device or emulator, the layout will appear as illustrated in Figure 36-1:

Figure 36-1

Clicking on the Show and Hide buttons will cause the Box to instantly appear and disappear without any animation effects. Default visibility animation effects can be added simply by replacing the *if* statement with a call to AnimatedVisibility as follows:

.

.

```
import androidx.compose.animation.*
```

.

.

```
    AnimatedVisibility(visible = boxVisible) {
        Box(modifier = Modifier
            .size(height = 200.dp, width = 200.dp)
            .background(Color.Blue))
    }
```

.

.

If the code editor reports that AnimatedVisibility is an experimental feature, add the following annotation to the MainScreen composable:

```
@OptIn(ExperimentalAnimationApi::class)
@Composable
fun MainScreen() {
```

.

.

When the app is now tested, the hiding and showing of the box will be subtly animated. The default behavior of AnimatedVisibility is so subtle it can be difficult to notice any difference. Fortunately, the Compose Animation API provides a range of customization options. The first option allows different animation effects to be defined when the child composables appear and disappear (referred to as the *enter* and *exit* animations).

36.3 Defining enter and exit animations

The animations to be used when children of an AnimatedVisibility composable appear and disappear are declared using the *enter* and *exit* parameters. The following changes, for example, configure the animations to fade the box into view and slide it vertically out of view:

```
AnimatedVisibility(visible = boxVisible,
    enter = fadeIn(),
    exit = slideOutVertically()
) {

    Box(modifier = Modifier
        .size(height = 200.dp, width = 200.dp)
        .background(Color.Blue))
    }
}
```

The full set of animation effects is as follows:

- **expandHorizontally()** - Content is revealed using a horizontal clipping technique. Options are available to control how much of the content is initially revealed before the animation begins.

- **expandVertically()** - Content is revealed using a vertical clipping technique. Options are available to control how much of the content is initially revealed before the animation begins.

- **expandIn()** - Content is revealed using both horizontal and vertical clipping techniques. Options are available to control how much of the content is initially revealed before the animation begins.

- **fadeIn()** - Fades the content into view from transparent to opaque. The initial transparency (alpha) may be declared using a floating-point value between 0 and 1.0. The default is 0.

- **fadeOut()** - Fades the content out of view from opaque to invisible. The target transparency before the content disappears may be declared using a floating-point value between 0 and 1.0. The default is 0.

- **scaleIn()** - The content expands into view as though a "zoom in" has been performed. By default, the content starts at zero size and expands to full size though this default can be changed by specifying the initial scale value as a float value between 0 and 1.0.

- **scaleOut()** - Shrinks the content from full size to a specified target scale before it disappears. The target scale is 0 by default but may be configured using a float value between 0 and 1.0.

- **shrinkHorizontally()** - Content slides from view behind a shrinking vertical clip bounds line. The target width and direction may be configured.

- **shrinkVertically()** - Content slides from view behind a shrinking horizontal clip bounds line. The target width and direction may be configured.

- **shrinkOut()** - Content slides from view behind shrinking horizontal and vertical clip bounds lines.

- **slideInHorizontally()** - Content slides into view along the horizontal axis. The sliding direction and offset within the content where sliding begins are both customizable.

- **slideInVertically()** - Content slides into view along the vertical axis. The sliding direction and offset within the content where sliding begins are both customizable.

- **slideIn()** - Slides the content into view at a customizable angle defined using an initial offset value.

- **slideOut()** - Slides the content out of view at a customizable angle defined using a target offset value.

- **slideOutHorizontally()** - Content slides out of view along the horizontal axis. The sliding direction and offset within the content where sliding ends are both customizable.

- **slideOutVertically()** - Content slides out of view along the vertical axis. The sliding direction and offset within the content where sliding ends are both customizable.

It is also possible to combine animation effects. The following, for example, combines the expandHorizontally and fadeIn effects:

```
AnimatedVisibility(visible = boxVisible,
    enter = fadeIn() + expandHorizontally(),
    exit = slideOutVertically()
) {
.
.
```

All of the above animations may be further customized by making use of *animation specs*.

36.4 Animation specs and animation easing

Animation specs are represented by instances of AnimationSpec, (or, more specifically, subclasses of AnimationSpec) and are used to configure aspects of animation behavior including the animation duration, start delay, spring, and bounce effects, repetition, and animation easing.

Compose Visibility Animation

As with Rows, Columns, and other container composables, AnimatedVisibility has its own scope (named AnimatedVisibilityScope). Within this scope, we have access to additional functions specific to animation. For example, to control the duration of an animation, we need to generate a DurationBasedAnimationSpec instance (a subclass of AnimationSpec) by calling the *tween()* function and passing it as a parameter to the animation effect function call. For example, modify our example *fadeIn()* call to pass through a duration specification:

.

.

```
import androidx.compose.animation.core.*
```
.

.

```
AnimatedVisibility(visible = boxVisible,
    enter = fadeIn(animationSpec = tween(durationMillis = 5000)),
    exit = slideOutVertically()
) {
```
.

.

Update the preview and hide and show the box, noting that the fade-in animation is now slow enough that we can see it.

The *tween()* function also allows us to specify animation easing. Animation easing allows the animation to speed up and slow down and can be defined either using custom *keyframe* positions for speed changes (a topic which will be covered in *"Compose State-Driven Animation"*) or using one of the following predefined values:

- FastOutSlowInEasing

- LinearOutSlowInEasing

- FastOutLinearEasing

- LinearEasing

- CubicBezierEasing

The following change uses LinearOutSlowInEasing easing for a slideInHorizontally effect:

```
AnimatedVisibility(visible = boxVisible,
    enter = slideInHorizontally(animationSpec =
                tween(durationMillis = 5000, easing = LinearOutSlowInEasing)),
    exit = slideOutVertically()
) {
```

When the box is shown, the animation gradually slows as it reaches the target position. Similarly, the following change bases the animation speed changes on four points within a Bezier curve:

```
AnimatedVisibility(visible = boxVisible,
    enter = slideInHorizontally(animationSpec = tween(durationMillis = 5000,
                    easing = CubicBezierEasing(0f, 1f, 0.5f,1f))),
    exit = slideOutVertically(),
) {
```

36.5 Repeating an animation

To make an animation repeat, we also need to use an animation spec, though in this case the RepeatableSpec subclass will be used, an instance of which can be obtained using the *repeatable()* function. In addition to the animation to be repeated, the function also accepts a RepeatMode parameter specifying whether the repetition should be performed from beginning to end (RepeatMode.Restart) or reversed from end to beginning (RepeatMode.Reverse) of the animation sequence. For example, modify the AnimatedVisibility call to repeat a fade-in enter animation 10 times using the reverse repeat mode:

```
AnimatedVisibility(visible = boxVisible,
    enter = fadeIn(
        animationSpec = repeatable(10, animation = tween(durationMillis = 2000),
                                    repeatMode = RepeatMode.Reverse)
    ),
    exit = slideOutVertically(),
.
.
```

36.6 Different animations for different children

When enter and exit animations are applied to an AnimatedVisibility call, those settings apply to all direct and indirect children. Specific animations may be added to individual children by applying the *animateEnterExit()* modifier to them. As is the case with AnimatedVisibility, this modifier allows both enter and exit animations to be declared. The following changes add vertical sliding animations on both entry and exit to the red Box call:

```
AnimatedVisibility(
    visible = boxVisible,
    enter = fadeIn(animationSpec = tween(durationMillis = 5500)),
    exit = fadeOut(animationSpec = tween(durationMillis = 5500))
) {
    Row {
        Box(Modifier.size(width = 150.dp, height = 150.dp)
                        .background(Color.Blue)
        )
        Spacer(modifier = Modifier.width(20.dp))
        Box(
            Modifier
                .animateEnterExit(
                    enter = slideInVertically(
                        animationSpec = tween(durationMillis = 5500)),
                    exit = slideOutVertically(
                        animationSpec = tween(durationMillis = 5500))
                )
                .size(width = 150.dp, height = 150.dp)
                .background(Color.Red)
        )
    }
}
```

When the above code runs, you will notice that the red box uses both fade and sliding animations. This is because the *animateEnterExit()* modifier animations are combined with those passed to the parent AnimatedVisibility instance. For example, the enter animation in the above example is equivalent to *fadeIn(...) + slideInVertically(...)*. If you only want the modifier animations to be used, the enter and exit settings for the parent AnimatedVisibility instance must be set to *EnterTransition.None* and *ExitTransition.None* respectively. In the following code, animation (including the default animation) is disabled on the parent so that only those specified by a call to the *animateEnterExit()* modifier are performed:

```
AnimatedVisibility(
    visible = boxVisible,
    enter = EnterTransition.None,
    exit = ExitTransition.None
) {
    Row {
        Box(
            Modifier
                .animateEnterExit(
                    enter = fadeIn(animationSpec = tween(durationMillis = 5500)),
                    exit = fadeOut(animationSpec = tween(durationMillis = 5500))
                )
                .size(width = 150.dp, height = 150.dp)
                .background(Color.Blue))
        Spacer(modifier = Modifier.width(20.dp))
        Box(
            Modifier
                .animateEnterExit(
                    enter = slideInVertically(
                            animationSpec = tween(durationMillis = 5500)),
                    exit = slideOutVertically(
                            animationSpec = tween(durationMillis = 5500))
                )
                .size(width = 150.dp, height = 150.dp)
                .background(Color.Red)
        )
    }
}
```

36.7 Auto-starting an animation

So far in this chapter, animations have been initiated in response to button click events. It is not unusual, however, to need an animation to begin as soon as the call to AnimatedVisibility is made. To trigger this, AnimatedVisibility can be passed a MutableTransitionState instance when it is called.

MutableTransitionState is a special purpose state which includes two properties named currentState and targetState. By default, both the current and target states are set to the same value which, in turn, is defined by passing through an *initial state* when the MutableTransitionState instance is created. The following, for example, creates a transition state initialized to false and passes it through to the AnimatedVisibility call via the visibleState parameter:

.

.

```
val state = remember {  MutableTransitionState(false)  }
```

```
    AnimatedVisibility(visibleState = state,
        enter = fadeIn(
            animationSpec = tween(5000)
        ),
        exit = slideOutVertically(),

    ) {
```

When tested, the Box composable will not appear until the show button is clicked because the initial state is set to false. To initiate the "enter" fade-in animation, we need to set the targetState property of the transition state instance to true when it is created. We do this by calling *apply()* on the state instance and setting the property in the trailing lambda as follows:

```
val state = remember { MutableTransitionState(true) }
```

```
state.apply { targetState = true }
```

Now when the app is run the fade-in animation starts automatically without user interaction.

36.8 Implementing crossfading

Crossfading animates the replacement of one composable with another and is performed using the Crossfade function. This function is passed a *target state* value that is used to decide which composable is to replace the currently visible component. A fading animation effect is then used to perform the replacement.

In our example app, we currently display both the show and hide buttons. In practice, only one of these buttons needs to be visible at any one time depending on the current visibility state of the Box component. It is not necessary, for example, to display the show button when the content is already visible. This is an ideal candidate for using cross fading to transition from one button to the other. To do this, we need to enclose the two CustomButton composables within a Crossfade call, passing through the *boxVisible* state value as the target state. We can then add some logic within the Crossfade lambda to decide which button is to be visible.

To implement this behavior, modify the MainScreen function so that it reads as follows:

```
fun MainScreen() {

    var boxVisible by remember { mutableStateOf(true) }

    val onClick = { newState : Boolean ->
        boxVisible = newState
    }

    Column(
        Modifier.padding(20.dp),
        horizontalAlignment = Alignment.CenterHorizontally
    ) {
        Row(
            Modifier.fillMaxWidth(),
```

```
            horizontalArrangement = Arrangement.SpaceEvenly
    ) {


        Crossfade(
            targetState = boxVisible,
            animationSpec = tween(5000)
        ) { visible ->
            when (visible) {
                true -> CustomButton(text = "Hide", targetState = false,
                        onClick = onClick, bgColor = Color.Red)
                false -> CustomButton(text = "Show", targetState = true,
                        onClick = onClick, bgColor = Color.Magenta)

            }

        }

    }
```

.

.

To enhance the effect of the crossfade, the above code also changes the background colors of the two buttons. We also use a *when* statement to decide which button to display based on the current *boxVisible* value.

Test the layout and check that clicking on the Show button initiates a crossfade to the Hide button and vice versa.

36.9 Summary

This chapter has explored the use of the Compose Animation API to animate the appearance and disappearance of components within a user interface layout. This requires the use of the *animatedVisibility()* function which may be configured to use different animation effects and durations, both for the appearance and disappearance of the target composable. The Animation API also includes crossfade support which allows the replacement of one component with another to be animated.

37. Compose State-Driven Animation

The previous chapter focused on using animation when hiding and showing user interface components. In this chapter, we will turn our attention to state-driven animation. The features of the Compose Animation API allow a variety of animation effects to be performed based on the change of state from one value to another. This includes animations such as rotation, motion, and color changes to name just a few options. This chapter will explain the concepts of state-driven animation, introduce the *animate as state* functions, spring effects, and keyframes, and explore the use of transitions to combine multiple animations.

37.1 Understanding state-driven animation

We already know from previous chapters that working with state is a key element of Compose-based app development. Invariably, the way that an app appears, behaves, and responds to user input are all manifestations of changes to and of state occurring behind the scenes. Using the Compose Animation API, state changes can also be used as the basis for animation effects. If a state change transforms the appearance, position, orientation, or size of a component in a layout, there is a good chance that visual transformation can be animated using one or more of the animate as state functions.

37.2 Introducing animate as state functions

The animate as state functions are also referred to as the *animate*AsState* functions. The reason for this is that the functions all use the same naming convention whereby the '*' wildcard is replaced by the type of the state value that is triggering the animation. For example, if you need to animate the background color change of a composable, you will need to use the *animateColorAsState()* function. At the time of writing, Compose provides state animation functions for Bounds, Color, Dp, Float, Int, IntOffset, IntSize, Offset, Rect, and Size data types which cover most animation requirements.

These functions animate the results of changes to a single state value. In basic terms, the function is given a target state value and then animates the change from the current value to the target value. The functions return special state values that can be used as properties for composables. Consider the following code fragment:

```
var temperature by remember { mutableStateOf(80) }

val animatedColor: Color by animateColorAsState(
    targetValue = if (temperature > 92) {
        Color.Red
    } else {
        Color.Green
    },
    animationSpec = tween(4500)
)
```

The above code declares a state variable named *temperature* initialized with a value of 80. Next, a call is made to animateColorAsState which uses the current temperature setting to decide whether the color should be red or green. Note that the animate as state functions also accept an animation spec, in this case, a duration of 4500 milliseconds. The *animatedColor* state can now be assigned as a color property for any composable in the layout. In the following code example it is used to control the background color of a Box composable:

```
Box(
    Modifier.size(width = 20.dp, height = 200.dp)
        .background(animatedColor)
)
```

If the temperature state value exceeds 92 at any point during execution, the background color of the Box will transition from green to red using the declared animation.

In the remainder of this chapter, we will create some more state-driven animation examples. Finally, we will close out the chapter by demonstrating the use of the *updateTransition()* function to combine multiple animations.

37.3 Creating the AnimateState project

Launch Android Studio and create a new *Empty Compose Activity* project named AnimateState, specifying *com.example.animatestate* as the package name, and selecting a minimum API level of API 26: Android 8.0 (Oreo). Within the *MainActivity.kt* file, delete the Greeting function and add a new empty composable named RotationDemo:

```
@Composable
fun RotationDemo() {

}
```

Next, edit the *onCreateActivity()* method and DefaultPreview function to call RotationDemo instead of Greeting.

37.4 Animating rotation with animateFloatAsState

In this first example, we will animate the rotation of an Image component. Since rotation angle in Compose is declared as a Float value, the animation will be created using the *animateFloatAsState()* function. Before writing code, a vector image needs to be added to the project. The image file is named *propeller.svg* and can be located in the *images* folder of the sample code download available from the following URL:

https://www.ebookfrenzy.com/retail/compose/index.php

Within Android Studio, display the Resource Manager tool window (*View -> Tool Windows -> Resource Manager*). Locate the *propeller.svg* image in the file system navigator for your operating system and drag and drop it onto the Resource Manager tool window. In the resulting dialog, click Next followed by the Import button to add the image to the project. The image should now appear in the Resource Manager as shown in Figure 37-1 below:

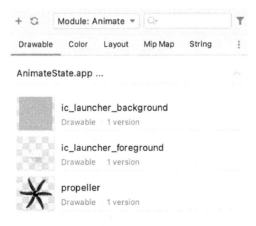

Figure 37-1

The image will also appear in the *res -> drawables* section of the Project tool window:

Figure 37-2

Edit the *MainActivity.kt* file and modify the RotationDemo function to design the user interface layout:

```kotlin
.
.
import androidx.compose.foundation.Image
import androidx.compose.foundation.layout.*
import androidx.compose.material.Button
import androidx.compose.runtime.*
import androidx.compose.ui.Alignment
import androidx.compose.ui.draw.rotate
import androidx.compose.ui.res.painterResource
import androidx.compose.ui.unit.dp
.
.
@Composable
fun RotationDemo() {

    var rotated by remember { mutableStateOf(false) }

    Column(horizontalAlignment = Alignment.CenterHorizontally,
                    modifier = Modifier.fillMaxWidth()) {
        Image(
            painter = painterResource(R.drawable.propeller),
            contentDescription = "fan",
            modifier = Modifier
                .padding(10.dp)
                .size(300.dp)
        )

        Button(
            onClick = { rotated = !rotated },
            modifier = Modifier.padding(10.dp)
        ) {
            Text(text = "Rotate Propeller")
        }
    }
}
```

Compose State-Driven Animation

The layout consists of a Column containing an Image configured to display the propeller drawing and a Button. The code includes a Boolean state variable named *rotated*, the value of which is toggled via the Button's onClick handler.

When previewed, the layout should resemble that illustrated in Figure 37-3 below:

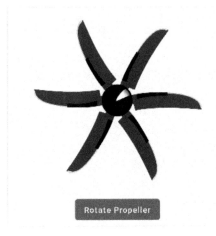

Figure 37-3

Although the button changes the *rotation* state value, that state has not yet been connected with an animation. We now need to make use of the *animateFloatAsState()* function by adding the following code:

```
.
.
import androidx.compose.animation.core.*
.
.
@Composable
fun RotationDemo() {

    var rotated by remember { mutableStateOf(false) }

    val angle by animateFloatAsState(
        targetValue = if (rotated) 360f else 0f,
        animationSpec = tween(durationMillis = 2500)
    )
.
.
```

Next, edit the Image declaration and pass the angle state through to the *rotate()* modifier as follows:

```
Image(
    painter = painterResource(R.drawable.propeller),
    contentDescription = "fan",
    modifier = Modifier
        .rotate(angle)
        .padding(10.dp)
        .size(300.dp)
```

)

This code calls *animateFloatAsState()* and assigns the resulting state value to a variable named *angle*. If the *rotated* value is currently set to true, then the target value for the animation is set to 360 degrees, otherwise, it is set to 0. All that remains now is to test the activity. Using either the Preview panel in interactive mode or an emulator or physical device for testing, click on the button. The propeller should rotate 360 degrees in the clockwise direction. A second click will rotate the propeller back to 0 degrees.

The rotation animation is currently using the default FastOutSlowInEasing easing setting where the animation rate slows as the propeller nears the end of the rotation. To see the other easing options outlined in the previous chapter in action, simply add them to the *tween()* call. The following change, for example, animates the rotation at a constant speed:

```
animationSpec = tween(durationMillis = 2500, easing = LinearEasing)
```

37.5 Animating color changes with animateColorAsState

In this example, we will look at animating color changes using the *animateColorAsState()* function. In this case, the layout will consist of a Box and Button pair. When the Button is clicked the Box will transition from one color to another using an animation. In preparation for this example, we will need to add an enumeration to the *MainActivity.kt* file to provide the two background color options. Edit the file and place the enum declaration after the MainActivity class:

```
.

.

enum class BoxColor {
    Red, Magenta
}


@Composable
fun RotationDemo() {

.

.
```

Add a new composable function to the *MainActivity.kt* file named ColorChangeDemo together with an @ Preview function so that it will appear in the Preview panel:

```
.

.

import androidx.compose.foundation.background
import androidx.compose.ui.graphics.Color

.

.

@Composable
fun ColorChangeDemo() {

    var colorState by remember { mutableStateOf(BoxColor.Red) }

    Column(horizontalAlignment = Alignment.CenterHorizontally,
            modifier = Modifier.fillMaxWidth()) {
        Box(
            modifier = Modifier
```

```
                .padding(20.dp)
                .size(200.dp)
                .background(Color.Red)
        )

        Button(
            onClick = {
                colorState = when (colorState) {
                    BoxColor.Red -> BoxColor.Magenta
                    BoxColor.Magenta -> BoxColor.Red
                }
            },
            modifier = Modifier.padding(10.dp)
        ) {
            Text(text = "Change Color")
        }
    }
}


@Preview(showBackground = true)
@Composable
fun ColorChangePreview() {
    AnimateStateTheme {
        ColorChangeDemo()
    }
}
.

.
```

Exit interactive mode, preview the layout and confirm that it resembles that shown in Figure 37-4:

Figure 37-4

The BoxColor enumeration contains two possible color selections, Red and Magenta. A state variable named *colorState* is declared and initialized to BoxColor.Red. Next, the Button onClick handler uses a *when* statement to toggle the *colorState* value between the Red and Magenta BoxColor enumeration values.

The ColorChangeDemo function now needs to use the *animateColorAsState()* function to implement and animate the Box background color change. The Box also needs to be modified to use the *animatedColor* state as the background color value:

```
import androidx.compose.animation.animateColorAsState

@Composable
fun ColorChangeDemo() {

    var colorState by remember { mutableStateOf(BoxColor.Red) }

    val animatedColor: Color by animateColorAsState(
        targetValue = when (colorState) {
                BoxColor.Red -> Color.Magenta
                BoxColor.Magenta -> Color.Red
        },
        animationSpec = tween(4500)
    )

    Column(horizontalAlignment = Alignment.CenterHorizontally,
            modifier = Modifier.fillMaxWidth()) {
        Box(
            modifier = Modifier
                .padding(20.dp)
                .size(200.dp)
                .background(animatedColor)
        )
    }
```

The code uses the current *colorState* color value to set the animation target value to the other color. This triggers the animated color change which is performed over a 4500-millisecond duration. Stop the current interactive session in the Preview panel if it is still running (only one preview can be in interactive mode at a time), locate the new composable preview, and run it in interactive mode. Once the preview is running, use the button to try out the color change animation.

37.6 Animating motion with animateDpAsState

In this, final example before looking at the *updateTransition()* function, we will use the *animateDpAsState()* function to animate the change in position of a composable. This will involve changing the x position offset of a component and animating the change as it moves to the new location on the screen. Using the same steps as before, add another composable function, this time named MotionDemo, together with a matching preview composable. As with the color change example, we also need an enumeration to contain the position options:

```
enum class BoxPosition {
    Start, End
```

```
}

@Composable
fun MotionDemo() {

    var boxState by remember { mutableStateOf(BoxPosition.Start)}
    val boxSideLength = 70.dp

    Column(modifier = Modifier.fillMaxWidth()) {
        Box(
            modifier = Modifier
                .offset(x = 0.dp, y = 20.dp)
                .size(boxSideLength)
                .background(Color.Red)
        )

        Spacer(modifier = Modifier.height(50.dp))

        Button(
            onClick = {
                boxState = when (boxState) {
                    BoxPosition.Start -> BoxPosition.End
                    BoxPosition.End -> BoxPosition.Start
                }
            },
            modifier = Modifier.padding(20.dp)
                .align(Alignment.CenterHorizontally)
        ) {
            Text(text = "Move Box")
        }
    }
}


@Preview(showBackground = true)
@Composable
fun MotionDemoPreview() {
    AnimateStateTheme {
        MotionDemo()
    }
}
```

This example is structured in much the same way as the color change animation except that this time we are working with density-independent pixel values instead of colors. The end goal is to animate the movement of the Box from the start of the screen to the end. Assuming that the code will potentially run on a variety of devices and screen sizes, we need to know the width of the screen to be able to find the end position. This information can be found by accessing properties of the LocalConfiguration instance. This is an object that is local to each Compose-based app and provides access to properties such as screen width, height and density, font scale information, and whether or not night mode is currently activated on the device. For this example we only need to know the width of the screen which can be obtained as follows:

```
.
.
import androidx.compose.ui.platform.LocalConfiguration
.
.
@Composable
fun MotionDemo() {

    val screenWidth = (LocalConfiguration.current.screenWidthDp.dp)
.
.
```

Next, we need to add the animation using the *animateDpAsState()* function:

```
.
.
import androidx.compose.ui.unit.Dp
.
.
@Composable
fun MotionDemo() {

    val screenWidth = (LocalConfiguration.current.screenWidthDp.dp)
    var boxState by remember { mutableStateOf(BoxPosition.Start)}
    val boxSideLength = 70.dp

    val animatedOffset: Dp by animateDpAsState(
        targetValue = when (boxState) {
            BoxPosition.Start -> 0.dp
            BoxPosition.End -> screenWidth - boxSideLength
        },
        animationSpec = tween(500)
    )
.
.
```

In the above code, the target state is set to either the start or end of the screen width, depending on the current boxState setting. In the case of the end position, the width of the Box is subtracted from the screen width so that the motion does not move beyond the edge of the screen.

Now that we have the *animatedOffset* state declared, we can pass it through as the x parameter to the Box *offset()* modifier call:

```
Box(
    modifier = Modifier
        .offset(x = animatedOffset, y = 20.dp)
```

```
        .size(boxSides)
        .background(Color.Red)
)
```

When the code is previewed in interactive mode, clicking the button should now cause the box to be animated as it moves back and forth across the screen.

37.7 Adding spring effects

The above example provides an ideal opportunity to introduce the spring animation effect. Spring behavior adds a bounce effect to animations and is applied using the *spring()* function via the animationSpec parameter. To understand the spring effect it helps to imagine one end of a spring attached to the animation start point (for example the left side of the screen or parent) and the other end attached to the corresponding side of the box. As the box moves, the spring stretches until the endpoint is reached, at which point the box bounces a few times on the string before finally resting at the endpoint.

The two key parameters to the *spring()* function are *damping ratio* and *stiffness*. The damping ratio defines the speed at which the bouncing effect decays and is declared as a Float value where 1.0 has no bounce and 0.1 is the highest bounce. Instead of using Float values, the following predefined constants are also available when configuring the damping ratio:

- DampingRatioHighBouncy

- DampingRatioLowBouncy

- DampingRatioMediumBouncy

- DampingRatioNoBouncy

To add a spring effect to the motion animation, add a *spring()* function call to the animation as follows:

```
.
  .
import androidx.compose.animation.core.Spring.DampingRatioHighBouncy
  .
  .
val animatedOffset: Dp by animateDpAsState(
    targetValue = when (boxState) {
        BoxPosition.Start -> 0.dp
        BoxPosition.End -> screenWidth - boxSideLength
    },
    animationSpec = spring(dampingRatio = DampingRatioHighBouncy)
)
```

When tested, the box will now bounce when it reaches the target destination.

The stiffness parameter defines the strength of the spring. When using a lower stiffness, the range of motion of the bouncing effect will be greater. The following, for example, combines a high bounce damping ratio with very low stiffness. The result is an animation that is so bouncy that the box bounces beyond the edge of the screen a few times before finally coming to rest at the endpoint:

```
.
  .
import androidx.compose.animation.core.Spring.StiffnessVeryLow
```

.

.

```
val animatedOffset: Dp by animateDpAsState(
    targetValue = when (boxState) {
        BoxPosition.Start -> 0.dp
        BoxPosition.End -> screenWidth - boxSides
    },
    spring(dampingRatio = DampingRatioHighBouncy, stiffness = StiffnessVeryLow)
)
```

The stiffness of the spring effect can be adjusted using the following constants:

- StiffnessHigh

- StiffnessLow

- StiffnessMedium

- StiffnessMediumLow

- StiffnessVeryLow

Take some time to experiment with the different damping and stiffness settings to learn more about the effects they produce.

37.8 Working with keyframes

Keyframes allow different duration and easing values to be applied at specific points in an animation timeline. Keyframes are applied to animation via the animationSpec parameter and defined using the *keyframes()* function which accepts a lambda containing the keyframe data and returns a KeyframesSpec instance.

A keyframe specification begins by declaring the total required duration for the entire animation to complete. That duration is then marked by timestamps declaring how much of the total animation should be completed at that point based on the state unit type (for example Float, Dp, Int, etc.). These timestamps are created via calls to the *at()* function.

As an example, edit the *animateDpAsState()* function call to add a keyframe specification to the animation as follows:

```
val animatedOffset: Dp by animateDpAsState(
    targetValue = when (boxState) {
        BoxPosition.Start -> 0.dp
        BoxPosition.End -> screenWidth - boxSides
    },
    animationSpec = keyframes {
        durationMillis = 1000
        100.dp.at(10)
        110.dp.at(500)
        200.dp.at(700)
    }
)
```

This keyframe declares a 1000 millisecond duration for the entire animation. This duration is then divided by three timestamps. The first timestamp occurs 10 milliseconds into the animation, at which point the offset value must have reached 100dp. At 500 milliseconds the offset must be 110dp and, finally, 200dp by the time 700 milliseconds have elapsed. This leaves 300 milliseconds to complete the remainder animation.

Try out the animation and observe the changes in the speed of the animation as each timestamp is reached.

The animation behavior can be further configured using the *with()* function to add easing settings to the timestamps, for example:

```
animationSpec = keyframes {
    durationMillis = 1000
    100.dp.at(10).with(LinearEasing)
    110.dp.at(500).with(FastOutSlowInEasing)
    200.dp.at(700).with(LinearOutSlowInEasing)
}
```

37.9 Combining multiple animations

Multiple animations can be run in parallel based on a single target state using the *updateTransition()* function. This function is passed the target state and returns a Transition instance to which multiple child animations may be added. When the target state changes, the transition will run all of the child animations concurrently. The *updateTransition()* call may also be passed an optional label parameter which can be used to identify the transition within the Animation Inspector (a topic that will be covered in the next section).

A Transition object configured to trigger its child animations in response to changes to a state variable named *myState* would typically be declared as follows:

```
val transition = updateTransition(targetState = myState,
                                  label = "My Transition")
```

The Transition class includes a collection of functions that are used to add animation to children. These functions use the naming convention of *animate<Type>()* depending on the unit type used for the animation such as *animateFloat()*, *animateDp()* and *animationColor()*. The syntax for these functions is as follows:

```
val myAnimation: <Type> by transition.animate<Type>(

    transitionSpec = {
        // anination spec (tween, spring etc)
    }

) { state ->
    // Code to identify new target state based on current state
}
```

To demonstrate updateTransitions in action, we will modify the example to perform both the color change and motion animations based on changes to the boxState value. Begin by adding a new function named TransitionDemo together with a corresponding preview composable (undefined symbol errors will be corrected in the next steps):

```
@Composable
fun TransitionDemo() {
    var boxState by remember { mutableStateOf(BoxPosition.Start)}
    var screenWidth = LocalConfiguration.current.screenWidthDp.dp
```

```
        Column(modifier = Modifier.fillMaxWidth()) {
            Box(
                modifier = Modifier
                    .offset(x = animatedOffset, y = 20.dp)
                    .size(70.dp)
                    .background(animatedColor)
            )
            Spacer(modifier = Modifier.height(50.dp))

            Button(
                onClick = {
                    boxState = when (boxState) {
                        BoxPosition.Start -> BoxPosition.End
                        BoxPosition.End -> BoxPosition.Start
                    }
                },
                modifier = Modifier.padding(20.dp)
                    .align(Alignment.CenterHorizontally)
            ) {
                Text(text = "Start Animation")
            }
        }
    }
}


@Preview(showBackground = true)
@Composable
fun TransitionDemoPreview() {
    AnimateStateTheme {
        TransitionDemo()
    }
}
```

Next, edit the new function to obtain a Transition instance configured to react to changes to *boxState*:

```
@Composable
fun TransitionDemo() {
    var boxState by remember { mutableStateOf(BoxPosition.Start)}
    val screenWidth = LocalConfiguration.current.screenWidthDp.dp
    val transition = updateTransition(targetState = boxState,
                label = "Color and Motion")
    .
    .
```

Finally, add the color and motion animations to the transition:

```
    .
    .
import androidx.compose.animation.animateColor
```

```
.

.

@Composable
fun TransitionDemo() {
.

.

    val transition = updateTransition(targetState = boxState,
                label = "Color and Motion")

    val animatedColor: Color by transition.animateColor(

        transitionSpec = {
            tween(4000)
        }

    ) { state ->
        when (state) {
            BoxPosition.Start -> Color.Red
            BoxPosition.End -> Color.Magenta
        }
    }


    val animatedOffset: Dp by transition.animateDp(

        transitionSpec = {
            tween(4000)
        }
    ) { state ->
        when (state) {
            BoxPosition.Start -> 0.dp
            BoxPosition.End -> screenWidth - 70.dp
        }
    }
.

.
```

When previewed, the box should change color as it moves across the screen.

37.10 Using the Animation Inspector

The Animation Inspector is a tool built into Android Studio that allows you to interact directly with the animation timeline and manually scroll back and forth through the animation sequences. The inspector is only available when a Transition-based animation is present and is accessed using the button highlighted in Figure 37-5 below:

Figure 37-5

If this button is not visible, select the *File -> Settings...* menu option (*Android Studio -> Preferences...* on macOS), click on the Experimental option and switch on the *Enable animation preview* option

Once enabled, the inspector panel will appear beneath the preview panel as illustrated in Figure 37-6:

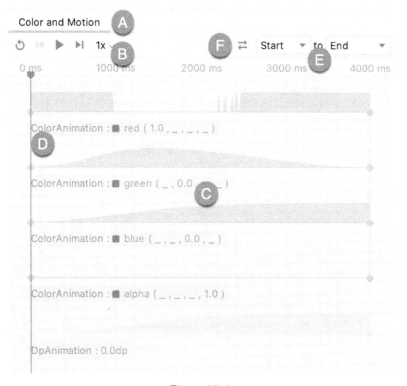

Figure 37-6

The area marked A contains tabs for each transition in the current source file. Since our example only contains a single transition, there is only one tab in the above image. Since a label was passed to the *updateTransition()* function call, this is displayed as the tab title.

The toolbar (B) provides options to play the animation, jump to the start or end of the timeline, loop repeatedly through the animation, and change the animation playback speed.

Compose State-Driven Animation

The transition's animation children are listed in the timeline panel (C). The blue vertical line (D) indicates the current position in the timeline which can be dragged to manually move through the animation. Finally, the drop-down menus (E) can be used to change the direction of the animation. Note that the options listed in these menus are taken from the BoxPosition enumeration. As an alternative to manually changing these menu settings, click on the button marked F as shown below to swap the direction settings:

Figure 37-7

37.11 Summary

The Compose Animation API provides several options for performing animation based on state changes. A set of animate as state functions are used to animate the results of changes to state values. These functions are passed a target state value and animate the change from the current value to the target value. Animations can be configured in terms of timeline linearity, duration, and spring effects. Individual animations are combined into a single Transition instance using the *updateTransition()* function. Android Studio includes the Animation Inspector for testing and manually scrolling through animation sequences.

38. Canvas Graphics Drawing in Compose

In this chapter, we will be introducing 2D graphics drawing using the Compose Canvas component. As we explore the capabilities of Canvas it will quickly become clear that, as with just about everything else in Compose, impressive results can typically be achieved with just a few lines of code.

38.1 Introducing the Canvas component

The Canvas component provides a surface on which to perform 2D graphics drawing. Behind the scenes, however, Canvas does much more than just provide a drawing area, including making sure that the state of the graphical content is maintained and managed automatically. Canvas also has its own scope (DrawScope) which gives us access to properties of the canvas area including the size dimensions and center point of the current bounds area, in addition to a set of functions that can be used to draw shapes, lines, and paths, define insets, perform rotations, and much more.

Given the visual nature of this particular Compose feature, the rest of this chapter will make use of a project to demonstrate many of the features of the Canvas component in action.

38.2 Creating the CanvasDemo project

Launch Android Studio and create a new *Empty Compose Activity* project named CanvasDemo, specifying *com.example.canvasdemo* as the package name, and selecting a minimum API level of API 26: Android 8.0 (Oreo). Within the *MainActivity.kt* file, delete the Greeting function and add a new empty composable named MainScreen:

```
@Composable
fun MainScreen() {


}
```

Next, edit the *onCreateActivity()* method and DefaultPreview function to call MainScreen instead of Greeting.

38.3 Drawing a line and getting the canvas size

The first drawing example we will look at involves drawing a straight diagonal line from one corner of the Canvas bounds to the other. To achieve this, we need to obtain the dimensions of the canvas by accessing the size properties provided by DrawScope. Edit the *MainActivity.kt* file to add a new function named DrawLine and add a call to this new function from within the MainScreen composable:

```
.

.
import androidx.compose.foundation.Canvas
import androidx.compose.foundation.layout.size
import androidx.compose.ui.geometry.Offset
import androidx.compose.ui.geometry.Size
import androidx.compose.ui.graphics.*
```

Canvas Graphics Drawing in Compose

```
import androidx.compose.ui.unit.dp
.

.

@Composable
fun MainScreen() {
    DrawLine()
}

@Composable
fun DrawLine() {
    Canvas(modifier = Modifier.size(300.dp)) {
        val height = size.height
        val width = size.width

    }
}
```

The DrawLine composable creates a fixed size Canvas and extracts the height and width properties from the DrawScope. All that remains is to draw a line via a call to the DrawScope *drawLine()* function:

```
@Composable
fun DrawLine() {
    Canvas(modifier = Modifier.size(300.dp)) {
        val height = size.height
        val width = size.width

        drawLine(
            start = Offset(x= 0f, y = 0f),
            end = Offset(x = width, y = height),
            color = Color.Blue,
            strokeWidth = 16.0f
        )
    }
}
```

The *drawLine()* API function needs to know the x and y coordinates of the start and endpoints of the line, keeping in mind that the top left-hand corner of the Canvas is position 0, 0. In the above example, these coordinates are packaged into an Offset instance via a call to the *Offset()* function. The *drawLine()* function also needs to know the thickness and color of the line to be drawn. After making the above changes, refresh the Preview panel where the drawing should be rendered as shown in Figure 38-1:

Figure 38-1

38.4 Drawing dashed lines

Any form of line drawing performed on a Canvas can be configured with dash effects by configuring a PathEffect instance and assigning it to the pathEffect argument of the drawing function call. To create a dashed line, we need to call the *dashPathEffect()* method of the PathEffect instance and pass it an array of floating-point numbers. The floating-point numbers indicate the "on" and "off" intervals in the line in pixels. There must be an even number of interval values with a minimum of 2 values. Modify the DrawLine composable to add a dashed line effect as follows:

```
@Composable
fun DrawLine() {
    Canvas(modifier = Modifier.size(300.dp)) {
        val height = size.height
        val width = size.width

        drawLine(
            start = Offset(x= 0f, y = 0f),
            end = Offset(x = width, y = height),
            color = Color.Blue,
            strokeWidth = 16.0f,
            pathEffect = PathEffect.dashPathEffect(
                    floatArrayOf(30f, 10f, 10f, 10f), phase = 0f)
        )
    }
}
```

The above path effect will draw a line beginning with a 30px dash and 10px space, followed by 10px dash and a 10px space, repeating this sequence until the end of the line as shown in Figure 38-2:

Figure 38-2

38.5 Drawing a rectangle

Rectangles are drawn on a Canvas using the *drawRect()* function which can be used in several different ways. The following code changes draw a rectangle of specific dimensions at the default position (0, 0) within the canvas area:

```
@Composable
fun MainScreen() {
    DrawRect()
}
```

Canvas Graphics Drawing in Compose

```
@Composable
fun DrawRect() {
    Canvas(modifier = Modifier.size(300.dp)) {
        val size = Size(600f, 250f)
        drawRect(
            color = Color.Blue,
            size = size
        )
    }
}
```

When rendered within the Preview panel, the rectangle will appear as shown in Figure 38-3:

Figure 38-3

Note that the dimensions of the Canvas are 300 x 300 while the rectangle is sized to 600 x 250. At first glance, this suggests that the rectangle should be much wider than it appears in the above figure relative to the Canvas. In practice, however, the Canvas size is declared in density-independent pixels (dp) while the rectangle size is specified in pixels (px). Density independent pixels are an abstract measurement that is calculated based on the physical density of the screen defined in dots per inch (dpi). Pixels, on the other hand, refer to the actual physical pixels on the screen. To work solely in pixels, start with dp values and then convert them to pixels as follows:

```
@Composable
fun DrawRect() {
    Canvas(modifier = Modifier.size(300.dp)) {
        val size = Size(200.dp.toPx(), 100.dp.toPx())
        drawRect(
            color = Color.Blue,
            size = size
        )
    }
}
```

Instead of specifying dimensions, the size of the rectangle can also be defined relative to the size of the Canvas. For example, the following code draws a square that is half the size of the Canvas:

```
@Composable
fun DrawRect() {
    Canvas(modifier = Modifier.size(300.dp)) {
        drawRect(
            color = Color.Blue,
```

```
            size = size / 2f
        )
    }
}
```

The above changes will result in the following drawing output:

The position of the rectangle within the Canvas area can be specified by providing the coordinates of the top left-hand corner of the drawing:

```
@Composable
fun DrawRect() {
    Canvas(modifier = Modifier.size(300.dp)) {
        drawRect(
            color = Color.Blue,
            topLeft = Offset(x=350f, y = 300f),
            size = size / 2f
        )
    }
}
```

Figure 38-4

Alternatively, the *inset()* function may be used to modify the bounds of the Canvas component:

.

.

import androidx.compose.ui.graphics.drawscope.inset

.

.

```
@Composable
```

Canvas Graphics Drawing in Compose

```
fun DrawRect() {
    Canvas(modifier = Modifier.size(300.dp)) {
        inset(100f, 200f) {
            drawRect(
                color = Color.Blue,
                size = size / 2f
            )
        }
    }
}
```

The *inset()* function can be called with a wide range of settings affecting different sides of the canvas. The function is also particularly useful because multiple drawing functions can be called from within the trailing lambda, with each adopting the same inset values.

The *drawRoundRect()* function is also available for drawing rectangles with rounded corners. In addition to size and position, this function also needs to be passed an appropriately configured CornerRadius component. It is also worth noting that rectangles (both with and without rounded corners) can be drawn in outline only by specifying a Stroke for the *style* property, for example:

```
.
.

import androidx.compose.ui.geometry.CornerRadius
import androidx.compose.ui.graphics.drawscope.Stroke

.
.

@Composable
fun DrawRect() {
    Canvas(modifier = Modifier.size(300.dp)) {

        val size = Size(
            width = 280.dp.toPx(),
            height = 200.dp.toPx())

        drawRoundRect(
            color = Color.Blue,
            size = size,
            topLeft = Offset(20f, 20f),
            style = Stroke(width = 8.dp.toPx()),
            cornerRadius = CornerRadius(
                x = 30.dp.toPx(),
                y = 30.dp.toPx()
            )
        )
    }
}
```

The above code produces an outline of a rectangle with rounded corners:

Figure 38-5

38.6 Applying rotation

Any element drawn on a Canvas component can be rotated via a call to the scope *rotate()* function. The following code, for example, rotates a rectangle drawing by 45°:

```
.

.

import androidx.compose.ui.graphics.drawscope.rotate

.

.

@Composable
fun DrawRect() {
    Canvas(modifier = Modifier.size(300.dp)) {
        rotate(45f) {
            drawRect(
                color = Color.Blue,
                topLeft = Offset(200f, 200f),
                size = size / 2f
            )
        }
    }
}
```

The above changes will render the drawing as shown in Figure 38-6 below:

Figure 38-6

38.7 Drawing circles and ovals

Circles are drawn in Compose using the *drawCircle()* function. The following code draws a circle centered within a Canvas. Note that we find the center of the canvas by referencing the DrawScope *center* property:

```
@Composable
fun MainScreen() {
    DrawCircle()
}


@Composable
fun DrawCircle() {
    Canvas(modifier = Modifier.size(300.dp)) {
        val canvasWidth = size.width
        val canvasHeight = size.height

        drawCircle(
            color = Color.Blue,
            center = center,
            radius = 120.dp.toPx()
        )
    }
}
```

When previewed, the canvas should appear as shown in Figure 38-7 below:

Figure 38-7

Oval shapes, on the other hand, are drawn by calling the *drawOval()* function. The following composable, for example, draws the outline of an oval shape:

```
@Composable
fun MainScreen() {
    DrawOval()
}


@Composable
fun DrawOval() {
    Canvas(modifier = Modifier.size(300.dp)) {
        val canvasWidth = size.width
```

```
    val canvasHeight = size.height
    drawOval(
        color = Color.Blue,
        topLeft = Offset(x = 25.dp.toPx(), y = 90.dp.toPx()),
        size = Size(
            width = canvasHeight - 50.dp.toPx(),
            height = canvasHeight / 2 - 50.dp.toPx()
        ),
        style = Stroke(width = 12.dp.toPx())
    )
    }
}
```

The above code will render in the Preview panel as illustrated in Figure 38-8:

Figure 38-8

38.8 Drawing gradients

Shapes can be filled using gradient patterns by making use of the Brush component which can, in turn, paint horizontal, vertical, linear, radial, and sweeping gradients. For example, to fill a rectangle with a horizontal gradient, we need a Brush initialized with a list of colors together with the start and end positions along the x-axis and an optional tile mode setting. The following example draws a rectangle that occupies the entire canvas and fills it with a horizontal gradient:

```
@Composable
fun MainScreen() {
    GradientFill()
}

@Composable
fun GradientFill() {

    Canvas(modifier = Modifier.size(300.dp)) {
        val canvasSize = size
        val colorList: List<Color> = listOf(Color.Red, Color.Blue,
                Color.Magenta, Color.Yellow, Color.Green, Color.Cyan)

        val brush = Brush.horizontalGradient(
            colors = colorList,
```

```
            startX = 0f,
            endX = 300.dp.toPx(),
            tileMode = TileMode.Repeated
        )

        drawRect(
            brush = brush,
            size = canvasSize
        )
    }
}
```

Try out the above example within the Preview panel where it should appear as follows:

Figure 38-9

The following example, on the other hand, uses a radial gradient to fill a circle:

```
@Composable
fun MainScreen() {
    RadialFill()
}

@Composable
fun RadialFill() {
    Canvas(modifier = Modifier.size(300.dp)) {

        val canvasWidth = size.width
        val canvasHeight = size.height
        val radius = 150.dp.toPx()
        val colorList: List<Color> = listOf(Color.Red, Color.Blue,
                Color.Magenta, Color.Yellow, Color.Green, Color.Cyan)

        val brush = Brush.radialGradient(
            colors = colorList,
            center = center,
            radius = radius,
            tileMode = TileMode.Repeated
        )
```

```
    drawCircle(
        brush = brush,
        center = center,
        radius = radius
    )
}
}
```

Note that the center parameter in the above *drawCircle()* call is optional in this example. In the absence of this parameter, the function will automatically default to the center of the canvas. When previewed, the circle will appear as shown in Figure 38-10:

Figure 38-10

Gradients are particularly useful for adding shadow effects to drawings. Consider, for example, the following horizontal gradient applied to a circle drawing:

```
@Composable
fun MainScreen() {
    ShadowCircle()
}

@Composable
fun ShadowCircle() {
    Canvas(modifier = Modifier.size(300.dp)) {
        val radius = 150.dp.toPx()
        val colorList: List<Color> =
            listOf(Color.Blue, Color.Black)

        val brush = Brush.horizontalGradient(
            colors = colorList,
            startX = 0f,
            endX = 300.dp.toPx(),
            tileMode = TileMode.Repeated
        )

        drawCircle(
            brush = brush,
```

```
            radius = radius
        )
    }
}
```

When previewed, the circle will appear with a shadow effect on the right-hand side as illustrated in Figure 38-11:

Figure 38-11

38.9 Drawing arcs

The *drawArc()* DrawScope function is used to draw an arc to fit within a specified rectangle and requires either a Brush or Color setting together with the start and sweep angles. The following code, for example, draws an arc starting at 20° with a sweep of 90° within a 250dp by 250dp rectangle:

```
@Composable
fun MainScreen() {
    DrawArc()
}


@Composable
fun DrawArc() {
    Canvas(modifier = Modifier.size(300.dp)) {
        drawArc(
            Color.Blue,
            startAngle = 20f,
            sweepAngle = 90f,
            useCenter = true,
            size = Size(250.dp.toPx(), 250.dp.toPx())
        )
    }
}
```

The above code will render the arc as shown in Figure 38-12:

Figure 38-12

38.10 Drawing paths

So far in this chapter, we have focused on drawing predefined shapes such as circles and rectangles. DrawScope also supports the drawing of paths. Paths are essentially lines drawn between a series of coordinates within the canvas area. Paths are stored in an instance of the Path class which, once defined, is passed to the *drawPath()* function for rendering on the Canvas.

When designing a path, the *moveTo()* function is called first to define the start point of the first line. A line is then drawn to the next position using either the *lineTo()* or *relativeLineTo()* functions. The *lineTo()* function accepts the x and y coordinates of the next position relative to the top left-hand corner of the parent Canvas. The *relativeLineTo()* function, on the other hand, assumes that the coordinates passed to it are relative to the previous position and can be negative or positive. The Path class also includes functions for drawing non-straight lines including Cubic and Quadratic Bézier curves.

Once the path is complete, the *close()* function must be called to end the drawing.

Within the *MainActivity.kt* file, make the following modifications to draw a custom shape using a combination of straight lines and Quadratic Bézier curves:

```
@Composable
fun MainScreen() {
    DrawPath()
}


@Composable
fun DrawPath() {
    Canvas(modifier = Modifier.size(300.dp)) {

        val path = Path().apply {
            moveTo(0f, 0f)
            quadraticBezierTo(50.dp.toPx(), 200.dp.toPx(),
                    300.dp.toPx(), 300.dp.toPx())
            lineTo(270.dp.toPx(), 100.dp.toPx())
            quadraticBezierTo(60.dp.toPx(), 80.dp.toPx(), 0f, 0f)
            close()
        }

        drawPath(
```

```
            path = path,
            Color.Blue,
        )
    }
}
```

Refresh the Preview panel where the drawing should appear as illustrated below:

Figure 38-13

38.11 Drawing points

The *drawPoints()* function is used to draw individual points at the locations specified by a list of Offset instances. The pointMode parameter of the *drawPoints()* function is used to control whether each point is plotted separately (using Points mode) or connected by lines using the Lines and Polygon modes. The *drawPoints()* function in Points mode is particularly useful for algorithm-driven drawing. The following code, for example, plots a sine wave comprised of individual points:

```
.
.
import java.lang.Math.PI
import java.lang.Math.sin
.
.
@Composable
fun MainScreen() {
    DrawPoints()
}

@Composable
fun DrawPoints() {
    Canvas(modifier = Modifier.size(300.dp)) {

        val height = size.height
        val width = size.width
        val points = mutableListOf<Offset>()

        for (x in 0..size.width.toInt()) {
            val y = (sin(x * (2f * PI /   width))
                * (height / 2) + (height / 2)).toFloat()
```

```
        points.add(Offset(x.toFloat(), y))
    }
    drawPoints(
        points = points,
        strokeWidth = 3f,
        pointMode = PointMode.Points,
        color = Color.Blue
    )
}
}
```

After making the above changes, the Canvas should appear as illustrated below:

Figure 38-14

38.12 Drawing an image

An image resource can be drawn onto a canvas via a call to the *drawImage()* function. To see this function in action, we first need to add an image resource to the project. The image is named *vacation.jpg* and can be found in the *images* folder of the sample code archive which can be downloaded from the following web page:

https://www.ebookfrenzy.com/retail/compose/index.php

Within Android Studio, display the Resource Manager tool window (*View -> Tool Windows -> Resource Manager*). Locate the *vacation.png* image in the file system navigator for your operating system and drag and drop it onto the Resource Manager tool window. In the resulting dialog, click Next followed by the Import button to add the image to the project. The image should now appear in the Resource Manager as shown in Figure 38-15 below:

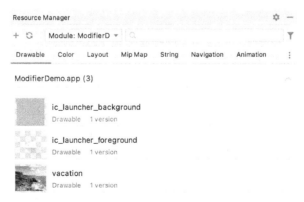

Figure 38-15

Canvas Graphics Drawing in Compose

The image will also appear in the *res -> drawables* section of the Project tool window:

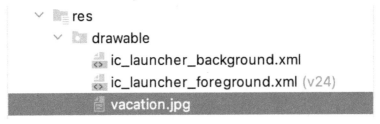

Figure 38-16

With the image added to the project, return to the *MainActivity.kt* file and make the following modifications:

```
.
.
import androidx.compose.ui.res.imageResource
.
.
@Composable
fun MainScreen() {
    DrawImage()
}

@Composable
fun DrawImage() {

    val image = ImageBitmap.imageResource(id = R.drawable.vacation)

    Canvas(
        modifier = Modifier
            .size(360.dp, 270.dp)
    ) {
        drawImage(
            image = image,
            topLeft = Offset(x = 0f, y = 0f)
        )
    }
}
```

The DrawImage composable begins by creating an ImageBitmap version of the resource image and then passes it as an argument to the *drawImage()* function together with an Offset instance configured to position the image in the top left-hand corner of the canvas area. Refresh the preview and confirm that the Canvas appears as follows:

Figure 38-17

The *drawImage()* function also allows color filters to be applied to the rendered image. This requires a ColorFilter instance which can be configured with tint, lighting, color matrix, and blend settings. A full explanation of color filtering is beyond the scope of this book, but more information can be found on the following web page:

https://developer.android.com/reference/kotlin/androidx/compose/ui/graphics/ColorFilter

For this example, add a tint color filter blending with a color matrix as follows:

```
.

.
drawImage(
    image = image,
    topLeft = Offset(x = 0f, y = 0f),
    colorFilter = ColorFilter.tint(
        color = Color(0xADFFAA2E),
        blendMode = BlendMode.ColorBurn
    )
)
.

.
```

When the canvas renders the image in the Preview panel, it will now do so with a yellowish hue.

38.13 Summary

The Compose Canvas component provides a surface on which to draw graphics. The Canvas DrawScope includes a set of functions that allow us to perform drawing operations within the canvas area, including the drawing of lines, shapes, gradients, images, and paths. In this chapter, we have explored some of the more common drawing features provided by Canvas and the DrawScope functions.

39. Working with ViewModels in Compose

Until a few years ago, Google did not recommend a specific approach to building Android apps other than to provide tools and development kits while letting developers decide what worked best for a particular project or individual programming style. That changed in 2017 with the introduction of the Android Architecture Components which became part of Android Jetpack when it was released in 2018. Jetpack has of course, since been expanded with the addition of Compose.

This chapter will provide an overview of the concepts of Jetpack, Android app architecture recommendations, and the ViewModel component.

39.1 What is Android Jetpack?

Android Jetpack consists of Android Studio, the Android Architecture Components, Android Support Library, and the Compose framework together with a set of guidelines that recommend how an Android App should be structured. The Android Architecture Components were designed to make it quicker and easier both to perform common tasks when developing Android apps while also conforming to the key principle of the architectural guidelines. While many of these components have been superseded by features built into Compose, the ViewModel architecture component remains relevant today. Before exploring the ViewModel component, it first helps to understand both the old and new approaches to Android app architecture.

39.2 The "old" architecture

In the chapter entitled *"An Example Compose Project"*, an Android project was created consisting of a single activity that contained all of the code for presenting and managing the user interface together with the back-end logic of the app. Up until the introduction of Jetpack, the most common architecture followed this paradigm with apps consisting of multiple activities (one for each screen within the app) with each activity class to some degree mixing user interface and back-end code.

This approach led to a range of problems related to the lifecycle of an app (for example an activity is destroyed and recreated each time the user rotates the device leading to the loss of any app data that had not been saved to some form of persistent storage) as well as issues such as inefficient navigation involving launching a new activity for each app screen accessed by the user.

39.3 Modern Android architecture

At the most basic level, Google now advocates single activity apps where different screens are loaded as content within the same activity.

Modern architecture guidelines also recommend separating different areas of responsibility within an app into entirely separate modules (a concept Google refers to as "separation of concerns"). One of the keys to this approach is the ViewModel component.

39.4 The ViewModel component

The purpose of ViewModel is to separate the user interface-related data model and logic of an app from the code responsible for displaying and managing the user interface and interacting with the operating system.

When designed in this way, an app will consist of one or more *UI Controllers,* such as an activity, together with ViewModel instances responsible for handling the data needed by those controllers.

A ViewModel is implemented as a separate class and contains *state* values containing the model data and functions that can be called to manage that data. The activity containing the user interface *observes* the model state values such that any value changes trigger a recomposition. User interface events relating to the model data such as a button click are configured to call the appropriate function within the ViewModel. This is, in fact, a direct implementation of the *unidirectional data flow* concept described in the chapter entitled *"An Overview of Compose State and Recomposition"*. The diagram in Figure 39-1 illustrates this concept as it relates to activities and ViewModels:

Figure 39-1

This separation of responsibility addresses the issues relating to the lifecycle of activities. Regardless of how many times an activity is recreated during the lifecycle of an app, the ViewModel instances remain in memory thereby maintaining data consistency. A ViewModel used by an activity, for example, will remain in memory until the activity finishes which, in the single activity app, is not until the app exits.

In addition to using ViewModels, the code responsible for gathering data from data sources such as web services or databases should be built into a separate *repository* module instead of being bundled with the view model. This topic will be covered in detail beginning with the chapter entitled *"Room Databases and Compose"*.

39.5 ViewModel implementation using state

The main purpose of a ViewModel is to store data that can be observed by the user interface of an activity. This allows the user interface to react when changes occur to the ViewModel data. There are two ways to declare the data within a ViewModel so that it is observable. One option is to use the Compose state mechanism which has been used extensively throughout this book. An alternative approach is to use the Jetpack LiveData component, a topic that will be covered later in this chapter.

Much like the state declared within composables, ViewModel state is declared using the *mutableStateOf* group of functions. The following ViewModel declaration, for example, declares a state containing an integer count value with an initial value of 0:

```
class MyViewModel {

    var customerCount by mutableStateOf(0)

}
```

With some data encapsulated in the model, the next step is to add a function that can be called from within the UI to change the counter value:

```
class MyViewModel {

    var customerCount by mutableStateOf(0)

    fun increaseCount() {
        customerCount++
    }
}
```

Even complex models are nothing more than a continuation of these two basic state and function building blocks.

39.6 Connecting a ViewModel state to an activity

A ViewModel is of little use unless it can be used within the composables that make up the app user interface. All this requires is to pass an instance of the ViewModel as a parameter to a composable from which the state values and functions can be accessed. Programming convention recommends that these steps be performed in a composable dedicated solely for this task and located at the top of the screen's composable hierarchy. The model state and event handler functions can then be passed to child composables as necessary. The following code shows an example of how a ViewModel might be accessed from within an activity:

```
class MainActivity : ComponentActivity() {
    override fun onCreate(savedInstanceState: Bundle?) {
        super.onCreate(savedInstanceState)
        setContent {
            ViewModelWorkTheme {
                Surface(color = MaterialTheme.colors.background) {
                    TopLevel()
                }
            }
        }
    }
}


@Composable
fun TopLevel(model: MyViewModel = MyViewModel()) {
    MainScreen(model.customerCount) { model.increaseCount() }
}


@Composable
fun MainScreen(count: Int, addCount: () -> Unit = {}) {
    Column(horizontalAlignment = Alignment.CenterHorizontally,
        modifier = Modifier.fillMaxWidth()) {
        Text("Total customers = $count",
        Modifier.padding(10.dp))
        Button(
            onClick = addCount,
        ) {
            Text(text = "Add a Customer")
```

```
            }

      }

}
```

In the above example, the first function call is made by the *onCreate()* method to the TopLevel composable which is declared with a default ViewModel parameter initialized with a MyViewModel instance:

```
@Composable
fun TopLevel(model: MyViewModel = MyViewModel()) {
.

.
```

It is, of course, also possible to create the view model within the body of the above TopLevel function as follows:

```
@Composable
fun TopLevel() {
      val model = MyViewModel()
.

.
```

While this is certainly valid code, it limits the re-usability of the function because it prevents a different view model from being passed as a parameter.

With access to the ViewModel instance, the TopLevel function is then able to obtain references to the view model *customerCount* state variable and *increaseCount()* function which it passes to the MainScreen composable:

```
MainScreen(model.customerCount) { model.increaseCount() }
```

As implemented, Button clicks will result in calls to the view model *increaseCount()* function which, in turn, increments the *customerCount* state. This change in state triggers a recomposition of the user interface, resulting in the new customer count value appearing in the Text composable.

The use of state and view models will be demonstrated in the chapter entitled *"A Compose ViewModel Tutorial"*.

39.7 ViewModel implementation using LiveData

The Jetpack LiveData component predates the introduction of Compose and can be used as a wrapper around data values within a view model. Once contained in a LiveData instance, those variables become observable to composables within an activity. LiveData instances can be declared as being mutable using the MutableLiveData class, allowing the ViewModel functions to make changes to the underlying data value. An example view model designed to store a customer name could, for example, be implemented as follows using MutableLiveData instead of state:

```
class MyViewModel {

    var customerName: MutableLiveData<String> = MutableLiveData("")

    fun setName(name: String) {
        customerName.value = name
    }

}
```

Note that new values must be assigned to the live data variable via the *value* property.

39.8 Observing ViewModel LiveData within an activity

As with state, the first step when working with LiveData is to obtain an instance of the view model within an initialization composable:

```
@Composable
fun TopLevel(model: MyViewModel = MyViewModel()) {


}
```

Once we have access to a view model instance, the next step is to make the live data observable. This is achieved by calling the *observeAsState()* method on the live data object:

```
@Composable
fun TopLevel(model: MyViewModel = MyViewModel()) {
    var customerName: String by model.customerName.observeAsState("")
}
```

In the above code, the *observeAsState()* call converts the live data value into a state instance and assigns it to the customerName variable. Once converted, the state will behave in the same way as any other state object, including triggering recompositions whenever the underlying value changes.

The use of LiveData and view models will be demonstrated in the chapter entitled *"A Compose Room Database and Repository Tutorial"*.

39.9 Summary

Until recently, Google has tended not to recommend any particular approach to structuring an Android app. That changed with the introduction of Android Jetpack which consists of a set of tools, components, libraries, and architecture guidelines. These architectural guidelines recommend that an app project be divided into separate modules, each being responsible for a particular area of functionality, otherwise known as "separation of concerns". In particular, the guidelines recommend separating the view data model of an app from the code responsible for handling the user interface. This is achieved using the ViewModel component. In this chapter, we have covered ViewModel-based architecture and demonstrated how this is implemented when developing with Compose. We have also explored how to observe and access view model data from within an activity using both state and LiveData.

40. A Compose ViewModel Tutorial

As outlined in the previous chapter, ViewModels are used to separate the data and associated logic used by an activity from the code responsible for rendering the user interface. Having covered the theory of modern Android app architecture, this chapter will create an example project that demonstrates the use of a ViewModel within an example project.

40.1 About the project

The project created in this chapter involves a simple app designed to perform temperature conversions between Celsius and Fahrenheit. Once the app is complete, it will appear as illustrated in Figure 40-1 below:

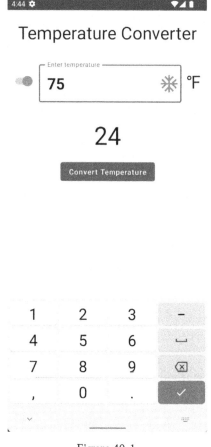

Figure 40-1

When a temperature value is entered into the OutlinedTextField and the button clicked, the converted value will appear in a result Text component. The Switch component is used to indicate whether the entered temperature is Fahrenheit or Celsius. The current switch setting, conversion result, and conversion logic will all be contained within a ViewModel.

40.2 Creating the ViewModelDemo project

Launch Android Studio and create a new *Empty Compose Activity* project named ViewModelDemo, specifying *com.example.viewmodeldemo* as the package name, and selecting a minimum API level of API 26: Android 8.0 (Oreo). Within the *MainActivity.kt* file, delete the Greeting function and add a new empty composable named ScreenSetup which, in turn, calls a function named MainScreen:

```
@Composable
fun ScreenSetup() {
    MainScreen()
}

@Composable
fun MainScreen() {

}
```

Next, edit the *onCreateActivity()* method function to call ScreenSetup instead of Greeting (we will modify the DefaultPreview composable later).

40.3 Adding the ViewModel

Within the Android Studio Project tool window, locate and right-click on the *app -> java -> com.example. viewmodeldemo* entry and select the *New -> Kotlin Class/File* menu option. In the resulting dialog, name the class *DemoViewModel* before tapping the keyboard Enter key.

The ViewModel needs to contain state values in which to store the conversion result and current switch position as follows:

```
package com.example.viewmodeldemo

import androidx.compose.runtime.getValue
import androidx.compose.runtime.mutableStateOf
import androidx.compose.runtime.setValue

class DemoViewModel {

    var isFahrenheit by mutableStateOf(true)
    var result by mutableStateOf("")
}
```

The class also needs to contain the logic for the model, starting with a function to perform the temperature unit conversion. Since the temperature is entered by the user into a text field it is passed to the function as a String. In addition to performing the calculation, code is also needed to convert between string and integer types. This code also needs to ensure that the user has entered a valid number. Remaining in the *DemoViewModel.kt* file, add a new function named *convertTemp()* so that it reads as follows:

.
.
.

```
import java.lang.Exception
import kotlin.math.roundToInt
```

```
class ViewModel {

.

.

    fun convertTemp(temp: String) {

        try {
            val tempInt = temp.toInt()

            if (isFahrenheit) {
                result = ((tempInt - 32) * 0.5556).roundToInt().toString()
            } else {
                result = ((tempInt * 1.8) + 32).roundToInt().toString()
            }
        } catch (e: Exception) {
            result = "Invalid Entry"
        }
    }

.

.
```

The above function begins by converting the temperature string value to an integer. This is performed within the context of a *try... catch* statement which reports invalid input if the text does not equate to a valid number. Next, the appropriate conversion is performed depending on the current *isFahrenheit* setting and the result is rounded to a whole number and converted back to a string before being assigned to the *result* state variable.

The other function that needs to be added to the view model will be called when the switch setting changes and simply inverts the current *isFahrenheit* state setting:

```
fun switchChange() {
    isFahrenheit = !isFahrenheit
}
```

The implementation of the view model is now complete and is ready to be used from within the main activity.

40.4 Accessing DemoViewModel from MainActivity

Now that we have declared a view model class, the next step is to create an instance and integrate it with the composables that make up our MainActivity. This project will involve creating a DemoViewModel instance as a parameter to the ScreenSetup function and then passing through the state variables and function references to the MainScreen function. Open the *MainActivity.kt* file in the code editor and make the following changes:

```
.

.

@Composable
fun ScreenSetup(viewModel: DemoViewModel = DemoViewModel()) {
    MainScreen(
        isFahrenheit = viewModel.isFahrenheit,
        result = viewModel.result,
        convertTemp = { viewModel.convertTemp(it) },
        switchChange = { viewModel.switchChange() }
    )
```

```
}


@Composable
fun MainScreen(
    isFahrenheit: Boolean,
    result: String,
    convertTemp: (String) -> Unit,
    switchChange: () -> Unit
) {


}
.
.
```

Before starting work on the user interface design, the DefaultPreview function also needs to be modified to make use of the view model:

```
@Preview(showBackground = true, showSystemUi = true)
@Composable
fun DefaultPreview(model: DemoViewModel = DemoViewModel()) {
    ViewModelDemoTheme {
        MainScreen(
            isFahrenheit = model.isFahrenheit,
            result = model.result,
            convertTemp = { model.convertTemp(it) },
            switchChange = { model.switchChange() }
        )
    }
}
```

40.5 Designing the temperature input composable

A closer look at the completed user interface screenshot shown in Figure 40-1 above will reveal the presence of a snowflake icon on the right-hand side of the OutlinedTextField component. Before writing any more code, this icon first needs to be added to the project. Within Android Studio, select the *Tools -> Resource Manager* menu option to display the Resource Manager tool window. Within the tool window click on the `+` button indicated by the arrow in Figure 40-2 and select the *Vector Asset* menu option to add a new resource to the project:

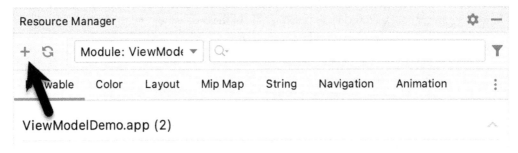

Figure 40-2

In the resulting dialog, click on the Clip Art box as shown in Figure 40-3 below:

Figure 40-3

When the icon selection dialog appears, enter "ac unit" into the search field to locate the clip art icon to be used in the project:

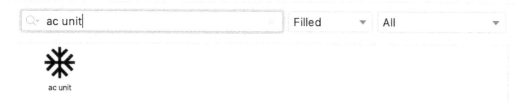

Figure 40-4

Select the icon and click on the OK button to return to the vector asset configuration dialog where the selected icon will now appear. Click Next followed by Finish to complete the addition of the icon to the project resources.

Double-click on the *ic_baseline_ac_unit_24.xml* vector asset file in the Project tool window to load it into the code editor and modify the android:tint property as follows:

.

.

```
android:tint="@color/purple_700">
```

.

.

40.6 Designing the temperature input composable

In the interests of avoiding the MainScreen function becoming cluttered, the Switch, OutlinedTextField, and unit indicator Text component will be placed in a separate composable named InputRow which can now be added to the *MainActivity.kt* file:

.

.

```
import androidx.compose.animation.Crossfade
import androidx.compose.animation.core.tween
import androidx.compose.foundation.layout.*
```

```
import androidx.compose.foundation.text.KeyboardOptions
import androidx.compose.material.*
import androidx.compose.ui.Alignment
import androidx.compose.ui.res.painterResource
import androidx.compose.ui.text.TextStyle
import androidx.compose.ui.text.font.FontWeight
import androidx.compose.ui.text.input.KeyboardType
import androidx.compose.ui.unit.dp
import androidx.compose.ui.unit.sp
.

.

@Composable
fun InputRow(
    isFahrenheit: Boolean,
    textState: String,
    switchChange: () -> Unit,
    onTextChange: (String) -> Unit
) {
    Row(verticalAlignment = Alignment.CenterVertically) {

        Switch(
            checked = isFahrenheit,
            onCheckedChange = { switchChange() }
        )

        OutlinedTextField(
            value = textState,
            onValueChange = { onTextChange(it) },
            keyboardOptions = KeyboardOptions(
                keyboardType = KeyboardType.Number
            ),
            singleLine = true,
            label = { Text("Enter temperature")},
            modifier = Modifier.padding(10.dp),
            textStyle = TextStyle(fontWeight = FontWeight.Bold,
                                    fontSize = 30.sp),
            trailingIcon = {
                Icon(
                    painter = painterResource(R.drawable.ic_baseline_ac_unit_24),
                    contentDescription = "frost",
                    modifier = Modifier
                        .size(40.dp)
                )
            }
        )
```

```
        Crossfade(
            targetState = isFahrenheit,
            animationSpec = tween(2000)
        ) { visible ->
            when (visible) {
                true -> Text("\u2109", style = MaterialTheme.typography.h4)
                false -> Text("\u2103", style = MaterialTheme.typography.h4)
            }
        }
    }
}
```

The InputRow function expects as parameters the state values and functions contained within the view model together with a *textState* state variable and onTextChange event handler. These last two parameters are used to display the text typed by the user into the text field and will be "hoisted" to the MainScreen function later in the chapter. The current *textState* value is also what gets passed to the *convertTemp()* function when the user clicks the button.

The composables that make up this section of the layout are contained within a Row which is configured to center its children vertically. The first child, the Switch component, simply calls the *switchChange()* function on the model to toggle the *isFahrenheit* state.

While many of the properties applied to the OutlinedTextField will be familiar from previous chapters, some require additional explanation. For example, since the temperature can only be entered as a number, the keyboardOptions keyboard type property is set to KeyboardNumber. This ensures that when the user taps within the text field, only the numeric keyboard will appear on the screen:

```
keyboardOptions = KeyboardOptions(
    keyboardType = KeyboardType.Number
)
```

Other keyboard type options include email address, password, phone number, and URI inputs.

The input is also limited to a single line of text using the singleLine property. As the name suggests, the OutlinedTextField component draws an outline around the text input area. When the component is not selected by the user (in other words it does not have "focus") the text assigned to the label property appears in slightly faded text within the text field as shown in Figure 40-5:

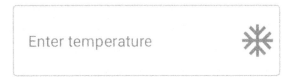

Figure 40-5

When the field has focus, however, the label appears as a title positioned within the outline:

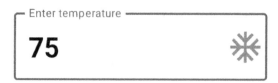

Figure 40-6

The result of a call to the TextStyle function is assigned to the textStyle property of the OutlinedTextField. TextStyle is used to group style settings into a single object that can be applied to other composables in a single operation. In this instance, we are only setting font weight and font style, but TextStyle may also be used to configure style settings including color, background, font family, shadow, text alignment, letter spacing, and text indent.

The trailingIcon property is used to position the previously added icon at the end of the text input area:

```
trailingIcon = {
    Icon(
        painter = painterResource(R.drawable.ic_baseline_ac_unit_24),
        contentDescription = "frost",
        modifier = Modifier
            .size(40.dp)
    )
}
```

Finally, crossfade animation (covered in the chapter titled *"Compose Visibility Animation"*) is used when switching the unit Text field between °F and °C (represented by Unicode values \u2109 and \u2103 respectively) based on the current *isFahrenheit* setting.

40.7 Completing the user interface design

The final task before testing the app is to complete the MainScreen function which now needs to read as follows:

.

.

```
import androidx.compose.runtime.getValue
import androidx.compose.runtime.mutableStateOf
import androidx.compose.runtime.setValue
import androidx.compose.runtime.remember
```

.

.

```
@Composable
fun MainScreen(
    isFahrenheit: Boolean,
    result: String,
    convertTemp: (String) -> Unit,
    switchChange: () -> Unit
) {
    Column(horizontalAlignment = Alignment.CenterHorizontally,
        modifier = Modifier.fillMaxSize()) {
```

```
    var textState by remember { mutableStateOf("") }

    val onTextChange = { text : String ->
        textState = text
    }

    Text("Temperature Converter",
        modifier = Modifier.padding(20.dp),
        style = MaterialTheme.typography.h4
    )

    InputRow(
        isFahrenheit = isFahrenheit,
        textState = textState,
        switchChange = switchChange,
        onTextChange = onTextChange
    )

    Text(result,
        modifier = Modifier.padding(20.dp),
        style = MaterialTheme.typography.h3
    )

    Button(
        onClick = { convertTemp(textState) }
    )
    {
        Text("Convert Temperature")
    }
  }
}
```

The MainScreen composable declares the *textState* state variable and an onTextChange event handler. The first child of the Column layout is a static Text component displaying a title. Next, the InputRow is called and passed the necessary parameters. The third child is another Text component, this time configured to display the content of the view model *result* state variable. Finally, a Button composable is configured to call the view model *convertTemp()* function, passing it *textState*. The *convertTemp()* function will calculate the converted temperature and assign it to the *result* state variable, thereby triggering a recomposition of the composable hierarchy.

40.8 Testing the app

Test the activity by running the app on a device or emulator, and tapping on the OutlinedTextField component. Note that the "Enter temperature" label moves to the outline leaving the input field clear to enter a temperature value. Verify that when the keyboard appears it only allows numerical selections. Enter a number and click on the Button at which point the converted temperature should be displayed.

Use the Switch to change from Fahrenheit to Centigrade and note the unit text to the right of the text field changes using cross-fade animation. Finally, test that attempting a conversion with a blank text field causes the

Invalid Entry text to appear.

40.9 Summary

This chapter has demonstrated the use of a view model to separate the data and logic of an application from the code responsible for displaying the user interface. The chapter also introduced the OutlinedTextField component and covered customization options including adding an icon, restricting keyboard input to numerical values, and setting style attributes using the TextStyle function.

41. An Overview of Android SQLite Databases

Mobile applications that do not need to store at least some amount of persistent data are few and far between. The use of databases is an essential aspect of most applications, ranging from applications that are almost entirely data-driven, to those that simply need to store small amounts of data such as the prevailing score of a game.

The importance of persistent data storage becomes even more evident when taking into consideration the somewhat transient lifecycle of the typical Android application. With the ever-present risk that the Android runtime system will terminate an application component to free up resources, a comprehensive data storage strategy to avoid data loss is a key factor in the design and implementation of any application development strategy.

This chapter will provide an overview of the SQLite database management system bundled with the Android operating system, together with an outline of the Android SDK classes that are provided to facilitate persistent SQLite-based database storage from within an Android application. Before delving into the specifics of SQLite in the context of Android development, however, a brief overview of databases and SQL will be covered.

41.1 Understanding database tables

Database *tables* provide the most basic level of data structure in a database. Each database can contain multiple tables and each table is designed to hold information of a specific type. For example, a database may contain a *customer* table that contains the name, address, and telephone number for each of the customers of a particular business. The same database may also include a *products* table used to store the product descriptions with associated product codes for the items sold by the business.

Each table in a database is assigned a name that must be unique within that particular database. A table name, once assigned to a table in one database, may not be used for another table except within the context of another database.

41.2 Introducing database schema

Database Schemas define the characteristics of the data stored in a database table. For example, the table schema for a customer database table might define that the customer name is a string of no more than 20 characters in length and that the customer phone number is a numerical data field of a certain format.

Schemas are also used to define the structure of entire databases and the relationship between the various tables contained in each database.

41.3 Columns and data types

It is helpful at this stage to begin to view a database table as being similar to a spreadsheet where data is stored in rows and columns.

Each column represents a data field in the corresponding table. For example, the name, address, and telephone data fields of a table are all *columns*.

Each column, in turn, is defined to contain a certain type of data. A column designed to store numbers would, therefore, be defined as containing numerical data.

41.4 Database rows

Each new record that is saved to a table is stored in a row. Each row, in turn, consists of the columns of data associated with the saved record.

Once again, consider the spreadsheet analogy described earlier in this chapter. Each entry in a customer table is equivalent to a row in a spreadsheet and each column contains the data for each customer (name, address, telephone, etc). When a new customer is added to the table, a new row is created and the data for that customer is stored in the corresponding columns of the new row.

Rows are also sometimes referred to as *records* or *entries* and these terms can generally be used interchangeably.

41.5 Introducing primary keys

Each database table should contain one or more columns that can be used to identify each row in the table uniquely. This is known in database terminology as the *Primary Key*. For example, a table may use a bank account number column as the primary key. Alternatively, a customer table may use the customer's social security number as the primary key.

Primary keys allow the database management system to identify a specific row in a table uniquely. Without a primary key, it would not be possible to retrieve or delete a specific row in a table because there can be no certainty that the correct row has been selected. For example, suppose a table existed where the customer's last name had been defined as the primary key. Imagine then the problem that might arise if more than one customer named "Smith" were recorded in the database. Without some guaranteed way to identify a specific row uniquely, it would be impossible to ensure the correct data was being accessed at any given time.

Primary keys can comprise a single column or multiple columns in a table. To qualify as a single column primary key, no two rows can contain matching primary key values. When using multiple columns to construct a primary key, individual column values do not need to be unique, but all the columns' values combined must be unique.

41.6 What is SQLite?

SQLite is an embedded, relational database management system (RDBMS). Most relational databases (Oracle, SQL Server, and MySQL being prime examples) are standalone server processes that run independently, and in cooperation with, applications that require database access. SQLite is referred to as *embedded* because it is provided in the form of a library that is linked into applications. As such, there is no standalone database server running in the background. All database operations are handled internally within the application through calls to functions contained in the SQLite library.

The developers of SQLite have placed the technology into the public domain with the result that it is now a widely deployed database solution.

SQLite is written in the C programming language and as such, the Android SDK provides a Java-based "wrapper" around the underlying database interface. This essentially consists of a set of classes that may be utilized within the Java or Kotlin code of an application to create and manage SQLite-based databases.

For additional information about SQLite refer to *https://www.sqlite.org*.

41.7 Structured Query Language (SQL)

Data is accessed in SQLite databases using a high-level language known as Structured Query Language. This is usually abbreviated to SQL and pronounced *sequel*. SQL is a standard language used by most relational database management systems. SQLite conforms mostly to the SQL-92 standard.

SQL is essentially a very simple and easy-to-use language designed specifically to enable the reading and writing of database data. Because SQL contains a small set of keywords, it can be learned quickly. In addition, SQL syntax is more or less identical between most DBMS implementations, so having learned SQL for one system, your skills will likely transfer to other database management systems.

While some basic SQL statements will be used within this chapter, a detailed overview of SQL is beyond the scope of this book. There are, however, many other resources that provide a far better overview of SQL than we could ever hope to provide in a single chapter here.

41.8 Trying SQLite on an Android Virtual Device (AVD)

For readers unfamiliar with databases in general and SQLite in particular, diving right into creating an Android application that uses SQLite may seem a little intimidating. Fortunately, Android is shipped with SQLite pre-installed, including an interactive environment for issuing SQL commands from within an *adb shell* session connected to a running Android AVD emulator instance. This is both a useful way to learn about SQLite and SQL and also an invaluable tool for identifying problems with databases created by applications running in an emulator.

To launch an interactive SQLite session, begin by running an AVD session. This can be achieved from within Android Studio by launching the Device Manager (*Tools -> Device Manager*), selecting a previously configured AVD, and clicking on the start button.

Once the AVD is up and running, open a Terminal or Command-Prompt window and connect to the emulator using the *adb* command-line tool as follows (note that the –e flag directs the tool to look for an emulator with which to connect, rather than a physical device):

```
adb -e shell
```

Once connected, the shell environment will provide a command prompt at which commands may be entered. Begin by obtaining superuser privileges using the *su* command:

```
Generic_x86:/ su
root@android:/ #
```

If a message appears indicating that superuser privileges are not allowed, the AVD instance likely includes Google Play support. To resolve this create a new AVD and, on the "Choose a device definition" screen, select a device that does not have a marker in the "Play Store" column.

Data stored in SQLite databases are stored in database files on the file system of the Android device on which the application is running. By default, the file system path for these database files is as follows:

```
/data/data/<package name>/databases/<database filename>.db
```

For example, if an application with the package name *com.example.MyDBApp* creates a database named *mydatabase.db*, the path to the file on the device would read as follows:

```
/data/data/com.examplc.MyDBApp/databases/mydatabase.db
```

For this exercise, therefore, change directory to /data/data within the adb shell and create a sub-directory hierarchy suitable for some SQLite experimentation:

```
cd /data/data
mkdir com.example.dbexample
cd com.example.dbexample
mkdir databases
cd databases
```

With a suitable location created for the database file, launch the interactive SQLite tool as follows:

An Overview of Android SQLite Databases

```
root@android:/data/data/databases # sqlite3 ./mydatabase.db
sqlite3 ./mydatabase.db
SQLite version 3.8.10.2 2015-05-20 18:17:19
Enter ".help" for usage hints.
sqlite>
```

At the *sqlite>* prompt, commands may be entered to perform tasks such as creating tables and inserting and retrieving data. For example, to create a new table in our database with fields to hold ID, name, address, and phone number fields the following statement is required:

```
create table contacts (_id integer primary key autoincrement, name text, address
text, phone text);
```

Note that each row in a table should have a *primary key* that is unique to that row. In the above example, we have designated the ID field as the primary key, declared it as being of type *integer,* and asked SQLite to increment the number automatically each time a row is added. This is a common way to make sure that each row has a unique primary key. On most other platforms, the choice of name for the primary key is arbitrary. In the case of Android, however, the key must be named *_id* for the database to be fully accessible using all of the Android database-related classes. The remaining fields are each declared as being of type *text.*

To list the tables in the currently selected database, use the *.tables* statement:

```
sqlite> .tables
contacts
```

To insert records into the table:

```
sqlite> insert into contacts (name, address, phone) values ("Bill Smith", "123
Main Street, California", "123-555-2323");
sqlite> insert into contacts (name, address, phone) values ("Mike Parks", "10
Upping Street, Idaho", "444-444-1212");
```

To retrieve all rows from a table:

```
sqlite> select * from contacts;
1|Bill Smith|123 Main Street, California|123-555-2323
2|Mike Parks|10 Upping Street, Idaho|444-444-1212
```

To extract a row that meets specific criteria:

```
sqlite> select * from contacts where name="Mike Parks";
2|Mike Parks|10 Upping Street, Idaho|444-444-1212
```

To exit from the sqlite3 interactive environment:

```
sqlite> .exit
```

When running an Android application in the emulator environment, any database files will be created on the file system of the emulator using the previously discussed path convention. This has the advantage that you can connect with adb, navigate to the location of the database file, load it into the sqlite3 interactive tool and perform tasks on the data to identify possible problems occurring in the application code.

It is also important to note that, while it is possible to connect with an adb shell to a physical Android device, the shell is not granted sufficient privileges by default to create and manage SQLite databases. Debugging of database problems is, therefore, best performed using an AVD session. Alternatively, databases can be inspected on both emulators and devices using the Android Studio Database Inspector, a topic that will be covered later.

41.9 The Android Room persistence library

SQLite is, as previously mentioned, written in the C programming language while Android applications are primarily developed using Java or Kotlin. To bridge this "language gap" in the past, the Android SDK included a set of classes that provide a layer on top of the SQLite database management system. Although still available in the SDK, the use of these classes involves writing a considerable amount of code and does not take advantage of the new architecture guidelines and features such as view models and LiveData. To address these shortcomings, the Android Jetpack Architecture Components include the Room persistent library. This library provides a high-level interface on top of the SQLite database system that makes it easy to store data locally on Android devices with minimal coding while also conforming to the recommendations for modern application architecture.

The next few chapters will provide an overview and tutorial of SQLite database management using the Room persistence library.

41.10 Summary

SQLite is a lightweight, embedded relational database management system that is included as part of the Android framework and provides a mechanism for implementing organized persistent data storage for Android applications. When combined with the Room persistence library, Android provides a modern way to implement data storage from within an Android app.

The goal of this chapter was to provide an overview of databases in general and SQLite in particular within the context of Android application development. The next chapters will provide an overview of the Room persistence library, after which we will work through the creation of an example application.

42. Room Databases and Compose

Included with the Android Architecture Components, the Room persistence library is designed specifically to make it easier to add database storage support to Android apps in a way that is consistent with the Android architecture guidelines. With the basics of SQLite databases covered in the previous chapter, this chapter will explore the concepts of the Room-based database management, the key elements that work together to implement Room support within an Android app, and how these are implemented in terms of architecture and coding. Having covered these topics, the next chapter will put this theory into practice in the form of an example Room database project.

42.1 Revisiting modern app architecture

The chapter entitled *"Working with ViewModels in Compose"* introduced the concept of modern app architecture and stressed the importance of separating different areas of responsibility within an app. The diagram illustrated in Figure 42-1 outlines the recommended architecture for a typical Android app:

Figure 42-1

With the top three levels of this architecture covered in some detail in earlier chapters of this book, it is now time to begin an exploration of the repository and database architecture levels in the context of the Room persistence library.

42.2 Key elements of Room database persistence

Before going into greater detail later in the chapter, it is first worth summarizing the key elements involved in working with SQLite databases using the Room persistence library:

42.2.1 Repository

The repository module contains all of the code necessary for directly handling all data sources used by the app. This avoids the need for the UI controller and ViewModel to contain code that directly accesses sources such as

Room Databases and Compose

databases or web services.

42.2.2 Room database

The room database object provides the interface to the underlying SQLite database. It also provides the repository with access to the Data Access Object (DAO). An app should only have one room database instance which may then be used to access multiple database tables.

42.2.3 Data Access Object (DAO)

The DAO contains the SQL statements required by the repository to insert, retrieve and delete data within the SQLite database. These SQL statements are mapped to methods that are then called from within the repository to execute the corresponding query.

42.2.4 Entities

An entity is a class that defines the schema for a table within the database and defines the table name, column names, and data types, and identifies which column is to be the primary key. In addition to declaring the table schema, entity classes also contain getter and setter methods that provide access to these data fields. The data returned to the repository by the DAO in response to the SQL query method calls will take the form of instances of these entity classes. The getter methods will then be called to extract the data from the entity object. Similarly, when the repository needs to write new records to the database, it will create an entity instance, configure values on the object via setter calls, then call insert methods declared in the DAO, passing through entity instances to be saved.

42.2.5 SQLite database

The SQLite database is responsible for storing and providing access to the data. The app code, including the repository, should never make direct access to this underlying database. All database operations are performed using a combination of the room database, DAOs, and entities.

The architecture diagram in Figure 42-2 illustrates how these different elements interact to provide Room-based database storage within an Android app:

Figure 42-2

The numbered connections in the above architecture diagram can be summarized as follows:

1. The repository interacts with the Room Database to get a database instance which, in turn, is used to obtain references to DAO instances.

2. The repository creates entity instances and configures them with data before passing them to the DAO for use in search and insertion operations.

3. The repository calls methods on the DAO passing through entities to be inserted into the database and receives entity instances back in response to search queries.

4. When a DAO has results to return to the repository it packages those results into entity objects.

5. The DAO interacts with the Room Database to initiate database operations and handle results.

6. The Room Database handles all of the low-level interactions with the underlying SQLite database, submitting queries and receiving results.

With a basic outline of the key elements of database access using the Room persistence library covered, it is now time to explore entities, DAOs, room databases, and repositories in more detail.

42.3 Understanding entities

Each database table will have associated with it an entity class. This class defines the schema for the table and takes the form of a standard Kotlin class interspersed with some special Room annotations. An example Kotlin class declaring the data to be stored within a database table might read as follows:

```
class Customer {

    var id: Int = 0
    var name: String? = null
    var address: String? = null

    constructor() {}

    constructor(id: Int, name: String, address: String) {
        this.id = id
        this.name = name
        this.address = address
    }
    constructor(name: String, address: String) {
        this.name = name
        this.address = address
    }

}
```

As currently implemented, the above code declares a basic Kotlin class containing several variables representing database table fields and a collection of getter and setter methods. This class, however, is not yet an entity. To make this class into an entity and to make it accessible within SQL statements, some Room annotations need to be added as follows:

```
@Entity(tableName = "customers")
class Customer {

    @PrimaryKey(autoGenerate = true)
    @NonNull
    @ColumnInfo(name = "customerId")
```

```
    var id: Int = 0

    @ColumnInfo(name = "customerName")
    var name: String? = null
    var address: String? = null

    constructor() {}

    constructor(id: Int, name: String, address: String) {
        this.id = id
        this.name = name
        this.address = address
    }

    constructor(name: String, address: String) {
        this.name = name
        this.address = address
    }
}
```

The above annotations begin by declaring that the class represents an entity and assigns a table name of "customers". This is the name by which the table will be referenced in the DAO SQL statements:

```
@Entity(tableName = "customers")
```

Every database table needs a column to act as the primary key. In this case, the customer id is declared as the primary key. Annotations have also been added to assign a column name to be referenced in SQL queries and to indicate that the field cannot be used to store null values. Finally, the id value is configured to be auto-generated. This means that the id assigned to new records will be automatically generated by the system to avoid duplicate keys.

```
@PrimaryKey(autoGenerate = true)
@NonNull
@ColumnInfo(name = "customerId")
var id: Int = 0
```

A column name is also assigned to the customer name field. Note, however, that no column name was assigned to the address field. This means that the address data will still be stored within the database, but that it is not required to be referenced in SQL statements. If a field within an entity is not required to be stored within a database, simply use the @Ignore annotation:

```
@Ignore
var MyString: String? = null
```

Annotations may also be included within an entity class to establish relationships with other entities using a relational database concept referred to as *foreign keys*. Foreign keys allow a table to reference the primary key in another table. For example, a relationship could be established between an entity named Purchase and our existing Customer entity as follows:

```
@Entity(foreignKeys = arrayOf(ForeignKey(entity = Customer::class,
    parentColumns = arrayOf("customerId"),
    childColumns = arrayOf("buyerId"),
```

```
    onDelete = ForeignKey.CASCADE,
    onUpdate = ForeignKey.RESTRICT)))
class Purchase {

    @PrimaryKey(autoGenerate = true)
    @NonNull
    @ColumnInfo(name = "purchaseId")
    var purchaseId: Int = 0

    @ColumnInfo(name = "buyerId")
    var buyerId: Int = 0
    .
    .
    .
}
```

Note that the foreign key declaration also specifies the action to be taken when a parent record is deleted or updated. Available options are CASCADE, NO_ACTION, RESTRICT, SET_DEFAULT, and SET_NULL.

42.4 Data Access Objects

A Data Access Object provides a way to access the data stored within an SQLite database. A DAO is declared as a standard Kotlin interface with some additional annotations that map specific SQL statements to methods that may then be called by the repository.

The first step is to create the interface and declare it as a DAO using the @Dao annotation:

```
@Dao
interface CustomerDao {
}
```

Next, entries are added consisting of SQL statements and corresponding method names. The following declaration, for example, allows all of the rows in the customers table to be retrieved via a call to a method named *getAllCustomers()*:

```
@Dao
interface CustomerDao {
    @Query("SELECT * FROM customers")
    fun getAllCustomers(): LiveData<List<Customer>>
}
```

Note that the *getAllCustomers()* method returns a List object containing a Customer entity object for each record retrieved from the database table. The DAO is also making use of LiveData so that the repository can observe changes to the database.

Arguments may also be passed into the methods and referenced within the corresponding SQL statements. Consider the following DAO declaration which searches for database records matching a customer's name (note that the column name referenced in the WHERE condition is the name assigned to the column in the entity class):

```
@Query("SELECT * FROM customers WHERE name = :customerName")
fun findCustomer(customerName: String): List<Customer>
```

In this example, the method is passed a string value which is, in turn, included within an SQL statement by prefixing the variable name with a colon (:).

A basic insertion operation can be declared as follows using the @Insert *convenience annotation*:

```
@Insert
fun addCustomer(Customer customer)
```

This is referred to as a convenience annotation because the Room persistence library can infer that the Customer entity passed to the *addCustomer()* method is to be inserted into the database without the need for the SQL insert statement to be provided. Multiple database records may also be inserted in a single transaction as follows:

```
@Insert
fun insertCustomers(Customer... customers)
```

The following DAO declaration deletes all records matching the provided customer name:

```
@Query("DELETE FROM customers WHERE name = :name")
fun deleteCustomer(String name)
```

As an alternative to using the @Query annotation to perform deletions, the @Delete convenience annotation may also be used. In the following example, all of the Customer records that match the set of entities passed to the *deleteCustomers()* method will be deleted from the database:

```
@Delete
fun deleteCustomers(Customer... customers)
```

The @Update convenience annotation provides similar behavior when updating records:

```
@Update
fun updateCustomers(Customer... customers)
```

The DAO methods for these types of database operations may also be declared to return an int value indicating the number of rows affected by the transaction, for example:

```
@Delete
fun deleteCustomers(Customer... customers): int
```

42.5 The Room database

The Room database class is created by extending the RoomDatabase class and acts as a layer on top of the actual SQLite database embedded into the Android operating system. The class is responsible for creating and returning a new room database instance and for providing access to the DAO instances associated with the database.

The Room persistence library provides a database builder for creating database instances. Each Android app should only have one room database instance, so it is best to implement defensive code within the class to prevent more than one instance from being created.

An example Room Database implementation for use with the example customer table is outlined in the following code listing:

```
import android.content.Context
import androidx.room.Database
import androidx.room.Room
import androidx.room.RoomDatabase


@Database(entities = [(Customer::class)], version = 1)
abstract class CustomerRoomDatabase: RoomDatabase() {


abstract fun customerDao(): CustomerDao
```

```
companion object {

    private var INSTANCE: CustomerRoomDatabase? = null

    fun getInstance(context: Context): CustomerRoomDatabase {
        synchronized(this) {
            var instance = INSTANCE

            if (instance == null) {
                instance = Room.databaseBuilder(
                    context.applicationContext,
                    CustomerRoomDatabase::class.java,
                    "customer_database"
                ).fallbackToDestructiveMigration()
                    .build()

                INSTANCE = instance
            }
            return instance
        }
    }
}
}
```

Important areas to note in the above example are the annotation above the class declaration declaring the entities with which the database is to work, the code to check that an instance of the class has not already been created, and the assignment of the name "customer_database" to the instance.

42.6 The Repository

The repository contains the code that makes calls to DAO methods to perform database operations. An example repository might be partially implemented as follows:

```
class CustomerRepository(private val customerDao: CustomerDao) {

    private val coroutineScope = CoroutineScope(Dispatchers.Main)
    .
    .

    fun insertCustomer(customer: Customer) {
        coroutineScope.launch(Dispatchers.IO) {
            customerDao.insertCustomer(customer)
        }
    }

    fun deleteCustomer(name: String) {
        coroutineScope.launch(Dispatchers.IO) {
            customerDao.deleteCustomer(name)
```

```
            }
        }
    .
    .
}
```

Once the repository has access to the DAO, it can make calls to the data access methods. The following code, for example, calls the *getAllCustomers()* DAO method:

```
val allCustomers: LiveData<List<Customer>>?
customerDao.getAllCustomers()
```

When calling DAO methods, it is important to note that unless the method returns a LiveData instance (which automatically runs queries on a separate thread), the operation cannot be performed on the app's main thread. In fact, attempting to do so will cause the app to crash with the following diagnostic output:

```
Cannot access database on the main thread since it may potentially lock the UI
for a long period of time
```

Since some database transactions may take a longer time to complete, running the operations on a separate thread avoids the app appearing to lock up. As will be demonstrated in the chapter entitled *"A Compose Room Database and Repository Tutorial"*, this problem can be easily resolved by making use of coroutines.

With all of the classes declared, instances of the database, DAO and repository need to be created and initialized, the code for which might read as follows:

```
private val repository: CustomerRepository
val customerDb = CustomerRoomDatabase.getInstance(application)
val customerDao = customerDb.customerDao()
repository = CustomerRepository(customerDao)
```

42.7 In-Memory databases

The examples outlined in this chapter involved the use of an SQLite database that exists as a database file on the persistent storage of an Android device. This ensures that the data persists even after the app process is terminated.

The Room database persistence library also supports *in-memory* databases. These databases reside entirely in memory and are lost when the app terminates. The only change necessary to work with an in-memory database is to call the *Room.inMemoryDatabaseBuilder()* method of the Room Database class instead of *Room.databaseBuilder()*. The following code shows the difference between the method calls (note that the in-memory database does not require a database name):

```
// Create a file storage-based database
instance = Room.databaseBuilder(
                context.applicationContext,
                CustomerRoomDatabase::class.java,
                "customer_database"
            ).fallbackToDestructiveMigration()
            .build()


// Create an in-memory database
instance = Room.inMemoryDatabaseBuilder(
                context.applicationContext,
```

```
        CustomerRoomDatabase::class.java,
    ).fallbackToDestructiveMigration()
    .build()
```

42.8 Database Inspector

Android Studio includes a Database Inspector tool window which allows the Room databases associated with running apps to be viewed, searched, and modified as shown in Figure 42-3:

Figure 42-3

Use of the Database Inspector will be covered in the chapter entitled *"A Compose Room Database and Repository Tutorial"*.

42.9 Summary

The Android Room persistence library is bundled with the Android Architecture Components and acts as an abstract layer above the lower-level SQLite database. The library is designed to make it easier to work with databases while conforming to the Android architecture guidelines. This chapter has introduced the different elements that interact to build Room-based database storage into Android app projects including entities, repositories, data access objects, annotations, and Room Database instances.

With the basics of SQLite and the Room architecture component covered, the next step is to create an example app that puts this theory into practice.

Chapter 43

43. A Compose Room Database and Repository Tutorial

This chapter will use the knowledge gained in the chapter entitled *"Working with ViewModels in Compose"* to provide a detailed tutorial demonstrating how to implement SQLite-based database storage using the Room persistence library. In keeping with the Android architectural guidelines, the project will make use of a view model and repository. The tutorial will also provide a demonstration of all of the elements covered in *"Room Databases and Compose"* including entities, a Data Access Object, a Room Database, and asynchronous database queries.

43.1 About the RoomDemo project

The project created in this chapter is a rudimentary inventory app designed to store the names and quantities of products. When completed, the app will provide the ability to add, delete and search for database entries while also displaying a scrollable list of all products currently stored in the database. This product list will update automatically as database entries are added or deleted. Once completed, the app will appear as illustrated in Figure 43-1 below:

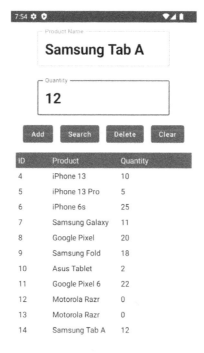

Figure 43-1

43.2 Creating the RoomDemo project

Launch Android Studio and create a new *Empty Compose Activity* project named RoomDemo, specifying *com.example.roomdemo* as the package name, and selecting a minimum API level of API 26: Android 8.0 (Oreo). Within the *MainActivity.kt* file, delete the Greeting function and add a new empty composable named ScreenSetup which, in turn, calls a function named MainScreen:

```
@Composable
fun ScreenSetup() {
    MainScreen()
}

@Composable
fun MainScreen() {

}
```

Next, edit the *onCreateActivity()* method function to call ScreenSetup instead of Greeting. Since this project will be using features that are not supported by the Preview panel, also delete the DefaultPreview composable from the file. To test the project we will be running it on a device or emulator session.

43.3 Modifying the build configuration

Before adding any new classes to the project, the first step is to add some additional libraries to the build configuration, including the Room persistence library. Locate and edit the module-level *build.gradle* file (*app -> Gradle Scripts -> build.gradle (Module: RoomDemo.app)*) and modify it as follows before clicking on the Sync Now link:

```
plugins {
    id 'com.android.application'
    id 'org.jetbrains.kotlin.android'
    id 'kotlin-kapt'
}
.

.

dependencies {
    .

    .

    implementation "androidx.room:room-runtime:2.4.0"
    implementation 'androidx.room:room-ktx:2.4.0'
    implementation "androidx.compose.runtime:runtime-livedata:1.0.5"
    annotationProcessor "androidx.room:room-compiler:2.4.0"
    kapt "androidx.room:room-compiler:2.4.0"
    .

    .

    .
}
```

43.4 Building the entity

This project will begin by creating the entity which defines the schema for the database table. The entity will consist of an integer for the product id, a string column to hold the product name, and another integer value to store the quantity. The product id column will serve as the primary key and will be auto-generated. Table 43-1 summarizes the structure of the entity:

Column	Data Type
productid	Integer / Primary Key / Auto Increment
productname	String
productquantity	Integer

Table 43-1

Add a class file for the entity by right-clicking on the *app -> java -> com.example.roomdemo* entry in the Project tool window and selecting the *New -> Kotlin File/Class* menu option. In the new class dialog, name the class *Product*, select the Class entry in the list and press the keyboard return key to generate the file.

When the *Product.kt* file opens in the editor, modify it so that it reads as follows:

```
package com.example.roomdemo

class Product {

    var id: Int = 0
    var productName: String = ""
    var quantity: Int = 0

    constructor() {}

    constructor(id: Int, productname: String, quantity: Int) {
        this.productName = productname
        this.quantity = quantity
    }
    constructor(productname: String, quantity: Int) {
        this.productName = productname
        this.quantity = quantity
    }
}
```

The class now has variables for the database table columns and matching getter and setter methods. Of course, this class does not become an entity until it has been annotated. With the class file still open in the editor, add annotations and corresponding import statements:

```
package com.example.roomdemo

import androidx.annotation.NonNull
import androidx.room.ColumnInfo
import androidx.room.Entity
import androidx.room.PrimaryKey

@Entity(tableName = "products")
```

```
class Product {

    @PrimaryKey(autoGenerate = true)
    @NonNull
    @ColumnInfo(name = "productId")
    var id: Int = 0

    @ColumnInfo(name = "productName")
    var productName: String = ""
    var quantity: Int = 0

    constructor() {}

    constructor(id: Int, productname: String, quantity: Int) {
        this.id = id
        this.productName = productname
        this.quantity = quantity
    }
    constructor(productname: String, quantity: Int) {
        this.productName = productname
        this.quantity = quantity
    }

}
```

These annotations declare this as the entity for a table named *products* and assign column names for both the *id* and *name* variables. The id column is also configured to be the primary key and auto-generated. Since a primary key can never be null, the @NonNull annotation is also applied. Since it will not be necessary to reference the quantity column in SQL queries, a column name has not been assigned to the *quantity* variable.

43.5 Creating the Data Access Object

With the product entity defined, the next step is to create the DAO interface. Referring once again to the Project tool window, right-click on the *app -> java -> com.example.roomdemo* entry and select the *New -> Kotlin File/ Class* menu option. In the new class dialog, enter *ProductDao* into the Name field and select *Interface* from the list as highlighted in Figure 43-2:

Figure 43-2

Click on OK to generate the new interface and, with the *ProductDao.kt* file loaded into the code editor, make the following changes:

```
package com.example.roomdemo

import androidx.lifecycle.LiveData
import androidx.room.Dao
import androidx.room.Insert
import androidx.room.Query

@Dao
interface ProductDao {

    @Insert
    fun insertProduct(product: Product)

    @Query("SELECT * FROM products WHERE productName = :name")
    fun findProduct(name: String): List<Product>

    @Query("DELETE FROM products WHERE productName = :name")
    fun deleteProduct(name: String)

    @Query("SELECT * FROM products")
    fun getAllProducts(): LiveData<List<Product>>
}
```

The DAO implements methods to insert, find and delete records from the products database. The insertion method is passed a Product entity object containing the data to be stored while the methods to find and delete records are passed a string containing the name of the product on which to operate. The *getAllProducts()* method returns a LiveData object containing all of the records within the database. This method will be used to keep the product list in the user interface layout synchronized with the database.

43.6 Adding the Room database

The last task before adding the repository to the project is to implement the Room Database instance. Add a new class to the project named *ProductRoomDatabase*, this time with the *Class* option selected.

Once the file has been generated, modify it as follows using the steps outlined in the *"Room Databases and Compose"* chapter:

```
package com.example.roomdemo

import android.content.Context
import androidx.room.Database
import androidx.room.Room
import androidx.room.RoomDatabase

@Database(entities = [(Product::class)], version = 1)
abstract class ProductRoomDatabase: RoomDatabase() {

abstract fun productDao(): ProductDao
```

```
    companion object {

        private var INSTANCE: ProductRoomDatabase? = null

        fun getInstance(context: Context): ProductRoomDatabase {
            synchronized(this) {
                var instance = INSTANCE

                if (instance == null) {
                    instance = Room.databaseBuilder(
                        context.applicationContext,
                        ProductRoomDatabase::class.java,
                        "product_database"
                    ).fallbackToDestructiveMigration()
                        .build()

                    INSTANCE = instance
                }
                return instance
            }
        }
    }
}
```

43.7 Adding the repository

Add a new class named *ProductRepository* to the project, with the *Class* option selected.

The repository class will be responsible for interacting with the Room database on behalf of the ViewModel and will need to provide methods that use the DAO to insert, delete and query product records. Except for the *getAllProducts()* DAO method (which returns a LiveData object) these database operations will need to be performed on separate threads from the main thread.

Remaining within the *ProductRepository.kt* file, make the following changes:

```
package com.example.roomdemo

import androidx.lifecycle.LiveData
import androidx.lifecycle.MutableLiveData
import kotlinx.coroutines.*

class ProductRepository(private val productDao: ProductDao) {

    val searchResults = MutableLiveData<List<Product>>()
}
```

The above declares a MutableLiveData variable named *searchResults* into which the results of a search operation are stored whenever an asynchronous search task completes (later in the tutorial, an observer within the ViewModel will monitor this live data object). When an instance of the class is created, it will need to be passed a reference to a ProductDao object.

The repository class now needs to provide some methods that can be called by the ViewModel to initiate database operations. To avoid performing database operations on the main thread, the repository will make use of coroutines where necessary. As such, some additional libraries need to be added to the project before work on the repository class can continue. Start by editing the *Gradle Scripts -> build.gradle (Module: RoomDemo.app)* file to add the following lines to the dependencies section:

```
dependencies {

.

.

    implementation 'org.jetbrains.kotlinx:kotlinx-coroutines-core:1.5.2'
    implementation 'org.jetbrains.kotlinx:kotlinx-coroutines-android:1.5.2'

.

.

}
```

After making the change, click on the *Sync Now* link at the top of the editor panel to commit the changes.

With a reference to the DAO stored and the appropriate libraries added, the methods are ready to be added to the ProductRepository class file as follows:

```
.

.

    val searchResults = MutableLiveData<List<Product>>()
    private val coroutineScope = CoroutineScope(Dispatchers.Main)

    fun insertProduct(newproduct: Product) {
        coroutineScope.launch(Dispatchers.IO) {
            productDao.insertProduct(newproduct)
        }
    }

    fun deleteProduct(name: String) {
        coroutineScope.launch(Dispatchers.IO) {
            productDao.deleteProduct(name)
        }
    }

    fun findProduct(name: String) {
        coroutineScope.launch(Dispatchers.Main) {
            searchResults.value = asyncFind(name).await()
        }
    }

    private fun asyncFind(name: String): Deferred<List<Product>?> =
        coroutineScope.async(Dispatchers.IO) {
            return@async productDao.findProduct(name)
        }
```

In the case of the find operation, the *asyncFind()* method makes use of a deferred value to return the search results to the *findProduct()* method. Because the *findProduct()* method needs access to the searchResults variable, the call to the *asyncFind()* method is dispatched to the main thread which, in turn, performs the database operation using the IO dispatcher.

One final task remains to complete the repository class. The LazyColumn which will be added to the user interface layout later will need to be able to keep up to date with the current list of products stored in the database. The ProductDao class already includes a method named *getAllProducts()* which uses a SQL query to select all of the database records and return them wrapped in a LiveData object. The repository needs to call this method once on initialization and store the result within a LiveData object that can be observed by the ViewModel and, in turn, by the main activity. Once this has been set up, each time a change occurs to the database table the activity observer will be notified and the LazyColumn recomposed with the latest product list. Remaining within the *ProductRepository.kt* file, add a LiveData variable and call to the DAO *getAllProducts()* method:

```
class ProductRepository(private val productDao: ProductDao) {

    val allProducts: LiveData<List<Product>> = productDao.getAllProducts()
    val searchResults = MutableLiveData<List<Product>>()
```

43.8 Adding the ViewModel

The ViewModel will be responsible for the creation of the database, DOA, and repository instances and for providing methods and LiveData objects that can be utilized by the UI controller to handle events.

Begin by adding a ViewModel class to the project by right-clicking on the *app -> java -> com.example.roomdemo* entry in the Project tool window and selecting the *New -> Kotlin File/Class* menu option. In the New Class dialog, name the class *MainViewModel*, select the Class entry in the list and press the keyboard return key to generate the file.

Within the *MainViewModel.kt* file, modify the class declaration to accept an application context instance together with some properties and an initializer block as outlined below. The application context, represented by the Android Context class, is used in application code to gain access to the application resources at runtime. In addition, a wide range of methods may be called on an application's context to gather information and make changes to the application's environment. In this case, the application context is required when creating a database and will be passed into the view model from within the activity later in the chapter:

```
import android.app.Application
import androidx.lifecycle.LiveData
import androidx.lifecycle.MutableLiveData

class MainViewModel(application: Application) {

    val allProducts: LiveData<List<Product>>
```

```
    private val repository: ProductRepository
    val searchResults: MutableLiveData<List<Product>>

    init {
        val productDb = ProductRoomDatabase.getInstance(application)
        val productDao = productDb.productDao()
        repository = ProductRepository(productDao)

        allProducts = repository.allProducts
        searchResults = repository.searchResults
    }
}
```

The initializer block creates a database which is used to create a DAO instance. We then use the DAO to initialize the repository:

```
val productDb = ProductRoomDatabase.getInstance(application)
val productDao = productDb.productDao()
repository = ProductRepository(productDao)
```

Finally, the repository is used to store references to the search results and allProducts live data objects so that they can be converted to states later within the main activity:

```
allProducts = repository.allProducts
searchResults = repository.searchResults
```

All that now remains within the ViewModel is to implement the methods that will be called from within the activity in response to button clicks. These need to be placed after the *init* block as follows:

```
.
.
init {
.
.
}

fun insertProduct(product: Product) {
    repository.insertProduct(product)
}

fun findProduct(name: String) {
    repository.findProduct(name)
}

fun deleteProduct(name: String) {
    repository.deleteProduct(name)
}
.
.
```

43.9 Designing the user interface

With the database, DOA, repository, and ViewModel completed, we are now ready to design the user interface. Start by editing the *MainActivity.kt* file and adding three composables to be used as the input text fields, column rows, and column title:

```
.
.

import androidx.compose.foundation.background
import androidx.compose.foundation.layout.*
import androidx.compose.foundation.text.KeyboardOptions
import androidx.compose.material.*
import androidx.compose.ui.graphics.Color
import androidx.compose.ui.text.TextStyle
import androidx.compose.ui.text.font.FontWeight
import androidx.compose.ui.text.input.KeyboardType
import androidx.compose.ui.unit.dp
import androidx.compose.ui.unit.sp

.
.

class MainActivity : ComponentActivity() {

.
.

@Composable
fun TitleRow(head1: String, head2: String, head3: String) {
    Row(
        modifier = Modifier
            .background(MaterialTheme.colors.primary)
            .fillMaxWidth()
            .padding(5.dp)
    ) {
        Text(head1, color = Color.White,
            modifier = Modifier
            .weight(0.1f))
        Text(head2, color = Color.White,
            modifier = Modifier
                .weight(0.2f))
        Text(head3, color = Color.White,
            modifier = Modifier.weight(0.2f))
    }
}


@Composable
fun ProductRow(id: Int, name: String, quantity: Int) {
    Row(
        modifier = Modifier
            .fillMaxWidth()
```

```
                .padding(5.dp)
    ) {
        Text(id.toString(), modifier = Modifier
            .weight(0.1f))
        Text(name, modifier = Modifier.weight(0.2f))
        Text(quantity.toString(), modifier = Modifier.weight(0.2f))
    }
}


@Composable
fun CustomTextField(
    title: String,
    textState: String,
    onTextChange: (String) -> Unit,
    keyboardType: KeyboardType
) {
    OutlinedTextField(
        value = textState,
        onValueChange = { onTextChange(it) },
        keyboardOptions = KeyboardOptions(
            keyboardType = keyboardType
        ),
        singleLine = true,
        label = { Text(title)},
        modifier = Modifier.padding(10.dp),
        textStyle = TextStyle(fontWeight = FontWeight.Bold,
            fontSize = 30.sp)
    )
}
```

Next, edit the ScreenSetup function to create a ViewModel instance and use it to convert the *allProducts* and *searchResults* live data objects to state values initialized with empty lists. These states, together with the view model also need to be passed to the MainScreen composable:

.

.

```
import android.app.Application
import androidx.compose.ui.platform.LocalContext
import androidx.compose.runtime.*
import androidx.compose.runtime.livedata.observeAsState
```

.

.

```
@Composable
fun ScreenSetup(
viewModel: MainViewModel =
        MainViewModel(LocalContext.current.applicationContext as Application)
) {
```

```
val allProducts by viewModel.allProducts.observeAsState(listOf())
val searchResults by viewModel.searchResults.observeAsState(listOf())

MainScreen(
    allProducts = allProducts,
    searchResults = searchResults,
    viewModel = viewModel
)
}


@Composable
fun MainScreen(
    allProducts: List<Product>,
    searchResults: List<Product>,
    viewModel: MainViewModel
) {

}
```

When creating the ViewModel instance above, note that we used the LocalContext object to obtain a reference to the application context and passed it to the view model so that it can be used when creating the database.

43.10 Completing the MainScreen function

Within the MainScreen function, add some state and event handler declarations as follows:

```
@Composable
fun MainScreen(
    allProducts: List<Product>,
    searchResults: List<Product>,
    viewModel: MainViewModel
) {
    var productName by remember { mutableStateOf("") }
    var productQuantity by remember { mutableStateOf("") }
    var searching by remember { mutableStateOf(false) }

    val onProductTextChange = { text : String ->
        productName = text
    }

    val onQuantityTextChange = { text : String ->
        productQuantity = text
    }
}
```

Continue modifying the MainScreen function to add a Column containing two CustomTextField composables and a Row containing four Button components as follows:

.

.

```
import androidx.compose.ui.Alignment.Companion.CenterHorizontally
.
.
@Composable
fun MainScreen(
    allProducts: List<Product>,
    searchResults: List<Product>,
    viewModel: MainViewModel
) {
.
.

    Column(
        horizontalAlignment = CenterHorizontally,
        modifier = Modifier
            .fillMaxWidth()
    ) {
        CustomTextField(
            title = "Product Name",
            textState = productName,
            onTextChange = onProductTextChange,
            keyboardType = KeyboardType.Text
        )

        CustomTextField(
            title = "Quantity",
            textState = productQuantity,
            onTextChange = onQuantityTextChange,
            keyboardType = KeyboardType.Number
        )

        Row(
            horizontalArrangement = Arrangement.SpaceEvenly,
            modifier = Modifier
                .fillMaxWidth()
                .padding(10.dp)
        ) {
            Button(onClick = {
                viewModel.insertProduct(Product(productName,
                                        productQuantity.toInt()))
                searching = false
            }) {
                Text("Add")
            }

            Button(onClick = {
```

```
                    searching = true
                    viewModel.findProduct(productName)
            }) {
                Text("Search")
            }

            Button(onClick = {
                searching = false
                viewModel.deleteProduct(productName)
            }) {
                Text("Delete")
            }

            Button(onClick = {
                searching = false
                productName = ""
                productQuantity = ""
            }) {
                Text("Clear")
            }
        }
    }
}
```

Finally, add a LazyColumn to the parent Column immediately after the row of Button components. This will display a single instance of the TitleRow followed by a ProductRow for each product. The *searching* state will be used to decide whether the list is to include all products or only those products that match the search criteria:

```
.
.
import androidx.compose.foundation.lazy.LazyColumn
import androidx.compose.foundation.lazy.items
.
.
@Composable
fun MainScreen(allProducts: List<Product>, searchResults: List<Product>,
viewModel: MainViewModel) {
.
.
        LazyColumn(
            Modifier
                .fillMaxWidth()
                .padding(10.dp)
        ) {
            val list = if (searching) searchResults else allProducts

            item {
```

```
        TitleRow(head1 = "ID", head2 = "Product", head3 = "Quantity")
    }

    items(list) { product ->
        ProductRow(id = product.id, name = product.productName,
                        quantity = product.quantity)
    }
  }
 }
}
```

43.11 Testing the RoomDemo app

Compile and run the app on a device or emulator where it should appear as illustrated in Figure 43-1 above. Add some products and make sure that they appear automatically in the LazyColumn. Perform a search for an existing product and verify that the matching result is listed. Click the Clear button to reset the list, then enter the name for an existing product, delete it from the database and confirm that it is removed from the product list.

43.12 Using the Database Inspector

As previously outlined in *"Room Databases and Compose"*, the Database Inspector tool may be used to inspect the content of Room databases associated with a running app and to perform minor data changes. After adding some database records using the RoomDemo app, display the Database Inspector tool using the *View -> Tool Windows -> App Inspection* menu option:

From within the inspector window, select the running app from the menu marked A in Figure 43-3 below:

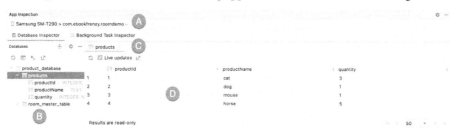

Figure 43-3

From the Databases panel (B) double-click on the *products* table to view the table rows currently stored in the database. Enable the *Live updates* option (C) and then use the running app to add more records to the database. Note that the Database Inspector updates the table data (D) in real-time to reflect the changes.

Turn off Live updates so that the table is no longer read-only, double-click on the quantity cell for a table row, and change the value before pressing the keyboard Enter key. Return to the running app and search for the product to confirm the change made to the quantity in the inspector was saved to the database table.

Finally, click on the table query button (indicated by the arrow in Figure 43-4 below) to display a new query tab (A), make sure that *product_database* is selected (B), and enter a SQL statement into the query text field (C) and click the Run button(D):

Figure 43-4

The list of rows should update to reflect the results of the SQL query (E).

43.13 Summary

This chapter has demonstrated the use of the Room persistence library to store data in an SQLite database. The finished project made use of a repository to separate the ViewModel from all database operations and demonstrated the creation of entities, a DAO, and a room database instance, including the use of asynchronous tasks when performing some database operations.

44. An Overview of Navigation in Compose

Very few Android apps today consist of just a single screen. In reality, most apps comprise multiple screens through which the user navigates using screen gestures, button clicks, and menu selections. Before the introduction of Android Jetpack, the implementation of navigation within an app was largely a manual coding process with no easy way to view and organize potentially complex navigation paths. This situation improved considerably, however, with the introduction of the Android Navigation Architecture Component which has now been extended to support navigation in Compose-based apps. This chapter will provide an overview of navigation within Compose including explanations of routes, navigation graphs, the navigation back stack, passing arguments, and the NavHostController and NavHost classes.

44.1 Understanding navigation

Every app has a home screen that appears after the app has launched and after any splash screen has appeared (a splash screen being the app branding screen that appears temporarily while the app loads). From this home screen, the user will typically perform tasks that will result in other screens appearing. These screens will usually take the form of other composables within the project. A messaging app, for example, might have a home screen listing current messages from which the user can navigate to either another screen to access a contact list, or to a settings screen. The contacts list screen, in turn, might allow the user to navigate to other screens where new users can be added or existing contacts updated. Graphically, the app's *navigation graph* might be represented as shown in Figure 44-1:

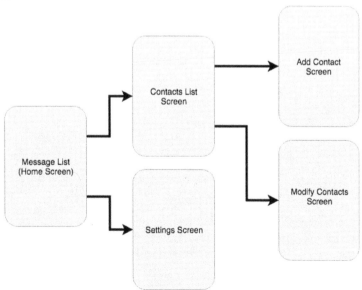

Figure 44-1

Each screen that makes up an app, including the home screen, is referred to as a *destination* and is usually a composable or activity. The Android navigation architecture uses a *navigation back stack* to track the user's path through the destinations within the app. When the app first launches, the home screen is the first destination placed onto the stack and becomes the *current destination*. When the user navigates to another destination, that screen becomes the current destination and is *pushed* onto the back stack above the home destination. As the user navigates to other screens, they are also pushed onto the stack. Figure 44-2, for example, shows the current state of the navigation stack for the hypothetical messaging app after the user has launched the app and is navigating to the "Add Contact" screen:

Figure 44-2

As the user navigates back through the screens using the system back button, each destination composable is *popped* off the stack until the home screen is once again the only destination on the stack. In Figure 44-3, the user has navigated back from the Add Contact screen, popping it off the stack and making the Contact List screen composable the current destination:

Figure 44-3

All of the work involved in navigating between destinations and managing the navigation stack is handled by a *navigation controller* which is represented by the NavHostController class. It is also possible to manually pop composables off the stack so that the app returns to a screen lower down the stack when the user navigates backward from the current screen.

Adding navigation to an Android project using the Navigation Architecture Component is a straightforward process involving a navigation host, navigation graph, navigation actions, and a minimal amount of code writing to obtain a reference to, and interact with, the navigation controller instance.

44.2 Declaring a navigation controller

The first step in adding navigation to an app project is to create a NavHostController instance. This is responsible for managing the back stack and keeping track of which composable is the current destination. So that the integrity of the back stack is maintained through recomposition, NavHostController is a stateful object and is created via a call to the *rememberNavController()* method as follows:

```
val navController = rememberNavController()
```

Once a navigation controller has been created it needs to be assigned to a NavHost instance.

44.3 Declaring a navigation host

The navigation host (NavHost) is a special component that is added to the user interface layout of an activity and serves as a placeholder for the destinations through which the user will navigate. Figure 44-4, for example, shows a typical activity screen and highlights the area represented by the navigation host:

Figure 44-4

When it is called, NavHost must be passed a NavHostController instance, a composable to serve as the *start destination,* and a *navigation graph*. The navigation graph consists of all the composables that are to be available as navigation destinations within the context of the navigation controller. These destinations are declared in the form of *routes*:

```
NavHost(navController = navController, startDestination = <start route>) {
    // Navigation graph destinations
}
```

44.4 Adding destinations to the navigation graph

Destinations are added to the navigation graph by making calls to the *composable()* method and providing a *route* and destination. The route is simply a string value that uniquely identifies the destination within the context of the current navigation controller and the destination is the composable to be called when the navigation is performed. The following NavHost declaration includes a navigation graph consisting of three destinations,

387

with the "home" route configured as the start destination:

```
NavHost(navController = navController, startDestination = "home") {

    composable("home") {
        Home()
    }

    composable("customers") {
        Customers()
    }

    composable("purchases") {
        Purchases()
    }
}
```

A more flexible alternative to hard coding the route strings into the *composable()* method calls is to define the routes in a sealed class:

```
sealed class Routes(val route: String) {
    object Home : Routes("home")
    object Customers : Routes("customers")
    object Purchases : Routes("purchases")
}
```

With the class declared, the NavHost will now reference the routes as follows:

```
NavHost(navController = navController, startDestination = Routes.Home.route) {

    composable(Routes.Home.route) {
        Home()
    }

    composable(Routes.Customers.route) {
        Customers()
    }

    composable(Routes.Purchases.route) {
        Purchases()
    }
}
```

The use of the sealed class approach gives us the advantage of a single location in which to make changes to the routes, and also adds syntax validation to avoid mistyping a route string when creating a NavHost or performing navigation.

44.5 Navigating to destinations

The primary mechanism for triggering navigation is via calls to the *navigate()* method of the navigation controller instance, specifying the route for the destination composable. The following code, for example, configures a

Button component to navigate to the Customers screen when clicked:

```
Button(onClick = {
    navController.navigate(Routes.Customers.route)
}) {
    Text(text = "Navigate to Customers")
}
```

The *navigate()* method also accepts a trailing lambda containing navigation options, one of which is the *popUpTo()* function. Consider, for example, a scenario where the user starts on the home screen and then navigates to the customer screen. The customer screen displays a list of customer names which, when clicked navigates to the purchases screen populated with a list of the selected customer's previous purchases. At this point, the back stack contains the customer and home destinations. If the user where to tap the back button located at the bottom of the screen, the app will navigate back to the customer screen. The *popUpTo()* navigation option allows us to pop items off the stack back to the specific destination. We could, for example, pop all destinations off the stack before navigating to the purchases screen so that only the home destination remains on the back stack as follows:

```
Button(onClick = {
    navController.navigate(Routes.Customers.route) {
        popUpTo(Routes.Home.route)
    }
}) {
    Text(text = "Navigate to Customers")
}
```

Now when the user clicks the back button on the purchases screen, the app will navigate directly to the home screen. The *popUpTo()* method also accepts options. The following, for example, uses the *inclusive* option to also pop the home destination off the stack before performing the navigation:

```
Button(onClick = {
    navController.navigate(Routes.Customers.route) {
        popUpTo(Routes.Home.route) {
            inclusive = true
        }
    }
}) {
    Text(text = "Navigate to Customers")
}
```

By default, an attempt to navigate from the current destination to itself will push an additional instance of the destination onto the stack. In most situations, this is unlikely to be the desired behavior. To prevent the addition of multiple instances of the same destination to the top of the stack, set the launchSingleTop option to true when calling the *navigate()* method:

```
Button(onClick = {
    navController.navigate(Routes.Customers.route) {
        launchSingleTop = true
    }
}) {
    Text(text = "Navigate to Customers")
}
```

The saveState and restoreState options, if set to true, will automatically save and restore the state of back stack entries when the user reselects a destination that has been selected previously.

44.6 Passing arguments to a destination

It is a common requirement when navigating from one screen to another to need to pass an argument to the destination. Compose supports the passing of arguments of a wide range of types from one screen to another and involves several steps. In our hypothetical example, we would probably need to pass the name of the selected customer from the customer screen to the purchases screen so that the correct purchase history can be displayed.

The first step in navigating with arguments involves adding the argument name to the destination route. We can, for example, add an argument named "customerName" to the purchases route as follows:

```
NavHost(navController = navController, startDestination = Routes.Home.route) {
.
.

    composable(Routes.Purchases.route + "/{customerName}") {
        Purchases()
    }
.
.
}
```

When the app triggers navigation to the customer destination, the value to be assigned to the argument will be stored within the corresponding back stack entry. The back stack entry for the current navigation is passed as a parameter to the trailing lambda of the *composable()* method where it can be extracted and passed to the Customer composable:

```
composable(Routes.Purchases.route + "/{customerName}") { backStackEntry ->

    val customerName = backStackEntry.arguments?.getString("customerName")

    Purchases(customerName)
}
```

By default, the navigation argument is assumed to be of String type. To pass arguments of different types, the type must be specified using the NavType enumeration via the *composable()* method *arguments* parameter. In the following example, the parameter type is declared as being of type Int. Note also that the argument now needs to be extracted from the back stack entry using *getInt()* instead of *getString()*:

```
composable(Routes.Purchases.route + "/{customerId}",
    arguments = listOf(navArgument("customerId") { type = NavType.IntType })) {
                        navBackStack ->
    Customers(navBackStack.arguments?.getInt("customerId"))
}
```

Returning to the original string argument example, the Purchases composable now needs to be modified to expect a String parameter:

```
@Composable
fun Customers(customerName: String?) {
.
.
```

}

The final step is to pass a value for the argument when making the *navigate()* method call. We do this by appending the argument value to the end of the destination route. Assuming that the value we need to pass to the purchases screen is stored as a state variable named selectedCustomer, the *navigate()* call would be written as follows:

```
var selectedCustomer by remember {
    mutableStateOf("")
}

// Code to identify selected customer here

Button(onClick = {
    navController.navigate(Routes.Customers.route + "/$selectedCustomer")
}) {
    Text(text = "Navigate to Customers")
}
```

When the button is clicked, the following sequence of events will occur:

1. A back stack entry is created for the current destination.

2. The current selectedCustomer state value is stored in the back stack entry.

3. The back stack entry is pushed onto the back stack.

4. The *composable()* method for the purchase route in the NavHost declaration is called.

5. The trailing lambda of the *composable()* method extracts the argument value from the back stack entry and passes it to the Purchases composable.

44.7 Working with bottom navigation bars

So far in this chapter, we have focused on navigation in response to click events on Button components. Another common form of navigation involves the bottom navigation bar.

The bottom navigation bar appears at the bottom of the screen and displays a list of navigation items usually comprising an icon and a label. Clicking on an item navigates to the different screen within the current activity. An example bottom navigation bar is illustrated in Figure 44-5 below:

Figure 44-5

The core components of bottom bar navigation are the Compose BottomNavigation and BottomNavigationItem components. Implementation typically involves a parent BottomNavigationBar containing a *forEach* loop which iterates through a list creating each BottomNavigationItem child. Each child is configured with the label and icon to be displayed and an onClick handler to perform the navigation to the corresponding destination. Typical syntax will read as follows:

```
BottomNavigation {

    <items list>.forEach { navItem ->
```

```
BottomNavigationItem(
    selected = <true | false>,
    onClick = {
        navController.navigate(navItem.route) {
            popUpTo(navController.graph.findStartDestination().id) {
                saveState = true
            }
            launchSingleTop = true
            restoreState = true
        }
    },

    icon = {
        <icon>
    },
    label = {
        <text>
    },
)
}
}
```

Note that the *PopUpTo()* method is called to make sure that if the user clicks the back button the navigation returns to the start destination. We can identify the start destination by calling the *findStartDestination()* method on the navigation graph:

```
navController.graph.findStartDestination()
```

Also, the launchSingleTop, saveState, and restoreState options need to be enabled when working with bottom bar navigation.

Each BottomNavigationItem needs to be told whether it is the currently selected item via the *selected* property. When working with bottom bar navigation, you will need to write code to compare the route associated with the item against the current route selection. The current route selection can be obtained by gaining access to the back stack via the *currentBackStackEntryAsState()* method of the navigation controller and accessing the destination route property, for example:

```
BottomNavigation {
    val backStackEntry by navController.currentBackStackEntryAsState()
    val currentRoute = backStackEntry?.destination?.route

    NavBarItems.BarItems.forEach { navItem ->

        BottomNavigationItem(
            selected = currentRoute == navItem.route
.
.
```

The two routes are then compared and the result assigned to the selected property. A more detailed example of bottom bar navigation will be demonstrated in the chapter entitled *"A Compose Bottom Navigation Bar Tutorial"*.

44.8 Summary

This chapter has covered the addition of navigation to Android apps using the Compose support built into the Jetpack Navigation Architecture Component. Navigation is implemented by creating an instance of the NavHostController class and associating it with a NavHost instance. The NavHost instance is configured with the starting destination and the navigation routes that make up the navigation graph for the current activity. Navigation is then performed by making calls to the *navigate()* method of the navigation controller instance, passing through the path of the destination composable. Compose also supports the passing of arguments to the destination composable. Navigation may also be added to screens using the Compose BottomNavigation and BottomNavigationItem components.

45. A Compose Navigation Tutorial

The previous chapter provided an overview of navigation using the Jetpack Navigation Architecture Component when developing with Compose. This chapter will build on this knowledge to create a project that uses navigation, including an example of passing an argument from one destination to another.

45.1 Creating the NavigationDemo project

Launch Android Studio and create a new *Empty Compose Activity* project named NavigationDemo, specifying *com.example.navigationdemo* as the package name, and selecting a minimum API level of API 26: Android 8.0 (Oreo). Within the *MainActivity.kt* file, delete the Greeting function and add a new empty composable named MainScreen:

```
@Composable
fun MainScreen() {


}
```

Next, edit the *onCreateActivity()* method and DefaultPreview function to call MainScreen instead of Greeting.

Before proceeding, we will also need to add the Compose navigation library to the project build settings. Within the Project tool window, locate and open the module level Gradle build file (*app -> Gradle Scripts -> build.gradle (Module: NavigationDemo.app)* file and add the following line to the *dependencies* section (keeping in mind that a more recent version of the library may now be available):

```
.
.
implementation   'androidx.navigation:navigation-compose:2.4.0'
.
.
```

45.2 About the NavigationDemo project

The completed project will comprise three destination screens named "home", "welcome" and "profile". The home screen will contain a text field into which the user will enter their name and a button which, when clicked, will navigate to the welcome screen, passing the user's name as an argument for inclusion in a welcome message. The welcome screen will also contain a button to navigate to the profile screen, the sole purpose of which is for experimenting with the *popUpTo()* navigation option method.

45.3 Declaring the navigation routes

The first step in implementing the navigation in the project is to add the routes for the three destinations which will be declared using a sealed class. Begin by right-clicking on the *app -> java -> com.example.navigationdemo* entry in the Project tool window and selecting the *New -> Kotlin File/Class* menu option. In the new class dialog, name the class *NavRoutes*, select the *Sealed Class* entry in the list and press the keyboard return key to generate the file. Edit the new file to add the destination routes as follows:

```
package com.example.navigationdemo


sealed class NavRoutes(val route: String) {
```

```
    object Home : NavRoutes("home")
    object Welcome : NavRoutes("welcome")
    object Profile : NavRoutes("profile")
}
```

45.4 Adding the home screen

The three destinations now need a composable, each of which we will declare in a separate file placed in a new package named *com.example.navigationdemo.screens*. Create this package now by right-clicking on the *com.example.navigationdemo* entry in the Project tool window and selecting the *New -> Package* menu option. In the resulting dialog, name the package *com.example.navigationdemo.screens* as shown in Figure 45-1 before tapping the keyboard enter key:

New Package

com.example.navigationdemo.screens

Figure 45-1

Right-click on the new package entry in the Project tool window, select the option to create a new Kotlin class file, name it *Home*, and modify it so that it reads as follows:

.

.

```
import androidx.compose.foundation.layout.*
import androidx.compose.material.*
import androidx.compose.runtime.*
import androidx.compose.ui.Alignment
import androidx.compose.ui.Modifier
import androidx.compose.ui.text.TextStyle
import androidx.compose.ui.text.font.FontWeight
import androidx.compose.ui.unit.dp
import androidx.compose.ui.unit.sp
import androidx.navigation.NavHostController

import com.example.navigationdemo.NavRoutes

@Composable
fun Home(navController: NavHostController) {

    var userName by remember { mutableStateOf("") }
    val onUserNameChange = { text : String ->
        userName = text
    }

    Box(
        modifier = Modifier
            .fillMaxSize(),
        contentAlignment = Alignment.Center
    ) {
```

```
    Column(horizontalAlignment = Alignment.CenterHorizontally) {
        CustomTextField(
            title = "Enter your name",
            textState = userName,
            onTextChange = onUserNameChange
        )

        Spacer(modifier = Modifier.size(30.dp))

        Button(onClick = { }) {
            Text(text = "Register")
        }
    }
}
}

@Composable
fun CustomTextField(
    title: String,
    textState: String,
    onTextChange: (String) -> Unit,
) {
    OutlinedTextField(
        value = textState,
        onValueChange = { onTextChange(it) },
        singleLine = true,
        label = { Text(title)},
        modifier = Modifier.padding(10.dp),
        textStyle = TextStyle(fontWeight = FontWeight.Bold,
            fontSize = 30.sp)
    )
}
```

45.5 Adding the welcome screen

Add a new class file to the screens package named *Welcome.kt*. Once the file has been created, edit it so that it reads as follows:

.

.

```
import androidx.compose.foundation.layout.*
import androidx.compose.material.*
import androidx.compose.runtime.*
import androidx.compose.ui.Alignment
import androidx.compose.ui.Modifier
import androidx.compose.ui.unit.dp
import androidx.navigation.NavHostController
```

```
import com.example.navigationdemo.NavRoutes

@Composable
fun Welcome(navController: NavHostController) {

    Box(
        modifier = Modifier
            .fillMaxSize(),
        contentAlignment = Alignment.Center
    ) {
        Column(horizontalAlignment = Alignment.CenterHorizontally) {
            Text("Welcome", style = MaterialTheme.typography.h5)

            Spacer(modifier = Modifier.size(30.dp))

            Button(onClick = { }) {
                Text(text = "Set up your Profile")
            }
        }
    }

}
```

45.6 Adding the profile screen

The profile screen is the simplest of the composables and consists of a single Text component. Once again, add a new class file to the screens package, this time named *Profile.kt*, and edit it to make the following changes:

.

.

```
import androidx.compose.foundation.layout.*
import androidx.compose.material.*
import androidx.compose.runtime.*
import androidx.compose.ui.Alignment
import androidx.compose.ui.Modifier

@Composable
fun Profile() {

    Box(
        modifier = Modifier
            .fillMaxSize(),
        contentAlignment = Alignment.Center
    ) {
            Text("Profile Screen", style = MaterialTheme.typography.h5)
    }
}
```

45.7 Creating the navigation controller and host

Now that the basic elements of the project have been created, the next step is to create the navigation controller (NavHostController) and navigation host (NavHost) instances. Edit the *MainActivity.kt* file and make the following modifications:

.

.

```
import androidx.navigation.compose.NavHost
import androidx.navigation.compose.composable
import androidx.navigation.compose.rememberNavController
import com.example.navigationdemo.screens.Home
import com.example.navigationdemo.screens.Profile
import com.example.navigationdemo.screens.Welcome
```

.

.

```
@Composable
fun MainScreen() {

    val navController = rememberNavController()

    NavHost(
        navController = navController,
        startDestination = NavRoutes.Home.route,
    ) {
        composable(NavRoutes.Home.route) {
            Home(navController = navController)
        }

        composable(NavRoutes.Welcome.route) {
            Welcome(navController = navController)
        }

        composable(NavRoutes.Profile.route) {
            Profile()
        }
    }
}
```

The above code changes to the MainScreen function begin by obtaining a navigation controller instance via a call to the *rememberNavController()* method. The NavHost component is called, assigning the home screen as the start destination. The *composable()* method is then called to add a route for each of the screens.

45.8 Implementing the screen navigation

Navigation needs to be initiated when the Button components in the home and welcome screens are clicked. Both composables have already been passed the navigation controller on which we will be calling the *navigate()* method. Starting with the *Home.kt* file, locate the Button component and add the navigation code to the onClick property using the route for the welcome screen:

.

.

```
Button(onClick = {
    navController.navigate(NavRoutes.Welcome.route)
}) {
    Text(text = "Register")
}
```

.

.

Next, edit the *Welcome.kt* file and add code to the Button onClick property to navigate to the profile screen:

.

.

```
Button(onClick = {
        navController.navigate(NavRoutes.Profile.route)
    }) {
        Text(text = "Set up your Profile")
    }
```

.

.

Take this opportunity to compile and run the app on a device or emulator and test that the buttons navigate to the correct screens when clicked.

45.9 Passing the user name argument

The welcome destination route in the NavHost declaration now needs to be extended so that the user name typed into the text field can be passed to the welcome screen during the navigation. First, edit the *Welcome. kt* file and modify the Welcome function to accept a user name String parameter and to display it in the Text component:

.

.

```
@Composable
fun Welcome(navController: NavHostController, userName: String?) {
```

.

.

```
        Column(horizontalAlignment = Alignment.CenterHorizontally) {
            Text("Welcome, $userName", style = MaterialTheme.typography.h5)
```

.

.

With the Welcome composable ready to accept and display the user name, the NavHost declaration needs to be changed to extract the parameter from the navigation back stack entry and pass it to the Welcome function. Return to the *MainActivity.kt* file and modify the Welcome route *composable()* call so that it reads as follows:

.

.

```
composable(NavRoutes.Welcome.route + "/{userName}") { backStackEntry ->

    val userName = backStackEntry.arguments?.getString("userName")
```

```
        Welcome(navController = navController, userName)
}
.
.
```

The final task before we test the app once again is to modify the onClick handler assigned to the home screen Button component to get the current user name state value and append it to the route in the *navigate()* method call. Edit the *Home.kt* file, locate the Button call and modify the onClick handler:

```
.
.
    Button(onClick = {
        navController.navigate(NavRoutes.Welcome.route + "/$userName")
    }) {
        Text(text = "Register")
    }
.
.
```

45.10 Testing the project

Compile and run the project on a device or emulator and enter a name into the text field on the home screen:

Figure 45-2

A Compose Navigation Tutorial

Click the Register button and verify that the name you entered appears in the Text component of the Welcome screen:

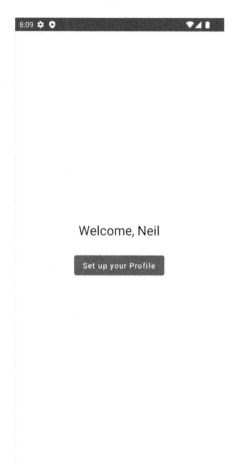

Figure 45-3

After clicking on the "Set up your Profile" button to reach the profile screen, the back button located in the bottom toolbar should navigate through the back stack (if you are using Android 12 or later, swipe right to navigate backwards), starting with the welcome screen followed by the home screen. If we want the backward navigation to return directly to the home screen we need to make sure everything except the home destination is popped off the navigation back stack using the *popUpTo()* method call. This needs to be called as an option to the *navigate()* method in the Button onClick handler in the Welcome composable:

```
Button(onClick = {
    navController.navigate(NavRoutes.Profile.route) {
        popUpTo(NavRoutes.Home.route)
    }
```

When the app runs, tapping the back button (or swiping right on newer Android versions) from the profile screen should now skip the welcome screen and return directly to the home screen.

45.11 Summary

In this chapter, we have created a project which makes use of navigation to switch between screens within an activity. This included creating a navigation controller and declaring a navigation host initialized with navigation routes for each destination. The tutorial also implemented a navigation argument to pass a string value from one navigation destination to another.

46. A Compose Bottom Navigation Bar Tutorial

Following on from the overview provided previously in the chapter entitled *"An Overview of Navigation in Compose"* this chapter will create a project that integrates navigation into an activity using the Compose BottomNavigation component. The project will also provide a brief introduction to the Scaffold component and demonstrate how it can be used to create a standard screen layout that conforms to the Material theme guidelines.

46.1 Creating the BottomBarDemo project

Launch Android Studio and create a new *Empty Compose Activity* project named BottomBarDemo, specifying *com.example.bottombardemo* as the package name, and selecting a minimum API level of API 26: Android 8.0 (Oreo). Within the *MainActivity.kt* file, delete the Greeting function and add a new empty composable named MainScreen:

```
@Composable
fun MainScreen() {


}
```

Next, edit the *onCreateActivity()* method and DefaultPreview function to call MainScreen instead of Greeting.

Before proceeding, we will also need to add the Compose navigation library to the project build settings. Within the Project tool window, locate and open the module level Gradle build file (*app -> Gradle Scripts -> build.gradle (Module: BottomBarDemo.app)* file and add the following line to the *dependencies* section:

```
implementation  'androidx.navigation:navigation-compose:2.4.0'
```

46.2 Declaring the navigation routes

When the project is completed, it will include a bottom bar containing three items which, when clicked, will navigate to different screens, each represented by a composable. The first step we need to complete is to add the routes for the three destinations which will be declared using a sealed class. Begin by right-clicking on the *app -> java -> com.example.bottombardemo* entry in the Project tool window and selecting the *New -> Kotlin File/ Class* menu option. In the new class dialog, name the class *NavRoutes*, select the *Sealed Class* entry in the list and press the keyboard return key to generate the file. Edit the new file to add the destination routes as follows:

```
package com.example.bottombardemo


sealed class NavRoutes(val route: String) {
    object Home : NavRoutes("home")
    object Contacts : NavRoutes("contacts")
    object Favorites : NavRoutes("favorites")
}
```

46.3 Designing bar items

Each item in the bottom bar will need a title string, an icon image, and the route to which the app should navigate when the item is clicked. To keep the *MainActivity.kt* file as simple as possible, we will also declare the bar item class as a separate file. Using the steps outlined above, add a new Kotlin Class file named *BarItem*, this time using the *Data Class* option, to the project and modify it so that it reads as follows:

```
package com.example.bottombardemo

import androidx.compose.ui.graphics.vector.ImageVector

data class BarItem(
    val title: String,
    val image: ImageVector,
    val route: String
)
```

46.4 Creating the bar item list

Now that we have the BarItem class providing a template for each bar item, the next step is to create a list containing the three bar items, each configured with the appropriate string, image, and route properties. Add another Kotlin class using the *Object* option, this time named *NavBarItems*, and implement the list as follows:

```
package com.example.bottombardemo

import androidx.compose.material.icons.*
import androidx.compose.material.icons.filled.Home
import androidx.compose.material.icons.filled.Favorite
import androidx.compose.material.icons.filled.Face

object NavBarItems {
    val BarItems = listOf(
        BarItem(
            title = "Home",
            image = Icons.Filled.Home,
            route = "home"
        ),
        BarItem(
            title = "Contacts",
            image = Icons.Filled.Face,
            route = "contacts"
        ),
        BarItem(
            title = "Favorites",
            image = Icons.Filled.Favorite,
            route = "favorites"
        )
    )
}
```

Note that the above declaration makes use of the built-in Material theme icons for the images. Although not as extensive as the Clip Art list available via the Resource Manager used in earlier chapters, these icons provide a quick and convenient way to add graphics to your project.

46.5 Adding the destination screens

Each of the three destinations now needs a composable. These will be simple functions that do nothing more than display the icon for the corresponding bar item selection. Each screen composable will be declared in a separate file, each of which will be placed in a new package named *com.example.bottombardemo.screens*. Create this package now by right-clicking on the *com.example.bottombardemo* entry in the Project tool window and selecting the New package menu option. In the resulting dialog, name the package *com.example.bottombardemo. screens* as shown in Figure 46-1 before tapping the keyboard enter key:

New Package

com.example.bottombardemo.screens

Figure 46-1

Right-click on the new package entry in the Project tool window, select the option to create a new Kotlin class named Home, and modify it so that it reads as follows:

.

.

```
import androidx.compose.foundation.layout.Box
import androidx.compose.foundation.layout.fillMaxSize
import androidx.compose.foundation.layout.size
import androidx.compose.material.Icon
import androidx.compose.material.icons.Icons
import androidx.compose.material.icons.filled.Home
import androidx.compose.runtime.Composable
import androidx.compose.ui.Alignment
import androidx.compose.ui.Modifier
import androidx.compose.ui.graphics.Color
import androidx.compose.ui.tooling.preview.Preview
import androidx.compose.ui.unit.dp


@Composable
fun Home() {

    Box(
        modifier = Modifier.fillMaxSize()
    ) {
        Icon(
            imageVector = Icons.Filled.Home,
            contentDescription = "home",
            tint = Color.Blue,
            modifier = Modifier.size(150.dp)
                .align(Alignment.Center)
        )
```

```
    }
}
```

Repeat these steps to add class files for the two remaining screens named Contacts and Favorites using the same code as that used for the home screen above, but changing the icon import, imageVector property, and contentDescription accordingly. In the case of the Contacts composable the following changes apply:

.

.

```
import androidx.compose.material.icons.filled.Face
```

.

.

```
@Composable
fun Contacts() {

    Box(
        modifier = Modifier.fillMaxSize()
    ) {
        Icon(
            imageVector = Icons.Filled.Face,
            contentDescription = "contacts",
            tint = Color.Blue,
            modifier = Modifier.size(150.dp)
                .align(Alignment.Center)
        )
    }
}
```

Similarly, the following changes will be needed for the *Favorites.kt* file:

.

.

```
import androidx.compose.material.icons.filled.Favorite
```

.

.

```
@Composable
fun Favorites() {

    Box(
        modifier = Modifier.fillMaxSize()
    ) {
        Icon(
            imageVector = Icons.Filled.Favorite,
            contentDescription = "favorites",
            tint = Color.Blue,
            modifier = Modifier.size(150.dp)
                .align(Alignment.Center)
        )
```

```
        }
}
```

46.6 Creating the navigation controller and host

Now that the basic elements of the project have been created, the next step is to create both the navigation controller (NavHostController) and navigation host (NavHost) instances. Edit the *MainActivity.kt* file and make the following modifications:

```
.

.

import androidx.navigation.compose.NavHost
import androidx.navigation.compose.composable
import androidx.navigation.compose.rememberNavController
import androidx.navigation.NavHostController
import com.example.bottombardemo.screens.Contacts
import com.example.bottombardemo.screens.Favorites
import com.example.bottombardemo.screens.Home

.

.

@Composable
fun MainScreen() {

    val navController = rememberNavController()
}


@Composable
fun NavigationHost(navController: NavHostController) {

    NavHost(
        navController = navController,
        startDestination = NavRoutes.Home.route,
    ) {
        composable(NavRoutes.Home.route) {
            Home()
        }

        composable(NavRoutes.Contacts.route) {
            Contacts()
        }

        composable(NavRoutes.Favorites.route) {
            Favorites()
        }
    }
}
```

46.7 Designing the navigation bar

The bottom navigation bar will be implemented in a separate composable named BottomNavBar which will need to be passed the navigation controller instance created in the NavSetup function. It will, of course, consist of a BottomNavigation component and a BottomNavigationItem child for each of the three destination screens. Start by adding the BottomNavBar function to the *MainActivity.kt* file as follows:

```
.
.
import androidx.compose.material.*
import androidx.compose.runtime.getValue
import androidx.navigation.compose.currentBackStackEntryAsState
import androidx.navigation.NavGraph.Companion.findStartDestination
.
.
@Composable
fun BottomNavigationBar(navController: NavHostController) {

    BottomNavigation {


    }
}
```

Within the BottomNavigation call, we will need to be able to identify the route of the currently selected navigation destination. We do this by calling the *currentBackStackEntryAsState()* method of the navigation controller to obtain the current back stack entry from which we can access the route:

```
@Composable
fun BottomNavigationBar(navController: NavHostController) {

    BottomNavigation {
        val backStackEntry by navController.currentBackStackEntryAsState()
        val currentRoute = backStackEntry?.destination?.route


    }
}
```

All that remains is to iterate through the items located in BarItems and use the title, image, and route settings for each item to configure BottomNavigationItem instances for each destination:

```
@Composable
fun BottomNavigationBar(navController: NavHostController) {

    BottomNavigation {
        val backStackEntry by navController.currentBackStackEntryAsState()
        val currentRoute = backStackEntry?.destination?.route

        NavBarItems.BarItems.forEach { navItem ->

            BottomNavigationItem(
```

```
            selected = currentRoute == navItem.route,
            onClick = {
                navController.navigate(navItem.route) {
                    popUpTo(navController.graph.findStartDestination().id) {
                        saveState = true
                    }
                    launchSingleTop = true
                    restoreState = true
                }
            },

            icon = {
                Icon(imageVector = navItem.image,
                        contentDescription = navItem.title)
            },
            label = {
                Text(text = navItem.title)
            },
        )
    }
}
}
```

46.8 Working with the Scaffold component

The final task before testing the project is to complete the layout in the MainScreen function. For this, we will be making use of the Compose Scaffold component. This component provides a template layout structure for the standard Material screen layout. Scaffold includes slots for standard layout elements including a top bar, content area, bottom bar, floating action button, snackbar, and a navigation drawer. For this example, we will be using the top bar, content area, and bottom bar scaffold slots. Edit the MainScreen function and add the Scaffold call as follows:

```
@Composable
fun MainScreen() {
    val navController = rememberNavController()

    Scaffold(
        topBar = { TopAppBar(title = {Text("Bottom Navigation Demo")}) },
        content = { NavigationHost(navController = navController) },
        bottomBar = { BottomNavigationBar(navController = navController)}
    )
}
```

For the top bar, we are using the TopAppBar component configured to display a Text composable while our NavigationHost composable is used for the content area of the screen. Finally, the bottom bar position is occupied by our BottomNavigationBar component.

46.9 Testing the project

At the time of writing, the Compose features used in this example were not supported in the Preview panel. To test the app, therefore, you will need to compile and run the project on a device or emulator where it should match the screen shown in Figure 46-2:

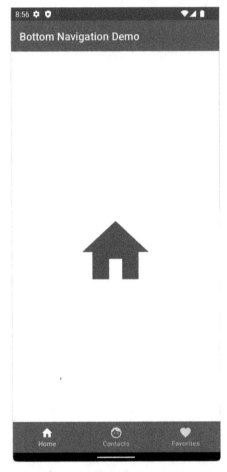

Figure 46-2

Test that the navigation works by clicking on the bottom bar items and verifying that the correct screen appears in each case. Also, check that the code to prevent duplicate back stack entries is working by clicking multiple times on the Contacts bar item followed by the back button (or a rightward swipe on newer Android versions). If the code is working as intended, the app should navigate back to the Home screen.

46.10 Summary

In this chapter, we have used the Compose BottomNavigation component to implement navigation between screens within an activity. This involves creating a BottomNavigationItem child for each screen together with a navigation controller and NavHost. A key step in implementing bottom bar navigation involves keeping track of the current destination route, a task which is achieved by accessing the current back stack entry via a call to the *currentBackStackEntryAsState()* method of the navigation controller. The project also made use of the Scaffold composable to create a layout that conforms to Material theme standards.

Chapter 47

47. Detecting Gestures in Compose

The term "gesture" is used to define a contiguous sequence of interactions between the touch screen and the user. A typical gesture begins at the point that the screen is first touched and ends when the last finger or pointing device leaves the display surface. When correctly harnessed, gestures can be implemented as a form of communication between user and application. Swiping motions to turn the pages of an eBook, or a pinching movement involving two touches to zoom in or out of an image are prime examples of how gestures can be used to interact with an application.

47.1 Compose gesture detection

Jetpack Compose provides mechanisms for the detection of common gestures within an application. In this chapter, we will cover a variety of gesture types including tap (click), double-tap, long press, and dragging, as well as multi-touch gestures such as panning, zooming, and rotation. Swipe gestures are also supported but require a little extra explanation, so will be covered independently in the next chapter.

In several instances, Compose provides two ways to detect gestures. One approach involves the use of gesture detection modifiers which provide gesture detection capabilities with built-in visual effects. An alternative option is to use the functions provided by the PointerInputScope interface which require extra coding but provide more advanced gesture detection capabilities. Where available, both of these options will be covered in this chapter.

This chapter will take a practical approach to exploring gesture detection by creating an Android Studio project that includes examples of the types of gesture detection.

47.2 Creating the GestureDemo project

Launch Android Studio and create a new *Empty Compose Activity* project named GestureDemo, specifying *com.example.gesturedemo* as the package name, and selecting a minimum API level of API 26: Android 8.0 (Oreo). Within the *MainActivity.kt* file, delete the Greeting function and add a new empty composable named MainScreen:

```
@Composable
fun MainScreen() {


}
```

Next, edit the *onCreateActivity()* method and DefaultPreview function to call MainScreen instead of Greeting.

47.3 Detecting click gestures

Click gestures, also known as taps, can be detected on any visible composable using the *clickable* modifier. This modifier accepts a trailing lambda containing the code to be executed when a click is detected on the component to which it has been applied, for example:

```
SomeComposable(
    modifier = Modifier.clickable { /* Code to be executed */ }
)
```

Within the *MainActivity.kt* file, add a new composable named ClickDemo and call it from the MainScreen function:

Detecting Gestures in Compose

```
import androidx.compose.foundation.*
import androidx.compose.foundation.gestures.*
import androidx.compose.foundation.layout.*
import androidx.compose.runtime.*
import androidx.compose.ui.graphics.*
import androidx.compose.ui.unit.dp

.

.

@Composable
fun MainScreen() {
    ClickDemo()
}

@Composable
fun ClickDemo() {

    var colorState by remember { mutableStateOf(true) }
    var bgColor by remember { mutableStateOf(Color.Blue) }

    val clickHandler = {

        colorState = !colorState

        if (colorState == true) {
            bgColor = Color.Blue
        }
        else {
            bgColor = Color.DarkGray
        }
    }

    Box(
        Modifier
            .clickable { clickHandler() }
            .background(bgColor)
            .size(100.dp)
    )
}
```

The ClickDemo composable contains a Box component the background color if which is controlled by the *bgColor* state. The Box also has applied to it a clickable modifier configured to call clickHandler which, in turn, toggles the current value of *colorState* and uses it to switch the current bgColor value between blue and gray. Use the Preview panel in interactive mode to test that clicking the Box causes the background color to change.

47.4 Detecting taps using PointerInputScope

While the clickable modifier is useful for detecting simple click gestures, it cannot distinguish between taps, presses, long presses, and double taps. For this level of precision, we need to utilize the *detectTapGestures()* function of PointerInputScope. This is applied to a composable via the *pointerInput()* modifier, which gives us access to the PointerInputScope as follows:

```
SomeComposable(
    Modifier
        .pointerInput(Unit) {
            detectTapGestures(
                onPress = { /* Press Detected */ },
                onDoubleTap = { /* Double Tap Detected */ },
                onLongPress = { /* Long Press Detected */ },
                onTap = { /* Tap Detected */ }
            )
        }
)
```

Edit the *MainActivity.kt* file as follows to add and call a composable named TapPressDemo:

```
.
.
import androidx.compose.ui.Alignment
import androidx.compose.ui.input.pointer.pointerInput
.
.
@Composable
fun MainScreen() {
    TapPressDemo()
}

@Composable
fun TapPressDemo() {

    var textState by remember {
        mutableStateOf("Waiting ....")
    }

    val tapHandler = { status : String ->
        textState = status

    }
    Column(
        horizontalAlignment = Alignment.CenterHorizontally,
        modifier = Modifier.fillMaxSize()
    ) {
        Box(
```

```
Modifier
    .padding(10.dp)
    .background(Color.Blue)
    .size(100.dp)
    .pointerInput(Unit) {
        detectTapGestures(
            onPress = { tapHandler("onPress Detected") },
            onDoubleTap = { tapHandler("onDoubleTap Detected") },
            onLongPress = { tapHandler("onLongPress Detected") },
            onTap = { tapHandler("onTap Detected") }
        )
    }
)
Spacer(Modifier.height(10.dp))
Text(textState)
    }
}
```

The TapPressDemo composable contains Box and Text components within a Column parent. The string displayed on the Text component is based on the current *textState* value. When a gesture is detected by the *detectTapGestures()* function, the tapHandler is called and passed a new string describing the type of gesture detected. This string is assigned to *textState* causing it to appear in the Text component. Refresh the Preview panel and use interactive mode to experiment with different tap and press gestures. While running, the user interface should match that shown in Figure 47-1:

onDoubleTap Detected

Figure 47-1

47.5 Detecting drag gestures

Drag gestures on a component can be detected by applying the *draggable()* modifier. This modifier stores the offset (or delta) of the drag motion from the point of origin as it occurs and stores it in a state, an instance of which can be created via a call to the *rememberDraggableState()* function. This state can then, for example, be used to move the position of the dragged component in coordination with the gesture. The *draggable()* call also needs to be told whether to detect horizontal or vertical gestures.

To see the *draggable()* modifier in action, make the following changes to the *MainActivity.kt* file:

.

.

```
import androidx.compose.ui.unit.IntOffset
```

```
import kotlin.math.roundToInt
```

```
.
.
@Composable
fun MainScreen() {
    DragDemo()
}

@Composable
fun DragDemo() {

    Box(modifier = Modifier.fillMaxSize()) {

        var xOffset by remember { mutableStateOf(0f) }

        Box(
            modifier = Modifier
                .offset { IntOffset(xOffset.roundToInt(), 0) }
                .size(100.dp)
                .background(Color.Blue)
                .draggable(
                    orientation = Orientation.Horizontal,
                    state = rememberDraggableState { distance ->
                        xOffset += distance
                    }
                )
        )
    }
}
```

The example creates a state to store the current x-axis offset and uses it as the x-coordinate of the draggable Box:

```
var xOffset by remember { mutableStateOf(0f) }
.
.
Box(
    modifier = Modifier
        .offset { IntOffset(xOffset.roundToInt(), 0) }
```

The draggable modifier is then applied to the Box with the orientation parameter set to horizontal. The state parameter is set by calling the *rememberDraggableState()* function, the trailing lambda for which is used to obtain the current delta value and add it to the xOffset state. This, in turn, causes the box to move in the direction of the drag gesture:

```
.draggable(
    orientation = Orientation.Horizontal,
    state = rememberDraggableState { distance ->
        xOffset += distance
    }
)
```

Detecting Gestures in Compose

Preview the design and test that the Box can be dragged horizontally left and right:

Figure 47-2

The *draggable()* modifier is only useful for supporting drag gestures in either the horizontal or vertical plane. To support multi-directional drag operations, the PointerInputScope detectDragGestures function needs to be used.

47.6 Detecting drag gestures using PointerInputScope

The PointerInputScope detectDragGestures function allows us to support both horizontal and vertical drag operations simultaneously and can be implemented using the following syntax:

```
SomeComposable() {

    .pointerInput(Unit) {

        detectDragGestures { _, distance ->

            xOffset += distance.x

            yOffset += distance.y

        }

    }
}
```

To see this in action, add and call a new function named PointerInputDrag in the *MainActivity.kt* file as follows:

```
@Composable
fun MainScreen() {

    PointerInputDrag()

}


@Composable
fun PointerInputDrag() {


    Box(modifier = Modifier.fillMaxSize()) {


        var xOffset by remember { mutableStateOf(0f) }
        var yOffset by remember { mutableStateOf(0f) }


        Box(
            Modifier
                .offset { IntOffset(xOffset.roundToInt(), yOffset.roundToInt()) }
                .background(Color.Blue)
                .size(100.dp)
                .pointerInput(Unit) {
                    detectDragGestures { _, distance ->
                        xOffset += distance.x
```

```
                    yOffset += distance.y
                }
            }
        )
    }
}
```

Since we are supporting both horizontal and vertical dragging gestures, we have declared states to store both x and y offsets. The detectDragGestures lambda passes us an Offset object which we have named *distance* and from which we can obtain the latest drag x and y offset values. These are added to the *xOffset* and *yOffset* states respectively, causing the Box component to follow the dragging motion around the screen:

```
.pointerInput(Unit) {
    detectDragGestures { _, distance ->
        xOffset += distance.x
        yOffset += distance.y
    }
}
```

Preview the design in interactive mode and test that it is possible to drag the box in any direction on the screen:

Figure 47-3

47.7 Scrolling using the scrollable modifier

Scrolling was introduced in the chapter entitled *"An Overview of Lists and Grids in Compose"* in relation to scrolling through lists of items. Using the *scrollable()* modifier, scrolling gestures are not limited to list components. As with the *draggable()* modifier, *scrollable()* is limited to support either horizontal or vertical gestures but not both in the same modifier declaration. Scrollable state is managed using the *rememberScrollableState()* function, the lambda for which gives us access to the distance traveled by the scroll gesture which can, in turn, be used to adjust the offset of one or more composables in the hierarchy. Make the following changes to implement scrolling in the *MainActivity.kt* file:

```
@Composable
fun MainScreen() {
    ScrollableModifier()
}


@Composable
fun ScrollableModifier() {

    var offset by remember { mutableStateOf(0f) }

    Box(
```

```
Modifier
    .fillMaxSize()
    .scrollable(
        orientation = Orientation.Vertical,
        state = rememberScrollableState { distance ->
            offset += distance
            distance
        }
    )
) {
    Box(modifier = Modifier
        .size(90.dp)
        .offset { IntOffset(0, offset.roundToInt()) }
        .background(Color.Red))
}
}
```

Preview the new composable and click and drag vertically on the screen. Note that the red box scrolls up and down in response to vertical scrolling gestures.

47.8 Scrolling using the scroll modifiers

As we saw in the previous example, the *scrollable()* modifier can only detect scrolling in a single orientation. To detect both horizontal and vertical scrolling, we need to use the scroll modifiers. These are essentially two modifiers named *verticalScroll()* and *horizontalScroll()* both of which must be passed a scroll state created via a call to the *rememberScrollState()* function, for example:

```
SomeComposable(modifier = Modifier
    .verticalScroll(rememberScrollState())
    .horizontalScroll(rememberScrollState())) {
}
```

In addition to supporting scrolling in both orientations, the scroll functions also have the advantage that they handle the actual scrolling. This means that we do not need to write code to apply new offsets to implement the scrolling behavior.

To demonstrate these modifiers, we will use a Box composable containing an image. The Box will be sized to act as a "viewport" through which only part of the image can be seen at any one time. We will, instead, use scrolling to allow the image to be scrolled within the box.

The first step is to add an image resource to the project. In previous chapters, we used the Resource Manager to add an image to the project resources. As we will demonstrate in this chapter, it is also possible to copy and paste an image file directly into the *drawables* folder within the Project tool window.

The image that will be used for the project is named *vacation.jpg* and can be found in the *images* folder of the sample code download available from the following URL:

https://www.ebookfrenzy.com/retail/compose/index.php

Locate the image in the file system navigator for your operating system and select and copy it. Right-click on the *app -> res -> drawable* entry in the Project tool window and select Paste from the resulting menu to add the file to the folder:

Figure 47-4

Next, modify the *MainActivity.kt* file as follows:

```
.

.
import androidx.compose.ui.geometry.Offset
import androidx.compose.ui.res.imageResource
.

.
@Composable
fun MainScreen() {
    ScrollModifiers()
}

@Composable
fun ScrollModifiers() {

    val image = ImageBitmap.imageResource(id = R.drawable.vacation)

    Box(modifier = Modifier
        .size(150.dp)
        .verticalScroll(rememberScrollState())
        .horizontalScroll(rememberScrollState())) {
        Canvas(
            modifier = Modifier
                .size(360.dp, 270.dp)
        )
        {
            drawImage(
                image = image,
                topLeft = Offset(
                    x = 0f,
                    y = 0f
                ),
            )
        }
    }
}
```

When previewed in interactive mode, only part of the image will be visible within the Box component. Clicking and dragging on the image will allow you to move the photo so that other areas of the image can be viewed:

Figure 47-5

47.9 Detecting pinch gestures

The remainder of this chapter will look at gestures that require multiple touch-points on the screen, beginning with pinch gestures. Pinch gestures are typically used to change the size (scale) of content and give the effect of zooming in and out. This type of gesture is detected using the *transformable()* modifier which takes as parameters a state of type TransformableState, an instance of which can be created by a call to the *rememberTransformableState()* function. This function accepts a trailing lambda to which are passed the following three parameters:

- **Scale change** - A Float value updated when pinch gestures are performed.

- **Offset change** - An Offset instance containing the current x and y offset values. This value is updated when a gesture causes the target component to move (referred to as *translations*).

- **Rotation change** - A Float value representing the current angle change when detecting rotation gestures.

All three of these parameters need to be declared when calling the *rememberTransformationState()* function, even if you do not make use of them in the body of the lambda. A typical TransformableState declaration that tracks scale changes might read as follows:

```
var scale by remember { mutableStateOf(1f) }

val state = rememberTransformableState { scaleChange, offsetChange,
                                         rotationChange ->
    scale *= scaleChange
}
```

Having created the state, it can then be used when calling the *transformable()* modifier on a composable as follows:

```
SomeComposable(modifier = Modifier
                    .transformable(state = state) {
}
```

As the pinch gesture progresses, the scale state will be updated. To reflect these changes we will need to make sure that the composable also changes in size. We can do this by accessing the graphics layer of the composable and setting the scaleX and scaleY properties to the current scale state. As we will demonstrate later, the rotation and translation transformations will also require access to the graphics layer.

Start this phase of the tutorial by making the following changes to the *MainActivity.kt* file to implement pinch gesture detection:

```
@Composable
fun MainScreen() {
    MultiTouchDemo()
}


@Composable
fun MultiTouchDemo() {

    var scale by remember { mutableStateOf(1f) }

    val state = rememberTransformableState {
                scaleChange, offsetChange, rotationChange ->
        scale *= scaleChange
    }

    Box(contentAlignment = Alignment.Center, modifier = Modifier.fillMaxSize()) {
        Box(
            Modifier
                .graphicsLayer(
                    scaleX = scale,
                    scaleY = scale,
                )
                .transformable(state = state)
                .background(Color.Blue)
                .size(100.dp)
        )
    }
}
```

To test out the pinch gesture the app will need to be run on a device or emulator because the Preview panel does not yet appear to support multi-touch gestures). Once running, perform a pinch gesture on the blue box to zoom in and out. If you are using an emulator, hold the keyboard Ctrl key (Cmd on macOS) while clicking and dragging to simulate multiple touches.

47.10 Detecting rotation gestures

We can now add rotation support to the example with just three additional lines of code:

```
@Composable
fun MultiTouchDemo() {

    var scale by remember { mutableStateOf(1f) }
    var angle by remember { mutableStateOf(0f) }

    val state = rememberTransformableState {
            scaleChange, offsetChange, rotationChange ->
        scale *= scaleChange
        angle += rotationChange
```

```
        }

    Box(contentAlignment = Alignment.Center, modifier = Modifier.fillMaxSize()) {
        Box(
            Modifier
                .graphicsLayer(
                    scaleX = scale,
                    scaleY = scale,
                    rotationZ = angle
                )
                .transformable(state = state)
                .background(Color.Blue)
                .size(100.dp)
        )
    }
}
```

Compile and run the app and perform both pinch and rotation gestures. Both the size and angle of the Box should now change:

Figure 47-6

47.11 Detecting translation gestures

Translation involves the change in the position of a component. As with rotation detection, we can add translation support to our example with just a few lines of code:

```
@Composable
fun MultiTouchDemo() {

    var scale by remember { mutableStateOf(1f) }
    var angle by remember { mutableStateOf(0f) }
    var offset by remember { mutableStateOf(Offset.Zero) }

    val state = rememberTransformableState {
                scaleChange, offsetChange, rotationChange ->
        scale *= scaleChange
        angle += rotationChange
        offset += offsetChange

    }
```

```
Box(contentAlignment = Alignment.Center, modifier = Modifier.fillMaxSize()) {
    Box(
        Modifier
            .graphicsLayer(
                scaleX = scale,
                scaleY = scale,
                rotationZ = angle,
                translationX = offset.x,
                translationY = offset.y
            )
            .transformable(state = state)
            .background(Color.Blue)
            .size(100.dp)
    )
}
}
```

Note that the translation gesture only works when testing on a physical device and requires two points of contact within the box to initiate. Also, since we are performing a pan gesture the box will move in the opposite direction to the gesture motion.

47.12 Summary

Gestures are a key form of interaction between the user and an app running on an Android device. Using the gesture detection features of Compose, it is possible to respond to a range of screen interactions including taps, long presses, scrolling, pinches, and rotations. Gestures are detected in Compose by applying modifiers to composables and responding to state changes.

48. Detecting Swipe Gestures in Compose

The preceding chapter demonstrated how to detect some common types of gestures including dragging, tapping, pinching, and scrolling. Detecting swipe gestures is a little more complicated than other gesture types which is why we are dedicating an entire chapter to the subject. This chapter will explain exactly what swipe gestures are and demonstrate how they can be detected.

48.1 Swipe gestures and anchors

A swipe gesture is a horizontal or vertical motion of a point of contact on the device screen. This motion is usually associated with a user interface component that moves in coordination with the swipe motion.

In Compose, a swiping motion serves to move a component from one *anchor* to another where an anchor is a fixed position on the screen along the axis of the swipe. A point between two anchors is declared as the *threshold*. If the swipe ends before the threshold is reached, the swiped component will return to the starting anchor. If, on the other hand, the swipe ends after passing the transition point, the component will continue moving until it reaches the destination anchor. These threshold-related movements can be configured to be instant (snapped) or animated.

48.2 Detecting swipe gestures

Swipe gestures are detected by applying the *swipeable()* modifier to the composable in which the gesture is to be detected. The following example shows the minimum requirements when calling the *swipeable()* modifier:

```
Box(
    modifier = Modifier
        .swipeable(
            state = <swipeable state>,
            anchors = <anchors>,
            thresholds = { _, _ -> FractionalThreshold(<value>) },
            orientation = <horizontal or vertical>
        )
)
```

Important parameters that can be specified when calling the *swipeable()* modifier can be summarized as follows:

- **state: SwipeableState** – Used to store the swipeable state through recompositions and obtained via a call to the *rememberSwipeableState()* function. This state contains the current offset of the swipe motion which can be used to change the position of the current or other composables.

- **anchors: Map** – A Map declaration that pairs anchor points and states. Anchor points are specified as pixels defining positions in the horizontal or vertical plane depending on the orientation setting.

- **orientation: Orientation** – The orientation of the swipe gesture. Must be set to either Orientation.Horizontal or Orientation.Vertical.

- **enabled: Boolean** – An optional setting that defaults to true and controls whether swipe detection is active.

- **reverseDirection: Boolean** – An optional setting that defaults to false. When set to true, this setting reverses the effect of the swipe direction. In other words, a downward swipe will behave as an upward swipe, a rightward swipe as a leftward swipe, and so on.

- **thresholds: (from, to)** – Specifies the position of thresholds between anchors. Declared as a lambda containing a call to either *FractionalThreshold(Float)* when declaring the transition point as a percentage of the distance between anchors, or *FixedThreshold(Dp)* when specifying a fixed position.

- **resistance: ResistanceConfig?** – An optional setting that defines the resistance that will be applied when the swiping motion passes beyond the first or last final anchor in the anchor map (referred to as the *bounds*). By default, the swipe will be allowed to move slightly beyond the bounds before springing back to the anchor. When set to null, the swipe cannot extend beyond the bounds.

- **velocityThreshold: Dp** – An optional setting defining the speed in dp per second that the swipe velocity has to exceed to move to the next state.

48.3 Declaring the anchors map

As previously outlined, swipe anchors are declared as map objects containing pairs of anchor positions and states. The anchors are declared using floating-point pixel values that correspond to a position along either the x or y-axis relative to the composable to which the *swipeable()* modifier is being applied. The corresponding state can be any valid state type that is supported by the Bundle class. For example, as each anchor point is reached, the text displayed on a text component may need to change. In this case, each state in an anchor pair would be a different string value setting. The anchor map can be declared using the Kotlin *mapOf()* function. Consider, for example, the following anchor declaration:

```
val swipeableState = rememberSwipeableState("On")
val anchors = mapOf(0f to "On", 150f to "Off", 300f to "Locked")
```

When the swipe reaches the anchors at the 150px and 300px position, the current value of the *swipeableState* will be set to "Off" and "Locked" respectively. A Text composable might be configured to display this current state as follows:

```
Text(swipeableState.currentValue)
```

48.4 Declaring thresholds

Thresholds are declared as lambdas which will be passed from and to states when called and must return a ThresholdConfig value. This ThresholdConfig instance can be generated via a call to either the *FractionalThreshold()* or *FixedThreshold()* function. The following code, for example, declares a threshold at a point 50% of the distance between two anchors:

```
{ _, _ -> FractionalThreshold(0.5f) }
```

The following declaration, on the other hand, sets a threshold at a fixed point 20dp along the distance between two anchors:

```
{ _, _ -> FixedThreshold(20.dp) }
```

48.5 Moving a component in response to a swipe

As with many of the gesture detection modifiers covered in the previous chapter, a swipe does not automatically move a component. Any position changes within the layout must therefore be programmed. Fortunately, this is simply a case of using the offset value of the swipeable state with the *offset()* modifier of any components in the layout that need to be moved in response to the gesture. If, for example, we need the Text view in the above example to move horizontally in response to the swipe gesture, we could do so with the following code change:

```
Text(
    swipeableState.currentValue,
    modifier = Modifier
        .offset { IntOffset(swipeableState.offset.value.roundToInt() , 0)
})
```

When executed, the Text component will now move in concert with the swiping motion.

With the basics of Compose swipe gesture detection covered, in the rest of this chapter we will create an example project that will help to clarify the information provided so far.

48.6 About the SwipeDemo project

The project created in the remainder of this chapter will implement horizontal swipe detection designed to move a Box between three anchor positions. At each anchor, the box will display a different letter signifying left (L), center (C), and right (R). Figure 48-1 shows the completed user interface:

Figure 48-1

48.7 Creating the SwipeDemo project

Launch Android Studio and create a new *Empty Compose Activity* project named SwipeDemo, specifying *com.example.swipedemo* as the package name, and selecting a minimum API level of API 26: Android 8.0 (Oreo). Within the *MainActivity.kt* file, delete the Greeting function and add a new empty composable named MainScreen:

```
@Composable
fun MainScreen() {


}
```

Next, edit the *onCreateActivity()* method and DefaultPreview function to call MainScreen instead of Greeting.

48.8 Setting up the swipeable state and anchors

Before designing the user interface layout, we need to set up some size constants, create the swipeable state and declare the anchor map. With the *MainActivity.kt* file loaded into the editor, locate and make the following changes to the MainScreen function:

```
.
.
import androidx.compose.material.*
import androidx.compose.ui.platform.LocalDensity
import androidx.compose.ui.unit.dp
.
.
@Composable
fun MainScreen() {
    val parentBoxWidth = 320.dp
```

```
    val childBoxSides = 30.dp

    val swipeableState = rememberSwipeableState("L")
    val widthPx = with(LocalDensity.current) {
            (parentBoxWidth - childBoxSides).toPx() }

    val anchors = mapOf(0f to "L", widthPx / 2 to "C", widthPx to "R")
}
```

In the above code, the parentBoxWidth value represents the width of the top-level Box within the component hierarchy we will be creating later in the tutorial. This is the component to which the *swipeable()* modifier will be applied. The parent box will contain a child box, the side lengths of which are defined via the childBoxSides declaration. Finally, the width in pixels of the swipeable area is calculated by taking the density of the display on which the app is running, then subtracting the width of the child box from the width of the parent box:

```
val widthPx = with(LocalDensity.current) {
            (parentBoxWidth - childBoxSides).toPx() }
```

The child box width is subtracted above to account for the fact that the child box will be centered on the anchor points, leaving an overhang equivalent to half the width of the child on the first and last anchors (these two halves combining to create a full child box width).

Finally, anchor points are configured at the start, mid-point, and end of the swipeable area. The states for these anchors are declared as strings set to "L", "C", and "R".

```
val anchors = mapOf(0f to "L", widthPx / 2 to "C", widthPx to "R")
```

At the time of writing, the *rememberSwipeableState()* function was an experimental feature. If the editor reports this error, add the @ExperimentalMaterialApi annotation above the @Composable directive for the MainScreen as shown below:

```
@OptIn(ExperimentalMaterialApi::class)
@Composable
fun MainScreen() {
```

48.9 Designing the parent Box

The next step is to design the composable hierarchy that makes up the user interface layout. As previously described, the layout will consist of a parent Box on which the swipeable modifier will be applied. Remaining within the MainScreen function add this component now:

```
    .
    .
import androidx.compose.foundation.gestures.Orientation
import androidx.compose.foundation.layout.*
    .
    .
Composable
fun MainScreen() {
    .
    .
    val anchors = mapOf(0f to "L", widthPx / 2 to "C", widthPx to "R")

    Box {
```

```
        Box (
            modifier = Modifier
                .padding(20.dp)
                .width(parentBoxWidth)
                .height(childBoxSides)
                .swipeable(
                    state = swipeableState,
                    anchors = anchors,
                    thresholds = { _, _ -> FractionalThreshold(0.5f) },
                    orientation = Orientation.Horizontal
                )
        ) {
        }
    }
}
```

Note that the thresholds are set to the halfway points between anchors.

The next step is to add the line graphic which is, itself, comprised of four Box components:

```
.
.
import androidx.compose.foundation.background
import androidx.compose.foundation.shape.CircleShape
import androidx.compose.ui.Alignment
import androidx.compose.ui.graphics.Color
.
.

Box (
    modifier = Modifier
        .padding(20.dp)
        .width(parentBoxWidth)
        .height(childBoxSides)
.
.
) {
    Box(Modifier.fillMaxWidth().height(5.dp).
        background(Color.DarkGray).align(Alignment.CenterStart))
    Box(Modifier.size(10.dp).background(Color.DarkGray,
        shape = CircleShape).align(Alignment.CenterStart))
    Box(Modifier.size(10.dp).background(Color.DarkGray,
        shape = CircleShape).align(Alignment.Center))
    Box(Modifier.size(10.dp).background(Color.DarkGray,
        shape = CircleShape).align(Alignment.CenterEnd))
}
.
.
```

Detecting Swipe Gestures in Compose

Take this opportunity to review the layout in the Preview panel where the line should now appear as shown in Figure 48-2:

Figure 48-2

Work on the parent Box implementation is now complete and we are ready to add the child box:

```
.
.

import androidx.compose.ui.unit.sp
import androidx.compose.ui.unit.IntOffset
import kotlin.math.roundToInt

.
.

Box(
    modifier = Modifier
        .padding(20.dp)
        .width(parentBoxWidth)
        .height(childBoxSides)

.
.

    Box(Modifier.size(10.dp).background(Color.DarkGray,
        shape = CircleShape).align(Alignment.CenterEnd))

        Box(
            Modifier
                .offset { IntOffset(swipeableState.offset.value.roundToInt(), 0)
}
                .size(childBoxSides)
                .background(Color.Blue),
            contentAlignment = Alignment.Center
        ) {
            Text(
                swipeableState.currentValue,
                color = Color.White,
                fontSize = 22.sp
            )
        }
    }
}

.
.

}
```

Before we try out the swiping behavior, some of the above code needs some explanation. First, the offset modifier is applied to the child Box to control the horizontal position. This is achieved by using the current offset value stored in *swipeableState* to control the position of the Box along the x-axis.

```
.offset { IntOffset(swipeableState.offset.value.roundToInt(), 0) }
```

The child Box contains a single child in the form of a Text component. The text displayed on this component is set based on the state value for the current anchor (in other words "L", "C" or "R"):

```
Text (
    swipeableState.currentValue,
    color = Color.White,
    fontSize = 22.sp
)
```

With the coding work completed, all that remains is to test that the swipe gesture detection works as intended.

48.10 Testing the project

With this phase of the project complete, we can now try out the swiping behavior. Using either the Preview panel in interactive mode or a device or emulator, click and swipe right anywhere within the bounds of the parent box. As you swipe, the child box will also move to the right. If you stop swiping before the child box reaches the mid-point between the first two anchors, it will animate back to the start anchor. Move the box beyond the mid-point, however, and the box will automatically animate to the second anchor, at which point the text will change from "L" to "C". From this point, the box can be swiped in either direction with the same threshold behavior.

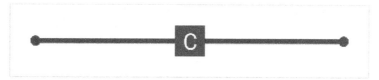

Figure 48-3

48.11 Summary

Swiping in Compose involves the movement of a component from one anchor point to another combined with a transition between different states. Swipe gestures are detected using the *swipeable()* modifier in conjunction with a map of anchors and state pairs. A threshold point is also declared between anchor points. If the swipe gesture ends before reaching the threshold, the target component moves back to the starting anchor, while the component will continue to the destination anchor if the swipe ends after the threshold.

49. Working with Compose Theming

The appearance of Android apps is intended to conform with a set of guidelines defined by Material Design. Material Design was developed by Google to provide a level of design consistency between different apps, while also allowing app developers to include their own branding in terms of color, typography, and shape choices (a concept referred to as *Material theming*). In addition to design guidelines, Material Design also includes a set of UI components for use when designing user interface layouts, many of which we have been using throughout this book.

In this chapter, we will provide an overview of how theming works within an Android Studio Compose project and explore how the default design configurations provided for newly created projects can be modified to meet your branding requirements.

49.1 Material Design 2 vs Material Design 3

Before beginning, it is important to note that Google is currently transitioning from Material Design 2 to Material Design 3 and that the current version of Android Studio defaults to Material Design 2. Material Design 3 provides the basis for Material You, a feature introduced in Android 12 that allows an app to automatically adjust theme elements to compliment preferences configured by the user on the device. Dynamic color support provided by Material Design 3, for example, allows the colors used in apps to automatically adapt to match the user's wallpaper selection.

So that this book will be useful for as long as possible, this chapter will focus on color and typography theming using Material Design 3. At the time of writing, shape theming was not yet supported by Material Design 3, though the concepts covered in this chapter for color and typography will apply to shapes when support is available.

49.2 Material Design 2 Theming

Before exploring Material Design 3, we first need to look at how Material Design 2 is used in an Android Studio project created using the Empty Compose Activity template. The first point to note is that both calls to the top-level composable in the *onCreate()* method and the DefaultPreview function are embedded in a theme composable. The following, for example, is the code generated for a project named MyApp:

```
class MainActivity : ComponentActivity() {
    override fun onCreate(savedInstanceState: Bundle?) {
.
.

        MyAppTheme {

.
.

                Greeting("Android")
            }
        }
    }
}
```

```
@Preview(showBackground = true)
@Composable
fun DefaultPreview() {
    MyAppTheme {
        Greeting("Android")
    }
}
```

All of the files associated with MyAppTheme are contained with the ui.theme sub-package of the project as shown in Figure 49-1:

Figure 49-1

The theme itself is declared in the *Theme.kt* file which begins by declaring different color palettes for use when the device is in light or dark mode. These palettes are created by calling the *darkColors()* and *lightColors()* builder function and specifying the colors for the different Material Theme color slots:

```
private val DarkColorPalette = darkColors(
    primary = Purple200,
    primaryVariant = Purple700,
    secondary = Teal200
)

private val LightColorPalette = lightColors(
    primary = Purple500,
    primaryVariant = Purple700,
    secondary = Teal200
}
```

This is just a subset of the slots available for color theming. For Material Design 3, for example, there is a total of 24 color slots available for use when designing a theme. In the absence of a slot assignment, the Material components use built-in default colors. More information about the color slots available in Material Design 2 can be found at the following URL:

https://material.io/design/color/the-color-system.html

These color slots are used by the Material components to set color attributes. For example, the *primary* color slot is used as the background color for the Material Button component. The actual colors assigned to the slots are declared in the *Colors.kt* file as follows:

```
val Purple200 = Color(0xFFBB86FC)
val Purple500 = Color(0xFF6200EE)
```

```
val Purple700 = Color(0xFF3700B3)
val Teal200 = Color(0xFF03DAC5)
```

Our example MyAppTheme composable is declared in the *Theme.kt* file as follows:

```
@Composable
fun MyApplicationTheme(
    darkTheme: Boolean = isSystemInDarkTheme(),
    content: @Composable () -> Unit
) {
    val colors = if (darkTheme) {
        DarkColorPalette
    } else {
        LightColorPalette
    }

    MaterialTheme(
        colors = colors,
        typography = Typography,
        shapes = Shapes,
        content = content
    )
}
```

Note that the theme makes use of the slot API (introduced in the chapter entitled *"An Overview of Compose Slot APIs"*) to display the content. The declaration begins by checking whether the device is in light or dark mode by calling the *isSystemInDarkTheme()* function. The result of this call is then used to decide if the dark or light color palette is to be passed as a parameter to the MaterialTheme call. In addition to the color palette, MaterialTheme is also passed typography and shape settings which are declared in the *Type.kt* and *Shape.kt* files respectively.

In terms of typography, Material Design has a set of type scales, three of which are declared in the *Type.kt* file (albeit with two commented out):

```
val Typography = Typography(
    body1 = TextStyle(
        fontFamily = FontFamily.Default,
        fontWeight = FontWeight.Normal,
        fontSize = 16.sp
    )
    /* Other default text styles to override
    button = TextStyle(
        fontFamily = FontFamily.Default,
        fontWeight = FontWeight.W500,
        fontSize = 14.sp
    ),
    caption = TextStyle(
        fontFamily = FontFamily.Default,
        fontWeight = FontWeight.Normal,
        fontSize = 12.sp
```

```
    )
    */
)
```

As with the color slots, this is only a subset of the type scales supported by Material Design. The full list can be found online at:

https://material.io/design/typography/the-type-system.html

The *Shape.kt* file is used to define how the corners of Material components are to be rendered:

```
val Shapes = Shapes(
    small = RoundedCornerShape(4.dp),
    medium = RoundedCornerShape(4.dp),
    large = RoundedCornerShape(0.dp)
)
```

The default rounded corners of an OutlinedTextField will, for example, be controlled by the above shape values.

Creating a custom theme simply involves editing these files to use different colors, typography, and shape settings. These changes will then be used by the Material components that make up the user interface of the app.

49.3 Material Design 3 Theming

The key difference between Material Design 2 (MD2) and Material Design 3 (MD3) is support for dynamic colors and the use of color schemes instead of palettes. Typography is implemented in the same way as with MD2 and we do not yet know how shapes will be supported. Color schemes are created via calls to the *lightColorScheme()* and *darkColorScheme()* builder functions, for example:

```
private val DarkColorPalette = darkColorScheme(
    primary = ...,
    onPrimary = ...,
    secondary = ....,
    .
    .
    .
)


private val LightColorPalette = lightColorScheme(
    .
    .
    .
}
```

When the theme is created, the color schemes are now assigned using the colorSchemes parameter instead of the colors parameter used in MD2:

```
@Composable
fun MyAppTheme(
    useDarkTheme: Boolean = isSystemInDarkTheme(),
    content: @Composable() () -> Unit
) {
    val colors = if (!useDarkTheme) {
        LightThemeColors
    } else {
```

```
        DarkThemeColors
    }

    MaterialTheme(
        colorScheme = colors,
        typography = AppTypography,
        content = content
    )
}
```

Although the typography and declaration of theme colors are much the same between MD2 and MD3, the color slots and typography types have different names in many cases. A full listing of MD3 color slot names can be found at:

https://developer.android.com/reference/kotlin/androidx/compose/material3/ColorScheme

Similarly, a list of typography options is available at the following URL:

https://developer.android.com/reference/kotlin/androidx/compose/material3/Typography

To add support for dynamic colors, dynamic color schemes need to be generated via calls to the *dynamicDarkColorScheme()* and *dynamicLightColorScheme()* functions passing through the current local context as a parameter. These functions will then generate color schemes that match the user's settings on the device (for example wallpaper selection). Since dynamic colors are only supported on Android 12 (S) or later, defensive code needs to be added when creating the MaterialTheme instance:

```
val useDynamicColor = Build.VERSION.SDK_INT >= Build.VERSION_CODES.S

val colors = when {
    useDynamicColor && useDarkTheme ->
                dynamicDarkColorScheme(LocalContext.current)
    useDynamicColor && !useDarkTheme ->
                dynamicLightColorScheme(LocalContext.current)
    useDarkTheme -> DarkColorScheme
    else -> LightColorScheme
}
```

Note that dynamic colors only take effect when enabled on the device by the user within the wallpaper and styles section of the Android Settings app.

49.4 Building a Custom Theme

As we have seen so far, the coding work in implementing a theme is relatively simple. The difficult part, however, is often choosing a set of complementary colors to make up the theme. Fortunately, Google has developed a tool that makes it easy to design custom color themes for your apps. This tool is called the Material Theme Builder and is available at:

https://material-foundation.github.io/material-theme-builder

From within the builder tool, select the Custom tab (marked A in Figure 49-2) and make a color selection for the primary color key (B) by clicking on the color rectangle to display the color selection dialog. Once a color has been selected, the theme panel (C) will change to reflect the recommended colors for all of the MD3 color slots. The generated colors for the Secondary, Tertiary, and Neutral slots can be overridden by clicking on the boxes

(D) and selecting different colors from the color selection panel:

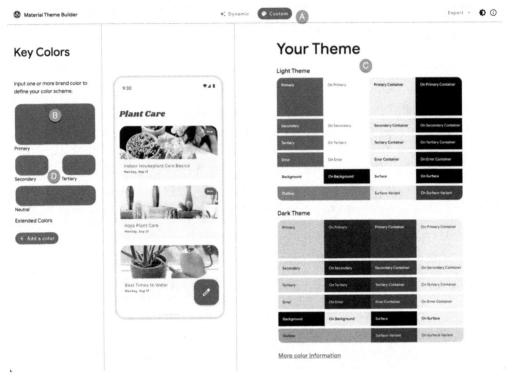

Figure 49-2

To incorporate the theme into your design, click on the Export button (F) and select the *Jetpack Compose (Theme.kt)* option. Once downloaded, place the *Color.kt*, *Theme.kt*, and *Type.kt* files into the ui.themes folder of your project, replacing the existing files if they are present. Note that the package names in each file and theme composable names in the *Theme.kt* file will need to be changed to match your project.

49.5 Summary

Material Design provides guidelines and components that define how Android apps look and appear. Individual branding can be applied to an app by designing themes that specify the colors, fonts, and shapes that should be used when the app is displayed. Google is currently introducing Material Design 3 which replaces Material Design 2 and supports the new features of Material Me including dynamic colors. For designing your own themes, Google also provides the Material Theme Builder which eases the task of choosing complementary theme colors. Once this tool has been used to design a theme, the corresponding files can be exported and used within an Android Studio project.

Chapter 50

50. A Material Design 3 Theming Tutorial

This chapter will demonstrate how to migrate an Android Studio project from Material Design 2 to Material Design 3 and create a new theme using the Material Theme Builder tool. The tutorial will also demonstrate how to add support for and test dynamic theme colors.

50.1 Creating the ThemeDemo project

Launch Android Studio and create a new *Empty Compose Activity* project named ThemeDemo, specifying *com.example.themedemo* as the package name, and selecting a minimum API level of API 26: Android 8.0 (Oreo). Within the *MainActivity.kt* file, delete the Greeting function and add a new empty composable named MainScreen:

```
@Composable
fun MainScreen() {


}
```

Next, edit the *onCreateActivity()* method and DefaultPreview function to call MainScreen instead of Greeting and enable the system UI preview option:

```
@Preview(showBackground = true, showSystemUi = true)
@Composable
fun DefaultPreview() {
.

.
```

50.2 Adding the Material Design 3 library

Assuming that you are running a version of Android Studio that defaults to Material Design 2, the first step in this project is to add the Material Design 3 library to the build configuration. Within the Project tool window, locate and open the module level *build.gradle* file (*app -> build -> build.gradle (Module: ThemeDemo)*) and add the library as follows (keeping in mind that a more recent version of the library may now be available):

```
dependencies {
    implementation "androidx.compose.material3:material3:1.0.0-alpha04"
.

.
```

After making the change, click on the *Sync Now* link to apply the new build configuration to the project.

50.3 Designing the user interface

The main activity will contain a simple layout containing some of the components provided with the MD3 alpha release that will enable us to see the effect of theming work performed later in the chapter. For the latest information on which MD3 components are available for use with Jetpack Compose, refer to the following web page:

A Material Design 3 Theming Tutorial

https://developer.android.com/jetpack/androidx/releases/compose-material3

Within the *MainActivity.kt* file, edit the MainScreen composable so that it reads as follows, including the OptIn annotation to enable the use of the experimental MD3 API. Also, delete any MD2 import directives:

```
.
.
import androidx.compose.material.Surface
import androidx.compose.material.Text
import androidx.compose.foundation.layout.Arrangement
import androidx.compose.foundation.layout.Column
import androidx.compose.material.icons.Icons
import androidx.compose.material.icons.filled.Favorite
import androidx.compose.material.icons.filled.Home
import androidx.compose.material.icons.filled.Settings
import androidx.compose.material3.*
import androidx.compose.runtime.*
import androidx.compose.ui.Alignment
.
.

@OptIn(ExperimentalMaterial3Api::class)
@Composable
fun MainScreen() {

    var selectedItem by remember { mutableStateOf(0) }
    val items = listOf("Home", "Settings", "Favorites")
    val icons = listOf(Icons.Filled.Home, Icons.Filled.Settings,
                               Icons.Filled.Favorite)

    Column(
        verticalArrangement = Arrangement.SpaceBetween,
        horizontalAlignment = Alignment.CenterHorizontally
    ) {

        SmallTopAppBar(title = { Text("ThemeDemo") }, scrollBehavior = null)

        Button(onClick = { }) {
            Text("MD3 Button")
        }

        Text("A Theme Demo")

        FloatingActionButton(onClick = { }) {
                Text("FAB")
        }

        NavigationBar {
```

```
        items.forEachIndexed { index, item ->
            NavigationBarItem(
                icon = { Icon(icons[index], contentDescription = null) },
                label = { Text(item) },
                selected = selectedItem == index,
                onClick = { selectedItem = index }
            )
        }
    }
}
}
```

When previewed, the MainScreen layout should appear as illustrated in Figure 50-1:

Figure 50-1

The completed design is currently using default theme colors and fonts. The next step is to build an entirely new theme for the app.

50.4 Building a new theme

The theme for the project will be designed and generated using the Material Theme Builder. Open a browser window and navigate to the following URL to access the builder tool:

A Material Design 3 Theming Tutorial

https://material-foundation.github.io/material-theme-builder/

Once you have loaded the builder, select the Custom button at the top of the screen and then click on the Primary color block in the Key Colors section to display the color selector. From the color selector, choose any color you feel like using as the basis for your theme:

Key Colors

Input one or more brand color to define your color scheme.

Figure 50-2

Review the color scheme in the My Theme panel and make any necessary color adjustments using the Color Key until you are happy with the color slots. Once the theme is ready, click on the Export button in the top right-hand corner and select the *Jetpack Compose (Theme.kt)* option. When prompted, save the file to a suitable location on your computer filesystem. The theme will be saved as a compressed file named *material-theme.zip*.

Using the appropriate tool for your operating system, unpack the theme file which should contain the following files in a folder with the path material-theme/ui/theme:

- Color.kt
- Theme.kt
- Type.kt

Now that the theme files have been generated, they need to be integrated into the Android Studio project.

50.5 Adding the theme to the project

Before we can add the new theme to the project we first need to remove the old MD2 theme files. Within the Android Studio Project tool window, select and delete the *Color.kt*, *Theme.kt*, and *Type.kt* files from the *ui.theme* folder. Once the files have been removed, locate the MD3 theme files in the *material-theme* folder on your local filesystem and drag and drop them onto the *ui.theme* folder in the Project tool window:

Figure 50-3

After adding the files, edit each one in turn and change the package declaration to match the current project which, assuming you followed the steps at the start of the chapter, will read as follows:

```
package com.example.themedemo.ui.theme
```

Next, edit the *Theme.kt* and change the name of the Theme composable from AppTheme to ThemeDemoTheme:

```
@Composable
fun ThemeDemoTheme(
useDarkTheme: Boolean = isSystemInDarkTheme(),
content: @Composable() () -> Unit
) {
val colors = if (!useDarkTheme) {
    LightThemeColors
} else {
    DarkThemeColors
.
.
```

Return to the *MainActivity.kt* file and refresh the Preview panel to confirm that the components are rendered using the new theme. Take some time to explore the *Colors.kt*, *Type.kt*, and *Theme.kt* files to see the different available theme settings. Also, experiment by making changes to different typography and color values.

50.6 Enabling dynamic colors

To test dynamic colors the app will need to be run on a device or emulator running Android 12 or later with the correct Wallpaper settings. On the device or emulator, launch the Settings app and select *Wallpaper & style* from the list of options. On the wallpaper settings screen click the option to change the wallpaper (marked A in Figure 50-4) and select a wallpaper image containing colors that differ significantly from the colors in your theme. Once selected, assign the wallpaper to the Home screen.

Return to the Wallpaper & styles screen and make sure that the *Wallpaper colors* option is selected (B) before trying out the different color scheme buttons (C). As each option is clicked the wallpaper example will change to reflect the selection:

Figure 50-4

Once you have made a choice, return to Android Studio, load the *Theme.kt* file into the code editor and make the following changes to the ThemeDemoTheme composable to add support for dynamic colors:

```
    .
    .
import android.os.Build
import androidx.compose.material3.*
import androidx.compose.ui.platform.LocalContext
    .
    .
@Composable
fun ThemeDemoTheme(
    useDarkTheme: Boolean = isSystemInDarkTheme(),
        content: @Composable() () -> Unit
) {

    val useDynamicColor = Build.VERSION.SDK_INT >= Build.VERSION_CODES.S

    val colors = when {
        useDynamicColor && useDarkTheme ->
            dynamicDarkColorScheme(LocalContext.current)
              useDynamicColor && !useDarkTheme ->
                dynamicLightColorScheme(LocalContext.current)
        useDarkTheme -> DarkThemeColors
            else -> LightThemeColors
```

```
    }

    MaterialTheme(
        colorScheme = colors,
        typography = AppTypography,
        content = content
    )
}
```

Build and run the app and note that the layout is now using a theme that matches the wallpaper color. Place the ThemeDemo app into the background, return to the *Wallpaper & styles* settings screen and choose a different wallpaper. Bring the ThemeDemo app to the foreground again at which point it will have dynamically adapted to match the new wallpaper.

50.7 Summary

In this chapter, we have demonstrated how to migrate an Android Studio project from Material Design 2 to Material Design 3. The project also made use of the Material Theme Builder to design a new theme and explained the steps to integrate the generated theme files into a project. Finally, the chapter showed how to implement and use the Material Me dynamic colors feature of Android 12.

51. Creating, Testing, and Uploading an Android App Bundle

Once the development work on an Android application is complete and it has been tested on a wide range of Android devices, the next step is to prepare the application for submission to Google Play. Before submission can take place, however, the application must be packaged for release and signed with a private key. This chapter explain how to obtain a private key, prepare the Android App Bundle for the project, and upload it to Google Play.

51.1 The release preparation process

Up until this point in the book, we have been building application projects in a mode suitable for testing and debugging. Building an application package for release to customers via Google Play, on the other hand, requires that some additional steps be taken. The first requirement is that the application is compiled in *release mode* instead of *debug mode*. Secondly, the application must be signed with a private key that uniquely identifies you as the application's developer. Finally, the application must be packaged into an *Android App Bundle*.

While each of these tasks can be performed outside of the Android Studio environment, the procedures can more easily be performed using the Android Studio build mechanism as outlined in this chapter. First, however, it is important to understand a little more about Android App Bundles.

51.2 Android app bundles

When a user installs an app from Google Play, the app is downloaded in the form of an APK file. This file contains everything needed to install and run the app on the user's device. Before the introduction of Android Studio 3.2, the developer would generate one or more APK files using Android Studio and upload them to Google Play. To support multiple device types, screen sizes, and locales this would require either the creation and upload of multiple APK files customized for each target device and locale or the generation of a large *universal APK* containing all of the different configuration resources and platform binaries within a single package.

Creating multiple APK files involved a significant amount of work that had to be repeated each time the app needed to be updated imposing a considerable time overhead on the app release process.

The universal APK option, while less of a burden to the developer, caused an entirely unexpected problem. By analyzing app installation metrics, Google discovered that the larger an installation APK file becomes (resulting in longer download times and increased storage use on the device), the fewer conversions the app receives. The conversion rate is calculated as a percentage of the users who completed the installation of an app after viewing that app on Google Play. Google estimates that the conversion rate for an app drops by 1% for each 6MB increase in APK file size.

Android App Bundles solve both of these problems by providing a way for the developer to create a single package from within Android Studio and have custom APK files automatically generated by Google Play for each individual supported configuration (a concept referred to as *Dynamic Delivery*).

An Android App Bundle is essentially a ZIP file containing all of the files necessary to build APK files for the devices and locales for which support has been provided within the app project. The project might, for example, include resources and images for different screen sizes. When a user installs the app, Google Play receives information about the user's device including the display, processor architecture, and locale. Using this information, the appropriate pre-generated APK files are transferred onto the user's device.

An additional benefit of Dynamic Delivery is the ability to split an app into multiple modules, referred to as *dynamic feature modules,* where each module contains the code and resources for a particular area of functionality within the app. Each dynamic feature module is contained within a separate APK file from the base module and is downloaded to the device only when that feature is required by the user. Dynamic Delivery and app bundles also allow for the creation of *instant dynamic feature modules* which can be run instantly on a device without the need to install an entire app.

Although it is still possible to generate APK files from Android Studio, app bundles are now the recommended way to upload apps to Google Play.

51.3 Register for a Google Play Developer Console account

The first step in the application submission process is to create a Google Play Developer Console account. To do so, navigate to *https://play.google.com/apps/publish/signup/* and follow the instructions to complete the registration process. Note that there is a one-time $25 fee to register. Once an application goes on sale, Google will keep 30% of all revenues associated with the application.

Once the account has been created, the next step is to gather together information about the application. To bring your application to market, the following information will be required:

- **Title** – The title of the application.

- **Short Description** - Up to 80 words describing the application.

- **Full Description** – Up to 4000 words describing the application.

- **Screenshots** – Up to 8 screenshots of your application running (a minimum of two is required). Google recommends submitting screenshots of the application running on a 7" or 10" tablet.

- **Language** – The language of the application (the default is US English).

- **Promotional Text** – The text that will be used when your application appears in special promotional features within the Google Play environment.

- **Application Type** – Whether your application is considered to be a *game* or an *application.*

- **Category** – The category that best describes your application (for example finance, health and fitness, education, sports, etc.).

- **Locations** – The geographical locations into which you wish your application to be made available for purchase.

- **Contact Details** – Methods by which users may contact you for support relating to the application. Options include web, email. and phone.

- **Pricing & Distribution** – Information about the price of the application and the geographical locations where it is to be marketed and sold.

Having collected the above information, click on the *Create app* button within the Google Play Console to begin the creation process.

51.4 Configuring the app in the console

When the *Create app* button is first clicked, the app details and declarations screen will appear as shown in Figure 51-1 below:

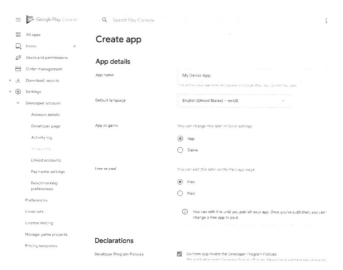

Figure 51-1

Once the app entry has been fully configured, click on the *Create app* button (highlighted in the above figure) to add the app and display the dashboards screen. Within the dashboard, locate the *Initial setup* section and unfold the list of steps to configure the app store listing:

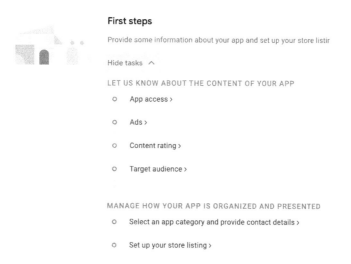

Figure 51-2

Work through the list of links and provide the requested information for your app, making sure to save the changes at each step.

51.5 Enabling Google Play app signing

Up until recently, Google Play uploads were signed with a release app signing key from within Android Studio and then uploaded to the Google Play console. While this option is still available, the recommended way to upload files is to now use a process referred to as *Google Play App Signing*. For a newly created app, this involves opting into Google Play App Signing and then generating an *upload key* that is used to sign the app bundle file within Android Studio. When the app bundle file generated by Android Studio is uploaded, the Google Play console removes the upload key and then signs the file with an app signing key that is stored securely within the Google Play servers.

Within the Google Play console, select the newly added app entry from the *All Apps* screen (accessed via the option located at the top of the left-hand navigation panel), unfold the Setup section (Marked A in Figure 51-3), and select the App Signing option (B).

Figure 51-3

Opt in to Google Play app signing by clicking on the *Create release* button (C). The console is now ready to create the first release of your app for testing. Before doing so, however, the next step is to generate the *upload* key from within Android Studio. This is performed as part of the process of generating a signed app bundle. Leave the current Google Play Console screen loaded into the browser as we will be returning to this later in the chapter.

51.6 Creating a keystore file

To create a keystore file, select the Android Studio *Build -> Generate Signed Bundle / APK...* menu option to display the Generate Signed Bundle or APK Wizard dialog as shown in Figure 51-4:

Figure 51-4

Verify that the *Android App Bundle* option is selected before clicking on the *Next* button.

If you have an existing release keystore file, click on the *Choose existing...* button on the next screen and navigate to and select the file. If you have yet to create a keystore file, click on the *Create new...* button to display the *New Key Store* dialog (Figure 51-5). Click on the button to the right of the Key store path field and navigate to a suitable location on your file system, enter a name for the keystore file (for example, *release.keystore.jks*) and click on the OK button.

The New Key Store dialog is divided into two sections. The top section relates to the keystore file. In this section, enter a strong password with which to protect the keystore file into both the *Password* and *Confirm* fields. The lower section of the dialog relates to the upload key that will be stored in the key store file.

Figure 51-5

Within the *Certificate* section of the New Key Store dialog, enter the following details:

- An alias by which the key will be referenced. This can be any sequence of characters, though only the first 8 are used by the system.

- A suitably strong password to protect the key.

- The number of years for which the key is to be valid (Google recommends at least 25 years).

In addition, information must be provided for at least one of the remaining fields (for example, your first and last name, or organization name).

Figure 51-6

Once the information has been entered, click on the *OK* button to proceed with the bundle creation.

51.7 Creating the Android app bundle

The next step is to instruct Android Studio to build the application app bundle file in release mode and then sign it with the newly created private key. At this point the *Generate Signed Bundle or APK* dialog should still be displayed with the keystore path, passwords, and key alias fields populated with information:

Figure 51-7

Make sure that the Export Encrypted Key option is enabled and, assuming that the other settings are correct, click on the *Next* button to proceed to the app bundle generation screen (Figure 51-8). Within this screen, review the *Destination Folder:* setting to verify that the location into which the app bundle file will be generated is acceptable. If you would prefer to use another location, click on the button to the right of the text field and navigate to the desired file system location.

Figure 51-8

Click on the *Finish* button and wait for the Gradle system to build the app bundle. Once the build is complete, a dialog will appear providing the option to open the folder containing the app bundle file in an explorer window, or to load the file into the APK Analyzer:

Generate Signed Bundle
App bundle(s) generated successfully:
Module 'app': locate or analyze the app bundle.

File Explorer

Figure 51-9

At this point, the application is ready to be submitted to Google Play. Click on the *locate* link to open a filesystem browser window. The file should be named *bundle.aab* and be located in the *app/release* sub-directory of the project folder unless another location was specified.

The private key generated as part of this process should be used when signing and releasing future applications and, as such, should be kept in a safe place and securely backed up.

51.8 Generating test APK files

An optional step at this stage is to generate APK files from the app bundle and install and run them on devices or emulator sessions. Google provides a command-line tool called *bundletool* designed specifically for this purpose which can be downloaded from the following URL:

https://github.com/google/bundletool/releases

At the time of writing, bundletool is provided as a .jar file which can be executed from the command-line as follows (noting that the version number may have changed since this book was published):

```
java -jar bundletool-all-0.9.0.jar
```

Running the above command will list all of the options available within the tool. To generate the APK files from the app bundle, the *build-apks* option is used. To generate APK files that can be installed onto a device or emulator the files will also need to be signed. To achieve this include the *--ks* option specifying the path of the keystore file created earlier in the chapter, together with the *--ks-key-alias* option specifying the alias provided when the key was generated.

Finally, the *--output* flag must be used to specify the path of the file (referred to as the APK Set) into which the APK files will be generated. This file must not already exist and is required to have a *.apks* filename extension. Bringing these requirements together results in the following command-line (allowing for differences in your operating system path structure):

```
java -jar bundletool-all-0.9.0.jar build-apks --bundle=/tmp/MyApps/app/release/
bundle.aab --output=/tmp/MyApks.apks --ks=/MyKeys/release.keystore.jks --ks-key-
alias=MyReleaseKey
```

When this command is executed, a prompt will appear requesting the keystore password before the APK files are generated into the specified APK Set file. The APK Set file is simply a ZIP file containing all of the APK files generated from the app bundle.

To install the appropriate APK files onto a connected device or emulator, use a command similar to the following:

```
java -jar bundletool-all-0.9.0.jar install-apks --apks=/tmp/MyApks.apks
```

This command will instruct the tool to identify the appropriate APK files for the connected device and install them so that the app can be launched and tested.

It is also possible to extract the APK files from the APK Set for the connected device without installing them. The first step in this process is to obtain the specification of the connected device as follows:

```
java -jar bundletool-all-0.9.0.jar get-device-spec --output=/tmp/device.json
```

Creating, Testing, and Uploading an Android App Bundle

The above command will generate a JSON file similar to the following:

```
{
  "supportedAbis": ["x86"],
  "supportedLocales": ["en-US"],
  "screenDensity": 420,
  "sdkVersion": 27
}
```

Next, this specification file is used to extract the matching APK files from the APK Set:

```
java -jar bundletool-all-0.9.0.jar extract-apks --apks=/tmp/MyApks.apks --output-
dir=/tmp/nexus5_apks --device-spec=/tmp/device.json
```

When executed, the directory specified via the *--output-dir* flag will contain correct APK files for the specified device configuration.

The next step in bringing an Android application to market involves submitting it to the Google Play Developer Console so that it can be made available for testing.

51.9 Uploading the app bundle to the Google Play Developer Console

Return to the Google Play Console and select the *Internal testing* option (marked A in Figure 51-10) located in the *Testing* section of the navigation panel before clicking on the *Create new release* button (B):

Figure 51-10

On the resulting screen, click on the Continue button (marked A below) to confirm the use of Google Play app signing, then drag and drop the bundle file generated by Android Studio onto the upload drop point (B):

App signing by Google Play

⊘ Google is protecting your app signing key

Google will create and protect the signing key for your app and use it to sign each release. This makes sure that any updates are from you. App signing is required to publish using Android App Bundles. Learn more

[Continue] Manage preferences

App bundles and APKs

ⓘ Complete the steps above to continue with your release

Ⓑ

⤒ Upload   🗐 Add from library

Figure 51-11

When the upload is complete, scroll down the screen and enter the release name and optional release notes. The release name can be any information you need to help you recognize the release and it is not visible to users.

After the app bundle file has uploaded, Google Play will generate all of the necessary APK files ready for testing. Once the APK files have been generated, scroll down to the bottom of the screen and click on the *Save* button. Once the settings have been saved, click on the *Review release* button.

51.10 Exploring the app bundle

On the review screen, click on the arrow to the right of the uploaded bundle as indicated in Figure 51-12:

New app bundles and APKs

File type	Version	API levels	Target SDK	Screen layouts	ABIs	Required features	
Android App Bundle	1 (1.0)	29+	29	4	All	1	→

Release notes

Figure 51-12

In the resulting panel, click on the *Explore bundle* link to load the app bundle explorer. This provides summary information relating to the API levels, screen layouts, and platforms supported by the app bundle:

Details   Downloads

Details

Releases	1 release View ⌄
Supported Android devices	1,298 Go to device catalog
Localizations	85 localizations View ⌄
Permissions	android.permission.USE_BIOMETRIC
Features	android.hardware.faketouch
Screen layouts	small, normal, large, xlarge
Native platforms	No restrictions
API levels	29+
Target SDK	29
OpenGL ES versions	0.0+
OpenGL textures	No textures required

Figure 51-13

Creating, Testing, and Uploading an Android App Bundle

Clicking on the *Go to device catalog* link will display the devices that are supported by the APK file:

Device catalog

View and manage the devices that are compatible with your app. Show more

Supported devices ▼   ☰ Add filter   🔍 Search devices

1,298 devices supported ⓘ   Manage devices ▼   ⬇ Download device list

Device	RAM (total memory)	System on Chip	Status	
A1 Alpha 20+	3,840 MB (3,726 MB)	Mediatek MT6771T	⊘ Supported	→
AT&T U318AA	1,024 MB (887 MB)	Mediatek MT6739WW	⊘ Supported	→
AT&T U705AA	2,816 MB (2,794 MB)	Mediatek MT6762	⊘ Supported	→

Figure 51-14

At this point, the app is ready for testing but cannot be rolled out until some testers have been set up within the console.

51.11 Managing testers

If the app is still in the Internal, Alpha, or Beta testing phase, a list of authorized testers may be specified by selecting the app from within the Google Play console, clicking on *Internal testing* in the navigation panel, and selecting the *Testers* tab as shown in Figure 51-15:

Figure 51-15

To add testers, click on the *Create email list* button, name the list and specify the email addresses for the test users either manually or by uploading a CSV file.

The "Join on the web" URL may now be copied from the screen and provided to the test users so that they accept the testing invitation and download the app.

51.12 Rolling the app out for testing

Now that an internal release has been created and a list of testers added, the app is ready to be rolled out for testing. Remaining within the *Internal testing* screen, select the Releases tab before clicking on the Edit button for the recently created release:

Figure 51-16

On the review screen, scroll to the bottom and click on the *Start rollout to Internal testing* button. After a short delay, while the release is processed, the app will be ready to be downloaded and tested by the designated users.

51.13 Uploading new app bundle revisions

The first app bundle file uploaded for your application will invariably have a version code of 1. If an attempt is made to upload another bundle file with the same version code number, the console will reject the file with the following error:

```
You need to use a different version code for your APK because you already have
one with version code 1.
```

To resolve this problem, the version code embedded into the bundle file needs to be increased. This is performed in the *module* level *build.gradle* file of the project, shown highlighted in Figure 51-17:

Figure 51-17

By default, this file will typically read as follows:

```
plugins {
    id 'com.android.application'
    id 'org.jetbrains.kotlin.android'
}

android {
    compileSdk 32

    defaultConfig {
        applicationId "com.example.demoapp"
```

```
minSdk 26
targetSdk 31
versionCode 1
versionName "1.0"
```
.

.

.
```
}
```

To change the version code, simply change the number declared next to *versionCode*. To also change the version number displayed to users of your application, change the *versionName* string. For example:

```
versionCode 2
versionName "2.0"
```

Having made these changes, rebuild the APK file and perform the upload again.

51.14 Analyzing the app bundle file

Android Studio provides the ability to analyze the content of an app bundle file. To analyze a bundle file, select the Android Studio *Build -> Analyze APK...* menu option and navigate to and choose the bundle file to be reviewed. Once loaded into the tool, information will be displayed about the raw and download size of the package together with a listing of the file structure of the package as illustrated in Figure 51-18:

unknown (version unknown)

APK size: **1.1 MB**, Download Size: **1.1 MB**   Compare with previous APK...

File	Raw File Size	Download Size	% of Total Download size
▼ base	1 MB	1 MB	96.8%
▼ dex	752.4 KB	751.2 KB	69.3%
classes.dex	752.4 KB	751.2 KB	69.3%
▶ res	216.3 KB	216.2 KB	20%
resources.pb	81.5 KB	81.1 KB	7.5%
▶ manifest	663 B	663 B	0.1%
▶ root	95 B	95 B	0%
▶ META-INF	34.6 KB	34.1 KB	3.1%
BundleConfig.pb	135 B	135 B	0%

Figure 51-18

Selecting the *classes.dex* file will display the class structure of the file in the lower panel. Within this panel, details of the individual classes may be explored down to the level of the methods within a class:

f m ◆ ▦ ▦ Load Proguard mappings...   This dex file defines **2142** classes with **16751** methods, and references **22365** methods.

Class	Defined Methods	Referenced Methods	Size
▶ android	16727	21813	2.3 MB
▶ java		503	12 KB
▶ com	24	28	36.3 KB
▶ org		18	434 B
▶ c float[]		1	20 B
▶ c int[]		1	20 B
▶ c long[]		1	20 B

Figure 51-19

Similarly, selecting a resource or image file within the file list will display the file content within the lower panel. The size differences between two bundle files may be reviewed by clicking on the *Compare with previous APK...* button and selecting a second bundle file.

51.15 Summary

Once an app project is either complete or ready for user testing, it can be uploaded to the Google Play console and published for production, internal, alpha, or beta testing. Before the app can be uploaded, an app entry must be created within the console including information about the app together with screenshots to be used within the Play Store. A release Android App Bundle file is then generated and signed with an upload key from within Android Studio. After the bundle file has been uploaded, Google Play removes the upload key and replaces it with the securely stored app signing key and the app is ready to be published.

The content of a bundle file can be reviewed at any time by loading it into the Android Studio APK Analyzer tool.

52. An Overview of Gradle in Android Studio

Up until this point it has, for the most part, been taken for granted that Android Studio will take the necessary steps to compile and run the application projects that have been created. Android Studio has been achieving this in the background using a system known as *Gradle*.

It is now time to look at how Gradle is used to compile and package together the various elements of an application project and to begin exploring how to configure this system when more advanced requirements are needed in terms of building projects in Android Studio.

52.1 An Overview of Gradle

Gradle is an automated build toolkit that allows the way in which projects are built to be configured and managed through a set of build configuration files. This includes defining how a project is to be built, what dependencies need to be fulfilled for the project to build successfully and what the end result (or results) of the build process should be.

The strength of Gradle lies in the flexibility that it provides to the developer. The Gradle system is a self-contained, command-line based environment that can be integrated into other environments through the use of plugins. In the case of Android Studio, Gradle integration is provided through the appropriately named Android Studio Plugin.

Although the Android Studio Plug-in allows Gradle tasks to be initiated and managed from within Android Studio, the Gradle command-line wrapper can still be used to build Android Studio based projects, including on systems on which Android Studio is not installed.

The configuration rules to build a project are declared in Gradle build files and scripts based on the Groovy programming language.

52.2 Gradle and Android Studio

Gradle brings a number of powerful features to building Android application projects. Some of the key features are as follows:

52.2.1 Sensible Defaults

Gradle implements a concept referred to as *convention over configuration*. This simply means that Gradle has a predefined set of sensible default configuration settings that will be used unless they are overridden by settings in the build files. This means that builds can be performed with the minimum of configuration required by the developer. Changes to the build files are only needed when the default configuration does not meet your build needs.

52.2.2 Dependencies

Another key area of Gradle functionality is that of dependencies. Consider, for example, a module within an Android Studio project which triggers an intent to load another module in the project. The first module has, in effect, a dependency on the second module since the application will fail to build if the second module cannot be located and launched at runtime. This dependency can be declared in the Gradle build file for the first module so that the second module is included in the application build, or an error flagged in the event the second module cannot be found or built. Other examples of dependencies are libraries and JAR files on which the project depends in order to compile and run.

Gradle dependencies can be categorized as *local* or *remote*. A local dependency references an item that is present on the local file system of the computer system on which the build is being performed. A remote dependency refers to an item that is present on a remote server (typically referred to as a *repository*).

Remote dependencies are handled for Android Studio projects using another project management tool named *Maven*. If a remote dependency is declared in a Gradle build file using Maven syntax then the dependency will be downloaded automatically from the designated repository and included in the build process. The following dependency declaration, for example, causes the AppCompat library to be added to the project from the Google repository:

```
implementation 'androidx.appcompat:appcompat:1.4.1'
```

52.2.3 Build Variants

In addition to dependencies, Gradle also provides *build variant* support for Android Studio projects. This allows multiple variations of an application to be built from a single project. Android runs on many different devices encompassing a range of processor types and screen sizes. In order to target as wide a range of device types and sizes as possible it will often be necessary to build a number of different variants of an application (for example, one with a user interface for phones and another for tablet sized screens). Through the use of Gradle, this is now possible in Android Studio.

52.2.4 Manifest Entries

Each Android Studio project has associated with it an *AndroidManifest.xml* file containing configuration details about the application. A number of manifest entries can be specified in Gradle build files which are then auto-generated into the manifest file when the project is built. This capability is complementary to the build variants feature, allowing elements such as the application version number, application ID and SDK version information to be configured differently for each build variant.

52.2.5 APK Signing

The chapter entitled *"Creating, Testing and Uploading an Android App Bundle"* covered the creation of a signed release APK file using the Android Studio environment. It is also possible to include the signing information entered through the Android Studio user interface within a Gradle build file so that signed APK files can be generated from the command-line.

52.2.6 ProGuard Support

ProGuard is a tool included with Android Studio that optimizes, shrinks and obfuscates Java byte code to make it more efficient and harder to reverse engineer (the method by which the logic of an application can be identified by others through analysis of the compiled Java byte code). The Gradle build files provide the ability to control whether or not ProGuard is run on your application when it is built.

52.3 The Property and Settings Gradle Build Files

The gradle build configuration consists a set of a configuration, property and settings files. The *gradle.properties* file, for example, contains mostly esoteric settings relating the command-line flags used by the Java Virtual Machine (JVM), whether or not the project uses the AndroidX libraries, and Kotlin coding style support. As a typical user, it is unlikely that you will need to change any of these settings in this file.

The *settings.gradle* file, on the other hand, defines which online repositories are to be searched when the build system needs to download and install any additional libraries and plugins required to build the project, as well as the project name. A typical *settings.gradle* file will read as follows:

```
pluginManagement {
    repositories {
        gradlePluginPortal()
        google()
        mavenCentral()
    }
}
dependencyResolutionManagement {
    repositoriesMode.set(RepositoriesMode.FAIL_ON_PROJECT_REPOS)
    repositories {
        google()
        mavenCentral()
    }
}
rootProject.name = "AndroidSample"
include ':app'
```

As with the *gradle.properties* file, it is unlikely that changes will need to made to this file.

52.4 The Top-level Gradle Build File

A completed Android Studio project contains everything needed to build an Android application and consists of modules, libraries, manifest files and Gradle build files.

Each project contains one top-level Gradle build file. This file is listed as *build.gradle (Project: <project name>)* and can be found in the project tool window as highlighted in Figure 52-1:

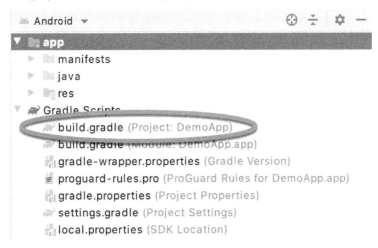

Figure 52-1

By default, the contents of the top level Gradle build file reads as follows:

```
buildscript {
    ext {
        compose_version = '1.0.5'
    }
}
```

```
// Top-level build file where you can add configuration options common to all sub-
projects/modules.
plugins {
    id 'com.android.application' version '7.1.0' apply false
    id 'com.android.library' version '7.1.0' apply false
    id 'org.jetbrains.kotlin.android' version '1.6.10' apply false
}

task clean(type: Delete) {
    delete rootProject.buildDir
}
```

As it stands all the file does is declare that remote libraries are to be obtained using the jcenter repository and that builds are dependent on the Android plugin for Gradle. In most situations it is not necessary to make any changes to this build file.

52.5 Module Level Gradle Build Files

An Android Studio application project is made up of one or more modules. Take, for example, a hypothetical application project named GradleDemo which contains two modules named Module1 and Module2 respectively. In this scenario, each of the modules will require its own Gradle build file. In terms of the project structure, these would be located as follows:

- Module1/build.gradle

- Module2/build.gradle

By default, the Module1 build.gradle file would resemble that of the following listing:

```
plugins {
    id 'com.android.application'
    id 'org.jetbrains.kotlin.android'
}

android {
    compileSdk 32

    defaultConfig {
        applicationId "com.ebookfrenzy.demoapp"
        minSdkVersion 26
        targetSdkVersion 32
        versionCode 1
        versionName "1.0"

        testInstrumentationRunner "androidx.test.runner.AndroidJUnitRunner"
    }

    buildTypes {
        release {
            minifyEnabled false
```

```
            proguardFiles getDefaultProguardFile('proguard-android-optimize.
txt'), 'proguard-rules.pro'
        }
    }
    compileOptions {
        sourceCompatibility JavaVersion.VERSION_1_8
        targetCompatibility JavaVersion.VERSION_1_8
    }
    kotlinOptions {
        jvmTarget = '1.8'
    }
}


dependencies {

    implementation "org.jetbrains.kotlin:kotlin-stdlib:$kotlin_version"
    implementation 'androidx.core:core-ktx:1.7.0'
    implementation 'androidx.appcompat:appcompat:1.4.1'
    implementation 'com.google.android.material:material:1.5.0'
    implementation 'androidx.constraintlayout:constraintlayout:2.1.3'
    testImplementation 'junit:junit:4.+'
    androidTestImplementation 'androidx.test.ext:junit:1.1.3'
    androidTestImplementation 'androidx.test.espresso:espresso-core:3.4.0'
}
```

As is evident from the file content, the build file begins by declaring the use of the Gradle Android application plug-in:

```
plugins {
    id 'com.android.application'
```

The *android* section of the file then states the version of the SDK to be used when building Module1.

```
android {
    compileSdkVersion 32
```

The items declared in the defaultConfig section define elements that are to be generated into the module's *AndroidManifest.xml* file during the build. These settings, which may be modified in the build file, are taken from the settings entered within Android Studio when the module was first created:

```
defaultConfig {
    applicationId "com.ebookfrenzy.demoapp"
    minSdkVersion 26
    targetSdkVersion 32
    versionCode 1
    versionName "1.0"


    testInstrumentationRunner "androidx.test.runner.AndroidJUnitRunner"
}
```

The buildTypes section contains instructions on whether and how to run ProGuard on the APK file when a release version of the application is built:

```
buildTypes {
    release {
        minifyEnabled false
        proguardFiles getDefaultProguardFile('proguard-android-optimize.txt'),
'proguard-rules.pro'
    }
}
```

As currently configured, ProGuard will not be run when Module1 is built. To enable ProGuard, the *minifyEnabled* entry needs to be changed from *false* to *true*. The *proguard-rules.pro* file can be found in the module directory of the project. Changes made to this file override the default settings in the *proguard-android.txt* file which is located on the Android SDK installation directory under *sdk/tools/proguard*.

Since no debug buildType is declared in this file, the defaults will be used (built without ProGuard, signed with a debug key and with debug symbols enabled).

An additional section, entitled *productFlavors* may also be included in the module build file to enable multiple build variants to be created.

Next, directives are included to specify the version of the Java compiler to be used when building the project:

```
compileOptions {
    sourceCompatibility JavaVersion.VERSION_1_8
    targetCompatibility JavaVersion.VERSION_1_8
}
kotlinOptions {
    jvmTarget = '1.8'
}
```

Finally, the dependencies section lists any local and remote dependencies on which the module is dependent. The dependency lines in the above example file designate the Android libraries that need to be included from the Android Repository:

```
.

.

implementation 'androidx.core:core-ktx:1.7.0'
implementation 'androidx.appcompat:appcompat:1.4.1'
.

.
```

Note that the dependency declarations include version numbers to indicate which version of the library should be included.

52.6 Configuring Signing Settings in the Build File

The *"Creating, Testing and Uploading an Android App Bundle"* chapter of this book covered the steps involved in setting up keys and generating a signed release APK file using the Android Studio user interface. These settings may also be declared within a *signingSettings* section of the build.gradle file. For example:

```
.

.

    defaultConfig {
```

```
    }
    signingConfigs {
        release {
            storeFile file("keystore.release")
            storePassword "your keystore password here"
            keyAlias "your key alias here"
            keyPassword "your key password here"
        }
    }
    buildTypes {
.
.
.
}
```

The above example embeds the key password information directly into the build file. An alternative to this approach is to extract these values from system environment variables:

```
signingConfigs {
    release {
        storeFile file("keystore.release")
        storePassword System.getenv("KEYSTOREPASSWD")
        keyAlias "your key alias here"
        keyPassword System.getenv("KEYPASSWD")
    }
}
```

Yet another approach is to configure the build file so that Gradle prompts for the passwords to be entered during the build process:

```
signingConfigs {
    release {
        storeFile file("keystore.release")
        storePassword System.console().readLine
                ("\nEnter Keystore password: ")
        keyAlias "your key alias here"
        keyPassword System.console().readLIne("\nEnter Key password: ")
    }
}
```

52.7 Running Gradle Tasks from the Command-line

Each Android Studio project contains a Gradle wrapper tool for the purpose of allowing Gradle tasks to be invoked from the command line. This tool is located in the root directory of each project folder. While this wrapper is executable on Windows systems, it needs to have execute permission enabled on Linux and macOS before it can be used. To enable execute permission, open a terminal window, change directory to the project folder for which the wrapper is needed and execute the following command:

```
chmod +x gradlew
```

Once the file has execute permissions, the location of the file will either need to be added to your $PATH environment variable, or the name prefixed by ./ in order to run. For example:

```
./gradlew tasks
```

Gradle views project building in terms of a number of different tasks. A full listing of tasks that are available for the current project can be obtained by running the following command from within the project directory (remembering to prefix the command with a ./ if running on macOS or Linux):

```
gradlew tasks
```

To build a debug release of the project suitable for device or emulator testing, use the assembleDebug option:

```
gradlew assembleDebug
```

Alternatively, to build a release version of the application:

```
gradlew assembleRelease
```

52.8 Summary

For the most part, Android Studio performs application builds in the background without any intervention from the developer. This build process is handled using the Gradle system, an automated build toolkit designed to allow the ways in which projects are built to be configured and managed through a set of build configuration files. While the default behavior of Gradle is adequate for many basic project build requirements, the need to configure the build process is inevitable with more complex projects. This chapter has provided an overview of the Gradle build system and configuration files within the context of an Android Studio project.

Index

Symbols

?. 95

2D graphics 319

@Composable 20, 141

@ExperimentalAnimationApi 290

@ExperimentalFoundationApi 286

:: operator 97

@Preview 21

  showSystemUi 21

A

Activity Manager 83

adb

  command-line tool 61

  connection testing 67

  device pairing 65

  enabling on Android devices 61

  Linux configuration 64

  list devices 61

  macOS configuration 62

  overview 61

  restart server 62

  testing connection 67

  WiFi debugging 65

  Windows configuration 63

  Wireless debugging 65

  Wireless pairing 65

AlertDialog 145

align() 209

alignByBaseline() 201

Alignment.Bottom 195, 200

Alignment.BottomCenter 207

Alignment.BottomEnd 207

Alignment.BottomStart 207

Alignment.Center 207

Alignment.CenterEnd 207

Alignment.CenterHorizontally 196

Alignment.CenterStart 207

Alignment.CenterVertically 195, 200

Alignment.End 196

alignment lines 217

Alignment.Start 196

Alignment.Top 195, 200

Alignment.TopCenter 207

Alignment.TopEnd 207

Alignment.TopStart 207

anchors 427

anchors map 428

android

  command-line tool 41

Android

  architecture 81

  runtime 82

  SDK Packages 6

Android Architecture Components 337

Android Debug Bridge. *See* ADB

Android Development

  System Requirements 3

Android Jetpack 337

Android Libraries 82

Android Monitor tool window 38

Android Native Development Kit 83

Android SDK Location

  identifying 9

Android SDK Manager 8, 10

Android SDK Packages

  version requirements 8

Android SDK Tools

  command-line access 9

  Linux 10

  macOS 10

  Windows 7 9

  Windows 8 9

Android Software Stack 81

Index

Android Studio

  Animation Inspector 316

  Asset Studio 174

  changing theme 60

  Database Inspector 383

  downloading 3

  Editor Window 55

  installation 4

  Layout Editor 137

  Linux installation 5

  macOS installation 4

  Main Window 54

  Menu Bar 54

  Navigation Bar 54

  Project tool window 55

  setup wizard 5

  Status Bar 55

  Toolbar 54

  Tool window bars 55

  tool windows 55

  updating 11

  Welcome Screen 53

  Windows installation 4

Android Support Library, 337

Android Virtual Device. *See* AVD

  overview 33

Android Virtual Device Manager 33

AndroidX libraries 464

animate as state functions 303

animateColorAsState() function 303, 307, 308

animateDpAsState() function 309, 313

AnimatedVisibility 293

  animation specs 297

  enter and exit animations 296

  expandHorizontally() 296

  expandIn() 296

  expandVertically() 296

  fadeIn() 297

  fadeOut() 297

  MutableTransitionState 300

  scaleIn() 297

  scaleOut() 297

  shrinkHorizontally() 297

  shrinkOut() 297

  shrinkVertically() 297

  slideIn() 297

  slideInHorizontally() 297

  slideInVertically() 297

  slideOut() 297

  slideOutHorizontally() 297

  slideOutVertically() 297

animateEnterExit() modifier 300

animateFloatAsState() function 304

animateScrollTo() function 263

animateScrollToItem(index: Int) 262

animateScrollTo(value: Int) 261

Animation

  auto-starting 300

  combining animations 314

  inspector 316

  keyframes 313

  KeyframesSpec 313

  motion 309

  spring effects 312

  state-based 303

  visibility 293

Animation damping

  DampingRatioHighBouncy 312

  DampingRatioLowBouncy 312

  DampingRatioMediumBouncy 312

  DampingRatioNoBouncy 312

Animation Inspector 316

AnimationSpec 297

  tween() function 298

Animation specs 297

Animation stiffness

  StiffnessHigh 313

  StiffnessLow 313

  StiffnessMedium 313

  StiffnessMediumLow 313

  StiffnessVeryLow 313

APK analyzer 460

APK file 454

APK File

analyzing 460

APK Signing 464

APK Wizard dialog 452

App Bundles 449

creating 454

overview 449

revisions 459

uploading 456

App Inspector 57

Application

stopping 38

Application Framework 83

Arrangement.Bottom 197

Arrangement.Center 196, 197

Arrangement.End 197

Arrangement.SpaceAround 198

Arrangement.SpaceBetween 198

Arrangement.SpaceEvenly 198

Arrangement.Start 196

Arrangement.Top 197

ART 82

as 97

as? 97

Asset Studio 174

AVD

command-line creation 33, 41

configuration files 43

creation 33

device frame 40

launch in tool window 40

overview 33

renaming 43

running an application 35

standalone 39

starting 34

Startup size and orientation 35

B

background modifier 188

barriers 247

Barriers 232

constrained views 232

baseline

alignment 200

baselines 219

BaseTextField 144

Bitwise AND 103

Bitwise Inversion 102

Bitwise Left Shift 104

Bitwise OR 103

Bitwise Right Shift 104

Bitwise XOR 103

Boolean 90

BottomNavigation 145, 391

Bottom Navigation Bar

tutorial 405

BottomNavigationItem 391, 410

Box 144

align() 209

alignment 207

Alignment.BottomCenter 207

Alignment.BottomEnd 207

Alignment.BottomStart 207

Alignment.Center 207

Alignment.CenterEnd 207

Alignment.CenterStart 207

Alignment.TopCenter 207

Alignment.TopEnd 207

Alignment.TopStart 207

BoxScope 209

contentAlignment 207

matchParentSize() 209

overview 205

tutorial 205

BoxScope

align() 209

matchParentSize() 209

modifiers 209

BoxWithConstraints 144

Build tool window 57

Build Variants 57, 464

tool window 57

Button 145

by keyword 150

Index

C

Canvas 144

  DrawScope 319

  inset() function 323

  overview 319

  size 319

Card 145

  example 266

C/C++ Libraries 82

centerAround() function 236

chain head 230

chaining modifiers 183

chains 230

chain styles 230

Char 90

Checkbox 145, 172

CircleShape 209

CircularProgressIndicator 145

clickable 188

clip 188

Clip Art 175

clip() modifier 209

  CircleShape 209

  CutCornerShape 209

  RectangleShape 209

  RoundedCornerShape 209

close() function 331

Code completion 72

Code editor 17

  Split mode 17

Code Editor

  basics 69

  Code completion 72

  Code folding 75

  Code Generation 74

  Code mode 71

  Code Reformatting 77

  Document Tabs 70

  Editing area 70

  Gutter Area 70

  Live Templates 78

  Parameter information 74

  Parameter name hints 74

  sample code 78

  Splitting 72

  Statement Completion 74

  Status Bar 71

Code folding 75

Code Generation 74

Code mode 71

Code reformatting 77

code samples

  download 1

Coil 278

  library 278

  rememberImagePainter() function 279

ColorFilter 335

color filtering 335

Column 144

  Alignment.CenterHorizontally 196

  Alignment.End 196

  Alignment.Start 196

  Arrangement.Bottom 197

  Arrangement.Center 197

  Arrangement.SpaceAround 198

  Arrangement.SpaceBetween 198

  Arrangement.SpaceEvenly 198

  Arrangement.Top 197

  Layout alignment 194

  list 259

  list tutorial 269

  overview 192

  scope 199

  scope modifiers 199

  spacing 198

  tutorial 191

  verticalArrangement 197

Column lists 259

ColumnScope 199

  Modifier.align() 199

  Modifier.alignBy() 199

  Modifier.weight() 199

combining modifiers 188

Communicating Sequential Processes (CSP) 262

Companion Objects 127

components 141

Composable

   adding a 24

   previewing 26

Composable function

   syntax 142

composable functions 141

composables

   add modifier support 184

Composables

   Foundation 144

   Material 144

Compose

   before 137

   components 141

   data-driven 138

   declarative syntax 137

   functions 141

   layout overview 213

   modifiers 181

   overview 137

   state 138

compose() method 387

CompositionLocal

   example 159

   overview 157

   state 160, 161

   syntax 158

constrainAs() modifier function 235

constrain() function 251

Constraint bias 240

Constraint Bias 229

ConstraintLayout 144

   adding constraints 236

   barriers 247

   Barriers 232

   basic constraints 238

   centerAround() function 236

   chain head 230

   chains 230

   chain styles 230

constrainAs() function 235

constrain() function 251

Constraint bias 240

Constraint Bias 229

Constraint margins 241

Constraints 227

constraint sets 250

createEndBarrier() 247

createHorizontalChain() 245

createRefFor() function 251

createRef() function 235

createRefs() function 235

createStartBarrier() 247

createTopBarrier() 247

createVerticalChain() 245

creating chains 245

generating references 235

guidelines 246

Guidelines 231

how to call 235

layout() modifier 251

library 237

linkTo() function 236

Margins 228

Opposing constraints 239

Opposing Constraints 228, 242

overview of 227

Packed chain 231

reference assignment 235

Spread chain 230

Spread inside chain 230

Weighted chain 230

Widget Dimensions 231

Constraint margins 241

constraints 222

constraint sets 250

contentAlignment 207

Content Provider 83

Coroutines 262

   coroutine scope 262

   CoroutineScope 262

   rememberCoroutineScope() 263

Index

coroutine scope 262

CoroutineScope 262

  rememberCoroutineScope() 263

createEndBarrier() 247

createHorizontalChain() 245

createRefFor() function 251

createRef() function 235

createRefs() 235

createStartBarrier() 247

createTopBarrier() 247

createVerticalChain() 245

Crossfading 301

CSP 262

currentBackStackEntryAsState() method 392, 410

Custom Accessors 125

Custom layout 221

  building 221

  constraints 222

  Layout() composable 222

  measurables 222

  overview 221

  Placeable 222

  syntax 221

custom layout modifiers 213

  alignment lines 217

  baselines 219

  creating 215

  default position 215

Custom layouts

  overview 213

  tutorial 213

Custom Theme

  building 439

CutCornerShape 209

D

DampingRatioHighBouncy 312

DampingRatioLowBouncy 312

DampingRatioMediumBouncy 312

DampingRatioNoBouncy 312

dark mode

  detecting 437

Dark Theme 38

  enable on device 38

dashPathEffect() method 321

Data Access Object (DAO) 360, 372

Data Access Objects 363

Database Inspector 367, 383

  live updates 383

  SQL query 383

Database Rows 354

Database Schema 353

Database Tables 353

data-driven 138

DDMS 38

Debugging

  enabling on device 61

declarative syntax 137

Default Function Parameters 117

default position 215

Device File Explorer 57

device frame 40

Device Manager 57

device pairing 65

draggable() modifier 416

drag gestures 416

drawable

  folder 174

drawArc() function 330

drawCircle() function 326

drawImage() function 333

Drawing

  arcs 330

  circle 326

  close() 331

  dashed lines 321

  dashPathEffect() 321

  drawArc() 330

  drawImage() 333

  drawPath() 331

  drawPoints() 332

  drawRect() 321

  drawRoundRect() 324

  gradients 327

images 333

line 319

oval 326

points 332

rectangle 321

rotate() 325

rotation 325

drawLine() function 320

drawPath() function 331

drawPoints() function 332

drawRect() function 321

drawRoundRect() function 324

DrawScope 319

DropdownMenu 145

DurationBasedAnimationSpec 298

Dynamic colors 438

enabling in Android 445

E

Elvis Operator 97

emit 141

Empty Compose Activity

template 14

Emulator 57

battery 48

cellular configuration 48

configuring fingerprints 50

directional pad 48

extended control options 47

Extended controls 47

fingerprint 48

location configuration 48

phone settings 48

resize 47

rotate 46

Screen Record 49

Snapshots 49

starting 34

take screenshot 46

toolbar 45

toolbar options 45

tool window mode 51

Virtual Sensors 49

zoom 46

enabling ADB support 61

enter animations 296

EnterTransition.None 300

Errata 2

Escape Sequences 91

ettings.gradle file 464

Event Log 57

exit animations 296

ExitTransition.None 300

expandHorizontally() 296

expandIn() 296

expandVertically() 296

Extended Control

options 47

F

fadeIn() 297

fadeOut() 297

Favorites

tool window 57

Files

switching between 70

fillMaxHeight 188

fillMaxSize 188

fillMaxWidth 188

findStartDestination() method 392

Fingerprint

emulation 50

firstVisibleItemIndex 264

Float 90

FloatingActionButton 145

FontWeight 25

forEach loop 224

Foundation components 144

Foundation Composables 144

Function Parameters

variable number of 117

Functions 115

G

Index

Gestures 413

  click 413

  drag 416

  horizontalScroll() 420

  overview 413

  pinch gestures 422

  PointerInputScope 415

  rememberScrollableState() function 419

  rememberScrollState() 420

  rememberTransformableState() 422

  rotation gestures 423

  scrollable() modifier 419

  scroll modifiers 420

  swipe 427

  taps 415

  translation gestures 424

  tutorial 413

  verticalScroll() 420

getStringArray() method 277

GNU/Linux 82

Google Play Developer Console 450

Google Play store 15

Gradient drawing 327

Gradle

  APK signing settings 468

  Build Variants 464

  command line tasks 469

  dependencies 463

  Manifest Entries 464

  overview 463

  sensible defaults 463

  tool window 57

Gradle Build File

  top level 465

Gradle Build Files

  module level 466

gradle.properties file 464

Graphics

  drawing 319

Grid

  overview 259

groupBy() function 263

guidelines 246

H

Higher-order Functions 119

horizontalArrangement 196, 198

horizontalScroll() 420

I

Image 144

  add drawable resource 174

  painterResource method 176

Immutable Variables 92

Initializer Blocks 125

In-Memory Database 366

Inner Classes 126

inset() function 323

InstrinsicSize.Max 257

InstrinsicSize.Min 257, 258

intelligent recomposition 147

IntelliJ IDEA 85

Interactive mode 30

Intrinsic measurements 253

IntrinsicSize 253

  intrinsic measurements 253

  Max 253

  Min 253

  tutorial 255

is 97

isInitialized property 97

isSystemInDarkTheme() function 437

item() function 260

items() function 260

itemsIndexed() function 260

J

Java

  convert to Kotlin 85

Java Native Interface 83

JetBrains 85

Jetpack Compose

  see Compose 137

K

keyboardOptions 349

Keyboard Shortcuts 58

keyframe 298

keyframes 313

  KeyframesSpec 313

keyframes() function 313

KeyframesSpec 313

Keystore File

  creation 452

Kotlin

  accessing class properties 125

  and Java 85

  arithmetic operators 99

  assignment operator 99

  augmented assignment operators 100

  bitwise operators 102

  Boolean 90

  break 110

  breaking from loops 109

  calling class methods 125

  Char 90

  class declaration 121

  class initialization 122

  class properties 122

  Companion Objects 127

  conditional control flow 111

  continue labels 110

  continue statement 110

  control flow 107

  convert from Java 85

  Custom Accessors 125

  data types 89

  decrement operator 100

  Default Function Parameters 117

  defining class methods 122

  do ... while loop 109

  Elvis Operator 97

  equality operators 101

  Escape Sequences 91

  expression syntax 99

  Float 90

for-in statement 107

function calling 116

Functions 115

groupBy() function 263

Higher-order Functions 119

if ... else ... expressions 112

if expressions 111

Immutable Variables 92

increment operator 100

inheritance 131

Initializer Blocks 125

Inner Classes 126

introduction 85

Lambda Expressions 118

let Function 95

Local Functions 116

logical operators 101

looping 107

Mutable Variables 92

Not-Null Assertion 95

Nullable Type 94

Overriding inherited methods 134

playground 86

Primary Constructor 122

properties 125

range operator 102

Safe Call Operator 94

Secondary Constructors 122

Single Expression Functions 116

String 90

subclassing 131

subStringBefore() method 279

Type Annotations 93

Type Casting 97

Type Checking 97

Type Inference 93

variable parameters 117

when statement 112

while loop 108

L

Lambda Expressions 118

Index

lateinit 96

Late Initialization 96

launchSingleTop 389

Layout alignment 194

Layout arrangement 196

Layout arrangement spacing 198

Layout components 144

Layout() composable 222

Layout Editor 137

Layout Inspector 57

layout modifier 188

layout() modifier 251

LazyColumn 144, 259

  creation 260

  scroll position detection 264

LazyList

  tutorial 275

Lazy lists 259

  Scrolling 261

LazyListScope 260

  item() function 260

  items() function 260

  itemsIndexed() function 260

  stickyHeader() function 263

LazyListState 264

  firstVisibleItemIndex 264

LazyRow 144, 259

  creation 260

  scroll position detection 264

LazyVerticalGrid 259

  adaptive mode 265

  fixed mode 265

let Function 95

libc 82

LinearProgressIndicator 145

lineTo() 331

lineTo() function 331

linkTo() function 236

Linux Kernel 82

list devices 61

Lists

  clickable items 282

enabling scrolling 261

  overview 259

literals

  live editing 26

LiveData 340

  observeAsState() 341

Live Edit

  disabling 26

  enabling 26

  of literals 26

Live Templates 78

Local Functions 116

Location Manager 83

Logcat

  tool window 57

M

MainActivity.kt file 17

  template code 23

map method 222

matchParentSize() 209

Material Composables 144

Material Design 2 435

Material Design 2 Theming 435

Material Design 3 435

  adding library 441

Material Design 3 Theming 438

Material Design components 145

Material Theme Builder 439

measurables 222

Minimum SDK

  setting 15

ModalDrawer 145

Modern Android architecture 337

modifier

  adding to composable 184

  chaining 183

  combining 188

  creating a 182

  ordering 184

  tutorial 181

Modifier.align() 199

Modifier.alignBy() 199

modifiers

  build-in 188

  overview 181

Modifier.weight() 199

multiple devices

  testing app on 37

MutableLiveData 340

MutableState 148

mutableStateOf function 141

mutableStateOf() function 149

MutableTransitionState 300

Mutable Variables 92

N

NavHost 387, 399

NavHostController 385, 399

navigate() method 389

Navigation 385

  BottomNavigation 391

  BottomNavigationItem 391

  compose() method 387

  controller 386

  currentBackStackEntryAsState() method 392

  declaring routes 395

  findStartDestination() method 392

  graph 387

  launchSingleTop 389

  library 405

  NavHost 387, 399

  NavHostController 385, 399

  navigate() method 389

  navigation graph 385

  NavType 390

  overview 385

  passing arguments

  popUpTo() method 389

  route 387

  stack 385, 386

  start destination 387

  tutorial 395

Navigation Architecture Component 385

Navigation bars 391

navigation controller 386

navigation graph 385, 387

Navigation Host 387

navigation library 405

NavType 390

Notifications Manager 83

Not-Null Assertion 95

Nullable Type 94

O

observeAsState() 341

Offset() function 320

offset modifier 188

offset() modifier 428

onCreate() method 21

OpenJDK 3

Opposing constraints 239

OutlinedButton 289

OutlinedTextField 343

P

Package Manager 83

Package name 15

Packed chain 231

padding 188

painterResource method 176

Parameter name hints 74

PathEffect 321

pinch gestures 422

Placeable 222

PointerInputScope 415

  drag gestures 418

  tap gestures 415

popUpTo() method 389

Preview panel 22

  build and refresh 22

  Interactive mode 30

Primary Constructor 122

Problems

  tool window 57

Profiler

Index

tool window 57

proguard-rules.pro file 468

ProGuard Support 464

project

  create new 14

  package name 15

Project

  tool window 57

Project tool window 16, 57

  Android mode 16

Q

Quick Documentation 77

R

RadioButton 145

Range Operator 102

Recent Files Navigation 59

recomposition 138

  intelligent recomposition 147

  overview 147

RectangleShape 209

relativeLineTo() function 331

release mode 449

Release Preparation 449

rememberCoroutineScope() 263

rememberDraggableState() function 416

rememberImagePainter() function 279

remember keyword 149

rememberSaveable keyword 156

rememberScrollableState() function 419

rememberScrollState() 420

rememberScrollState() function 261

rememberTransformableState() 422

rememberTransformationState() function 422

repeatable() function 299

RepeatableSpec

  repeatable() 299

RepeatMode.Reverse 299

Repository

  tutorial 369

Resource Manager 58, 83

Room

  Data Access Object (DAO) 360

  entities 360, 361

  In-Memory Database 366

  Repository 359

Room Database 360

  tutorial 369

Room Database Persistence 359

Room persistence library 370

Room Persistence Library 357

rotate modifier 188

rotation gestures 423

RoundedCornerShape 209

Row 144

  Alignment.Bottom 195

  Alignment.CenterVertically 195

  Alignment.Top 195

  Arrangement.Center 196

  Arrangement.End 197

  Arrangement.SpaceAround 198

  Arrangement.SpaceBetween 198

  Arrangement.SpaceEvenly 198

  Arrangement.Start 196

  horizontalArrangement 196

  Layout alignment 194

  Layout arrangement 196

  list 259

  list example 274

  overview 192

  scope 199

  scope modifiers 199

  spacing 198

  tutorial 191

Row lists 259

RowScope 199

  Modifier.align() 200

  Modifier.alignBy() 200

  Modifier.alignByBaseline() 200

  Modifier.paddingFrom() 200

  Modifier.weight() 200

Run

  tool window 58

S

Safe Call Operator 94

Scaffold 145

scaleIn() 297

scale modifier 188

scaleOut() 297

Scope modifiers

   weights 203

scrollable modifier 188

scrollable() modifier 419, 420

Scroll detection

   example 285

scroll modifiers 420

ScrollState

   rememberScrollState() function 261

scrollToItem(index: Int) 262

scrollTo(value: Int) 261

SDK Packages 6

SDK settings 15

Secondary Constructors 122

Secure Sockets Layer (SSL) 82

Shape 145

Shape.kt file 437

Shapes

   CircleShape 209

   CutCornerShape 209

   RectangleShape 209

   RoundedCornerShape 209

showSystemUi 21, 270

shrinkHorizontally() 297

shrinkOut() 297

shrinkVertically() 297

size modifier 188

slideIn() 297

slideInHorizontally() 297

slideInVertically() 297

slideOut() 297

slideOutHorizontally() 297

slideOutVertically() 297

Slider 145

Slider component 27

Slot APIs

calling 166

   declaring 166

   overview 165

   tutorial 169

Snackbar 145

Snapshots

   emulator 49

Spread chain 230

Spread inside chain 230

Spring effects 312

spring() function 312

SQL 354

SQLite 353

   AVD command-line use 355

   Columns and Data Types 353

   overview 354

   Primary keys 354

start destination 387

state 138

   basics of 147

   by keyword 150

   configuration changes 155

   declaring 148

   hoisting 153

   MutableState 148

   mutableStateOf() function 149

   overview 147

   remember keyword 149

   rememberSaveable 156

   Unidirectional data flow 151

stateful 147

stateful composables 141

State hoisting 153

stateless composables 141

Statement Completion 74

stickyHeader 286

stickyHeader() function 263

Sticky headers

   adding 286

   example 285

   stickyHeader() function 263

StiffnessHigh 313

Index

StiffnessLow 313

StiffnessMedium 313

StiffnessMediumLow 313

StiffnessVeryLow 313

String 90

Structure

  tool window 58

Structured Query Language 354

Structure tool window 58

subStringBefore() method 279

Surface component 20, 207

swipeable() modifier 427

swipeable state 429

Swipe gestures

  anchors 427

  anchors map 428

  detecting 427

  swipeable() modifier 427

  swipeable state 429

  thresholds 428

  tutorial 429

Swipe Gestures 427

Switch 145

Switcher 59

system requirements 3

T

Telephony Manager 83

Terminal

  tool window 58

Text 145

Text component 142

TextField 145

TextStyle 350

Theme

  building a custom 439

Theming 435

  Material Theme Builder 439

  tutorial 441

thresholds 428

TODO

  tool window 58

Tool window bars 55

Tool windows 55

TopAppBar 145

trailingIcon 350

TransformableState 422

translation gestures 424

tween() function 298

Type Annotations 93

Type Casting 97

Type Checking 97

Type Inference 93

Type.kt file 437

U

UI Controllers 338

Unidirectional data flow 151

updateTransition() function 304, 309, 314

USB connection issues

  resolving 64

V

Vector Asset

  add to project 174

verticalArrangement 197, 198

verticalScroll() 420

ViewModel

  example 344

  LiveData 340

  observeAsState() 341

  overview 337

  tutorial 343

  using state 338

View System 83

Virtual Device Configuration dialog 34

Virtual Sensors 49

Visibility animation 293

W

Weighted chain 230

Welcome screen 53

while Loop 108

Widget Dimensions 231

WiFi debugging 65

Wireless debugging 65

Wireless pairing 65

X

XML resource

reading an 275